The Sacred Landscape of the Inca

The Sacred Landscape of the Inca

The Cusco Ceque System

Brian S. Bauer

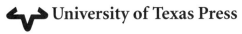 **University of Texas Press**

Austin

Requests for permission to reproduce material from this
work should be sent to Permissions, University of Texas Press,
Box 7819, Austin, TX 78713-7819.

♾The paper used in this publication meets the minimum
requirements of American National Standard for Information
Sciences–Permanence of Paper for Printed Library Materials,
ANSI Z 39.48-1984.

Library of Congress Cataloging-in-Publication Data

Bauer, Brian S.

   The sacred landscape of the Inca : the Cusco ceque system /
Brian S. Bauer. — 1st University of Texas Press ed.

        p.   cm.

   Includes bibliographical references and index.

   ISBN 0-292-70865-3 (alk. paper)

   1. Incas—Religion. 2. Sacred space—Peru—Cuzco.
3. Indians of South America—Andes Region—Religion.
4. Incas—Social life and customs. 5. Indians of South America—Andes Region—Social life and customs.
6. Cuzco (Peru)—Antiquities.   I. Title.

F3429.3.R3B38   1998

299'.88323—dc21   97-49914

This work is dedicated to Manuel Chávez Ballón,
an early explorer of the Cusco ceque system.

. . . the city of Cusco was the house and dwelling place of gods, and thus there was not in all of it, a fountain, or road, or wall that they did not say contained a mystery, which can be seen from the list of shrines in that city, of which there were more than four hundred. All this endured until the Spanish came . . .

. . . Ciudad del Cuzco era casa y morada de dioses, e ansí no avía en toda ella fuente ny paso ny pared que no dixesen que tenya mysterio como paresçe en cada manyfestaçión de los adoratorios de aquella Ciudad y carta que dellos manifestaron que pasauan de quatrocientos y tantos: todo esto duró hasta que vinyeron los españoles . . .

Juan Polo de Ondegardo 1916c: 55 [1571]

Contents

Contents

Illustrations and Tables

Photographs

Maps

Figures

Tables

Preface

In this book I examine, and attempt to reconstruct, the Cusco ceque system, a ritual system composed of several hundred shrines in the heartland of the Inca. Although this complex of shrines and ritual lines (ceques) came under scrutiny during the Spanish campaigns against autochthonous religions in the 1560s and 1570s, recent archaeological and archival research has yielded new information on its physical form and internal structure. By studying the Cusco ceque system, insights are gained about the organization of one of the New World's largest indigenous societies.

The book is divided into eleven chapters. The introduction provides background information necessary for understanding the system and the organization of the city of Cusco at the time of the Spanish invasion. In Chapter 2, the probable date and author of the original ceque-system manuscript are discussed. Chapter 3 provides information on shrine worship by Andean people and outlines the different types of shrines included in the ceque system and how and when offerings were made. The third chapter also includes a discussion of the research methods used to identify the ancient shrines of the Cusco region. Chapter 4 is divided into two sections. In the first, the prestige-ranking terms *collana, payan,* and *cayao* are explored. In the second, the ritual organization of the ceque system and that of the Cusco kin groups are analyzed. Of principal interest is how the maintenance responsibilities for the shrines and ceques were divided between the kin groups of the city.

Chapters 5 through 8 provide descriptions of the shrines and the courses of the ceques for the four indigenous divisions of the Cusco Valley: Chinchaysuyu, Antisuyu, Collasuyu, and Cuntisuyu. The shrine descriptions are accompanied by photographs. Historical references to individual shrines recorded by the Spanish chroniclers and references recovered in the course of archival research are included in these shrine descriptions. The goal of these four chapters is to develop an empirical understanding of the shrines and the directions of the ceques, and to test models of the system provided by earlier researchers against the actual distribution of the shrines and ceques across the Cusco region. A translation of the *Relación de las huacas,* the major source of information on the Cusco ceque system, is included in Appendix 2 as a reference guide for these chapters.

In the ninth chapter, the thirty-seven shrines of the Chinchaysuyu region in Cusco, as described by Cristóbal de Albornoz around 1582, are presented. Albornoz's shrine information is critical because it represents the only detailed description of the Cusco ceque system apart from that presented in the *Relación de las huacas.* As an alternative and independent source, Albornoz's text furnishes locational, descriptional, and mythological information on shrines of the Cusco system that is not preserved elsewhere.

In the first half of Chapter 10, the evidence for other prehistoric ceque systems, as inferred by archaeologists, is examined. In the second half, I look at the evidence, as presented by ethnographers, for the continued use of ceque-like systems in various communities in Bolivia and Chile. In the concluding chapter, the data presented in the book are reviewed and their implications for the development of larger models of Inca state society are addressed.

Many individuals and organizations aided me in developing this book. Before submitting the first proposal to begin the project, I visited Tom Zuidema and we discussed the system shrine by shrine. That discussion has continued over the years, and I am most grateful for his many insights into the system. I am also grateful to John H. Rowe for sharing documents that he found in Lima and Cusco and for permission to reproduce his English translation of Cobo's account of the ceque system. Furthermore, David Dearborn guided me through the astronomical aspects of the system and provided personal support when it was needed.

Perhaps I owe the greatest debt to the members of my archival and field teams. Over the course of three separate field seasons, Wilton Barrionuevo Orosco, Luis Guevara Carazas, and Silvia Flores Delgado spent hundreds of hours walking the hills of Cusco interviewing local informants. They each have become experts in segments of the system. Archival research was conducted by Jean-Jacques Decoster, José Luis Mendoza, and Margarita Castro. They examined thousands of manuscripts in ten separate archives, locating and transcribing information on Cusco kin groups, landholdings, and shrines. This book could not have been completed without their help.

Shackled by dyslexia, I have relied on friends and colleagues to help me see this project to its completion. Monica Barnes and David Fleming provided much-needed advice in improving and organizing the manuscript. Chapters were also read by Peter Bürge, MariAnn Carr, Lisa Cipolla, Paul Goldstein, Veronica Laverallo, Michael Malpass, Martina Munsters, Johan Reinhard, Jack Rossen, and Charles Stanish. Their criticisms and suggestions are gratefully acknowledged. I have also been aided at various stages by Anthony Aveni, Gayle Bauer, William Bauer, Clark Erickson, Mary Glowacki, Patricia J. Lyon, Theresa May, Susan Niles, Nancy Orr, Jeanette Sherbondy, Maarten Van de Guchte, Gary Urton, and Nancy Warrington. Jean-Jacques Decoster, Evan Franke, Roland Hamilton, and Martín Giesso helped prepare the translations.

Permission for this project was granted by the Instituto Nacional de Cultura (INC): Lima and Cusco. The members of the INC in Cusco—including Percy Ardiles Nieves, Fernando Astete Victoria, Arminda Gibaja Oviedo, Wilbert San Román Luna, and Wilfredo Yépez Valdez—were particularly helpful. Members of the Cusco academic community also aided me over the course of this study. I would especially like to thank Luis Barreda Murillo, Raymundo Béjar Navarro, Manuel Chávez Ballón, José Gonzales Corrales, Italo Oberti Rodríguez, Alfredo Valencia Zegarra, and Julinho Zapata.

I am also indebted to a wide range of funding organizations that supported this project. Major funding was provided by The L. J. Skaggs and Mary C. Skaggs Foundation, the Fulbright-Hays fellowship committee, the National Endowment for the Humanities (grant nos. RO-22282-91 and FB-30115-93), The Guttman Foundation, The Institute for the Humanities (The University of Illinois at Chicago), The Institute for New World Archaeology, The National Science Foundation (grant no. 9307513), The Dudley Observatory, and the University of Chicago Housing System. Their assistance is gratefully acknowledged.

1

Introduction

This book is about an elaborate system of shrines that surrounded the city of Cusco, the capital of the Inca Empire in the fifteenth century. It is about the Inca, both noble and common, who maintained and worshipped at the shrines, and the Spaniards, who systematically destroyed the shrines in their campaigns against idolatry. In many ways, the book is also about contemporaries: the people of Cusco today who still remember and respect many of the shrines, and a generation of Andean scholars who have labored to reconstruct and comprehend this complex ritual system.

The distribution of Inca shrines surrounding Cusco is known as the "Cusco ceque system." We have learned of this shrine system primarily through the writings of a meticulous Jesuit scholar named Bernabé Cobo. In his 1653 chronicle, *Historia del Nuevo Mundo* (History of the New World), Cobo presents an extraordinary account of indigenous culture and religion in the Inca heartland. Four chapters of his chronicle are devoted to describing 328 *huacas* (shrines) that encircled Cusco, and the 42 *ceques* (lines) along which the huacas were organized. In addition, these unusually detailed chapters record the objects offered to the huacas, the huacas' relative order along the ceques, and how the huacas were maintained and worshipped by the Inca. Cobo's list of shrines and lines is the most complete description of Inca huaca worship available to scholars today.

Despite the importance of the ceque system in understanding the pre-Hispanic organization of Cusco, there has never been a large-scale, systematic study aimed at identifying the shrines and ceques of the city as described by Cobo. Accordingly, current models of the system's physical form and its relation to the social, political, and territorial organization of Cusco remain hypothetical and untested. From 1990 to 1995, I directed a project in Cusco to provide ground documentation of the ceque system. The project included extensive survey work in the Cusco region to identify the location of the huacas and the course of the ceques described in Cobo's work. It also comprised archival research in Cusco, Lima, and Seville to recover additional documentation on the social groups of the Cusco region, their landholdings, and the positions of the huacas. In other words, archival research supported, complemented, and extended the regional survey data by providing concise information on specific huacas and by providing additional information on the landholdings of Cusco-based kin groups. This information provided a means to study how the ceque system actually extended across the Cusco region, and how it was maintained by the various kin groups that surrounded the Inca capital at the time of the Spanish conquest.

The major findings recovered and developed in the course of my field and archival research into the Cusco ceque system are presented in this book. Using the information on this shrine system handed down to us by Cobo, as well as data recovered in the course of extensive archaeological and archival research, the physical distribution of the huacas and ceques across the Cusco Valley is documented and the sacred geography of the Inca is reconstructed for the first time. From this empirical understanding of the ceque system, new insights are gained into the historical and political organization of Inca society. Furthermore, by examining the Cusco ceque system, we can explore both the sacred landscape of the Inca heartland and the basic organizing principles of the New World's largest empire.

The Shrines and Ceques of Cusco

At its height in the early sixteenth century, the Inca Empire encompassed a population of at least six million people and a territory that stretched from modern-day Colombia to Chile (Map 1.1). The Inca ruled their empire, which they called Tahuantinsuyu (the four parts together), from the highland city of Cusco. Located at the northern end of a

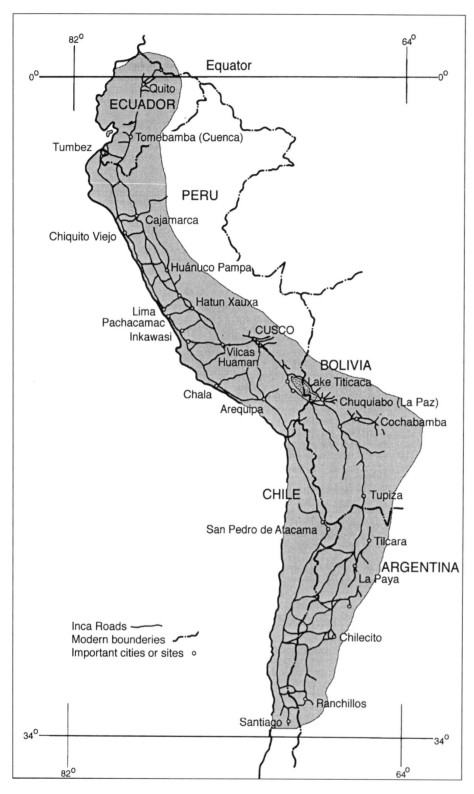

Map 1.1. The Inca Empire. At its height in the early sixteenth century, the Inca Empire encompassed the territory that stretched from modern-day Colombia to Chile. A complex system of roads connected the city of Cusco with all parts of the empire. (After Hyslop 1990)

Table 1.1. The Thirteen Dynastic Rulers Who Reigned before the Arrival of the Spaniards in 1532

Ruler
(1) Manco Capac
(2) Sinchi Roca
(3) Lloque Yupanqui
(4) Mayta Capac
(5) Capac Yupanqui
(6) Inca Roca
(7) Yahuar Huacac
(8) Viracocha Inca
(9) Pachacuti Inca Yupanqui
(10) Topa Inca Yupanqui
(11) Huayna Capac
(12) Huascar
(13) Atahualpa
(European Invasion of 1532)
(14) Manco Inca
(15) Paullu Inca

large and agriculturally rich valley, Cusco was the ancestral home of the thirteen dynastic rulers who are said to have reigned before the arrival of the Spaniards in 1532 (Table 1.1).

Besides being the royal seat for the ruling dynasty and the political core of the Inca polity, Cusco represented the geographical and spiritual center of the empire. At the very heart of the city stood the Coricancha (Golden Enclosure), or what the Spaniards later referred to as the "Templo del Sol" (Temple of the Sun). This elaborate complex, built with the finest Inca stone masonry and metalwork, was the focal point for the major imperial religious rites that were staged in the city (Photo 1.1). However, Cusco was also filled with lesser shrines, each of which held its own special place in the capital's ritual organization. As Juan Polo de Ondegardo (1916c: 55 [1571]) wrote, ". . . the city of Cusco was the house and dwelling place of gods, and thus there was not in all of it, a fountain, or road, or wall that they did not say contained a mystery. . . ."[1] Indeed, the entire city was considered sacred, and travelers offered prayers and sacrifices

Photo 1.1. The Coricancha (Golden Enclosure) was the focal point for the major religious rites that occurred in the city. It was also the vortex of the Cusco ceque system. The church of Santo Domingo now stands over the remains of this temple.

to Cusco on the mountain passes when it first came into view (Photo 1.2).

Like all Andean communities, Cusco was surrounded by sacred objects and places known generally as huacas. These sacred items and locations held critical roles in defining the topography of the Andes and the lives of the indigenous peoples who lived there. As the contemporary scholar Michael J. Sallnow writes, "The Andean landscape is imbued with sacredness. Human destinies are in part determined by chthonian powers, in the spirits of mountain, rocks, springs, rivers, and other topographic features, and generalized in the earth matrix, Pachamama" (1991: 141). In other words,

cosmological powers were worshipped by the natives of Peru in specific objects and landscape features in and around their communities.

Many of the early chroniclers of Peru define the Quechua word *huaca* as equivalent to "idol."[2] Garcilaso de la Vega (1966: 76–77 [1609: Vol. 1, Bk. 2, Ch. 4]), reacting to this limited definition, gave an expanded description of the term, stating that the word *huaca* means "a sacred thing." According to this Cusco-born chronicler, a huaca was anything in nature that was out of the ordinary. This definition includes objects of outstanding beauty or elegance, as well as those of ugly or monstrous proportions. Garcilaso de la

Photo 1.2. The Cusco Valley. The city of Cusco is located at the northern end of a long valley. The entire city was considered sacred, and travelers offered prayers and sacrifices when they first saw it. (Courtesy Servicio Aerofotográfico Nacional, Perú)

Vega provided various examples of objects that were considered unusual and were thus called huacas. These covered an enormous range of observations, from the snow-capped mountains of the Andes to harelipped individuals. Cobo's (1990: 47 [1653: Bk. 13, Ch. 12]) definition for the word *huaca* (or *guaca*) adds an important additional dimension: "... the Peruvian Indians used the term *guaca* for all of the sacred places designated for prayers and sacrifices, as well as for all of the gods and idols that were worshipped in these places."[3] While recognizing that the term *huaca* can be used to describe a variety of unusual objects, Cobo's definition, which emphasizes the fact that prayers and offerings were made to these unique objects and locations, will be focused on in this study.

A number of sixteenth- and seventeenth-century writers mention the word *ceque* in their works and indicate that it can be glossed as "line." The earliest Quechua-Spanish lexicon was written by Domingo de Santo Tomás and was published less than thirty years after the arrival of the Spaniards in Peru. Santo Tomás (1951: 159, 196, 259 [1560: 71, 89, 121]) equates *ceque* [cepque, çeque, zeque] with the Spanish word *raya* (line or mark), suggesting that ceques had special importance in discussions of field boundaries. The anonymous *Arte y vocabulario en la lengua general del Perú...* (1951: 30, 178 [1586]) and Diego González Holguín's (1989: 81–82, 652 [1608]) vocabulary also gloss *ceque* as *raya*. Cristóbal de Albornoz (1984 [ca. 1582]) describes ceques as marks, and offers advice on how to destroy them, which suggests that some of the ceques may have been trails or other markings that could be physically destroyed. Furthermore, in his discussion of Quechua kinship terminology, the Jesuit parish priest Juan Pérez Bocanegra (1631: 609, 610) states that the term *checan çequep* incorporates the concepts of "straight line of consanguinity," while *pallcarec çeque* denotes "transversal" or "collateral" lines of relations (Zuidema 1977c: 260).

Soon after initial contact, the pan-Andean pattern of huaca worship and its pivotal role in indigenous worldviews drew the attention of the Spaniards. The most important shrines of the Inca Empire, such as the Temple of Pachacamac on the coast of Peru and the Coricancha in Cusco, were looted and destroyed by Europeans even before they established absolute rule over the Inca Empire. Then, in less than seven years after initial contact, the Spaniards gained control of most of the important cities in Peru, and the former rulers of Tahuantinsuyu retreated into the mountainous

jungles northeast of Cusco. In 1539, sensing that the momentum of the conquest was irreversible, the Spaniards began a series of campaigns targeted specifically against what they deemed as idolatrous activities. One of their first acts in these campaigns was to execute the Villca Umu, who was the chief priest of the Temple of the Sun in Cusco.

Realizing the importance of shrines in Andean rituals, the Spaniards focused much of the first decades of the anti-idolatry campaigns on the discovery and destruction of huacas. Spanish clergy wrote specific instructions to help their fellow Christians in this task. For example, Pablo Joseph de Arriaga (1968a [1621: Ch. 15]), one of the most active and effective agents of the anti-idolatry movement, outlined thirty-six questions concerning huacas and their attendants that were to be asked on entering a village. He also gave specific instructions on how information on the shrines should be recorded, and detailed the manner in which the shrines were to be destroyed. He emphasized that all the attendants and worshippers of a huaca were to be prosecuted, that the foundations for the shrine needed to be dug out, that the specific object of worship was to be destroyed, and that anything flammable associated with it was to be burnt. A cross was then to be built on the same spot as the destroyed huaca to conclude its razing. Albornoz (1984 [ca. 1582]) provided similar advice, and even instructed his fellow Christians to record the names and locations of the huacas at the time of destruction so that they could later be revisited and inspected for evidence of continued worship.

The Spanish campaigns against the autochthonous religions of the Andes met with intense resistance and provided the catalyst for numerous millenarian cults. For example, starting around 1560, the indigenous peoples of the Central Andes were swept by the ten-year-long Taqui Oncoy movement, which called for a return to huaca worship and for the casting out of Spanish ideology from the highlands. Such social unrest, however, only increased the Europeans' efforts to impose their religion on the Andean peoples and to uproot and destroy huaca worship. Nevertheless, although hundreds of thousands of local shrines were destroyed, and an untold number of people were prosecuted in the Early Colonial period, ritual observations at specific locations on the landscape continued, and today, the worship of place-specific sacred powers plays a discreet but important role in the lives of many rural inhabitants. In the following pages, the ancient huacas of the Cusco region will be revisited nearly four hundred and fifty years after their destruction, and the role that these sacred objects and locations played in defining the social, political, and territorial organization of the Inca heartland will be explored.

The Organization of Cusco and the Ceque System

The spatial organization of the Inca Empire is discussed in a number of chronicles, and there is general agreement on its broadest geopolitical divisions. The Inca divided the Cusco Valley (and, by extension, their empire) into four regions, or *suyus*. The city of Cusco was at the junction of these four parts and was, for the Inca, the axis and center of Andean cosmological order (Map 1.2). The physical partitioning of the city, and the surrounding valley, echoed a division of society into moieties (or halves). The upper half of Cusco, Hanansaya (Upper part), was occupied by two quarters. The northwest quarter was referred to as Chinchaysuyu and the northeast was named Antisuyu. The lower half of Cusco, Hurinsaya (Lower part), also contained two quarters, with Collasuyu lying to the southeast and Cuntisuyu to the southwest (Map 1.3).

While most of the Spanish chronicles provide information on the moiety and suyu divisions of Cusco Valley,

Cobo's 1653 work goes further and describes a related, but vastly more complex, Inca partitioning system (Cobo 1956: 169–186, 1980: 14–61, 1990: 51–84 [1653: Bk. 13, Ch. 13–16]; also see Rowe 1980, 1981a). In addition to the moieties of Cusco (Hanansaya and Hurinsaya) and the quarters of the valley (Chinchaysuyu, Antisuyu, Collasuyu, and Cuntisuyu), Cobo states that the Cusco region was further partitioned by 42 abstract lines, or ceques, that radiated from the center of the city. He also indicates that the orientations of the ceques were determined by the locations of not less than 328 shrines that surrounded Cusco:

> From the Temple of the Sun as from the center there went out certain lines which the Indians call ceques: they formed four parts corresponding to the four royal roads which went out from Cuzco. On each one of those ceques were arranged in order the guacas and shrines which there were in Cuzco and its district, like stations of holy places, the veneration of which was common to all. (Cobo 1980: 15 [1653: Bk. 13, Ch. 13])[4]

In the course of his account, Cobo describes the ceques contained in each of the four suyus, as well as the individual shrines that formed the organizational lines. His account indicates that the first three divisions, Chinchaysuyu, Antisuyu, and Collasuyu, contained nine ceques each. The

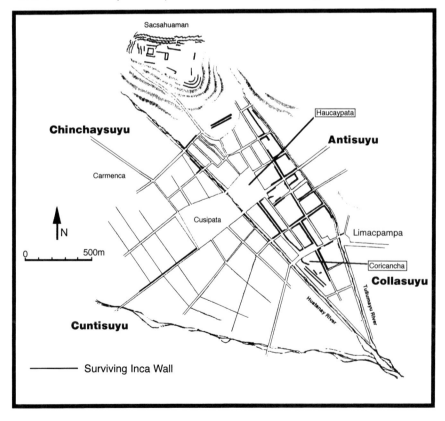

Map 1.2. The ancient city of Cusco was located at the junction of the four great *suyus* (Chinchaysuyu, Antisuyu, Collasuyu, and Cuntisuyu). The city was, for the Inca, the center of Andean cosmological order. The two most important locations in the city were the Coricancha and Haucaypata (now the Plaza de Armas).

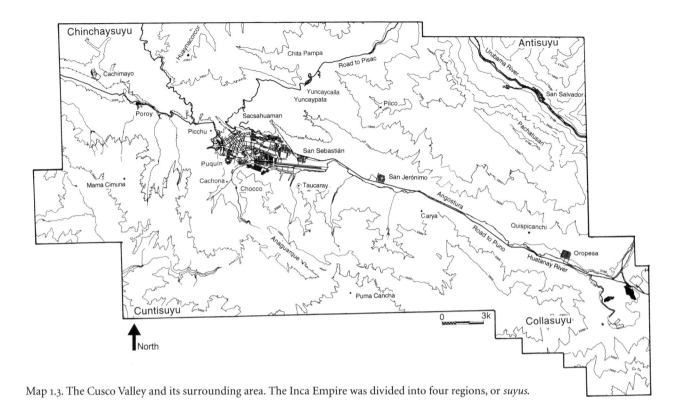

Map 1.3. The Cusco Valley and its surrounding area. The Inca Empire was divided into four regions, or *suyus*.

organization of ceques in Cuntisuyu, the fourth suyu, is more complex. Cobo lists fourteen ceques in this suyu, but he states that one ceque, the eighth, was divided and called by two different names: *collana* and *cayao*. Field research in Cusco has found that this ceque actually formed two separate lines radiating out from Cusco. Accordingly, the total number of ceques in Cuntisuyu was fifteen rather than the fourteen reported by Cobo.

Cobo's description of the Cusco ceque system, here called the *Relación de las huacas* (Report of the shrines), is divided into four chapters, each characterizing the ceques and huacas in a specific suyu. The huacas along each ceque are presented according to their relative distance from the Temple of the Sun. The first shrine of a ceque is generally within the city of Cusco, often in or near the Coricancha. The last huaca of a ceque is always outside of the city, frequently near or just beyond the border of the Cusco Valley.

At the beginning of each of the four chapters of the *Relación de las huacas*, Cobo describes the approximate location of the suyu and the number of ceques and shrines found within it. For example, for Chinchaysuyu Cobo writes:

Beginning, then, with the Road of Chinchaysuyu, which leaves the city through the precinct of Carmenga, there were in [the part corresponding to] it nine ceques on which were included eighty-five guacas, . . . (Cobo 1980: 15 [1653: Bk. 13, Ch. 13])[5]

Cobo is not consistent, however, in his presentation of ceque information. The Chinchaysuyu ceques are discussed in a counterclockwise order, while those of Antisuyu, Collasuyu, and Cuntisuyu are enumerated in a clockwise direction (Figure 1.1). It is generally suggested by researchers, such as Zuidema (1964) and Rowe (1985), who have studied the system that Cobo's ordering of the Chinchaysuyu ceques is a peculiarity of his presentation, not of the system itself.[6] It should also be noted that according to the *Relación de las huacas*, the ceques in each of the four suyus were enumerated in groups of three, a pattern I will call "ceque clusters." The lines within each ceque cluster were ranked by the terms (1) *collana*, (2) *payan*, and (3) *cayao* (Zuidema 1964: 2–5, 1983a; Rowe 1985).

Overall, Cobo presents a clear and well-organized description of the Cusco ceque system. The precision of his ac-

Chinchaysuyu   Antisuyu

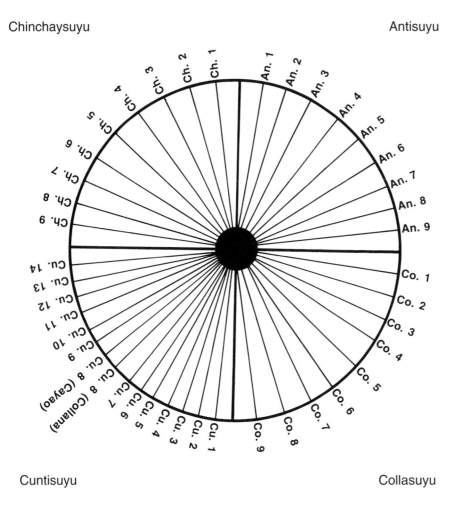

Cuntisuyu   Collasuyu

Figure 1.1. The Cusco ceques. In Cobo's description of the Cusco ceques, the Chinchaysuyu ceques
are discussed in a counterclockwise order, while those of Antisuyu, Collasuyu, and Cuntisuyu are
enumerated in a clockwise direction.

count suggests that the original information on the system came from an individual who kept track of what offerings were to be presented to the Cusco shrines. Albornoz (1984: 200 [ca. 1582]) notes the existence of such people, calling them *camayocs* (specialists). Molina (1989: 127–128 [ca. 1575]) and other writers are more specific, calling them *huacacamayocs* (huaca specialists) and *vilcacamayocs* (sacred object specialists). These individuals helped to coordinate shrine worship in the Cusco region and ensured that appropriate offerings were made to each of the huacas at the appropriate times. The information now preserved within the folios of Cobo's *History of the New World* may have been recorded on a *quipu*, a system of knotted strings used as a counting or mnemonic device by the Inca (Rowe 1946, 1980;

Zuidema 1977a, 1988a, 1989c; Aveni 1990c). The speculation that huaca and offering information was recorded on quipus is supported by Juan de Matienzo (1967: 119 [1567: Ch. 36]), who notes that the royal *quipucamayocs* (quipu specialists) were interviewed soon after the conquest for information on the huacas of Cusco (Photo 1.3).

The shrines of the Cusco region, as described by Cobo, included natural features of the landscape, such as caves, boulders, and springs, as well as artificial features, like houses, fountains, and canals. The number of huacas associated with individual ceques seems to have varied greatly. For example, two ceques in Cuntisuyu are listed in the *Relación de las huacas* as containing only three shrines each, while a third ceque in the same suyu held fifteen. Cobo's ac-

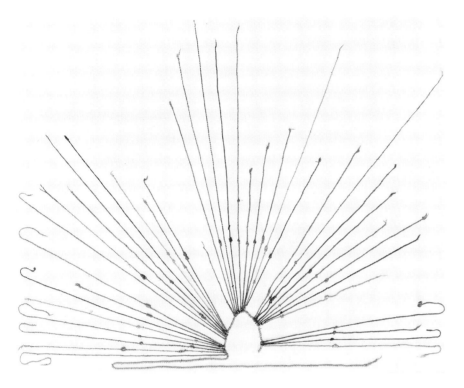

Photo 1.3. A quipu. Information on the Cusco ceque system may once have been recorded on a quipu. (Courtesy The Field Museum, negative A81973)

count also contains fragments of oral traditions concerning the origins of the huacas, and information on what offerings were made at them. Many of the shrines gained status as holy places for the inhabitants of Cusco through their association with events in the mythic history of the Inca. Other shrines became the focus of worship because of their relationships with specific Inca rulers; several were palaces, and others marked places where important events in an Inca's life were said to have taken place. A number of huacas served as land boundaries between social groups or were related to the irrigation systems of the Cusco region (Sherbondy 1982, 1986; Zuidema 1986b). Certain shrines marked symbolically important locations, such as mountain passes from whence Cusco was first seen by travelers approaching the city. Others represented astronomical sighting points in the Inca calendar; for example, three huacas are said to have been sets of towers on hills surrounding Cusco that marked sunsets on important days in the Inca ritual calendar (Bauer and Dearborn 1995).

Cobo specifically notes that attendants and servants of the various Cusco-based kin groups (*panacas* and *ayllus*) were responsible for making offerings to the huacas on specific ceques (Cobo 1980: 14 [1653: Bk. 13, Ch. 13]). Accord-

ingly, it seems that the spatial divisions of the Cusco Valley, as defined by the courses of ceques, were directly linked to the social organization of the capital by the ritual responsibilities held by certain kin groups (Zuidema 1964, 1990b; Rowe 1985). As such, the Cusco ceque system is perhaps the most complex ritual system to be recorded during the Early Conquest period of the Americas, and it has been used by scholars to develop a number of social and political models of the Inca capital.

Studies of the Cusco Ceque System

The Cusco ceque system first appeared as a topic of scholarly research in an article by Paul Kirchhoff (1949) and in a number of unpublished works by the Cusco archaeologist Manuel Chávez Ballón. The first extensive investigation of the system was conducted by R. Tom Zuidema in the mid-1950s and was translated and published in 1964 under the title *The ceque system of Cuzco: The social organization of the capital of the Inca.* This seminal study of the Cusco ceque system, written during the process of discovery, presents a highly complex analysis, much of which has yielded to reinterpretation by Zuidema himself in recent years.

Since the publication of Zuidema's monograph, interest in the Cusco ceque system has grown to become one of the most widely debated, and perhaps most misunderstood, aspects of Andean studies. Zuidema has been especially active in continued research on the social and political dimensions of Inca society as reflected in the Cusco ceque system. Other prominent scholars—including Chávez Ballón (1970), Nathan Wachtel (1973), John H. Rowe (1980, 1985), Santiago Agurto Calvo (1980, 1987), Gary D. Urton (1984), John Hyslop (1990), and Ian S. Farrington (1992)—have examined various organizational aspects of the Cusco ceques. These studies are largely historical in nature, attempting to construct models of the system from information provided in the *Relación de las huacas*. Importantly, these investigations include only limited ground verification of the locations of the shrines or the organization of the ceques, and are, consequently, not empirically grounded analyses.

Field research can make important contributions to understanding the ceque system. Jeanette Sherbondy's (1982, 1986, 1987) study of the irrigation system of Hanan Cusco provides one of the best examples. By analyzing Cobo's writing and by drawing on information recovered in the archives of Cusco as well as during limited reconnaissance work, Sherbondy examined the relationships between Inca social organization, traditional Inca land and water rights, and the ceque system in the Chinchaysuyu and Antisuyu regions of Cusco. She identified a number of shrines and developed a series of maps showing possible ceque courses in these two suyus.

Another investigation that illustrates how fieldwork can advance our understanding of the Cusco ceque system is Maarten Van de Guchte's (1984, 1990) study of Inca carved stones. In his work, Van de Guchte supplies detailed descriptions of all known carved rocks in the Cusco region, some of which represented huacas in the ceque system. He also provides a collection of maps that portray possible projections of ceques in Chinchaysuyu and Antisuyu. Sherbondy's and Van de Guchte's work assumes, however, that the Cusco ceques formed perfectly straight lines, an assumption that has generally been accepted in the literature since the time of Zuidema's initial research on the system.

The Ceques as Straight Lines

Cobo (1980: 15 [1653: Bk. 13, Ch. 13]) begins his description of the Cusco ceque system by stating, "From the Temple of the Sun as from the center there went out certain lines which the Indians call ceques ... ," and he proceeds to list the huacas of each ceque in an order proceeding away from the Coricancha. Cobo's description of the Cusco ceque system has frequently been compared with Cristóbal de Molina's (1989 [ca. 1575]) description of the Capac Cocha ritual. During this Inca celebration, offerings were gathered in Cusco and then redistributed to all the huacas of the empire. Of special interest to this study is that Molina indicates that the individuals who made the offerings traveled directly from shrine to shrine:

> ... all the people with the Capac Cocha, which by another name is called Cachaguaes, ... went separated from one another, without going by the royal road directly, but without turning anywhere, traversing the gorges and mountains that they found before them, until each one reached the part and place that ... were waiting to receive the said sacrifices ... [7]

Zuidema (1977a: 231), quite reasonably, has used this account to suggest that ceques formed straight lines. The notion of straight Cusco ceque lines is further bolstered by the many comparisons that have been made between the ceque system and the Nazca Lines on the coast of Peru (Morrison 1978; Reinhard 1985a; Aveni 1990c), and it has been reinforced by the numerous hypothetical reconstructions of the system that have been published (Zuidema 1964, 1977a, 1983b, 1990a; Chávez Ballón 1970; Wachtel 1973; Sherbondy 1982, 1986; Urton 1984; Van de Guchte 1984, 1990; Aveni 1990c; Farrington 1992).

The straight-line proposal becomes a definitive feature of the system within the context of Zuidema's work on the possible calendrical functions of the ceques. Since the mid-1970s, Zuidema and Anthony F. Aveni have developed a complex argument suggesting that some of the ceques were used as sight lines for observing astronomical events on the horizon (Zuidema 1977a: 220; Aveni 1981a, 1981b). The proposition that some of the ceques were sight lines has profound implications for understanding the role and sacred nature of the shrines that Cobo recorded. The theory suggests that various objects and locations were selected as huacas because they fell along certain *preconceived* lines. In other words, various shrines were incorporated into the ceque system not because of some innate power they possessed or their specific significance in events in Inca mythic history or their importance in defining territorial boundaries between ethnic groups, but rather because of their usefulness in defining lines from the center of Cusco to the horizon (Zuidema 1977a: 251, 1981b: 325, 1988a: 341). This is specifically discussed in an article on Inca calendrics:

> As far as we have been able to study these directions, called *ceques*, "lines," they were based on sightlines towards the horizon. Ceques to the nearby horizon could pass beyond it, while ceques to the faraway horizon would end before. The directions were known with the help of natural or man made markers along the ceques, in numbers varying from 3 to 15, *whose locations normally were chosen as close as possible to the directions. For this reason they were worshipped as sacred and called huacas.* (Zuidema 1982c: 59; emphasis added)

It is important to note, however, that Zuidema and Aveni do not state that all of the ceques were straight. Nevertheless, their discussions of the system and their diagrams of "known" ceques (Zuidema 1977a, 1982b, 1982c, 1990a; Aveni 1981a) indicate that they believe a good many of them did represent straight lines. This straight-line assumption has been accepted and further advanced by other researchers trained by Zuidema (Sherbondy 1982, 1986, 1987; Van de Guchte 1984, 1990).

Rowe (1979, 1981b) appears to have been the first to question the straight-line assumption. Additional field data recovered by Susan A. Niles necessitates reconsideration of the straight-line ceque proposition. In 1977, Niles began an intensive archaeological study of a small section of Antisuyu, northeast of Cusco. Her shrine identifications were based on huaca descriptions provided by Cobo, surviving placenames, and the courses of Inca roads. Precise locations, descriptions, and photographs were given for each candidate. The ceques defined from these proposed identifications are far from straight, and the huacas of individual ceques are spread across nearly forty degrees as viewed from the Coricancha. Subsequently, it was recognized that these huacas and their respective ceques appeared to be located in radically different positions than predicted by straight-line representations of the system (Niles 1987: 180, 204–205; Dearborn and Schreiber 1989). Niles (1987: 171–206) concluded that many of the huacas that defined the fourth, fifth, and sixth ceques of Antisuyu (An. 4, An. 5, and An. 6) were scattered across the region in a nonlinear fashion. In addition, her findings indicate that the ceques could change directions as they zigzagged their way through the landscape. The research presented in this book supports Niles's findings and indicates that many of the ceques did not form straight lines. In this model of the Cusco ceque system, it is the specific *locations* of the huacas that define the course of the lines and not vice versa. In other words, while the connotative model of the system by the Inca may have included the notion of ceques as straight lines, researchers cannot presume that the actual form of the system on the landscape reproduced this restrictive framework.

While Niles and I present evidence indicating that the ceques were not necessarily straight, we both believe that they generally did not cross over one another. In the course of this study, I have identified a number of huacas that seem to be well away from the general course of their ceque, and their inclusion would mean that the ceque crossed over one or more adjacent lines. These exceptional shrines and their unusual ceques require special attention and discussion.

Numbering and Naming the Huacas

The presence of 42 lines and at least 328 shrines requires that a classification system be developed and used in discussions of the Cusco ceque system. In this study, I use Rowe's (1980) numbering method of the ceques and huacas to describe their locations in the system. In this method, ceques and huacas are identified according to the order in which Cobo presents them in his description of the system. For example, Co. 1:2 signifies the second shrine on the first ceque of Collasuyu, while Co. 9:13 designates the thirteenth shrine on the ninth ceque of Collasuyu. This system is both simple and neutral. Zuidema (1964) has developed an alternative numbering system for the Cusco ceques and their huacas based on the division of the region into four quarters and the clustering of the ceques into sets of three. A conversion table for the two numbering systems is provided in Appendix 1.

To aid the reader in understanding the Cusco ceque system, I have provided an English translation of the *Relación de las huacas* in Appendix 2. This translation, by John H. Rowe (1980), first appeared in *Ñawpa Pacha*. It is reproduced here with his permission. A modified version of this translation also appears in Cobo 1990. Spanish editions of the *Relación de las huacas* can be found in Cobo 1954, 1964, 1980, and 1981.

The Quechua terms, toponyms, and personal names contained in this work are written according to their Hispanicized spelling as found in the Spanish chronicles and on modern maps. The English and Spanish plural form *s* is used in this text rather than the Quechua form (*kuna* or *cuna*). For example, I discuss *huacas* rather than *huacakuna*.

When I compare the descriptions of a shrine found in different historical texts, *the reader will find the name of a huaca spelled a number of different ways, even within the same paragraph.* For example, in the discussion of Sanca Cancha and Hurin Sanca (Ch. 7:2), one finds the same location spelled as Sancay Uaci, Sanzahuaci, and Cangaguase; or in the case of Chacuaytapara (Ch. 8:5) there is also Chaguaytapra, Chanaytapra, and Chaquaitapra; or for Pachatusa (An. 2:2) there is Payatusan and Pachatusan. In other places, the reader will find that the spacing and capitalization used in huaca names is different as well. For example, Poma Chupa (Cu. 1:3) is also written as Poma chupan as well as puma chupa and Pumapchupan. In these and other cases, I have retained the *original* spelling, spacing, and capitalization as found in each of the primary sources.

Margot Beyersdorff has provided English glosses for the huaca names. Although this was an extremely challenging, and at times highly speculative, task, we feel it is important to offer possible translations. Many of the names are derived from the physical form of the huaca (e.g., Anaypampa [Co. 3:5 Exquisite Plain], Cachipuquiu [An. 5:2 Salt Spring], Nina [Ch. 3:1 Flame], Mayu [Co. 1:9 River], Tipcpuquiu [An. 1:8 Boiling Spring], Totorguaylla [Ch. 9:12 Reed Meadow]), while other names suggest activities that were once carried out at them (e.g., Ayllipampa [An 7:1 Maize Song Plain], Caynaconga [An. 2:7 Resting Place], Chiquinapampa [An. 1:1 Weaning of Animals Plain]). Some names address the supernatural powers that were localized in the shrine. For example, Co. 9:3 was called Pactaguañui [Careful, Death!], and we learn from Cobo that "it was a much venerated place; they sacrificed to it to be preserved from sudden death." Likewise, Ch. 4:2 was named Puñui [Sleep] because it was ". . . a very solemn shrine . . . held to be the cause of sleep," and Ch. 6:4 Guayra [Wind] was "where sacrifices were made to the wind." There are other names, however, for which meanings have become lost. Additional information on the suggested glosses of huaca names is offered in Appendix 3, along with their spelling in modern Quechua orthography. We note that these glosses are a starting point for understanding the names of the Cusco huacas, and we encourage others to expand on this effort.

2

The Original Ceque System Manuscript

THE CUSCO CEQUE SYSTEM is known to us primarily through the 1653 work of Cobo. It is widely recognized, however, that Cobo was not the original author of his ceque system information and that he gained his data by copying an older document. Although there has been considerable speculation on the primary source of Cobo's ceque system information, the author and date of what will be called here the "original ceque system manuscript" have not been clearly identified. The purpose of this chapter is to address and resolve the authorship and date issues by determining which Spaniards were aware of the Cusco ceque system, and by examining the historical context in which the original ceque system manuscript was recorded. In the first section of this chapter, possible dates for the original ceque system manuscript and Cobo's editing of this document will be discussed. In the second section, references to the Cusco ceque system contained in other chronicles will be presented. The chapter concludes with an examination of possible authors for the original ceque system manuscript.

The Date of the Original Ceque System Manuscript

Cobo extracted much of his information on the history and religious practices of the Inca from earlier documents. One of these sources discussed the ceques of the Cusco region in unprecedented detail. Cobo included the ceque material in his chronicle, not because of a personal interest in the ceque system per se, but to illustrate that the Inca worshiped a range of objects (Rowe 1980:8). Writing at the end of his huaca list, he is very direct on this point:

> I very nearly refrained from listing, even in their brief fashion, the guacas named in these four chapters, and I would have done so, except that I judge it necessary to enumerate them to explain more clearly the gullibility of these people . . . (Cobo 1980:61 [1653:Bk. 13, Ch. 16])

Determining the date and author of Cobo's original source on the ceque system and identifying the changes that Cobo made while extracting data from it are difficult because the original manuscript has not been found. Nevertheless, through a detailed examination of Cobo's account, some conclusions can be reached.

Cobo used manuscripts stored in secular and ecclesiastical archives of various cities in Peru, including Lima, Cusco, and Arequipa, as well as Juli, the center for Jesuit studies in the Andes, but, like most writers of his time, he was inconsistent in acknowledging his sources. Furthermore, in some sections he mixed information from different sources, while in other places he reproduced entire blocks of data (Rowe 1980:2–3). When Cobo did copy blocks of text into his chronicle, he tended to make few changes in the spelling of the indigenous words. The numerous spelling errors and irregularities in Cobo's description of the ceque system suggest the source of Cobo's data was written by an individual who was not a Quechua expert (Rowe 1980:3). It also appears that the document was written in the city of Cusco because the fourth shrine on the ninth ceque of Collasuyu (Co. 9:4) is described as "a spring which is this side of Membilla"; that is to say, between Cusco and Membilla (or what is now called Wimpillay).

There are other clues within Cobo's text to the author and date of the original ceque system manuscript. For example, many of the huaca descriptions are vague, suggesting that the original author was not sure of the shrines' locations. For example, the account of the sixth shrine on the fifth ceque of Chinchaysuyu (Ch. 5:6) reads as follows:

> The sixth guaca was named Sabacurinca; it was a well-carved seat where the Incas sat. It was very venerated, and solemn sacrifices were made to it. On account of this seat, the whole fortress was worshiped; for it [the seat] must have been inside or next to [the fortress]. (Cobo 1980:23 [1653:Bk. 13, Ch. 13])[1]

This passage, and others like it in the account, suggests that the writer of the original ceque system manuscript obtained his information through interviews rather than through countryside inspections. The most likely source of information on the shrines of the Cusco region would have been the imperial quipu specialists who, as we are told by Cobo and other chroniclers, kept track of the Cusco shrines and of the offerings made to them. Based on this information, it seems that the author of the original ceque system manuscript was in Cusco early enough to have interviewed the state quipu keepers but was not an expert in Quechua.

A clue to the date of the original ceque system manuscript is contained within Cobo's description of the seventh shrine on the eighth ceque of Chinchaysuyu (Ch. 8:7). This huaca consisted of two pillars that marked an important sunset in the Inca ritual calendar. Cobo (1980:27 [1653:Bk. 13, Ch. 13]) describes the pillars as being on "a hill by way of which the water channel from Chinchero comes." These pillars, which are also described by a number of other early colonial writers, stood on the hill of Picchu, which forms the northwest horizon as seen from central Cusco (Bauer and Dearborn 1995). The Chinchero channel mentioned by Cobo in relation to this shrine crossed Picchu. The act to begin construction of this channel was passed in Cusco on 1 July 1557 (Esquivel y Navía 1980:192 [1749]), indicating that the ceque account was written no earlier than this date.

Other possible aids in dating the original ceque system manuscript are the land-title descriptions contained within the account. Nearly forty huacas are described as being on or near land owned by prominent early Spanish colonists. For example, Ch. 3:3, a spring called Ticicocha, is said to have been inside the house of Diego Maldonado, an extremely wealthy and influential early citizen of Spanish Cusco who died in 1570. These references are not as helpful in dating Cobo's source as they might initially seem because Maldonado and other prominent inhabitants of Cusco often owned more than one house in the city. Furthermore, many of these houses continued to be identified with the original owners long after their deaths.[2]

Nevertheless, one land-title reference within the description of the fifth shrine on the second ceque of Collasuyu (Oscollo [Co. 2:5]) is helpful in dating the original manuscript. It reads:

> The fifth was a flat place called Oscollo, which belonged to Garcilaso. They offered it the usual things. (Cobo 1980:43 [1653:Bk. 13, Ch. 15])[3]

This shrine was located on the plain of Oscollopampa, between the modern communities of San Jerónimo and San Sebastián, along the south bank of the Huatanay River (Bauer 1992a). We know from local land documents that Oscollopampa (Huzcollabamba) was purchased by Captain Garcilaso de la Vega in 1559 from the *caciques* (leaders) of the Uro, Acamana, and Cayra (Guevara Gil 1993:392). If the information recorded in the description of Co. 2:5 is from the original ceque system manuscript, and not added later by Cobo, then it must have been recorded after Garcilaso de la Vega's purchase of the land in 1559.

Rowe (1980, 1981a) suggests that one of the most useful clues in dating the original ceque system manuscript lies in the description of the fourth huaca of the seventh ceque of Antisuyu (An. 7:4), which reads:

> The fourth was a large plaza named Colcapampa, where the parish of the Martyrs was made, at the end of which there was a stone which was an important idol, to whom children were offered along with other things. (Cobo 1980:37 [1653:Bk. 13, Ch. 14])[4]

As he has gleaned from information provided in the Libro de Cabildos del Cuzco (1559–1560), Rowe (1981a:213) points out that the initial five parish churches of Cusco were established in 1559, during Polo de Ondegardo's first term as *corregidor* (chief magistrate). However, one of these, the parish church of the Martyrs (parroquia de los Mártires), established in honor of "san fabian y san sevastian" (AHD/Libro de Cabildos, 1559–1560: f. 63v, cited by Rowe 1981a:213), had become known as the parish church of San Sebastián by the time Francisco de Toledo's reduction movement began in 1572. Accordingly, Rowe suggests that the original manuscript, which mentions the parish church of the Martyrs, was written sometime in the thirteen years between 1559 and 1572.

Based on the information available at this time, Rowe's suggested range of dates seems entirely possible. It is clear that the *Relación de las huacas* was first recorded after 1559. The only way that the original ceque system manuscript could have been written before this date is if the references to the parish church of the Martyrs and to the ownership of Oscollopampa by Garcilaso were added later by Cobo. The 1572 date is less well founded, however. San Fabián and San Sebastián are, after all, the martyrs. It is unclear when exactly the popular name of the parish church changed from that of the Martyrs to that of San Sebastián. Furthermore, older Spanish inhabitants of the valley might have continued to use the traditional name even after it had been changed.

Sixteenth-Century Writings on the Cusco Ceque System

When Cobo finished his *Historia del Nuevo Mundo,* the Spaniards had occupied the Peruvian highlands for more than one hundred years. During these four or five generations of Hispanic rule, the existence of Andean ceque systems had come to the attention of a number of church and Spanish crown administrators, including Cristóbal de Albornoz, Cristóbal de Molina, Juan Polo de Ondegardo, José de Acosta, Francisco de Toledo, and Pedro de Córdoba Mexía. Several of these individuals were personally familiar with the Cusco system. It is worthwhile to examine the reports of these officials because they provide data unavailable in Cobo's chronicle and information on the possible author of the original ceque system manuscript.

Cristóbal de Albornoz (ca. 1530–1583)

One of the principal leaders in the Spanish campaigns against the autochthonous religions of the Andes in the immediate postconquest era was Cristóbal de Albornoz. From 1568 until his death in 1583, Albornoz led a series of campaigns in the Peruvian highlands to identify and destroy native shrines, and to punish individuals and communities who worshiped them. One of the most comprehensive of these anti-idolatry campaigns was in the Huamanga (modern Ayacucho) area, where from 1568 through 1571 Albornoz crusaded against the millenarian Taqui Oncoy movement.[5] During this period he was personally responsible for the destruction of thousands of huacas and for the persecution of many individuals. He recorded the names and locations of many of the shrines so that other Spaniards could revisit and inspect them for evidence of continued use. Albornoz writes, for example, that he found over two thousand shrines in the area of the Chanca and Aymara ethnic groups, in the central Andes, and that he recorded the names of the destroyed huacas in the parishes' records.[6]

Soon after his Huamanga campaign, Albornoz (1984 [ca. 1582]) wrote an essay, *Instrucción para descubrir todas las guacas del Pirú y sus camayos y haziendas* (Instructions for discovering all the huacas of Peru and their *camayos* [specialists] and activities), and encouraged fellow Spaniards to destroy Andean shrines. In this small treatise, Albornoz explicitly states that many Andean shrines were organized along ceques and provides a list of thirty-seven huacas in the Chinchaysuyu region of Cusco, the majority of which are also mentioned in Cobo's chronicle. Given Albornoz's knowledge of the Cusco shrines and the nature of ceques, it is reasonable to assume that he had a basic understanding of the Cusco ceque system. There is, however, no evidence to suggest that Cobo had access to any of Albornoz's works. Furthermore, as will be discussed in Chapter 9, the order, names, and spellings of Albornoz's list of Cusco shrines suggest that it was composed independently of the original ceque system manuscript.[7]

Cristóbal de Molina (?–1585)

Father Cristóbal de Molina, like Albornoz, was a well-known religious figure in the postconquest era. Molina lived most of his life as a priest in the Hospital de Naturales de Nuestra Señora de los Remedios (Indian Hospice of Our Lady of Succor), and he was known to his contemporaries as an outstanding Quechua scholar (Guaman Poma de Ayala 1980:580 [1615:611 (625)]). Molina shared a long-term association with Albornoz, aiding him in the extirpation of idolatry in the Cusco region, and he is specifically mentioned in Albornoz's 1577 and 1584 reports (Millones 1990: 180, 182, 223, 228). Because Albornoz knew of the Cusco ceque system, the close interaction between these two men in the Cusco region makes it likely that Molina was also familiar with it.

Molina was the author of a number of documents on the Inca. One report, concerning the origin, lives, and customs of the Inca, was written before 1575 but is now lost.[8] Another work, *Relación de las fábulas i ritos de los Ingas* (An account of the fables and rites of the Inca), was written around 1575 and was used extensively by Cobo in his *Historia del Nuevo Mundo.* This report provides detailed descriptions of Inca rituals in Cusco. Furthermore, it indicates that an account (*relación*) on the shrines of Cusco existed (Molina 1989:126 [ca. 1575]), and that this report was considered important enough to be sent to Don Sebastián de Lartaun, the bishop of Cusco. Molina writes:

> There were so many places which they had dedicated to sacrifice in Cusco that if they were to be added here it would be very tedious, and because in the "Account of the Huacas" that I sent to your Most Reverend Lordship, they are all set down in the manner that they were sacrificed; I do not put that here.[9]

This passage has led some researchers to suggest that Molina was the author of the original ceque system manuscript (Rowe 1946:300; Porras Barrenechea 1962:277; Zuidema 1964:1 n. 1). Rowe (1980:7) later pointed out, however, that Molina does not specifically claim authorship of the report that he sent to the bishop. Accordingly, it is possible that Molina may have sent the bishop a report on the shrines that was written by another person.

Three discrepancies between information given in Molina's *Relación de las fábulas . . .* and that recorded in Cobo's chronicle have also been identified. Although it is difficult to say just how much emphasis should be placed on such discrepancies, they argue against the likelihood that Molina was the author of the original ceque system manuscript. The first discrepancy is that the eighth shrine on the eighth ceque of Chinchaysuyu (Ch. 8:8) is described in Cobo's chronicle as a temple that contained certain stones thought to be the women of Ticci Viracocha (the Creator). This contrasts with information provided by Molina (1989:78 [ca. 1575]), who specifically states that women were not allowed to serve this deity (Rowe 1980:7).[10] The second is that Molina (1989:118 [ca. 1575]) suggests that the field of Sausero belonged to Mama Huaco, while Cobo's chronicle indicates that it was a field of the Sun (Rowe 1980:8). The third discrepancy concerns the belvedere (or *mirador*) of Santo Domingo. Molina (1989:100 [ca. 1575]) writes that the quarters of the huaca of the moon, Passamama, were located where the belvedere of Santo Domingo was built. This contrasts with information contained in Cobo's account of the ceque system, which records that a stone called Sabaraura (Cu. 1.1) was located there.

On the other hand, there are some interesting correlations between information presented in Molina's *Relación de las fábulas . . .* and that presented in Cobo's account of the ceque system. For example, Cobo's chronicle describes the first huaca of the fifth ceque of Antisuyu (An. 5:1), situated near the Plaza of Limacpampa, as Aucaypata (Haucaypata). While numerous Conquest period documents refer to the central plaza of Cusco as Haucaypata, Molina (1989:72 [ca. 1575]) is the only author other than Cobo to specifically report that Limacpampa also shared this name.

Juan Polo de Ondegardo (ca. 1510–1575)

Juan Polo de Ondegardo was a prominent lawyer who held a number of public positions in what is now Bolivia and

Peru during the mid- to late-sixteenth century. He was the corregidor of Potosí, served twice as the corregidor of Cusco, and wrote treatises and legal briefs for men such as Jerónimo de Loayza (the first archbishop of Lima) and for Viceroys Hurtado de Mendoza, Conde de Nieva, and Toledo (Polo de Ondegardo 1916a–e, 1917, 1940, 1965a–e).[11] His writings were extensively used by the Catholic Church's Provincial Councils of Lima and were major sources of information for Cobo and Acosta.

As corregidor of Cusco (1558–1560 and 1571–1572), Polo de Ondegardo was in an unusually powerful position to conduct interviews with surviving royal Incas and their entourages, and he won praise from his compatriots for the often spectacular results of his investigations. For example, one early inquiry on the noble lineages of the Inca led to the discovery of the royal Inca mummies, which were still being housed and worshipped in the environs of Cusco. It is also apparent that Polo de Ondegardo was extremely interested in the huacas and ceques of Cusco because they are mentioned in most of his major works.

The earliest treatise of Polo de Ondegardo (1916b [1585]) to mention the ceque system of Cusco was published in 1585, by order of the Third Provincial Council of Lima under the directorship of Acosta, with the title *De los errores y supersticiones de los indios, sacados del tratado y averiguación que hizo el Licenciado Polo* (About the errors and superstitions of the Indians; taken from the work and investigation done by Licentiate Polo). The publication is, as the title indicates, an extract from a much longer work that Polo de Ondegardo wrote on Inca religion in 1559 during his first term as corregidor of Cusco. In this 1559 account—which Cobo claimed to have the original copy of, with the author's own signature—Polo de Ondegardo (1916b:43 [1585]) notes that there were 340 shrines within a few leagues of Cusco:

> Since Cuzco and its province had large numbers of idols, *huacas, villcas,* places of worship, and shrines erected in various places, thus, too, in every province there were individual *huacas* or shrines, and each one had some particular object of worship: and each family had the bodies of the dead to venerate. Finally, each land and province had a great diversity of temples, and although now the idols, stones, instruments of sacrifices, and many other things which they had for their rituals have been removed, yet the hills, knolls, fountains, springs, rivers, lakes, ocean, gorges, rocks, *apachetas* [sacred

cairns], and other such things are still there. They are still worshipped today, and much vigilance is necessary to extirpate their impious worship from their hearts. The huacas and places of worship in Cuzco, and within a few leagues of it, number three hundred forty of various names, and there must have been more. Among them, many have been forgotten, yet there are bound to be survivals, especially where there are old men and women, and even more so where there are principals and *curacas* [leaders] inclined toward these. (Polo de Ondegardo 1965b:52–53 [1585]; translation modified)[12]

Because the number of shrines mentioned by Polo de Ondegardo in this report is so close to that listed in Cobo's chronicle, it is likely that Polo de Ondegardo either used the same principal informant(s) as the author of the original ceque system manuscript, or that he had read, or written, that very document.

A second reference to the Cusco ceque system by Polo de Ondegardo may be found in an extensive report he wrote for Licenciado Briviesca de Muñatones on the *encomiendas*[13] of Peru. In this document, finished and signed in Lima on 12 December 1561, Polo de Ondegardo (1940:183–184 [1561]) again mentions the huacas of Cusco, and notes that these shrines were organized along ceques:

... it will appear in the map that I made of the ceques and shrines of the city of Cusco, which is in the hands of many religious leaders[14] of that town, there was in that city, within one and a half leagues of it, about 400 places where sacrifices were made and a great quantity of property was wasted on them for different effects that Indians have imagined, ...[15]

From the above statement it seems that Polo de Ondegardo spent time studying the Cusco ceque system. It is also interesting to note that in this report, written some two years after *De los errores y supersticiones de los indios . . .*, he indicates that there were more than 400 shrines in the Cusco region, and he claims to have made a map (*carta*) of the system.[16]

There is no doubt that Polo de Ondegardo did draw a map of the ceque system because he refers to it several times in a 1571 document, *Relación de los fundamentos acerca del notable daño que resulta de no guardar a los Indios sus fueros* (A report on the causes relating to serious harm to the Indians which results from not keeping their traditional laws). This monumental work, written ten years after his encomienda study, discussed the traditional rights of the Inca.

In one section, Polo de Ondegardo (1916c:133–134 [1571]) describes how the Inca Empire was divided into four general regions (suyus) and explains how he marked these areas on his map of the Cusco huacas:

... in addition to another and more general division which they called *Tahuantinsuyu*, which is to say, four parts into which the whole realm was divided, which they called *colca suyo, zincha suyo, ande suyo, inde suyo*,[17] and which division begins from Cuzco, from which city come four roads, each one going to one of these parts, as appears in the map of the huacas, ... (Polo de Ondegardo 1965c:142–143 [1571]; translation modified)[18]

Polo de Ondegardo's (1916c:55 [1571]) 1571 report also states that aside from that of Cusco, he personally investigated other ceque systems in different parts of the highlands:

... the city of Cusco was the house and dwelling place of gods, and thus there was not in all of it, a fountain, or road, or wall that they did not say contained a mystery, which can be seen from the list of shrines in that city, of which there were more than four hundred. All this endured until the Spanish came, and even today they venerate every one of them when not watched, and the whole country keeps and worships the huacas which the Incas gave them. Following their own records, and to test the list, I have removed many in the province of Omasuyo and Collasuyo. (Polo de Ondegardo 1965c: 64–65 [1571]; translation modified)[19]

In this same 1571 report, arguably the most concise description of the ceque system outside of Cobo's work, Polo de Ondegardo (1916c:56–57 [1571]) stresses that he personally documented ceque systems in a large number of towns and showed these systems to other Spanish administrators. Although he does not specifically say so, his presentation suggests that the complexity of these systems varied according to the size and importance of the individual communities:

In each village the organization was the same; the district was crosscut by *ceques* and lines connecting shrines or various consecrations and all the things which seemed notable: wells and springs and stones, hollows and valleys and summits which they call *apachetas* [sacred cairns]. To each thing they assigned their people and showed them the way to follow in sacrificing to each of them and to what end and at what time and with what kinds of things and assigned people to teach it to them. Finally, although nowhere were there so many shrines as at Cuzco, the organization was the same and seeing the map of the huacas of Cuzco in every village no matter how small, they drew it in the same way and showed the *ceques* and the permanent *huacas* and shrines, and it is important to know this for their conversion. I have tested this matter in more than a hundred towns, and the Lord Bishop of the Charcas, doubting that the matter was so universal, when we traveled together by order of His Majesty in the matter of perpetuity [of the encomiendas], was shown it in Pocona[20] and the Indians themselves drew there the same map and there is no doubt about it because they were found there, as I say, without error, . . . (Polo de Ondegardo 1965c:67–68 [1571]; translation modified)[21]

In his final reference to the Cusco ceque system in this document, Polo de Ondegardo (1916c:113–114 [1571]) states that it was important for Spanish priests to understand that these extensive systems of shrines were maintained by all Andean communities, and he encouraged Spaniards to preach against the adoration of huacas and to punish those Indians who continued to worship them:

I put this down so that it may be understood that thus are their conceptions in everything, and how simple and uncomplicated they are. Many others, men and women, have charge of the permanent huacas, of which particular account is given in the general letter[22] about Cuzco, which is common in the whole realm and includes all of the places which are distinguished from the others in some way, whether near the village or even as far away as the mountain peaks, if it is rugged country, and which they call *apachetas* [sacred cairns], such as some large stones, and all the *puquios* [springs], and sources of water, or some level places which they build on some slope, or some specific trees, or the places where they sow the maize for the sacrifices, because all of these things are divided off by their *ceques* and boundaries around every village and are in the charge of persons who make within them different sacrifices and for diverse effects in some so that women may become pregnant, in others because they say that from them come the ice or the hail, and in others so that it might rain. Thus in this way does the Inca teach them this division of places in all that was conquered, charging them greatly with the benefit which they would receive in notifying everyone in his land of what they had and could make use of for their necessities, which today they do by the same system and have persons designated who understand this, and thus it is necessary in all the villages to have them make a map,[23] and, seeing the map of

Cuzco, they will do it, . . . (Polo de Ondegardo 1965c:123 [1571]; translation modified)[24]

The sum of these quotes, dating from 1559, 1561, and 1571, makes it clear that Polo de Ondegardo possessed a singularly broad knowledge of Andean ceque systems. His two terms as corregidor of Cusco gave him the opportunity, power, and motivation to conduct research on the huacas in the Inca heartland, and his travels across the Andes enabled him to examine ceque systems in many communities. It is clear that during his first term as corregidor of Cusco, Polo de Ondegardo had become aware of about 340 shrines, and he suggests that there were even more to be found. At that time he recorded the nature of the Cusco ceque system in a written account. In addition, it is clear that Polo de Ondegardo was aware of other such systems by 1561, because he showed the bishop of the Charcas one in the community of Pocona. Furthermore, by 1561 Polo de Ondegardo had increased his Cusco shrine number from 340 to 400 and had made a map of the system. Ten years later, he was still using his original report on the shrines of Cusco, referring to it several times in a 1571 document. In this same 1571 account, he advises all Spanish officials to make shrine maps during their inspections of communities. This recommendation seems to have been accepted by Viceroy Toledo and, as will be seen in the case of Pedro de Córdoba Mexía, was a task assigned to lower-level village inspectors.

On the basis of much of this information, Polo de Ondegardo has been credited with recording the original manuscript (Urteaga 1916; Zuidema 1977a, 1982c; Sherbondy 1982). Philip Means (1928:431, 432) credits Polo de Ondegardo with writing the original ceque system manuscript, and he even indicates that a copy of it, or perhaps the original draft, was housed in the Biblioteca Nacional in Lima. Means's wording suggests, however, that he never actually saw the manuscript, but was relying on second-hand information.[25]

There are also a number of discrepancies between information given in Polo de Ondegardo's works and that recorded in the *Relación de las huacas* that should be discussed. For example, Cobo's chronicle states that the second huaca of the sixth ceque of Chinchaysuyu (Ch. 6:2) was located in the Temple of the Creator, whereas Polo de Ondegardo writes in 1571 that he was unable to discover the house of the Creator (Polo de Ondegardo 1872:59, cited by Rowe 1980:7). Furthermore, Polo de Ondegardo (1916b:43 [1585], 1916c:

56–57 [1571]), when describing the various objects worshipped as huacas by the Inca, habitually uses the term *apachetas*. This term is completely absent from Cobo's account of the Cusco ceque system.

Pedro de Córdoba Mexía

During Viceroy Toledo's general inspections of indigenous communities (1570–1573) he gave specific instructions to Spanish officials to collect information on the "order" of huacas in various regions. Some of these instructions can be found in a work of Licenciado Pedro de Córdoba Mexía (1900:395–396 [ca. 1572]):

> Furthermore, look with much attention if in the towns . . . there is any huaca or shrine; and for more information inform yourselves about the *caciques* [leaders] and older ones of the aforementioned division and about the boys of the parish or constables; and yielding nothing clear you will make use of a plan and order which this Inca reign had of the huacas and shrines which were in each province, and the way they had sacrifices, and the other ceremonies that they made in their heathenism, and although they tell you that they [the huacas] are destroyed and that there is no memory or trace of them, you will personally see by the plan the places where they were and if they are destroyed and who destroyed them, asking about the rituals and ceremonies that each of these made, and who is the sorcerer or sorcerers that each one had, and what duty they did at the said huaca, and what they gave to the said sorcerer priests; and if they had special fields, gold, or other things and what has been done with them. Of everything that you do make a complete account writing the names of the huacas and sorcerers in a way that takes care that they do not relapse, and that there be amends made, and put crosses on them, being a respectable place for them.[26]

In this passage Córdoba Mexía indicates that inspectors should: (1) record the "order" of shrines in different provinces, (2) take extensive notes on the offerings and ceremonies associated with each shrine, and (3) make a *traza* (plan) of the shrine locations.[27] If these instructions were followed, then it is possible that a large number of maps and documents recording the shrines of various Andean villages were drafted during the latter part of the sixteenth century, and that some of these may still exist in public and private archives. It is worth considering that Cobo may have obtained such a study for the Cusco region and incorporated it into his chronicle.

Juan de Matienzo (ca. 1530–1579)

Licenciado Juan de Matienzo was a well-respected lawyer in the Spanish colony during the mid- to late-sixteenth century who spent time in Cusco attempting to negotiate a peaceful end to the war between the Spaniards and the last Inca rulers in Vilcabamba. He was also widely known for writing *Gobierno del Perú* (Government of Peru) in 1567, a treatise that presented a program for Spanish political reform in the Andes. While arguing that the shrines of the Inca must be systematically found, recorded, and destroyed, Matienzo (1967:119 [1567:Ch. 36]) states that Polo de Ondegardo, during his time as corregidor of Cusco, obtained and wrote down extensive information on the huacas of the Inca from the imperial quipu specialists:

> . . . first take from them the huacas and shrines that they have, and idols that they worship, something that until now has not been done, although the Licenciado Polo de Ondegardo, citizen and *encomendero* of this city [La Plata], a man of very good understanding, and who has served your Majesty very well in this reign, being corregidor in Cuzco investigated all the huacas and idols that the Indians have, which they worshipped, according to quipus of the Incas and superstitions they used, which is written down . . . [28]

Since *Gobierno del Perú* was finished by Matienzo in 1567, Polo de Ondegardo's interviews with the imperial quipu specialists concerning the huacas of the city must have occurred during his first term as corregidor (1558–1560). This concurs with information provided by Cobo (1979:99 [1653: Bk. 12, Ch. 2]), who stated that he had Polo de Ondegardo's 1559 report, written while the latter was corregidor of Cusco, which was based on interviews with former Inca rulers, priests, and quipucamayocs (quipu specialists). In other words, while it is clear that Matienzo did not write the report that was later copied by Cobo, he does provide evidence suggesting that Polo de Ondegardo did.

José de Acosta (ca. 1540–1600)

José de Acosta, a well-known and influential member of the Society of Jesus, lived in Peru and Mexico for most of his adult life. He wrote a number of theological and historical works, including *De procurinda indorum salute, o Predicación del evangelio en las Indias* [1580] and *Historia natural y moral de las Indias* [1590]. These works are important for the study of the Cusco ceque system because Acosta used

Polo de Ondegardo's writings in his discussions of the Inca, and Cobo had access to Acosta's works while writing his own chronicle. In fact, Acosta was a leading participant of the Provincial Councils of Lima, which published several excerpts from Polo de Ondegardo's original works, including the one dating to 1585.

Acosta mentions the Cusco ceque system and Polo de Ondegardo in two separate sections of his *De procurinda indorum salute.* . . . In one passage, he indicates that Polo de Ondegardo recorded the Cusco ceque system and was the principal destroyer of its huacas (Acosta 1954a:562 [1580:Bk. 5, Ch. 10]). In another passage, Acosta states that Polo de Ondegardo wrote a history of the Inca that included a description of the Cusco ceque system:

> [Superstition] is so strong among the Indians, that one can not count the kinds of sacrifices and huacas: mountains, hills, prominent rocks, useful springs, swiftly running rivers, high rocky peaks, large mountains of sand, an opening of a dark hole, a giant and ancient tree, a vein of ore, the odd and elegant form of any little stone; . . . then instantly they take it for divine and without delay they worship it. The mountains are full of this pernicious pestilence of idolatry, the valleys are full, the villages, the houses, and roads and there is not a portion of land in Peru which is free of this superstition. As the victims, the libations, the order of the ceremonies with which they followed all these principal cults of the Incas, are infinite; whoever wants should read the history of this that the Licenciado Polo [de Ondegardo], a serious and prudent man, carefully wrote, [and] you will see that within the boundaries of the city of Cuzco alone, there were more than 360 huacas counted, all of which were given divine honors, to some they offered fruit of the land; to others precious wools and gold and silver, and in honor of others much blood of innocent children was spilled in sacrifice.[29]

It is interesting to note in this passage that Acosta does not mention the 340 huacas described by Polo de Ondegardo (1916b:43 [1585]) in his 1559 investigation, nor the more than 400 listed in the latter's subsequent reports (Polo de Ondegardo 1940:183–184 [1561], 1916c:133–134 [1571]). Instead, Acosta writes that there were some 360 huacas in the Cusco region, but how he arrived at this summation is unclear. Nevertheless, it can be concluded that Acosta's work, like Matienzo's, provides circumstantial evidence suggesting that Polo de Ondegardo was the author of the original ceque system manuscript.

Martín de Murúa

Martín de Murúa was a Mercedarian priest who finished a work called *Historia del origen y genealogía real de los reyes Inças del Perú* (History of the origin and royal genealogy of the Inca kings of Peru) in Cusco in May of 1590. It is considerably difficult to summarize Murúa's work, however, because it was rewritten at least two times after the original manuscript was completed. The texts of the three manuscripts overlap, but each contains unique information not found in the others. The shortest Murúa manuscript, referred to as the Loyola Manuscript, contains two brief references to the huacas of the Cusco ceque system. The first reference (Murúa 1946:67 [1590:Pt. 1, Ch. 9]) was copied from the 1585 abstract of Polo de Ondegardo's 1559 document and states that there were more than 340 shrines in the Cusco area. In the second reference, Murúa (1946:78 [1590:Pt. 1, Ch. 14]) suggests that there were more than 450 shrines in the Cusco area:

> . . . the huacas and idols of this city and a few leagues around it were more than four hundred and fifty of various names, and there must have been many more. Each was venerated, used for sacrifice and ceremonies, like when they were sick and when they wanted to die . . . [30]

The second Murúa (1987 [ca. 1615]) manuscript, frequently called the Wellington Manuscript, is currently owned by the Getty Museum. There are no direct references to the Cusco ceque system in the Loyola Manuscript. Little is known concerning the third manuscript of Murúa except that it has a considerable number of illuminated pages. It is now privately owned and remains unpublished.

Viceroy Francisco de Toledo (ca. 1515–1584)

Additional information on Inca huacas is contained in a 1572 letter from Viceroy Francisco de Toledo to King Philip II that summarizes the materials the viceroy was sending to Spain in response to the king's requests of the previous year. In this letter, Toledo (1924:394 [1572]) mentions that a report on huacas ordered by Philip II was being sent along with the letter:

> The report that your Majesty commands on the huacas and that I ordered and provided is sent with this dispatch.[31]

This short entry indicates that Philip II ordered Viceroy Toledo in 1571 to conduct a huaca study, and that the report was completed and sent to Spain in 1572. It is possible that this investigation was conducted in Cusco under Toledo's supervision because the viceroy arrived in Cusco in March of 1571 and left in late September or early October of 1572, after the execution of Tupa Amaru. Toledo's inquiry on huacas may well have been supervised by Polo de Ondegardo, who was then serving his second term as corregidor of Cusco. It is not impossible that this 1571 report, written by order of the king of Spain, was the document that Cobo later used in his own chronicle.

Summary and Discussion

Although the original ceque system manuscript has been lost, information on it and its author can be drawn from Cobo's *Historia del Nuevo Mundo* and from the works of other earlier Spanish writers on Inca religion. Of the various Spaniards described above who appear to have known about Andean ceque systems, Molina and Polo de Ondegardo have both been suggested as the most likely author of the original ceque system manuscript (Urteaga 1916; Rowe 1946:300; Porras Barrenechea 1962:277; Zuidema 1964:1 n. 1, 1977a, 1982c; Sherbondy 1982). Rowe (1980:6–8) has, however, identified discrepancies between information presented in the writings of these two Spaniards, and information contained in the account of the huacas preserved in Cobo's chronicle. On the basis of these discrepancies, Rowe argues against the likelihood that *either* Polo de Ondegardo or Molina was the principal author of the original ceque system manuscript, concluding, "From the scanty evidence available, no other name stands out as a likely candidate for the authorship of Cobo's source, so the question of authorship must be left open for the time being" (Rowe 1980:8).

While there are certain discrepancies in information, words used, and spelling between Cobo's account of the ceque system and the various reports issued by Polo de Ondegardo, there is strong circumstantial evidence suggesting that Polo de Ondegardo was the author of the original ceque system manuscript. In the introduction to Books 12, 13, and 14 of the *Historia del Nuevo Mundo*, Cobo (1979: 98–102 [1653:Bk. 12, Ch. 2]) describes the three major sources that he used in this section of his chronicle. By citing these three sources and stressing that his information was extracted from experts on Inca history and religion, Cobo hoped to give greater credence and authority to his own

writings.[32] Cobo (1979:100 [1653:Bk. 12, Ch. 2]) recognizes his debt to Molina by indicating that he used Molina's "copious account of the rites and fables that the Peruvian Indians practiced in pagan times," a clear reference to Molina's *Relación de las fábulas. . . .* Cobo also states that he made extensive use of a report—now apparently lost—on the history and government of the Inca, written for Viceroy Toledo sometime between the work of Polo de Ondegardo (1559) and that of Molina (ca. 1575). Moreover, Cobo cited as a major source of information a 1559 report by Polo de Ondegardo (i.e., *De los errores y supersticiones de los indios*), written after interviews with Cusco quipu specialists. In fact, Cobo had in his possession the original manuscript, with Polo de Ondegardo's own signature, that was sent to Archbishop Jerónimo de Loayza. As noted above, Matienzo states directly that Polo de Ondegardo, during his first term as corregidor of Cusco, interviewed the imperial quipu specialists concerning the huacas of Cusco. Furthermore, the only surviving portion of that report states that the Inca had at least 340 shrines in the Cusco region, a number which is close to that reported in Cobo's account of the ceque system. Together these constitute strong circumstantial evidence that Polo de Ondegardo was the author of the original ceque system manuscript.

The Cusco ceque system is specifically mentioned by Albornoz, Molina, Polo de Ondegardo, Acosta, and Murúa, yet each of these authors provides a different number of huacas in the system. Albornoz and Molina simply indicate that there were a large number of shrines in the system, without providing any specific numbers. Polo de Ondegardo, Acosta, and Murúa (the latter two of whom used Polo de Ondegardo's reports) are more specific, but give inconsistent numbers. In his 1559 report, Polo de Ondegardo states that there were 340 shrines in the ceque system. About three years later he (Polo de Ondegardo 1940:183–184 [1561]) mentions that there were more than 400 huacas in Cusco, a claim that is repeated ten years later (Polo de Ondegardo 1916c:55, 133–134 [1571]). This situation is made more complex by the fact that Acosta (1954b:560–561 [1580:Bk. 5, Ch. 9]) has Polo de Ondegardo identifying some 360 shrines in Cusco, while Murúa (1946:78 [1590:Pt. 1, Ch. 14]) claims that there were 450.

There are various potential explanations for the discrepancy in the number of shrines mentioned in these reports. For example, it is possible that Polo de Ondegardo continued to find more huacas in the Cusco ceque system after

1559, so that he mentions a larger number in the later reports. Alternatively, the earlier 340 number may represent the total number of huacas that Polo de Ondegardo thought were in the ceque system, while the later sums refer to the number of shrines in Cusco found by him, not all of which were necessarily part of the ceque system. We may never know why different numbers of huacas are presented in various reports by Polo de Ondegardo, Acosta, and Murúa; however, it seems likely that Polo de Ondegardo was the author of the original ceque system manuscript, and that this information was contained in his 1559 report, which was later copied by Cobo.

3

Huacas

THE SHRINES of the Cusco region primarily encompassed natural features of the landscape, specific structures associated with former Inca rulers, and the putative locations of important mythohistorical events. In this chapter, I will review information on the physical nature of the Cusco huacas, and the homage given to them. In the first section, the objects and locations included as shrines in the Cusco ceque system are examined, and the manner in which these huacas were worshipped is discussed. In the second section, the archaeological and historical research conducted in the course of this investigation is outlined, and the research methods used to identify the shrines are presented.

The Huacas of the Cusco Ceque System

It is important to take stock of the overall physical nature of the shrines in the Cusco ceque system. Of the 328 huacas presented in the main section of Cobo's report, 96 (29%) are springs or sources of water and approximately 95 (29%) are standing stones. Together these springs and stones represent nearly 60 percent of the shrines in the *Relación de las huacas*. Other major shrine categories include hills and mountain passes (32 [10%]), palaces of the royal Incas and temples (28 [9%]), fields and flat places (28 [9%]), tombs (10 [3%]), and ravines (7 [2%]). Sacred objects or places that occur less frequently in the ceque system account are caves (3 [1%]), quarries (3 [1%]), stone seats (3 [1%]), sunset markers (3 [1%]), trees (2 [1%]), and roads (2 [1%]). The exact number of huacas in different categories cannot be determined, however, because many of the huaca descriptions are ambiguous. What's more, Cobo was not consistent in presenting information on the Cusco shrines. Rowe (1980:8) notes that the earliest entries in the *Relación de las huacas* are relatively detailed, but there is a drop in specificity after the fourth shrine on the second ceque of Chinchaysuyu (Ch. 2:4). With the exception of especially important huacas, such as Huanacauri (Co. 6:7), progressively less information is provided on the form, origin, utility, and location of the shrines throughout the remainder of the manuscript.

All huacas, no matter how large or small, facilitated communication with the supernatural world (Van de Guchte 1990:271). Most, if not all, of the huacas in the Cusco ceque system represented contact points with important chthonic powers that were thought to have shaped the lives of the inhabitants of the region. For example, elaborate offerings were made at Guaracince (Ch. 2:1), a flat area in the Temple of the Sun, to prevent earthquakes:

> The first guaca was called Guaracince, which was in the plaza of the Temple of the Sun, [a plaza] called Chuqui-pampa (it means "plain of gold"). It was a bit of flat ground which was there, in which they said that the earthquake was formed. At it they made sacrifices so that it would not quake, and they were very solemn [ones], because when the earth quaked children were killed, and ordinarily sheep and clothing were burned and gold and silver was buried. (Cobo 1980:17 [1653:Bk. 13, Ch. 13])[1]

Several huacas helped to guard against death. For example, Puñui (Ch. 4:2) was venerated by those who were unable to sleep and by others who were afraid of dying in their sleep. Offerings were made to the shrine of Pactaquañui (Co. 9:3) to prevent sudden death. The huaca of Guamanguachanca (Ch. 5:8) was worshipped to prevent children from dying, while the dead were thought to assemble once a year at the shrine of Taucaray (Co. 4:2). Two huacas were related to hail, two to wind, one to rain, and one to the preservation of corn after harvest. Many shrines were associated with the health of the Inca and with victory in war. Springs received offerings to prevent them from drying up, and sacrifices were made to quarries so that they would continue to produce stone. Offerings for a safe journey were made by travelers at several shrines, and the major Inca deities (the Sun, the Thunder, and Ticci Viracocha [the Creator]) were paid homage at other huacas. However, because the information in the *Relación de las huacas* was not recorded systematically, the exact forms of many of the huacas, and the reasons why offerings were made to them, remain unknown.

The two most important huacas in the Cusco region were the mountain of Huanacauri (Co. 6:7) and the temple of Coricancha, both of which are included within the Cusco ceque system. Huanacauri was worshipped because it was believed that a brother of the mythical first Inca, Manco Capac, had been transformed into stone on its summit. This shrine was visited during the major Cusco festivals, and it is listed by Cobo among the huacas of Cuntisuyu. The Coricancha was the most important ritual complex in the imperial city, but its position in the ceque system is more ambiguous. The *Relación de las huacas* identifies various parts of this temple as representing separate huacas in the system. Moreover, descriptions of shrines such as Guaracince (Ch. 2:1), a flat bit of ground in the plaza of the Temple of the Sun, and Sabaraura (Cu. 1:1), a stone where the belvedere of Santo Domingo was built, indicate that different parts of this temple were assigned to separate suyus. Albornoz (1984:204 [ca. 1582]), on the other hand, lists the Coricancha as a single entity, according it the status of the first and most important huaca of Cusco in his account of the sacred locations of Chinchaysuyu.

Origins of the Shrines

Many huacas of the Cusco ceque system were considered sacred because of their association with legendary events. Some of the myths have not been preserved and others are difficult to understand. Take, for example, the description of the shrine of Aucaypata Paccha (Ch. 8:3):

> The third guaca was a fountain named Aucaypata [Paccha] which was next to where the house of the cabildo [municipal council] is now. In it the priests of Chucuilla said that the Thunder bathed, and they made up a thousand other absurdities. (Cobo 1980:7 [1653:Bk. 13, Ch. 13])[2]

In other cases, such as Cascasayba (An. 2:9), even less is revealed concerning the origin myth of the shrine:

> The ninth was named Cascasayba; it consisted of certain stones which were on the hill of Quisco. It was an important guaca and had a certain long origin [story] which the Indians tell. They offered it all kinds of things and children as well. (Cobo 1980:33 [1653:Bk. 13, Ch. 14])[3]

Some huacas, however, figure in well-known legends. Numerous shrines are related to the mythical conquest of the

Cusco Valley by Manco Capac. He is said to have emerged with his three brothers (Ayar Auca, Ayar Cache, and Ayar Ucho) and their four sisters (Mama Ocllo, Mama Huaco, Mama Ipacura, and Mama Raua) from a cave south of Cusco in the region of Pacariqtambo. Several of these mythical personages are believed to have been converted into stone during their journey to Cusco (Urbano 1981; Bauer 1991, 1996). These stones, and many of the places the first mythical Incas are thought to have visited, are incorporated into the ceque system as huacas.[4]

Fifteen of the standing stone huacas in the system are specifically described as "Pururaucas" and are related to the Inca legend of the Chanca War.[5] According to this legend, the Chanca, an aggressive ethnic group located in an area that is today the modern departments of Ayacucho and Apurimac, attacked the Cusco region during the reign of the eighth Inca king, Viracocha Inca. In response to the impending invasion, Viracocha Inca fled Cusco, and Pachacuti Inca Yupanqui usurped political authority from his father as well as his older brother, the appointed heir. In the legend, Pachacuti Inca Yupanqui appealed to the various groups of the Cusco region for help, and then attacked the advancing Chanca forces. It is said that the turning point of the battle came when the large stones of the Cusco area transformed themselves into warriors to fight alongside the young Inca. These stone-warriors were called "Pururaucas."

Other elements of the Chanca War are also represented in the Cusco ceque system. For example, the shrines of Cutirsaspampa (Ch. 9:7), Queachili (Ch. 9:8), and Quishuarpuquiu (Ch. 9:9) mark important locations of the final battle between the Inca and the Chanca, and Illanguarque (Ch. 8:1) is described as a building where Pachacuti Inca Yupanqui kept certain weapons to use against his enemies.[6] There are many shrines closely associated with Pachacuti Inca Yupanqui besides those related to the Chanca War. This largely legendary figure is credited with reorganizing Inca society and the Cusco region after the Chanca War. At least nineteen shrine descriptions specifically mention him.[7]

In addition to Manco Capac and Pachacuti Inca Yupanqui, various other Inca rulers are associated with shrines mentioned in the ceque system document. The body of the second Inca, Sinchi Roca, was said to have been kept in a house called Acoyguaci (Co. 6:3). Mayta Capac, the fourth Inca, is associated with the shrines of Sancacancha (Co. 8:1) and Tampucancha (Co. 9:1). Viracocha Inca, the eighth ruler of Cusco, is mentioned in association with the descriptions of Guayllaurcaja (Ch. 2:8) and Taxanamaro (Ch. 8:11). The house of the younger son of Pachacuti Inca Yupanqui, Topa Yupanqui, who was chosen as the tenth Inca, is mentioned in relation to Cugiguaman (Ch. 3:9) and Quinoapuquiu (Ch. 3:10). The elder son of Pachacuti Inca Yupanqui, Amaru Topa, who did not succeed his father as ruler but who still retained considerable power, is mentioned in the descriptions of Chacuaytapara (Ch. 8:5) and Amaromarcaguaci (An. 1:7). Huayna Capac, the eleventh Inca, grandson of Pachacuti Inca Yupanqui, is associated with five shrines. The last Inca, Paullu, who was crowned under Spanish supervision, figures in three huaca descriptions.[8]

Some of the queens (*coyas*) of the Inca rulers are mentioned in the *Relación de las huacas*. The mummy of Mama Anaguarque, Pachacuti Inca Yupanqui's wife, was kept at Pomamarca (An. 6:6), and one ceque (Cu. 1) may have been named after her. The house of Cori Ocllo, wife of Amaru Topa, is listed as Ch. 4:3. There are three shrines associated with Mama Ocllo, wife of Huayna Capac: Ticicocha (Ch. 3.3), Picchu (Ch. 9:2), and Anaypampa (Co. 3:5). Managuananunca Guaci (Cu. 8:9), which can be translated as "the house that will never die," is also presented as the house of an unnamed coya.

Other shrines are related to large Inca festivals such as the most important ritual in Cusco, the Capac Raymi celebration of the December solstice. Several huacas are associated with activities related to this celebration. During the month of Capac Raymi, the annual Warachikoy ritual was also held. This was an elaborate ceremony initiating Inca youths into manhood that involved, among other things, visiting various shrines of the system.[9]

Colonial documents make it clear that some Andean shrines were portable. There are numerous descriptions of huacas being carried into battle or being brought to Cusco (Figure 3.1). In addition, Albornoz (1984:199 [ca. 1582]) states that when the Inca resettled groups in different areas, new rock formations were dedicated to represent the huacas of their previous area. Although most of the shrines of the system seem to have been worshipped in their original places, the *Relación de las huacas* does suggest that a few shrines were deliberately positioned by an Inca along particular ceques. For example, Cugiguaman (Ch. 3:9) is described as being placed on a ceque by Pachacuti Inca Yupanqui:

> The ninth guaca was named Cugiguaman. It was a stone shaped like a falcon which Inca Yupanqui said had appeared to him in a quarry, and he ordered that it be placed on this ceque and that sacrifices be made to it. (Cobo 1980:19 [1653:Bk. 13, Ch. 13])[10]

Rowe (1980, 1981a, 1985) has used references like this to "reconstruct" the system during various reigns. It is unclear, however, whether such descriptions reflect actual historic acts or mythical events. Since the historicity of these statements is questioned, no attempt will be presented in this

Figure 3.1. Meeting of the huacas. The indigenous writer Guaman Poma de Ayala (1980:235 [1615: 261 [263]]) depicts an assemblage of huacas brought to Cusco by Tupa Inca. The caption reads: "Chapter of the Idols, Sacred Shrines of the Inca" and "The Inca speaks with all the shrines." In the drawing, Topa Inca asks, "Shrines, sacred ones, which of you has said, let it not rain, let it freeze, let it hail? Answer me now!" The shrines reply, "It was not us, Inca."

study to analyze the system during different periods of Inca rule. Nevertheless, I believe that the system should be seen as a dynamic one, able to change and expand in the course of imperial development.

Maintenance of the Huacas

Contact with a huaca required signs of respect: a prayer or an offering, or more typically both. The most powerful huacas of the Andean world were attended by hundreds of individuals and needed conspicuous amounts of goods for their maintenance. The system for supporting these shrines involved the control of large numbers of camelids and considerable amounts of agricultural land. Offspring of the animals and produce from the fields were sacrificed to the huaca and used to support its attendants. Maintenance of even smaller, regional shrines required the control of various land and animal resources and the activities of a number of full-time specialists. For example, a small shrine called Llatabamba in the area of Yanaoca—about one hundred aerial kilometers southeast of Cusco—which was reported to Polo de Ondegardo in 1560, was served by four villagers who controlled several maize fields and a set of corrals on behalf of the shrine (La Lone 1985). At times, fields dedicated to the shrine were located a considerable distance from it. Pablo José Arriaga reports that fourteen small coca fields in the lowland area of Huamanmayu belonged to huacas in the sierra. He also notes, "Indians are set to guard these fields, to gather the coca, and take it to the ministers of the huaca at the proper time, for it is a universal offering for huacas on all occasions" (Arriaga 1968b:43 [1621]).

Some of the resources associated with certain huacas were considered important enough to be sacred locations in their own right. According to Cobo, the field of Sausero (Co. 2:3) yielded corn that was offered to the Sun, and the field of Añaypampa (An. 3:5) belonged to the coya Mama Ocllo. Another example is the field of Mancochuqui (Ch. 8:2), about which Cobo writes:

> The second was called Mancochuqui. It was a chacara of Huanacauri, and what was harvested from it was sacrificed to him. (Cobo 1980:27 [1653:Bk. 13, Ch. 13])[11]

Even so, the majority of the huacas of the Cusco ceque system appear not to have had specific lands, livestock, or attendants dedicated to them. Instead, responsibility for their maintenance, as will be discussed in the following chapter, was spread among the various kin groups of the city.

Remembrance and Renewal

Because the huacas embodied supernatural properties, prayers and offerings were presented to them.[12] According to Cobo, people showed their devotion in the following manner:

> Facing their gods or their temples and *guacas,* they lowered their heads and their bodies in a profound show of humility, and they would stretch their arms out in front of themselves, keeping them parallel to each other from the beginning to the end, with the hands open and the palms out, a little above the level of their heads. Then they would make a kissing sound with their lips. Next they would bring their hands to their mouths and kiss the inside of their fingertips. (Cobo 1990:118 [1653:Bk. 13, Ch. 23])[13]

Homage was given to the shrine at the time of an offering. Cobo indicates that prayers frequently began with a general call to Ticci Viracocha, the Creator god, followed by an appeal to the specific huaca. An example of such a prayer, presented to a spring so that it would continue to flow, may be preserved within Cobo's chronicle:

> Lord, who created all things and among them you saw fit to create me, and you created the water of this spring for my sustenance, I beseech you to keep it from drying up and keep water flowing as you have done in past years so that we can harvest the crops we have sown. . . .
>
> O source of water who have irrigated my field for so many years, and by means of this benefaction that you confer upon me I obtain my food, do the same this year, and even increase the amount of water so that the harvest will be more abundant. (Cobo 1990:111 [1653:Bk. 13, Ch. 21])[14]

Arriaga also describes a prayer said before a huaca, as well as other activities:

> Señor X (naming the huaca, and making the usual sound with his lips as if sucking them in, which they call *mochar*), Here I come bringing the things your children and creatures offer you. Accept them and do not be angry. Give them life, health, and good fields.
>
> Saying this and similar things, he pours out the chicha [corn beer] in front of the huaca, or over it, or sprinkles the huaca with it as if he were giving it a rap on the nose. He anoints the huaca with the blood of guinea pigs or llamas and then burns, or blows towards it, the rest of the offerings, according to the nature of each one. (Arriaga 1968b:47 [1621])

The offerings presented to the huacas varied according to the importance of the shrine. It is well documented that the most significant huacas of the Andes received the consummate offering: human sacrifices. These sacrifices generally involved children and were at times associated with the Capac Cocha ritual of the Inca, a complex festival during which all the major huacas of the empire were visited (see Chapter 10). More inconsequential huacas could receive just a few coca leaves. For example, Cobo (1980:57 [1653: Bk. 13, Ch. 16]) writes of Cachicalla (Cu. 8:7) that "they did not offer anything to it except the coca which passers-by cast from the mouth."[15]

While documentary evidence makes it clear that specific kin groups bore the responsibility for maintaining the huacas on particular ceques, the *Relación de las huacas* provides only sketchy information on the timing and nature of the offerings. The account suggests that most of the offerings were either burned or buried, although at some huacas, as in the case of rivers and ravines, the offerings were thrown into them. In several instances, the *Relación de las huacas* states that the last shrine on a ceque was offered "what was left over" from the other huacas of that ceque.[16] From this we can infer that offerings were made to sequential shrines along the ceques during a single ritual. Furthermore, these descriptions indicate that, following the order of the shrines provided in the ceque account, the offerings were made from the center of the system (i.e., the Coricancha) to the periphery. In addition, an unusual statement contained in the description of Oyaraypuquiu (An. 5:5)—"They offered it shells of all colors according to the times"[17] (Cobo 1980:35 [1653: Bk. 13, Ch. 14])—implies that offerings could be made at different times of the year.

Because many of the descriptions are incomplete, it is difficult to analyze the full range of items given as offerings to the Cusco huacas from the information presented in the *Relación de las huacas*. There are only a few extensive discussions of what was offered to particular shrines. For instance, at Mantocalla (An. 3:6) the Inca "placed on the said hill many bundles of carved firewood dressed as men and women and a great quantity of maize ears made of wood. After great drunken feasts, they burned many sheep with the said firewood and killed some children" (Cobo 1980:33 [1653:Bk. 13, Ch. 14).[18] Or in the case of Guaracince (Ch. 2:1), "children were killed, and ordinarily sheep and clothing were burned and gold and silver was buried" (Cobo 1980:17 [1653:Bk. 13, Ch. 13).[19] More frequently, however, the *Rela-*

ción de las huacas provides no details, simply stating that "ordinary," "great," or "very solemn" sacrifices were made (Niles 1987:174).

The mentioning of animal sacrifice in the *Relación de las huacas* seems especially sparse. It is known from other works that a large number of llamas (misidentified in most Spanish documents as sheep) and guinea pigs (called *quis*) were offered to huacas (Molina 1989 [ca. 1575]; Polo de Ondegardo 1916b [1585], 1916c [1571]; Guaman Poma de Ayala 1980 [1615]; Arriaga 1968a [1621]; Cobo 1990 [1653]). Nevertheless, there are no references in the ceque system document to guinea pigs being offered and only a few huaca descriptions mention sheep (i.e., llama) sacrifices.

The most common offering mentioned in the *Relación de las huacas* is seashells. These were regularly presented to water-related shrines. The reason for this ubiquitous offering is that the shells and the water shrines were felt to be related. Polo de Ondegardo (1916b:39 [1585]) provides information on this relationship:

> . . . they sacrificed or offered sea shells called *mullu*. And they offered them to the wells and springs, saying that the shells were daughters of the sea, mother of all waters. They have different names according to color, and thus they serve different purposes, they used these shells in almost all the manners of sacrifice . . .[20]

While the term *mullu* was used for a variety of different seashells, it was most frequently used for the *Spondylus*. This mollusk is generally red and inhabits the warm waters of the Ecuadorian coast and regions farther north. The shells were offered to the huacas of the Cusco ceque system in various ways: in their natural forms, cut into pieces, ground into powder, or carved into figurines.

Child sacrifice is recorded in the ceque system document, having occurred especially at those shrines related to the Sun. Numerous huacas received precious metals (gold and silver), most commonly in the form of human (Photo 3.1), llama, or alpaca figurines (Photos 3.2 and 3.3). Textiles, often described as miniature women's clothes, are frequently listed among the items offered to the Cusco huacas (Photo 3.4). From the descriptions in the document, coca offerings seem to have been more rare and were generally associated with mountain passes. The coca leaves could be burnt, presented in small bags, or offered straight from the mouth.

Because of the extensive looting of shrines in the Cusco region, there is little hope that offerings made to the hua-

Photo 3.1. Female silver figurine. This figure was found on the Island of the Moon (Lake Titicaca). Similar figurines were offered to the shrines of Cusco. (Courtesy Department of Library Services, American Museum of Natural History. Photograph by Lee Boltin, negative 323437.)

Photo 3.2. Silver llama. This llama was found on the Island of the Sun (Lake Titicaca). Similar figurines were offered to the shrines of Cusco. (Courtesy Department of Library Services, American Museum of Natural History. Photograph by Rota, negative 327112.)

Photo 3.4. Figurine with preserved textiles, original provenience unknown. This figurine has a miniature tunic and coca bag. Similar items were offered to the shrines of the Cusco ceque system. (Courtesy Department of Library Services, American Museum of Natural History. Photograph by Lee Boltin, negative 329851.)

Photo 3.3. Silver alpaca. This alpaca was found on the Island of the Sun (Lake Titicaca). (Courtesy Department of Library Services, American Museum of Natural History. Photograph by Lee Boltin, negative 322739.)

cas of the ceque system will be recovered for scientific study.[21] However, examples of similar offerings have been identified elsewhere in the Inca Empire (Pardo 1941; Beorchia 1973, 1978, 1987; McEwan and Van de Guchte 1992; Reinhard 1992a, 1992b, 1996). For example, Adolph Bandelier's (1910) collections from the Islands of the Sun and the Moon in Lake Titicaca contain a number of miniature gold and silver humans, llamas, and alpacas, as well as textiles. Other collections made in areas where natural preservation processes are better, such as on the coast of Peru and on mountain summits, have yielded more complete offering inventories. For example, a child sacrifice was found in 1985 on the mountain of El Plomo. Along with the mummified remains of a well-dressed boy, several gold, silver, and shell figurines were found, as well as miniature textiles:

> Three were male human figures: one of gold (formed by hammering and soldering sheet metal), one of solid silver-copper alloy, and one of *Spondylus* shell. . . . Averaging about two inches high, all the human figures were clothed, had plume crests, and carried little bags containing fragments of coca leaves. . . . The other three statuettes, one of gold, and two of *Spondylus,* were stylized llamas, colored red on one side and white on the other. (Schobinger 1991:63)

More recently, Alfredo Narváez (Heyerdahl et al. 1995: 101–115) has excavated a remarkable huaca in the ancient city of Tucumé on the coast of Peru. The huaca is a large unworked stone housed in a specially constructed building near the gate of the city. Excavations revealed a host of offering materials, including miniature metal and ceramic items, carved and natural *Spondylus* shells, adult llamas, and human burials. Perhaps most intriguing was the recovery of three *Spondylus* and two silver figurines finely dressed in miniature clothing. One of the silver figurines is nearly identical to that found at El Plomo. The huaca appears to have been actively attended and maintained for several hundred years, and may still have been functioning on the eve of the Spanish invasion. These extraordinary finds serve as vivid examples of the types of offerings that were left at the shrines of the Cusco ceque system.

Identifying Huacas: A Research Method

The identification of huacas in the field is a difficult and time-consuming task. It was made even more complex in the case of the Cusco region after it was determined that the Cusco ceques do not necessarily travel in straight lines (Niles 1987; Bauer 1992a). This section presents the research method used to find and identify the physical remains of the shrines. As will be discussed, the huaca identifications have varying degrees of confidence. Certain huacas described by Cobo are unique or unusual features of the Cusco landscape, some of which not only have physically survived into our time but also have maintained their traditional toponyms over the past several centuries. These shrines are identified with little ambiguity. In many more cases, however, the exact location of a shrine cannot be determined, even though field and archival research can help determine the general area where it once stood. In other instances, a number of possible candidates for the same shrine may be found. In such cases, one site may be preferred over another, but the full range of options must be considered.

The relative completeness of the shrine list presented by Cobo, and the known form of the system (lines of huacas radiating from central Cusco), suggests that locating the huacas would be relatively simple (Niles 1987:176–177). This impression is strengthened by the many details included in the *Relación de las huacas* concerning the location of certain shrines. Cobo frequently writes that huacas were "beside," "next to," "near," "below," or "inside" features of colonial Cusco that were widely known at the time of writing. For example, Ticicocha (Ch. 3:3) is described as "inside the house which belonged to the said Diego Maldonado"; Coracora (Ch. 5:5) is listed as "where the cabildo houses are now"; and Sacas[gu]aylla Puquiu (An. 8:1) is presented as "next to the mill of Pedro Alonso [Carrasco]." Furthermore, Cobo provides topographic information that relates the shrines of certain ceques to each other and to geographical features of the Cusco region. For instance, Pirquipuquiu (An 8:2) "is in a ravine lower down" from the shrine before it; Corcorpuquiu (An. 9:3) "is in the puna above the Angostura"; and Micaya Puquiu (Co. 1:5) "is on the slope of the hill of Guanacauri." Some of the place-names mentioned in the *Relación de las huacas* are still used in the Cusco region; however, many have been forgotten. In the words of Niles (1987:177), "Much of the list of *huacas* reads like a map, with references to hills, ravines, flat places, cliffs, rocks, caves, quarries, rivers, lakes, and springs that no longer carry their ancient names and that have not yet been identified." Each year that passes makes the reconstruction of the system more difficult.

Field Research

Field research on the ceque system began in 1990 under the auspices of the Cusco Ceque System Research Project. The goal of the project was to provide, through ethnographic and archival research as well as field survey, systematic documentation of the ceque system. Research began by gathering data on the locations of former Inca shrines from the Spanish chronicles, especially that of Cobo. Archaeological surveys were then conducted in areas of the Cusco Valley thought to have contained particular huacas, based on documentary research. Survey crews were composed of archaeology students trained in archaeological reconnaissance from the Universidad San Antonio Abad del Cusco. Local inhabitants were interviewed in Quechua to find shrines that had retained their original names. A toponym was confirmed when three informants independently provided similar answers. Positive identification of a huaca occurred when a description provided by Cobo matched the physical features of a specific object (e.g., a cave, spring, or outcrop) that had also retained the name of a shrine. Working from these points, teams surveyed the surrounding area to identify other possible shrines that had not retained their toponyms.

The shrines and shrine candidates were photographed, and their positions were noted on a map. A plan of the huaca was drawn when appropriate, and a collection of surface artifacts was made. Large looters' pits were found at some of the locations thought to represent shrines of the Cusco ceque system (Photo 3.5). Looters had exposed human skeletal remains at three possible huaca locations (Photo 3.6). Because of the looting, it was not possible to determine whether these remains represented normal burials or the remains of sacrificed individuals

During the survey work, interviews were held with village officials to gather more toponymic information and to gain access to early land documents still retained by some communities. Furthermore, crew members met with former hacienda owners of the Cusco region and sought permission to examine documents held in their

Photo 3.5. Looters' pit at a possible shrine site.

Photo 3.6. Skull fragments found beside looters' pit at a possible shrine site.

Photo 3.7. The stone of Condorrumi along the trail from Cusco to Chanan.

private archives. They were also questioned about local land divisions, boundary markers, and toponyms.

Field researchers collected information on the current shrines of the region including their names, objects offered to them, when and how the offerings are made, and the function of the shrines. It was found that many of the locations visited during the survey are still considered to be sacred places. Some of these are notable topographic features, such as prominent springs and tops of high hills, while others represent far less impressive forms. For example, one small unworked stone called Condorrumi (condor stone), located along the trail from Cusco to Chanan, is widely respected by those who frequent this path (Photo 3.7).

Survey work found various small stone cairns (Photo 3.8) and the remains of burnt offerings beside many of the shrines (Photo 3.9). On one of our many trips to the mountain of Huanacauri (Cu. 6:8) the remains of an offering just a few hours old were found, with a candle still burning (Photo 3.10). Prepackaged offerings can be purchased in the Cusco market and contain a variety of items including different types of seeds, silver foil, gold foil, cloth, and seashells. These contents mirror many of the offerings listed in the *Relación de las huacas*. The burning of these modern offerings destroys most of the items, but the seashells tend to survive and can frequently be seen among the ashes (Photo 3.11).

Photo 3.8. A small cairn on a mountain slope near Cusco.

Photo 3.11. Remains of seashells in a modern offering.

Photo 3.9. Remains of a burnt offering on a mountain summit near Cusco. Note the seashells among the ashes.

Photo 3.10. Burnt offering on Huanacauri Mountain. This offering was made the night before our arrival at the summit. Note the still-burning candle in the background.

Several factors affected our ability to locate and identify huacas. The approximate locations for many of the huacas within the boundaries of colonial Cusco could be identified with some certainty through information provided in chronicles, such as Garcilaso de la Vega's (1966:427 [1609: Vol. 1, Bk. 7, Ch. 10]) description of the homes of prominent Spaniards in 1560, and various property documents found during our archival research. Similarly, many of the shrines in the countryside far from the center of the city could be found because their names continue to be used. The most difficult regions to survey and to recover topographic information about were the more recently settled zones of Cusco. Large tracts of land have been urbanized since the late 1940s, and many topographic features in these areas have been destroyed. In addition, these zones now contain first- or second-generation immigrants from different parts of the department of Cusco who do not know the traditional names used for areas in their neighborhoods. Accordingly, the location of many of the huacas surrounding the city of Cusco have been lost forever.

To correct popular belief, it should be noted that some of the most spectacular natural features in the Cusco region are not mentioned as huacas in the *Relación de las huacas*. For example, the mountain of Mama Cimuna (4342 masl), which is one of the highest mountains adjacent to the Cusco Valley, is absent from the list. Furthermore, many of the best-known Inca sites in the region, and most of the carved rocks in the Sacsahuaman area, are not present among the shrines described by Cobo.

Archival Research

A major aspect of the Cusco Ceque System Research Project was the identification of huacas that surrounded the imperial city of the Inca. Project goals included the formulation of new models for explaining how the system was maintained and how it was related to the social divisions of Inca kin groups in the Cusco Valley. These research issues required a database that went beyond the archaeological documentation of the system and necessitated extensive archival research. Accordingly, data on the huacas of the Cusco ceque system and the social organization of the imperial city were collected by project members in the Archivo Arzobispal del Cusco (AAC), the Archivo Histórico Depar-

tamental del Cusco (AHD)[22], the Archivos del Ministerio de Agricultura del Cusco (AMAC), the Biblioteca Nacional (BN) in Lima, the Archivo General de la Nación (AGN) in Lima, and the Archivo General de las Indias (AGI) in Seville. The archival teams were composed of history students trained in archival research from the Universidad San Antonio Abad del Cusco, under the supervision of Jean-Jacques Decoster and the author. Members of the archival teams systematically worked through sections of the archives looking for documents containing information on huaca locations and on the pre-Hispanic social divisions of the Cusco Valley. As mentioned above, research was also conducted in the private archives of various communities as well as those of former hacienda owners living in Cusco. When relevant information was located, transcriptions and photocopies were made of the original document.

The archival research greatly expanded the available information on the shrines mentioned in the *Relación de las huacas*. It identified toponyms that had been forgotten or had changed, and helped resolve whether or not specific toponyms were used for two different features of the landscape over time. In a few cases, maps were recovered that actually show the location of certain shrines and communities listed by Cobo.

Some of the suggested huaca locations presented in this work are speculative. The very nature of the shrines, the systematic campaigns led by the Spaniards to destroy them, and the 450 years that separate us from the Incaic system have left little evidence from which to draw conclusions. Nevertheless, I have been able to identify likely possibilities for many of the huacas of the system. Chapters 5 through 8 provide detailed discussions, photographs, maps, and historical references for each shrine candidate. I encourage additional research to verify these huacas and to provide new, or alternative, shrine identifications. Following the protocols set forth by Niles (1987) and continued in this book, it is hoped that future investigators will provide detailed descriptions and illustrations of newly identified shrines. Furthermore, they should consider and discuss the implications that the location of a newly identified shrine has for the course of its particular ceque as well as for the courses of the other ceques continued in the same suyu.

4

The Social Organization of Cusco and Its Ceque System

THE LOCAL SOURCES of sacredness scattered across the Cusco landscape in the form of springs, outcrops, mountaintops, and the like required prayers and offerings. The ritual responsibilities for the maintenance of these huacas were divided among the kin groups of the city. Accordingly, the Cusco ceque system played an important role in the identity of these groups as well as in the unification of the region's population. The purpose of this chapter is to discuss various theories concerning the organization of the Cusco ceque system and how it was maintained. This is not an easy task because many huacas, ceques, and kin groups were involved in the system. It is made even more difficult by the fact that the information we have on the system is fragmentary. Nevertheless, several models of increasing complexity and decreasing certainty can be developed from material preserved in the *Relación de las huacas*. In the first section of this chapter, the terms *collana, payan,* and *cayao* will be discussed. These are important words to understand because the Inca used them to characterize, or rank, the different lines of the system. In the second and third sections, the ritual responsibilities that various Cusco kin groups held for the huacas along particular ceques will be explored.[1]

Collana, Payan, Cayao

In his description of the Cusco ceque system, Cobo repeatedly used the indigenous terms *collana, payan,* and *cayao* to enumerate the ceques.[2] This classificatory scheme creates tripartite ceque groups, which I call "ceque clusters." Three of the four suyus of the Cusco region (Chinchaysuyu, Antisuyu, and Collasuyu) each contained nine ceques. The nine lines within each of these suyus were organized into

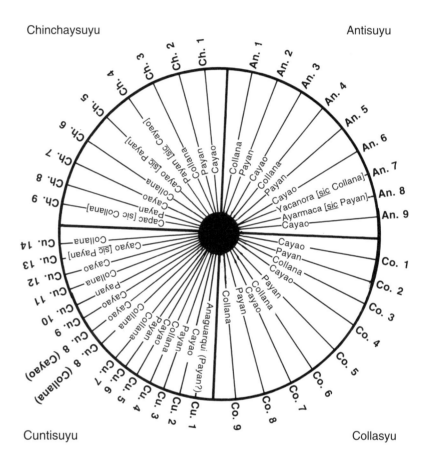

Figure 4.1. The ceques in the Cusco system were classified as either collana, payan, or cayao. This classificatory scheme creates clusters of three lines. Chinchaysuyu, Antisuyu, and Collasuyu each contained three ceque clusters, while Cuntisuyu contained five.

three ceque clusters (Figure 4.1, Table 4.1). The fourth quarter (Cuntisuyu), in contrast, held fifteen ceques, which were organized into five clusters.

Although the terms *collana, payan,* and *cayao* are found throughout the text of the *Relación de las huacas*, Cobo provides no definition of their meanings. Fortunately, these terms are also contained within various early colonial

Table 4.1. The Classification of Ceques into Collana, Payan, and Cayao

Chinchaysuyu		Antisuyu	
Ch. 1	Cayao	An. 1	Collana
Ch. 2	Payan	An. 2	Payan
Ch. 3	Collana	An. 3	Cayao
Ch. 4	Payan [*sic* Cayao]	An. 4	Collana
Ch. 5	Cayao [*sic* Payan]	An. 5	Payan
Ch. 6	Collana	An. 6	Cayao
Ch. 7	Cayao	An. 7	Yacanora [*sic* Collana]
Ch. 8	Payan	An. 8	Ayarmaca [*sic* Payan]
Ch. 9	Capac [*sic* Collana]	An. 9	Cayao

Collasuyu		Cuntisuyu	
Co. 1	Cayao	Cu. 1	Anaguarqui (Payan?)
Co. 2	Payan		
Co. 3	Collana	Cu. 2	Cayao
		Cu. 3	Payan
Co. 4	Cayao	Cu. 4	Collana
Co. 5	Payan		
Co. 6	Collana	Cu. 5	Cayao
		Cu. 6	Payan
Co. 7	Cayao	Cu. 7	Collana
Co. 8	Payan		
Co. 9	Collana	Cu. 8	Cayao
		Cu. 8	Collana
		Cu. 9	Cayao
		Cu. 10	Payan
		Cu. 11	Collana
		Cu. 12	Cayao
		Cu. 13	Cayao [*sic* Payan]
		Cu. 14	Collana

Quechua/Spanish vocabularies, liturgical materials, and administrative documents. I will review these sources below so that we may begin to understand what these terms mean and why they were used by the Inca to classify the Cusco ceques.

In the earliest Andean lexicon, Santo Tomás (1951:192, 267 [1560:86, 124]) defines *collanan* as "the best or most principal thing in whatever class." The *Arte y vocabulario en la lengua general del Perú* (1951:144, 174 [1586]) defines *collana* and *collanan* as an "excellent, first, or principal thing." González Holguín (1952:521, 642 [1608]), in his monumental Quechua dictionary, provides a nearly identical definition. Because in Andean villages today the word *collana* carries an equivalent meaning and is frequently used to refer to the preeminent kin group of a community, it can be suggested that *collana* was used to mark the most prestigious line in each ceque cluster.

The terms *payan* and *cayao* are more difficult to define because they do not appear in exactly these forms in the early vocabularies of Peru. The closest match for *payan* is *paya*, which Santo Tomás (1951:22, 335 [1560:2, 159]), the *Arte y vocabulario en la lengua general del Perú* (1951:69 [1586]), and González Holguín (1952:282 [1608]) define as "grandmother." There is no clear gloss in Santo Tomás or González Holguín for *cayao*; however, the *Arte y vocabulario en la lengua general del Perú* (1951:24 [1586]) translates *cayan* as "spleen," and Zuidema (1964:107 n.73, 165 n.159; 1977c; 1982d) suggests that it means "origin" or "base."

The words *collana, payan,* and *cayao* can also be found, with the additional terms of *caru* and *hucayllulla,* in the liturgical writings of the Jesuit Juan de Pérez Bocanegra (1631:613) in his discussions of Inca kinship:

Carurunamacij: is a distant relation or relative in the fourth degree.

Collana: is he who is not so distant a relative or relation.

Payan: is the close relation.

Cayaurunamacij: is the last of the relatives or relations, very much closer than the other first two.

Hucayllulla, hacpanacalla: are all those who belong to the same family or caste.[3]

Pérez Bocanegra suggests that *collana, payan,* and *cayao* represent kin terms that reflect increased genealogical distance (Zuidema 1964, 1977c). In a four-grade kinship descent system, *cayao* would designate one's most immediate relatives (parents and siblings), *payan* would include one's grandparents and their descendants, and *collana* would represent one's great-grandparents and their descendants (Rowe 1985:42).

The terms *collana* (*collona*), *payan* (*pasana*), and *cayao* also appear in a 1585 document describing the political organization of the province of Collaguas (Kirchhoff 1949: 303; Rowe 1985:42).[4] In this passage, Ulloa Mogollón (1885:45

[1585]) classifies the three separate social units, or what he calls "ayllus," of the province with these terms. Although each of these three ayllus had a separate leader, they were united under the direction of a single authority whose right to rule was passed from father to son.

A similar situation is described for two groups, the Ayarmaca and Pumamarca, who lived in the area of the ceque system in the Cusco Valley and were resettled into the community of San Sebastián. Archival documents indicate that they were divided into two moieties, called Hanan Cusco and Hurin Cusco. Both divisions were further subdivided into three separate social units called collana, payan, and cayao (AHD/Intendencia, Real Hacienda: Leg. 177, 1786–1787, f. 172).

Another document containing the terms *collana, payan,* and *cayao* presents a list of twenty-two individuals who were members of Capac Ayllu, said to be composed of the descendants of Topa Inca Yupanqui (Rowe 1986:194, 222–223). This manuscript, written in Cusco in 1569, indicates that Topa Inca Yupanqui's ayllu was made of three separate sublineages classified as collana, payan, and cayao. The collana group, the most prestigious, was composed of the descendants of Topa Inca Yupanqui himself. The payan group contained the descendants of Amaru Topa Inca, an older brother of Topa Inca Yupanqui. This sublineage of Capac Ayllu must have also held considerable prestige in Cusco because Amaru Topa Inca is said to have helped Topa Inca Yupanqui rule the empire.[5] The third group, cayao, comprised the descendants of Topa Yupanqui Inca, another brother of Topa Inca Yupanqui. The cayao group would have held less prestige than the other two. In this case, the terms *collana, payan,* and *cayao* are used to designate three separate sublineages within a single royal clan and to classify them according to their relative prestige.

Were the lineages of each of the ruling Incas divided in a similar manner? While it is currently not possible to answer this question, it is important to note that documentary evidence does suggest that at least one other royal Cusco kin group was divided into three subsets. During independent research, both Rowe (AHD/Corregimiento, Causas Ordinarias: Leg. 18, 1671–1673; Rowe, pers. com. 1992) and the author (AMAC/Community Files for Collana Chahuancuzco) recovered information on a dispute over the lands of Surama (An. 9:2) near the eastern end of the Cusco Valley. The documents suggest that the kin group of Pachacuti Inca Yupanqui, like that of his sons, was also divided into three sublineages called collana, payan, and cayao.

Zuidema (1964, 1977c) has also proposed that these terms can be used to distinguish social classes among the Inca of Cusco. He suggests that the collana represented the primary kin of the Inca ruler. According to his theory, the payan classification would be used for the offspring of Inca (or collana) men and non-Inca women, and the cayao was used for non-Inca people.

In summary, collana, payan, and cayao are ranking terms that begin with collana, the most principal, and end with cayao. In each of the above examples, they have been used to divide groups of individuals into subsets, which possess different degrees of prestige primarily based on descent. The terms *collana, payan,* and *cayao* appear to have been used in this same generalized context in the ceque system, establishing a hierarchical order within sets of three lines that were maintained by various Cusco kin groups.

Problematic Ceque Classifications

A number of interesting irregularities and possible omissions of the terms *collana, payan,* and *cayao* in the *Relación de las huacas* need to be examined if we are to understand the source document and the system itself (Figure 4.1, Table 4.1). For example, in three cases (An. 7, An. 8, and Cu. 1) these general terms have been replaced by more specific ones (Zuidema 1964:1). The seventh and eighth ceques of Antisuyu were called Yacanora and Ayarmaca, respectively. These are the names of two ethnic groups of the Cusco Valley that occupied areas in Antisuyu.[6] From the general ordering of the other ceques in Antisuyu, it appears that An. 7 and An. 8 held the positions of collana and payan. Similarly, Cu. 1 is listed as Anahuarqui, a name derived from a mountain close to Cusco and the wife of the ninth Inca. The hierarchical order of Cu. 1 is more difficult to determine because of the unusual composition of this suyu. Zuidema (1964) suggests that this ceque was payan and that it was paired with Cu. 8, which was classified as both collana and cayao. Rowe (1985), on the other hand, proposes that Cu. 1 was termed cayao.

Although it is currently not known why these three ceques, of the forty-two in the system, should be singled out with unique names, a preliminary explanation can be presented. Cobo states that specific kin groups of the Cusco

Valley were responsible for maintaining individual ceques. It is possible that rather than being part of the tripartite ranking system, the unique names of An. 7 (Yacanora), An. 8 (Ayarmaca), and Cu. 1 (Anahuarqui) are meant to identify the kin groups responsible for maintaining these ceques. In other words, each of the ceques of the system may have been classified with the terms *collana, payan,* and *cayao* as well as with the name of the specific kin group that maintained the shrines along its course. This explanation brings to mind the work of Albornoz (1984:218 [ca. 1582]), who notes that the ceques immortalized the names of the individuals who offered them sacrifices. The unusual pattern of hierarchical terms and unique names preserved in the *Relación de las huacas* may well reflect a misunderstanding between the indigenous informant(s) and the author of the original ceque manuscript (or an error in the re-recording of the document by Cobo decades later) in which ranking terms were confused with kin group names.

There are other recording irregularities in the *Relación de las huacas* regarding the tripartitioning of the ceques into collana, payan, and cayao. For example, Ch. 9 is listed as Capac. The position of the ceque in the system suggests, however, that it also may have been classified as collana. But it should be noted that Ch. 9 is in the "last" ceque cluster of Chinchaysuyu (Ch. 7, Ch. 8, and Ch. 9) and that the *Relación de las huacas* indicates that Ch. 7, which is a cayao, was the responsibility of Capac Ayllu. As discussed above, early colonial documents from Cusco indicate that Capac Ayllu incorporated the extended family of Topa Inca Yupanqui, and that this kin group was divided into three sublineages called collana, payan, or cayao according to their relative prestige. Given this information, it is understandable how the most prestigious ceque (collana) of a ceque cluster could also be called by the name of the kin group that maintained the ceques in that cluster.

Additional examples of unusual ceque classifications include Cu. 12 and Cu. 13, both of which are classified as cayao. It is evident from the order of the other ceques in Cuntisuyu that Cu. 13 held the position of payan rather than that of cayao. A similar case can be found in Chinchaysuyu, where Ch. 4 is labeled as payan and Ch. 5 is presented as cayao. The order of the ceques in this suyu suggest that the names of these two ceques have been mistakenly reversed; Ch. 4 should be classified as cayao and Ch. 5 as payan (Table 4.1, Figure 4.1).

A final observation made by Zuidema (1964:3) is that the two moieties of Cusco contain symmetrical patterns of collana, payan, and cayao ceques despite the fact that the numbering of the Chinchaysuyu ceques in the *Relación de las huacas* ran opposite to those of Antisuyu, Collasuyu, and Cuntisuyu (Figure 4.1). In the upper (Hanan) moiety of Cusco, the classifications of the ceques into collana, payan, and cayao ran in a clockwise direction. The westernmost ceque (Ch. 9) was called Capac (or collana), which was followed by a payan (Ch. 8) and a cayao (Ch. 7). This pattern of collana, payan, and cayao is repeated across upper Cusco as one moves from west to east. The lower moiety of Cusco (Hurin) presents a similar collana, payan, and cayao pattern, but it runs in a counterclockwise direction. The westernmost ceque (Cu. 14) is classified as collana and the easternmost is cayao (An. 1).

The Hierarchy of Ceque Clusters

It has been noted that three of the suyus (Chinchaysuyu, Antisuyu, and Collasuyu) contained three sets of ceque clusters each and that the fourth suyu (Cuntisuyu) contained five. Zuidema (1964), followed by Rowe (1985), has suggested that the ceque clusters of the suyus can also be classified with the terms *collana, payan,* and *cayao.* If this is the case, then the first three ceques of Antisuyu, in the upper moiety, would have been classified as collana, the middle three as payan, and the final three as cayao. The order in Collasuyu, located in the lower moiety, would have been the reverse, with Co. 9–Co. 7 called collana, Co. 6–Co. 4 payan, and Co. 3–Co. 1 cayao. The ranking of the ceques of Chinchaysuyu is more speculative because its ceques are presented in a counterclockwise order in the *Relación de las huacas.* Both Zuidema and Rowe suggest that the last three ceques of Chinchaysuyu, as numbered by Cobo, would have been collana, the middle three payan, and the first three cayao.

The classification of ceque clusters in Cuntisuyu is even more difficult to determine because it contained fifteen ceques rather than nine. Zuidema (1964) proposes the following arrangements: Cu. 14, Cu. 13, Cu. 12 (collana); Cu. 11, Cu. 10, Cu. 9 (payan); Cu. 8 and Cu. 1 (cayao); Cu. 7, Cu. 6, Cu. 5 (collana); and Cu. 4, Cu. 3, Cu. 2 (payan). In this ordering, Zuidema suggests that two clusters in Cuntisuyu are classified as collana, two as payan, and one as cayao. Rowe (1985) prefers an alternative ordering: Cu. 14, Cu. 13, Cu. 12 (collana); Cu. 11, Cu. 10, Cu. 9 (payan); Cu. 8 (cayao); Cu. 7, Cu. 6, Cu. 5 (collana); Cu. 4, Cu. 3, Cu. 2 (payan); and Cu. 1 (cayao). Rowe's listing differs from Zuidema's in that Cu. 8 and Cu. 1 are defined as separate ceque clusters. This model is based on the proposition that Cu. 1, like Cu. 8, incorporated two different ceques (Rowe 1985:47). In Rowe's proposed counting system, two clusters are classified as collana, two as payan, and two as cayao. Both of these hierarchical systems for the Cuntisuyu ceques have merit. The critical difference between them is that Zuidema's model suggests that two widely separate ceques (Cu. 1 and Cu. 8) were considered a single cluster, while Rowe's model proposes that not all the ceque clusters of the system contained three ceques, and he suggests that Cu. 1 was composed of two lines of huacas.

Rowe's proposition that Cu. 1 may have contained two separate lines of huacas, like that of Cu. 8, can be tested with field data. Ground documentation of the huacas of Cuntisuyu, presented in Chapter 7, indicates that the huacas of Cu. 1 form one continuous line. These findings do not support Rowe's model of Cuntisuyu. Accordingly, until further research has been conducted, I have adopted Zuidema's ranking system for the ceque clusters (Table 4.2).

Kings, Ayllus, and Ceques

The spatial divisions of the Cusco Valley, as defined by the projections of ceques across the region, were linked to the social organization of the capital by the ritual responsibilities that various kin groups held for huacas along particular lines. According to Cobo, members of the Cusco kin groups held ritual obligations to maintain the shrines along certain ceques at specified times:

> Each ceque was the responsibility of the partialities and families of the city of Cuzco, from within which came the attendants and servants who cared for the guacas of their ceque and saw to offering the established sacrifices at the proper times. (Cobo 1980:15 [1653:Bk. 13, Ch. 13])[7]

Table 4.2. The Hypothetical Classification of Ceque Clusters with the Terms *Collana*, *Payan*, and *Cayao*

Chinchaysuyu		Antisuyu	
Ch. 1, Ch. 2, Ch. 3	Cayao	An. 1, An. 2, An. 3	Collana
Ch. 4, Ch. 5, Ch. 6	Payan	An. 4, An. 5, An. 6	Payan
Ch. 7, Ch. 8, Ch. 9	Collana	An. 7, An. 8, An. 9	Cayao
Collasuyu		**Cuntisuyu**	
Co. 1, Co. 2, Co. 3	Cayao	Cu. 1	Cayao
Co. 4, Co. 5, Co. 6	Payan	Cu. 2, Cu. 3, Cu. 4	Payan
Co. 7, Co. 8, Co. 9	Collana	Cu. 5, Cu. 6, Cu. 7	Collana
		Cu. 8	Cayao
		Cu. 9, Cu. 10, Cu. 11	Payan
		Cu. 12, Cu. 13, Cu. 14	Collana

Furthermore, within the text of the ceque system document, Cobo occasionally notes which kin group was responsible for a particular ceque. For example, for the first ceque of Chinchaysuyu (Ch. 1) he writes:

> The first ceque was called Cayao; it was the responsibility of the partiality and ayllo of Goacaytaqui and had the following five guacas. (Cobo 1980:15 [1653:Bk. 13, Ch. 13])[8]

From an analysis of the various kin-group names included in the *Relación de las huacas*, it can be deduced that the obligation of maintaining and worshipping the shrines along the ceques was divided between two broadly defined social divisions of the Cusco Valley: (1) the panacas of the ruling Incas and (2) the nonroyal ayllus of Cusco.[9] The panacas, or what can also be referred to as "royal ayllus," were composed of the direct descendants of Inca kings. The nonroyal ayllus of Cusco comprised the lower-level citizens of the imperial city. The goal of this section is to analyze the social organization of the Cusco Valley, as defined by its various royal and nonroyal ayllus, and to determine which of the lines of the Cusco ceque system were the responsibility of each of these groups.

The Panacas of Cusco

At the time of the European invasion of Tahuantinsuyu, the royal Incas of Cusco traced their ancestry back eleven generations from the last undisputed ruler of the empire, Huayna Capac, to the mythical founder of Cusco, Manco Capac. It is widely recognized that the Incas subdivided this dynastic list into two groups: rulers associated with Hurin Cusco and those associated with Hanan Cusco (Table 4.3).[10] The first five Incas, Manco Capac through Capac Yupanqui, were affiliated with Hurin Cusco (Collasuyu and Cuntisuyu), while the last five Incas, Inca Roca through Topa Inca Yupanqui, were associated with Hanan Cusco (Chinchaysuyu and Antisuyu).[11]

The social elite of Cusco, or what Garcilaso de la Vega classifies as the "Incas of royal blood," was composed of the ruling Inca and his sister/wife, as well as the direct descendants of all previous Inca rulers. Generally, at the death of an Inca king, his eldest son inherited the position of Inca, and the other male descendants of the dead Inca formed a royal descent group called a *panaca* (or *panaca ayllu*) dedicated to supporting the cult, lands, and prestige of their father.

Many colonial sources provide information on the names of the Inca kings that ruled Cusco before the arrival of the

Table 4.3. Traditional List of Inca Rulers
before Huayna Capac

Inca Dynastic Succession	Moiety Association
1) Manco Capac	Hurin Cusco
2) Sinchi Roca	Hurin Cusco
3) Lloque Yupanqui	Hurin Cusco
4) Mayta Capac	Hurin Cusco
5) Capac Yupanqui	Hurin Cusco
6) Inca Roca	Hanan Cusco
7) Yahuar Huacac	Hanan Cusco
8) Viracocha Inca	Hanan Cusco
9) Pachacuti Inca	Hanan Cusco
10) Topa Inca	Hanan Cusco

Spaniards and the names of their respective panacas (Table 4.4). Five independent sources are presented here for illustrative purposes.[12] The earliest systematic description of the Inca kings and their panacas is provided in a 1542 document based on an inquest of Licenciado Vaca de Castro in Cusco (Callapiña et al. 1974 [1542/1608]).[13] Another early source on the Inca dynasty and its lineages was written by Diego Fernández (1963:84 [1571:Bk. 3, Ch. 7]). Although Fernández published his summary in Spain in 1571, it is believed to be based on information that he gathered in Cusco in the late 1550s (Means 1928:365). A third source is Pedro Sarmiento

de Gamboa's 1572 report, which presents extensive information on the Cusco kings and their descent groups, as he discusses the life of each Inca (Sarmiento de Gamboa 1906 [1572]). Another account of the Cusco panacas is contained in a 1603 letter to Garcilaso de la Vega (1966:626 [1609:Vol 1, Bk. 9, Ch. 40]) from the royal Inca descendants, requesting that he contact the king of Spain on their behalf.

However, the most important source of data on Inca panacas for this study is Molina's (1989 [ca. 1575]) description of the Cusco Citua festival. During this elaborate celebration, held in the ninth month of the Inca calendar, the imperial city was ritually cleaned. At its close, four groups of one hundred warriors carrying ashes ran out from the central plaza of Cusco along the four royal roads of the empire. When the runners reached the edge of the Cusco Valley, the ashes were passed to representatives of other groups, who threw them into the major rivers of the region. The Cusco participants in this event are listed by Molina according to their social rank as members of the panacas and the nonroyal ayllus of the capital city:

> The Indians who went out shouting and left Cusco in the direction of Collasuyu, were of the lineage of Usca Mayta Ayllu, Apu Mayta Ayllu, Hahuanina and Sutic and Maras Ayllu, Cuycusa Ayllu.
>
> Those who left to the west, which is in the direction of Chinchaysuyu, went out shouting the same cries and were of the lineage of Capac Ayllu y Hatun Ayllu and Vicaquirao and Chavin Cuzco Ayllu and Arayraca Ayllu and others of Uro . . .

Table 4.4. The Royal Descent Groups (Panacas) of the Inca from Selected Chronicles

Founder	Callapito et al. (1542)	Fernandez (1571)	Sarmiento de Gamboa (1572)	Molina (ca. 1575)	Garcilaso de la Vega (1609)
(1) Manco Capac	Chima	Chima	Chima	China (Cuntisuyu)	Chima
(2) Sinchi Roca	Raorao	Piauragua	Raura	Raura (Cuntisuyu)	Rauraua
(3) Lloque Yupanqui	Chigua Yuin	Aguanin	Avayni	Yahuaymin (Collasuyu)	Hahuanina
(4) Mayta Capac	Uscamaitas	Uzcamaita	Usca Mayta	Uscaymata (Collasuyu)	Usca Maita
(5) Capac Yupanqui	Apomaitas	Apomaita	Apu Mayta	Yapo may ho (Collasuyu)	Apu Maita
(6) Inca Roca	Vicaquirao	Vica Cupa	Vicaquirao	Uicaquicao (Chinchaysuyu)	Uncaquirau
(7) Yahuar Huacac	Aucayllo	Aoca	Aucaylli	Aucaylli (Antisuyu)	Ailli
(8) Viracocha Inca	Sucsu	Cococ	Çocço	Cuscu (Antisuyu)	Socso
(9) Pachacuti Inca	Innaca	Hatren	Inaca (or Hatun)	Atun (Chinchaysuyu)	Inca
(10) Topa Inca	Capac	Capac	Capac	Capac (Chinchaysuyu)	Cápac Aillu
(11) Huayna Capac		Tome Bamba	Tumipampa		Tumi Pampa

Those who carried the cries to the part of Antisuyu were of the following lineages: Socso Ayllu, Aucaylli Ayllu, Tarpuntay Ayllu, Saño Ayllu, . . .

Those who left towards Cuntisuyu were of the following lineages: Raura Panaca Ayllu and Chima Panaca Ayllu and Masca Panaca Ayllu and Quesco Ayllu . . .[14]

In this description of the Citua ritual, Molina presents the names of ten panacas and ten nonroyal ayllus of Cusco according to their suyu: three panacas and three nonroyal ayllus in Collasuyu, three panacas and three nonroyal ayllus in Chinchaysuyu, two panacas and two nonroyal ayllus in Antisuyu, and two panacas and two nonroyal ayllus in Cuntisuyu.

In his description of the Citua ritual, Molina writes that members of the first two Inca descent groups, Chima (descendants of Manco Capac, the first Inca) and Raurau (descendants of Sinchi Roca, the second Inca), ran with members of two nonroyal ayllus, the Masca and Quesco, toward Cuntisuyu. The warriors from the panacas of Hahuanina (descendants of Lloque Yupanqui, the third Inca), Usca Mayta (descendants of Mayta Capac, the fourth Inca), and Apu Mayta (descendants of Capac Yupanqui, the fifth Inca) left with runners from the nonroyal ayllus of Sutic, Maras, and Cuycusa and headed into Collasuyu. Representatives of panacas Aucaylli (descendants of Yahuar Huacac, the seventh Inca) and Sucsu (descendants of Viracocha Inca, the eight Inca) went with those of the nonroyal ayllus Tarpuntay and Sañoc into Antisuyu. And finally, warriors from the panacas of Vicaquirao (descendants of Inca Roca, the sixth Inca), Hatun (descendants of Pachacuti Inca Yupanqui, the ninth Inca), and Capac (descendants of Topa Inca Yupanqui, the tenth Inca) left Cusco with members of the nonroyal ayllus of Chavin Cusco, Arayraca, and Uro toward Chinchaysuyu. Tumi Bamba, the panaca of Huayna Capac, the eleventh king of Cusco (who died shortly before Pizarro and his forces landed on the shores of Peru), appears not to have been included in either the Citua festival or the ceque system. Given the general economic and social confusion of the immediate preconquest period, this is not surprising.

Molina's division of the Cusco panacas into suyus is reproduced in the *Relación de las huacas,* as Cobo describes which ceques were the responsibility of the royal kin groups of the Inca (Table 4.5). According to Cobo, the descendants of the first Inca (Chima Panaca) were responsible for Cu. 5. Representatives of the third, fourth, and fifth rulers of Cusco (Hahuanina, Usca Mayta, and Apu Mayta Panacas)

Table 4.5. The Cusco Ceque System and the Panacas

Ceque		Responsibility	Notes
Chinchaysuyu			
Ch. 1	Cayao	Guacaytaqui	
Ch. 2	Payan	Vicaquirao	(Inca Roca: 6th Inca)
Ch. 3	Collana		
Ch. 4	Payan [*sic* Cayao]		
Ch. 5	Cayao [*sic* Payan]	Iñaca (or Hatun)	(Pachacuti Inca: 9th Inca)
Ch. 6	Collana		
Ch. 7	Cayao	Capac	(Topac Inca: 10th Inca)
Ch. 8	Payan		
Ch. 9	Capac [*sic* Collana]		
Antisuyu			
An. 1	Collana	Suscu	(Viracocha Inca: 8th Inca)
An. 2	Payan		
An. 3	Cayao		
An. 4	Collana	Aucaylli	(Yahuar Huacac: 7th Inca)
An. 5	Payan		
An. 6	Cayao		
An. 7	Collana ?	Yacanora	
An. 8	Payan ?	Ayarmaca	
An. 9	Cayao	Cari	
Collasuyu			
Co. 1	Cayao	Aguini	
Co. 2	Payan	Hahuanina	(Lloque Yupanqui: 3d Inca)
Co. 3	Collana		
Co. 4	Cayao	Apu Mayta	(Capac Yupanqui: 5th Inca)
Co. 5	Payan		
Co. 6	Collana		
Co. 7	Cayao	Usca Mayta	(Mayta Capac: 4th Inca)
Co. 8	Payan		
Co. 9	Collana		
Cuntisuyu[1]			
Cu. 1	Anaguarque		
Cu. 2	Cayao	Quisco	
Cu. 3	Payan		
Cu. 4	Collana		
Cu. 5	Cayao	Chima	(Manco Capac: 1st Inca)
Cu. 6	Payan		
Cu. 7	Collana		
Cu. 8	Cayao and Collana		
Cu. 9	Cayao		
Cu. 10	Payan		
Cu. 11	Collana		
Cu. 12	Cayao		
Cu. 13	Cayao [*sic* Payan]		
Cu. 14	Collana		

1. Raurau, the panaca of the second Inca, Sinchi Roca, was also in Cuntisuyu; however, its exact position is not known.

maintained the shrines along Co. 2, Co. 7, and Co. 4, respectively. Members of the sixth king's descent group (Vicaquirao Panaca) served the huacas of Ch. 2. The ancestral kin of the seventh and eighth kings (Aucaylli and Sucsu Panacas) attended the shrines of ceques An. 4 and An. 1, and those of the tenth Inca (Capac Panaca) were responsible for Ch. 7.

In an apparent recording error, only eight of the ten panacas of Cusco are listed in the *Relación de las huacas* as having responsibility for ceques within the system. Nevertheless, the ceques of the missing two panacas, that of the ninth Inca, Pachacuti Inca Yupanqui, and that of the second Inca, Sinchi Roca, can be suggested from available data. It can be proposed that Pachacuti Inca Yupanqui's panaca, Iñaca (also called Hatun), was responsible for Ch. 5, because the *Relación de las huacas* indicates that members of this panaca made sacrifices at its first huaca, Cusi Chanca (Ch. 5:1), which was the birthplace of Pachacuti Inca Yupanqui. It can also be inferred that members of Sinchi Roca's panaca, Raurau, attended a ceque in Cuntisuyu, since this panaca is associated with this suyu by Molina. Zuidema (1964:9–10) suggests that the most likely candidate for the ceque of Raurau Panaca is Cu. 13, while Rowe (1985: 47–48) proposes Cu. 14. I see both of these positions as equally valid solutions to the problem of the Raurau's ceque in Cuntisuyu. However, a number of other possibilities could also be suggested, because the only constraint on Raurau's ceque in Cuntisuyu is that it not fall among those included in the ceque cluster of Cu. 5, which was assigned to Chima Panaca, or the ceque cluster of Cu. 1, which was maintained by Quisco Ayllu (see below).

A pattern emerges from the positions of the panacas in the ceque system. As noted earlier, the ceque system is divided into a series of ceque clusters, composed of three lines each, that are classified as cayao, payan, and collana. Following Cobo's description of the system, it appears that the responsibilities of panacas were distributed across the system in such a way that no single ceque cluster included more than one panaca (Zuidema 1964; Rowe 1985).

Rowe also suggests that the positions of the panacas in the *Relación de las huacas* may be related to Pérez Bocanegra's (1631:613) description of the terms *cayao, payan,* and *collana* as indicators of relative genealogical distance. Rowe believes that the position of each panaca in the Cusco ceque system is determined by its genealogical distance from Huayna Capac (Table 4.6).

> The ego or point of reference in this system must necessarily have been Huayna Capac, the eleventh monarch, who was the son of Tupac Inca. For Huayna Capac, the members of his father's group were indeed cayau, the members of the group of his grandfather Pachacuti, payan, and the members of the group of his great-grandfather Viracocha Inca, collana.[15]

It should be noted, however, that the panacas for the tenth, ninth, and eighth, as well as those for the fourth, third, and presumably the second, Cusco kings were classified as cayao, payan, and collana, whereas the panacas of

Table 4.6. Inca Kings, Panacas, Ceques, and Their Classifications

Inca	Panaca	Ceque	Classification
Topa Inca: 10th Inca	Capac	Ch. 7	Cayao
Pachacuti Inca: 9th Inca	Inaca (or Hatun)	Ch. 5	Cayao [*sic* Payan]
Viracocha Inca: 8th Inca	Suscu	An. 1	Collana
Yahuar Huacac: 7th Inca	Aucailli	An. 4	Collana
Inca Roca: 6th Inca	Vicaquirao	Ch. 2	Payan
Capac Yupanqui: 5th Inca	Apu Mayta	Co. 4	Cayao
Mayta Capac: 4th Inca	Usca Mayta	Co. 7	Cayao
Lloque Yupanqui: 3d Inca	Hahuanina	Co. 2	Payan
Sinchi Roca: 2d Inca	Raurau	Cu. ?	Collana ?
Manco Capac: 1st Inca	Chima	Cu. 5	Cayao

the seventh, sixth, and fifth Incas were classified in the reverse order: collana, payan, and cayao. Reasons for this anomaly are open to debate.

The Nonroyal Ayllus of Cusco

There were ten nonroyal ayllus in the area of Cusco. The fact that there were ten nonroyal ayllus as well as ten panacas suggests that these groups were somehow paired (Zuidema 1964; Rowe 1985). The distribution of the ten panacas across the Cusco ceque system has been discussed above. In this section, the relation of the nonroyal ayllus to that same system will be explored. The results are more ambiguous, however, because there is less information available on the nonroyal ayllus than on the panacas.

The nonroyal ayllus of Cusco are best described in three independent accounts written in that city in the early to mid-1570s. One of these is Sarmiento de Gamboa's (1906 [1572]) description of Manco Capac's journey from the Inca origin place of Tambotoco to Cusco, which contains information on the mythical origins of the nonroyal ayllus. The second account is an untitled report written for Viceroy Francisco de Toledo by Gabriel de Loarte (1882 [1572]). This little-used document furnishes information on the territories in Cusco thought to have been occupied by the nonroyal ayllus in some vague, if not mythical, pre-Inca period and on their composition during the Early Colonial period. The third account containing extensive information on the nonroyal ayllus of Cusco is Molina's portrayal of the Citua festival, which describes the social positions of the royal, as well as the nonroyal, ayllus of the region in relation to the four suyus.[16]

Sarmiento de Gamboa (1906:34 [1572:Bk. 11]) indicates that some six leagues to the south-southwest of Cusco was a place called Pacariqtambo, where there was a hill called Tambotoco with three caves. The caves were called Marastoco, Sutictoco, and Capactoco. Four men and four women, the first Incas, are said to have emerged from the central cave of Capactoco. The men were named Manco Capac, Ayar Auca, Ayar Cache, and Ayar Ucho, while the four women were called Mama Ocllo, Mama Huaco, Mama Ipacura, and Mama Raua. The movement of these eight Incas from the Pacariqtambo region to the Cusco Valley was followed by that of ten groups, which are here called the nonroyal ayllus of Cusco. Sarmiento de Gamboa writes:

Whereupon were moved by greed ten groups or *ayllos,* which among those barbarians means lineages or groups. The names of those groups are as follows:

Chavin Cuzco Ayllo: of the lineage of Ayar Cache; there are today some of this group in Cuzco. Their leaders are named Martín Chucumbi and Don Diego Guaman Paucar,

Arayraca Ayllo Cuzcocallan: presently from this ayllo are Juan Pizarro Yupangui, Don Francisco Quipi, Alonso Tarma Yupangui of the lineage of Ayar Uchu,

Tarpuntay Ayllo: there is in Cuzco presently from this ayllo,

Guacaytaqui Ayllo: of those, a few live today in Cuzco,

Sañoc Ayllo: of those, there are some in Cuzco.

Those five groups are *Hanan Cuzcos,* which means the group of Upper Cuzco.

Sutictoco Ayllo: which is the lineage, that came out of one of the windows called Sutictoco, as mentioned above. There are presently in Cuzco some of them and their leaders, who watch over them, Don Francisco Avca Micho Avri Sutic and Don Alonso Gualpa,

Maras Ayllo: those are the ones who claim to have come out of the window Marastoco. There are some of them in Cuzco, and their leaders are Don Alonso Llama Oca and Don Gonzalo Ampura Llama Oca,

Cuycusa Ayllo: there are some of them in Cuzco and their head is Christóbal Acllari,

Masca Ayllo: there is from this lineage in Cuzco Juan Quispi,

Oro Ayllo: there is today from this lineage Don Pedro Yucay.

I declare that all those lineages have been preserved in such a way that their memory has not been lost, and given that there are more than the ones mentioned above, I refer only to their heads, who are protectors and leaders of the lineage, and through whom the group is being maintained. And each of them has the duty and obligation to protect the others and to know the matters and deeds of their ancestors.[17]

Sarmiento de Gamboa's list of nonroyal ayllus in Cusco resembles that of Molina's description of the Citua ritual in a number of interesting ways. First, both authors register ten nonroyal groups evenly divided between Hanan (Chinchaysuyu and Antisuyu) and Hurin (Collasuyu and Cuntisuyu) Cusco; second, the names of their nonroyal groups are very similar; and third, the ayllus are presented in approximately the same order in both lists.

Gabriel de Loarte's (1882 [1572]) report for Viceroy Toledo is less concise, and only the points relative to this study will be summarized here. On 26 January 1572, Gabriel de Loarte interviewed approximately fifteen men from three of the ten nonroyal ayllus of Cusco (Sauasiray Ayllu, Antasayac Ayllu, and Ayar Ucho Ayllu) concerning the history of the Inca.[18] During this interview, members of Sauasiray Ayllu stated that their founding ancestor emerged from the cave of Sutictoco and first settled the area around the Temple of the Sun. Since a group called Sutic Ayllu is recorded by both Molina and Sarmiento de Gamboa, it can be suggested that this ayllu had at least two names: Sauasiray and Sutic. Representatives of Antasayac Ayllu declared that their founding ancestor was called Quesco, an ayllu name found in Molina's account, and that he settled the area of Cusco called Santa Clara by the Spaniards. Accordingly, it seems that the Quesco Ayllu mentioned by Molina was also known as Antasayac Ayllu.[19] Furthermore, individuals of Ayar Ucho Ayllu claimed direct descent from a brother of Manco Capac. Loarte notes that this group originally occupied an area near the center of Cusco called Pucamarca, and that they were also called the Alcaviza. Sarmiento de Gamboa specifically states, however, that the descendants of Ayar Ucho were referred to as Arayraca Ayllu, a name that also appears in Molina's account. Because members from Ayar Ucho Ayllu (or Alcaviza) and Arayraca Ayllu claim, in separate documents, to be the direct descendants of the mythical Ayar Ucho, it can be suggested that these are alternative names for the same kin group. This proposition is supported by the fact that two of the individuals described by Sarmiento de Gamboa as the leaders of Arayraca Ayllu, Juan Pizarro Yupanqui and Francisco Quispi, are also listed in Loarte's report as the leaders of Ayar Ucho (or Alcaviza) Ayllu.

Table 4.7 summarizes the information on nonroyal ayllus of Cusco as presented by Molina, Sarmiento de Gamboa, and Loarte. A comparison of these three sources reveals a number of inconsistencies that need to be examined. Molina suggests that Uro Ayllu, along with those of Chavin Cusco and Arayraca, was in Chinchaysuyu, while Sarmiento de Gamboa records only the latter two kin groups in this suyu. On the other hand, Sarmiento de Gamboa places Guacaytaqui Ayllu in Antisuyu, between Taruntay and Sañoc, while Molina does not. Furthermore, Molina ends his list with Quesco Ayllu, yet Sarmiento de Gamboa ends his with Uro. Some of these inconsistencies are reconcilable using additional information provided in the *Relación de las huacas,* while others are not.

Table 4.7. The Nonroyal Ayllus of Cusco

Molina [ca. 1575]	Sarmiento de Gamboa [1572]	Loarte [1572]
Chinchaysuyu		
1) Chavin Cusco	Chavin Cusco	
2) Arayraca	Arayraca Cusco-callan	Aray Ucho Ayllu (also called Arayraca and Alcaviza)
3) Uro		
Antisuyu		
Tarpuntay	Taruntay	
	Guacaytaqui [*sic*][1]	
Sañoc	Sañoc	
Collasuyu		
Sutic	Sutic	Sauasiray Ayllu (also called Sutic)
Maras	Maras	
Cuycusa	Cuycusa	
Cuntisuyu		
Masca	Masca	
Quesco	Uro	Antasayac Ayllu (also called Quizco)

1. Guacaytaqui should be in Chinchaysuyu after Arayraca.

44

The *Relación de las huacas* specifically lists the names of two nonroyal ayllus mentioned by Molina and Sarmiento de Gamboa as being responsible for the huacas along two ceques, and it indicates that members of Goacaytaqui (Guacaytaqui) Ayllu were responsible for the huacas along the first ceque of Chinchaysuyu (Ch. 1). Given this information, it seems logical to suggest that Guacaytaqui was incorrectly placed in Sarmiento de Gamboa's list between Taruntay and Sañoc in Antisuyu, when it should have been after Arayraca in Chinchaysuyu. The *Relación de las huacas* also notes that shrines along the second ceque of Cuntisuyu (Cu. 2) were maintained by Quisco (Quesco) Ayllu. On the basis of this data, it can be suggested that Molina is correct in placing this ayllu in Cuntisuyu. The proper position of Uro Ayllu, recorded by Molina as in Chinchaysuyu and by Sarmiento de Gamboa as in Cuntisuyu, is more ambiguous. Because it is known that many ayllus in Cusco held multiple names, it is possible that Uro may have been an alternative name for either Quesco Ayllu or Guacaytaqui Ayllu (Zuidema 1964:8; Rowe 1985:53).[20] Without additional archival data, however, it is difficult to suggest which of these ayllus is the better candidate.

Possible Positions of the Nonroyal Ayllus in the Cusco Ceque System

Using information provided in the *Relación de las huacas*, it can be concluded that two of the nonroyal ayllus of Cusco were directly involved in maintaining shrines along ceques: Quisco (Quesco) Ayllu was responsible for the shrines of Cu. 2, and Goacaytaqui (Guacaytaqui) Ayllu maintained those of Ch. 1. Given that all of the panacas were incorporated into the ceque system, it is reasonable to suggest that each of the nonroyal ayllus was also responsible for a ceque, even though the majority of the nonroyal ayllus are not specifically mentioned in the ceque document.

Having identified the names of the nonroyal ayllus of the Cusco region and determined their relative positions in the four suyus, researchers have speculated on the role that these groups played in maintaining the Cusco shrines.[21] Since Molina's description of the Citua festival lists the same number of panacas and nonroyal ayllus in each suyu, some scholars suggest that each of the royal kin groups of Cusco was paired with a nonroyal one, and that the pairing can be understood through the hierarchical presentations of panaca and nonroyal ayllu names in Molina's account

(Zuidema 1964; Rowe 1985). For example, for Chinchaysuyu Molina (1989:75 [ca. 1575])writes:

> Those that left to the west, which is towards Chinchaysuyu, left shouting in the same manner and these were of the lineage of Capac Ayllu y Hatun Ayllu and Vicaquirao and Chavin Cuzco Ayllu and Arayraca Ayllu and others of Uro . . .[22]

It has been proposed that the first panaca (Capac) of this list was paired with the first nonroyal ayllu (Chavin Cusco), that the second panaca (Hatun [also called Iñaca]) was associated with the second nonroyal ayllu (Arayraca), and that the third panaca (Vicaquirao) was linked to the third nonroyal ayllu (Uro).

There is some evidence that a similar pairing of royal and nonroyal ayllus may have occurred in specific ceque clusters, because Cobo's documentation of the system indicates that Guacaytaqui Ayllu[23] was responsible for the first ceque of Chinchaysuyu (Ch. 1) and that the panaca, Vicaquirao, of the sixth ruler of Cusco maintained those of the second ceque (Ch. 2). Extrapolating from this *single* apparent pairing, researchers have proposed that each ceque cluster that contained a panaca also contained a nonroyal ayllu (Zuidema 1964:8). If this assumption is correct, then in Chinchaysuyu, Hatun (Iñaca) Panaca (Ch. 5) was paired with Arayraca, which was responsible for either Ch. 4 or Ch. 6, and Capac Panaca (Ch. 7) was matched with Chavin Cusco, which maintained the shrines along either Ch. 8 or Ch. 9. In Antisuyu, Sucsu Panaca (An. 1) was coupled with Tarpuntay, keepers of An. 2 or An. 3, and Aucaylli Panaca (An. 4) was associated with Sañoc, who looked after the huacas of An. 5 or An. 6. In Collasuyu, Hahuanina Panaca (Co. 2) would have been paired with Cuycusa, which may have maintained the shrines of Co. 3, since Cobo writes that another group called Aguini cared for those of Co. 1. Alternatively, Zuidema (1964:8) and Rowe (1985:51) suggest that Aguini is synonymous with Cuycusa. Apu Mayta Panaca (Co. 4) would have been matched with Maras Ayllu, which made offerings along Co. 5 or Co. 6, and Usca Mayta Panaca (Co. 7) with Sutic, which was responsible for Co. 8 or Co. 9 (Table 4.8, Figure 4.2).

The possible positions of royal and nonroyal ayllus in Cuntisuyu are more difficult to predict because this quarter of Cusco contains an unusual number of ceques. Cobo writes that Quesco Ayllu was responsible for the shrines along Cu. 2, and that Chima Panaca maintained those along

Table 4.8. The Social Organization of Cusco and the Ceque System

The Ceques and Panacas of Hanan Cuzco
Chinchaysuyu

Ceque	Classification	Responsibility	Notes
Ch. 1	Cayao	Goacaytaqui	Nonroyal ayllu, noted by Cobo and Sarmiento de Gamboa
Ch. 2	Payan	Vicaquirao	Panaca of Inca Roca: 6th Inca
Ch. 3	Collana	?[1]	
Ch. 4	Payan [sic Cayao]	?	
Ch. 5	Cayao [sic Payan]	Inaca (or Hatun)	Panaca of Pachacuti Inca: 9th Inca
Ch. 6	Collana	Arayraca?	Nonroyal ayllu, noted by Molina and Sarmiento de Gamboa
Ch. 7	Cayao	Capac	Panaca of Topa Inca: 10th Inca
Ch. 8	Payan	Chavin Cuzco?	Nonroyal ayllu, noted by Molina and Sarmiento de Gamboa
Ch. 9	Capac [sic Collana]	?	

Antisuyu

Ceque	Classification	Responsibility	Notes
An. 1	Collana	Socso	Panaca of Viracocha Inca: 8th Inca
An. 2	Payan	Tarpuntay?	Nonroyal ayllu, noted by Molina and Sarmiento de Gamboa
An. 3	Cayao	?	
An. 4	Collana	Aucailli	Panaca of Yahuar Huacac: 7th Inca
An. 5	Payan	Sanoc?	Nonroyal ayllu, noted by Molina and Sarmiento de Gamboa
An. 6	Cayao	?	
An. 7	Yacanora [sic Collana]	Yacanora	Kin group
An. 8	Ayarmaca [sic Payan]	Ayarmaca	Kin group
An. 9	Cayao	Cari	Kin group?[2]

The Ceques and Panacas of Hurin Cuzco
Collasuyu

Ceque	Classification	Responsibility	Notes
Co. 1	Cayao	Aguini	Kin group?
Co. 2	Payan	Hahuanina	Panaca of Lloque Yupanqui: 3d Inca
Co. 3	Collana	Cuycusa?	Nonroyal ayllu, noted by Molina and Sarmiento de Gamboa[3]
Co. 4	Cayao	Apu Mayta	Panaca of Capac Yupanqui: 5th Inca
Co. 5	Payan	Maras?	Nonroyal ayllu, noted by Molina and Sarmiento de Gamboa
Co. 6	Collana	?	
Co. 7	Cayao	Usca Mayta	Panaca of Mayta Capac: 4th Inca
Co. 8	Payan	Sutic?	Nonroyal ayllu, noted by Molina and Sarmiento de Gamboa
Co. 9	Collana	?	

Cuntisuyu[4]

Ceque	Classification	Responsibility	Notes
Cu. 1	Anaguarqui	Anaguarqui?	Kin group, perhaps related to the village of Chocco (Payan?)
Cu. 2	Cayao	Quisco	Nonroyal ayllu, noted by Molina and Cobo
Cu. 3	Payan	?	
Cu. 4	Collana	?	
Cu. 5	Cayao	Chima	Panaca of Manco Capac: 1st Inca
Cu. 6	Payan	?	
Cu. 7	Collana	?	
Cu. 8a	Cayao	?	
Cu. 8b	Collana	?	
Cu. 9	Cayao	?	
Cu. 10	Payan	?	
Cu. 11	Collana	?	
Cu. 12	Cayao	?	
Cu. 13	Cayao [sic Payan]?		
Cu. 14	Collana	?	

1. ? = Information unknown or speculative.

2. There is an area between Cusco and San Sebastián that is traditionally called Cari, which may be related to this term.

3. A huaca with this name is listed as Co. 8:5 by Cobo.

4. Raurau, the panaca of the second Inca, Sinchi Roca, was also in Cuntisuyu; however, its exact position is not known.

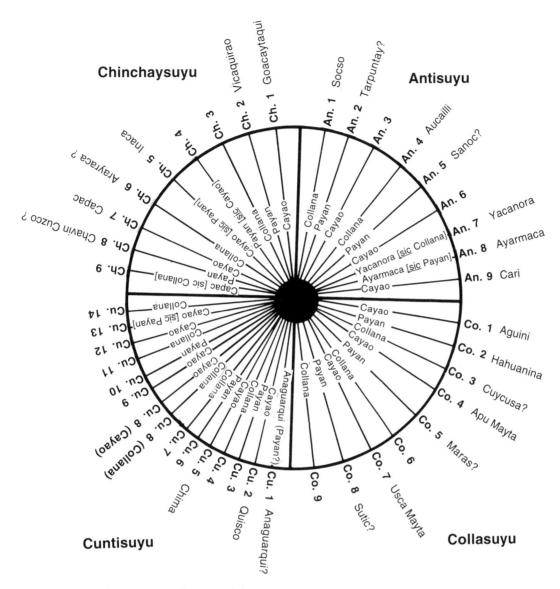

Figure 4.2. The social organization of Cusco and the ceque system.

Cu. 5.[24] Accordingly, Raurau Panaca and Masca Ayllu may have been caretakers of two other ceques in this suyu. It must be emphasized, however, that since only one royal and nonroyal pair is explicitly mentioned in the *Relación de las huacas,* the above pairings should be considered speculative at best.

Other Cusco Ayllus and Problematic Ceques

Besides the ten panacas and the ten nonroyal ayllus, there were also other populations that controlled territories in the Cusco Valley that do not seem to have been incorporated into the social hierarchy of the city. Yet there is tentative evidence to suggest that some of these groups were responsible for ceques in the system. For example, An. 7 and An. 8 are classified as Ayarmaca and Yacanora, rather than as collana, payan, or cayao like most of the other ceques in the system. The Ayarmaca and Yacanora were two kin groups that occupied separate areas near San Sebastián. It is possible that this irregularity reflects a recording "error," and that the document should indicate that the shrines along An. 7 and An. 8 were maintained by the Ayarmaca and Yacanora. Another possible transcription error may have occurred in

Cobo's description of Cu. 1, which he names Anaguarque. The ridge of Anaguarque, over which Cu. 1 runs, is a major shrine of the village of Chocco, and inhabitants of this village are traditionally thought to be the descendants of a woman named Mama Anaguarque (principal wife of Pachacuti Inca Yupanqui). Since there appears to be a relationship between the name and course of Cu. 1 and the village of Chocco, it is possible that members of Chocco were responsible for the huacas along this ceque. This idea is supported by parish records of San Jerónimo, which list Anahuarque as the name of a separate group in the Chocco region (Rowe, pers. com. 1992).

There are also two groups listed by Cobo as responsible for certain ceques that are not listed in any other account: Aguini (Co. 1) and Cari (An. 9). Earlier researchers have proposed that the name Cari may be synonymous with Sañoc (Rowe 1985:53) and that Aguini is synonymous with Cuycusa (Zuidema 1964:8; Rowe 1985:53). While this may be the case, I have classified Cari and Aguini as currently unidentified kin groups because there is no independent documentation that directly supports the earlier suggestions.

Summary and Discussion

The *Relación de las huacas* indicates that the shrines along individual lines of the Cusco ceque system were the responsibility of different kin groups. Attendants and servants from these groups cared for the huacas of their ceque and saw that the required sacrifices were made at the appropriate times (Cobo 1980:14 [1653:Bk. 13, Ch. 13]). From the fragmentary data provided in Cobo's chronicle and from information contained in other documents, I have attempted to outline which Cusco groups were responsible for certain ceques and to illustrate how the order of the lines in the ceque system may have reproduced the social organization of the imperial capital. Zuidema (1964) and Rowe (1985) have also presented hypothetical reconstructions of the kin groups responsible for maintaining shrines in the ceque system. Although many of their observations have been incorporated in this chapter, I have developed a slightly different model of the system. The fact that three alternative models can be constructed is not surprising because the available data is fragmentary and open to different interpretations.

While our understanding of the Cusco ceque system is still rudimentary, it is clear that the system included a re-

markable reproduction of the Inca panaca system. Traditionally, a series of ten Incas—five from Hanan Cusco and five from Hurin Cusco—were thought to have ruled the imperial city before the arrival of the Spaniards. After their deaths, the social status of these rulers was carried on by their descendants in the form of ten panacas. The *Relación de las huacas* specifically mentions eight of these panacas as being responsible for the huacas along eight ceques, and ceques for the other two panacas can be suggested. Furthermore, it is evident that each of the ten panacas was associated with ceques in separate ceque clusters.

The ten ceques that were maintained by the panacas are not, however, randomly scattered across the system. Their positions in the ceque system closely conform to their standing in the social order of Cusco. The panacas of the first five Incas were traditionally associated with Hurin Cusco, and the second five Incas were affiliated with Hanan Cusco. The ceques that these Hanan and Hurin Cusco panacas maintained were located in their appropriate moiety division.

It is also documented that there were ten nonroyal ayllus in the imperial city: five in Hanan Cusco and five in Hurin Cusco. Researchers suggest that each of these nonroyal ayllus was conceptually paired with a particular panaca. If this is the case, then it is possible to speculate that the ceque clusters that contained a panaca also contained a nonroyal ayllu. In other words, the hierarchical, yet paired, relationships that may have existed between the panacas and the nonroyal ayllus of Cusco could have determined which ceques these groups maintained. One possible pairing of the panacas and the nonroyal ayllus is presented in Table 4.8 and Figure 4.2.

Nevertheless, this speculative reconstruction of the ritual responsibilities of the panacas and nonroyal ayllus of Cusco leaves nearly half of the ceques of the system unaccounted for. Circumstantial evidence suggests that several other kin groups of the Cusco Valley may also have been responsible for some of the ceques of the system. Yet, even with these kin groups included, it is still unclear what groups maintained some eighteen ceques. Did certain kin groups maintain the shrines along more than one ceque? Were there additional groups responsible for ceques that were not recorded in the *Relación de las huacas*? Did other categories of royal or nonroyal Inca peoples (*camayocs, mitima, yanacuna,* etc.) maintain ceques of the system? These questions will remain unanswered until additional data on the organization of Cusco become available.

5

The Huacas and Ceques of Chinchaysuyu

THE ORGANIZATION of the sacred topography of Cusco was both highly centralized and ritualized. In the previous chapter, the relationship between the social organization of Cusco and the ceque system was explored. But what was the relationship between the concrete form of the system on the ground and its idealized representations as expressed in the *Relación de las huacas*? A major research goal is to answer this question by providing the first empirical understanding of the system. This was accomplished through extensive archaeological fieldwork in the Cusco Valley and archival research in Cusco, Lima, and Seville. The results of that research are contained in the following four chapters, which present the distribution of huacas and the directions of the ceques according to the four suyus of the Cusco region.

Chinchaysuyu, the largest of the suyus, lay to the north and northwest of Cusco. Its large size and its location in the upper moiety of Cusco made Chinchaysuyu the most prestigious suyu. The *Relación de las huacas* indicates that Chinchaysuyu contained nine ceques and at least eighty-five shrines. Unlike those of Antisuyu, Collasuyu, and Cuntisuyu, the ceques of Chinchaysuyu are presented in a counterclockwise order. The first ceque (Ch. 1), defining the division between Chinchaysuyu and Antisuyu, extended north from the imperial city toward the ruins of Kenko Grande. The ninth ceque (Ch. 9) marked the division between Chinchaysuyu and Cuntisuyu, and the western boundary between Hanan and Hurin Cusco. This ceque projected from Cusco toward the hacienda of Picchu and may have ended more than fifty kilometers away on the far side of the Vilcaconga Pass.

Chinchaysuyu is especially interesting in the study of Andean ceque systems because it is the only area for which we have two separate huaca lists. Besides the account preserved within the *Relación de las huacas,* a second record of Chinchaysuyu huacas is provided by Albornoz in his *Instrucción*

para descubrir . . . In this document, Albornoz records the names of thirty-seven shrines in Chinchaysuyu, twenty-four of which match shrines described in the *Relación de las huacas.* An examination of the information presented by Cobo for Chinchaysuyu is presented here, and an analysis of Albornoz's data is offered in Chapter 9.

Despite the unprecedented amount of information available for Chinchaysuyu, only tentative identifications can be presented for most of its huacas. Ground confirmation of the Chinchaysuyu shrines was frustrated by a number of unique features of this region. One of these complicating features is that many of the traditional toponyms have changed over the past century. This is especially true for the area around Sacsahuaman. Another complicating feature is that much of the Chinchaysuyu landscape near Cusco has been modified. The region immediately north of Sacsahuaman is particularly affected because its outcrops have been quarried for centuries and numerous roads have been built across it. The modification of large sections of Chinchaysuyu has resulted in the destruction of various huacas and the loss of traditional toponyms. Another important feature of Chinchaysuyu is its great number of carved rocks, which vary in size and intricacy from the large archaeological complex of Kenko Grande to isolated outcrops measuring only a few meters across. Although not all huacas were carved outcrops, and not all carved rocks were huacas in the ceque system, the presence of scores of these features in Chinchaysuyu made survey work more complex than in the other regions of the Cusco Valley.

On the other hand, research in Chinchaysuyu was aided by the work of Sherbondy (1982, 1986) and Van de Guchte (1984, 1990). Sherbondy investigated the irrigation system of Hanan Cusco and identified a number of possible huaca locations. She also found archival references to many of the Chinchaysuyu huacas. Van de Guchte studied the carved outcrops of the Inca Empire and provided detailed descriptions of the major archaeological sites and most of the sculpted rocks in the Chinchaysuyu region of Cusco. Like Sherbondy, Van de Guchte identified several possible shrines and found previously unrecognized historical references to huacas of the Cusco ceque system. Aveni (1980, 1981a) and Zuidema (1981c) have also suggested possible locations for shrines along the sixth and eighth ceques of Chinchaysuyu (Ch. 6 and Ch. 8). Although in some cases I present alternative huaca locations and ceque courses to those suggested by these scholars, I remain in debt to them for their studies of this complex region.

The First Ceque of Chinchaysuyu

The first ceque of Chinchaysuyu contained five huacas and is reported to have been the responsibility of Goacataqui (Guacaytaqui) Ayllu. Cobo indicates that the first shrine, a rock called Michosamaro (Ch. 1:1), was a brother of Manco Capac transformed into stone and that it stood against the slope of Totocache (Tococache). Albornoz (1984:205 [ca. 1582]) describes this shrine as follows: "Luchus Amaro was a stone in Tococache." Although it is recognized that the modern Cusco district of San Blas was formally called Tococache, the exact location of Ch. 1:1 is unknown.

Cobo states that Ch. 1:2 (Patallacta) was a house of [Pachacuti] Inca Yupanqui and that this Inca died there.

Several other writers also link Patallacta with Pachacuti Inca Yupanqui. Acosta (1954:201 [1590:Ch. 21]), using an early report by Polo de Ondegardo, states that the body of Pachacuti Inca Yupanqui was moved from Patallacta to Tococache. Betanzos (1987:150 [1557:Pt. 1, Ch. 32]) indicates that the body of Pachacuti Inca Yupanqui was kept there, and Sarmiento de Gamboa (1906:92 [1572:Ch. 47]) includes a description of Pachacuti Inca Yupanqui's death in which he asks that his body be placed in Patallacta. Albornoz (1984:205 [ca. 1582]) also included this huaca in his list of shrines of Chinchaysuyu; however, he calls it by another name: "Ancas pata is a steep rock where the house of Viracocha Inca was."[1] The large hill and hacienda of Patallacta stand immediately north of the city, and there are a number of Inca remains on this hill, including the extensive ruins of Kenko Grande and Kenko Chico.[2] Kenko Grande, one of the best-known ruins in the Cusco region, is a spectacularly sculpted outcrop with several carved crevices and a monolith in the center of a semicircular terraced area (Photo 5.1). Kenko Chico, a low-lying oval hill, lies across a small ravine from Kenko Grande, and a large stone stairway leads to its flat summit. The sides of Kenko Chico are lined with enormous stone blocks comparable to those of Sacsahuaman, and a series of impressive terraces can be found on its southern slope (Photo 5.2). Sherbondy (1982:49, 189 n. 78) has proposed that Kenko Grande and Kenko Chico

Photo 5.1. Kenko Grande is a spectacularly sculpted outcrop with several carved crevices and a monolith in the center of a semicircular terraced area. It may represent Patallacta (Ch. 1:2).

Photo 5.2. Kenko Chico is across a small ravine from Kenko Grande. The ravine may have held the shrine of Pilcopuquio (Ch. 1:3).

Photo 5.3. The cave of Tambomachay, with its Inca platform and staircase at one corner, offers an impressive view of the Cusco Valley. It is the best candidate for Cirocaya (Ch. 1:4).

are the two most likely locations for Patallacta (Ch. 1:2), a conclusion supported by our survey results.

According to the *Relación de las huacas*, [Pachacuti] Inca Yupanqui created a spring named Pilcopuquio (Ch. 1:3) beside Patallacta. Albornoz (1984:205 [ca. 1582]) simply describes this shrine as a spring. References to a spring called Pilcopuquiu can be found in a number of documents concerning the lands immediately north of Cusco (AGN/Títulos de Propiedad: Leg. 3, c. 58). Sherbondy (1982:49, 189 n. 78) suggests that among the numerous springs and ravines north of the city, the small ravine that runs between the ruins of Kenko Grande and Kenko Chico is the best candidate for Pilcopuquio (Ch. 1:3).[3] Evidence supporting this shrine location was recovered by our surveyors, who found recently made offerings beside the spring in 1991, even though it has been capped with cement for decades.

The fourth shrine of this ceque is listed as a cave called Cirocaya (Ch. 1:4) where offerings were made so that hail would not damage the crops. A similar description is provided by Albornoz (1984:205 [ca. 1582]): "Sico cayan, a cave guaca from which they say the hail came out." There are numerous caves in the region northwest of Cusco. The two largest will be presented here as possible locations for Ch. 1:4. The first is Llanllakuyoc, a mazelike outcrop with many large carved crevices, approximately two kilometers north

of Kenko Grande.[4] The second is the principal cave of the Tambomachay area, which offers an impressive view of the Cusco Valley (Photo 5.3). Located in the northwest corner of the valley, the entrance to this wide, shallow cave contains an Inca platform with a staircase at one corner.[5] I favor the cave of Tambomachay—because of its view and the stone platform at its entrance—over that of Llanllakuyoc as the shrine of Cirocaya.[6]

The final shrine of Ch. 1 is described as a hill called Sonconancay (Ch. 1:5). The cave of Tambomachay stands at the base of Catunque, one of the highest hills in the Cusco Valley (Photo 5.4). The summit of this hill contains several looters' trenches and traces of a stone wall. The surface of the site holds fragments of Killke (Early Inca) and Inca pottery, as well as human cranial remains. Because Catunque is still considered to be a major *apu* (sacred mountain) of the region, it is possible that these looted remains represent the place that Cobo records as Sonconancay (Maps 5.1 and 5.2).

The Second Ceque of Chinchaysuyu

The eight shrines of Ch. 2 are reported to be the responsibility of Vicaquirao Panaca, the descent group of Inca Roca, the sixth Inca king. The initial huaca, Guaracince (Ch. 2:1),

Photo 5.4. The summit of Catunque, which may represent Sonconancay (Ch. 1:5), contains several looters' trenches and a stone wall. The cave of Tambomachay can be seen in the center of this photograph.

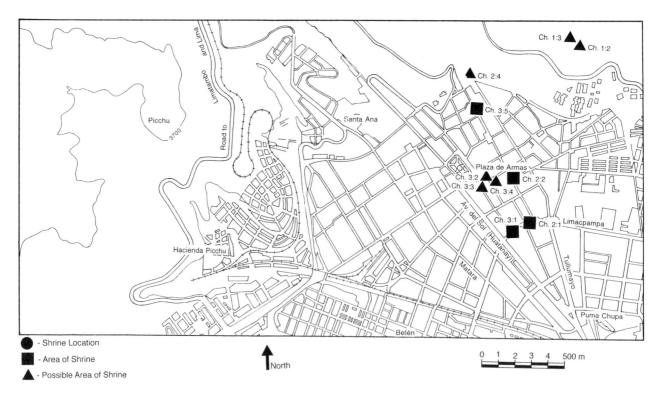

Map. 5.1. Possible locations of Ch. 1, Ch. 2, and Ch. 3 shrines in the city of Cusco.

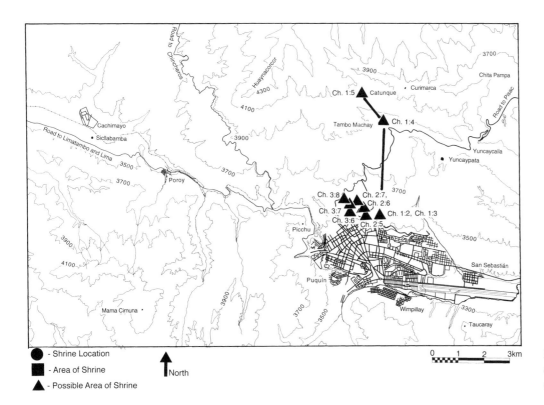

Map. 5.2. Suggested courses of ceques Ch. 1, Ch. 2, and Ch. 3.

was a flat piece of ground within the Temple of the Sun where offerings were made so that the earth would not quake. Albornoz (1984:205 [ca. 1582]) also includes this huaca in his list of Chinchaysuyu shrines, writing, "Guaracinci, a worked stone in the door of the sun." The second shrine, Racramirpay (Ch. 2:2), is described as a stone in a window a little way below the monastery of San Agustín, where sacrifices were made when the Inca went to war. The approximate position of Racramirpay can be suggested because the monastery of San Agustín stood two blocks north of the Temple of the Sun.

The third shrine is characterized as a gold idol called Intiillapa (Ch. 2:3), set on a gold litter in a house or temple in the precinct of Toto Cachi (Tococache). It is said that [Pachacuti] Inca Yupanqui took this huaca to be his symbolic brother. Cobo provides a similar description of the shrine elsewhere in his chronicle:

The Thunder also has a separate temple in the Tococache district. Inside the temple there was a gold statue of the Thunder placed on a litter of the same metal. This statue was made by the Inca Pachacuti in honor of the Thunder, and he called the statue Inti Illapa. Pachacuti took this statue as a brother, and during his lifetime he carried

it with him whenever he went to war. This idol was greatly venerated, and it was served in a very stately and ceremonious fashion. (Cobo 1990:32 [1653:Bk. 14, Ch. 7])[7]

The *Relación de las huacas* also notes that the body of [Pachacuti] Inca Yupanqui was found in the same house.[8] The exact location of this important structure remains to be identified.

The fourth shrine, a canal called Viroypacha (Ch. 2:4), must have been a well-known feature of Cusco because two of Guaman Poma de Ayala's drawings contain locations labeled Uiruypaccha (1980:289, 970 [1615:316 (318), 1051 (1059)]), which he describes as a pond and a fountain in one of the palaces of the Inca (1980:306 [1615:334 (336)]).[9] There are also numerous references to Viroypacha in local land documents, the earliest of which dated to 1629 (ADC/Protocolos Notariales: Domingo de Oro, Prot. 257, f. 680). Sherbondy (1982:49) suggests that this huaca was a segment of the river that flows from Sacsahuaman through Cusco to join the Huatanay River at Puma Chupa (see Cu. 1:3).[10] Perhaps the best possible location for Ch. 2:4 along this river is a waterfall and carved rock currently called Sapantiana, which also contains a series of Inca structures and terraces beside it.[11]

Photo 5.5. The area north and east of Sacsahuaman (lower right corner) held a number of shrines. For example, Chuquibamba (Ch. 2:5) is described as a flat place next to the fortress of Sacsahuaman. This plain may have been near the center of this photograph. (Courtesy Department of Library Services, American Museum of Natural History. Shippee-Johnson Expedition, negative 334794.)

Chuquibamba (Ch. 2:5), a flat place next to the fortress of Sacsahuaman, is reported to be the next huaca along this ceque (Photo 5.5). Chuquibamba is mentioned in a land document dating to 1593 as being beside the fort of Sacsahuaman (AGN/Títulos de Propiedad: Leg. 7, c. 47, fs. 4, 1648), and other documents present it as a large agricultural area immediately north of Cusco.[12] In all likelihood, Chuquibamba corresponds to the plain west of Kenko Chico and east of Sacsahuaman.

The positions of the next two huacas along this ceque are very tenuous. Macasayba (Ch. 2:6), registered as a large stone next to Chuquibamba, may be a carved stone on the plain thought to be Chuquibamba. Guayrangallay (Ch. 2:7), a quarry above the fortress, could be located on the hill northeast of Sacsahuaman, which has been quarried for centuries. The location of the final shrine, Guayllaurcaja (Ch. 2:8), is not known (Map. 5.1 and Map 5.2).

The Third Ceque of Chinchaysuyu

The first of the ten shrines of Ch. 3 was called Nina (Ch. 3:1). It is described as a stone brazier next to the Temple of the Sun that held the fire used for all sacrifices. The brazier is mentioned again by Cobo as he describes how sacrifices were offered each day to the Sun:

> Likewise, every morning they made the Sun a fire of carved wood, and as the Sun appeared in the sky, the fire was lighted, and food prepared in the same way as for the Inca was brought there for the Sun, and as they threw part of the food into the fire, they would say, "Eat this, Lord Sun, in recognition of the fact that we are your children." (Cobo 1990:113–114 [1653 Book 13, Ch. 21])[13]

Elsewhere in his chronicle Cobo writes:

> The fire for the sacrifices that were made in Cuzco was taken from a stone brazier which was located next to the Temple of the Sun, and the flame could not be taken from any other place. This fire was not started and fed with just any wood, it was done with a certain kind of wood which was scented, carefully carved, and very colorful. (Cobo 1990:117 [1653 Bk. 13, Ch. 22])[14]

This shrine is mentioned by Albornoz (1984:205 [ca. 1582]) as Nina, ". . . a brazier that always burned," as well as by Betanzos (1987:51 [1557:Pt. 1, Ch. 11]) and Murúa (1946: 370 [1590:Bk. 14, Ch. 2]). It is also referred to by an anonymous writer (*Antigüedades* 1992:59, 90 [1590]), who notes, "Here (at the Temple of the Sun) there was a fire which they called eternal, in the manner of the Romans, because it was to burn perpetually, night and day . . ."[15] as well as, "The principal task of these [Chosen Women] was to keep and preserve the fire of the sacrifices, that they called *nina villka*, sacred fire."[16] The huaca may also correspond with either Nina Soyuma or Nina Amaro, two shrines presented in Albornoz's (1984:216 [ca. 1582]) list of the six most important huacas of the Cusco area. Although the exact location of this shrine is not known, it was near the Temple of the Sun.

The positions of the second and third huacas of Ch. 3 are listed in relation to the property of Diego Maldonado, one of the wealthiest encomenderos in early colonial Peru. Canchapacha (Ch. 3:2) was a spring on Diego Maldonado's street, while Ticicocha (Ch. 3:3) was a spring inside Maldonado's house that belonged to Mama Ocllo.[17] The fourth huaca, Condorcancha (Ch. 3:4), is described as a house of [Pachacuti] Inca Yupanqui. These three shrines appear to have been near one other, because Garcilaso de la Vega (1966:424 [1609:Vol. 1, Bk. 7, Ch. 9]) states that the house of Diego Maldonado was south of the cathedral in an area called Hatun Cancha that included the palace of Pachacuti Inca Yupanqui. The exact location of Condorcancha (Ch. 3:4) is, however, not known.

There can be little doubt that Ch. 3:5, presented as a house of Huayna Capac called Pomacorco, stood somewhere on Pumacorco Street, which leads from Cusco to the base of Sacsahuaman. Pomacorco is mentioned by Tito Cussi Yupangui (1988:170 [1570]) as well as in numerous archival documents, one of which specifically mentions that Huayna Capac held a house there. There are still several well-preserved stone buildings and doorways along this street.

The next three shrines, Ch. 3:6, Ch. 3:7, and Ch. 3:8, are all described in relation to a flat place called Calispuquio. The sixth shrine, Mollaguanca (Ch. 3:6), was a stone in the middle of Calispuquio; the seventh, Calispuquio Guaci (Ch. 3:7), was a house of Topa Inca; and the eighth was the spring of Calispuquio itself (Ch. 3:8), which was below the house of Topa Inca. Cobo specifically notes in his description of Calispuquio that the initiates to manhood washed there and that water was taken from this spring for use by the Inca.[18] This is supported by other writers who also link Calispuquio with the male initiation rites of the Inca. For example, Betanzos describes the use of the spring by the young men of Cusco near the end of the month of Capac Raymi:

The Inca ordered that after the thirty days had elapsed the relatives of these neophytes should assemble there in the square and bring the neophytes with them. After thrusting the halberd into the ground, the neophytes remain standing, hold the halberd in their hands, and extend their arms; their relatives will then beat them with slings on their arms so that they will remember this. Next they will go from there to a fountain called Calizpuquio, which means spring of the *caliz* [health]. They will go to this spring, where they all bathe, at nightfall. (Betanzos 1996:63 [1557:Pt. 1, Ch. 14])[19]

Molina, like Betanzos, describes initiates bathing in Calispuquio during the final days of the Capac Raymi festival. In doing so, he mentions that this spring was about a quarter of a league behind Sacsahuaman:

Then on the twenty-first day of this month, all those who had been knighted would go to bathe in a spring called Calispuquio, located behind the fortress of Cusco, nearly a quarter of a league away. There, they would remove the clothes in which they had been knighted, and put on others called *uauaclla*, which are black and yellow with a red cross in the center. From there, they would return to the plaza . . .[20]

Guaman Poma de Ayala (1980:310 [1615:337 (339)]) briefly mentions Calispuquio in a description of Sacsahuaman, suggesting that it was behind Sacsahuaman near the Suchuna (a smooth rock outcrop now referred to as the Rodadero) and a more jagged outcrop called the Chincana (labyrinth).[21] Numerous land documents also mention the area of Calispuquio. One 1601 document describes Calispuquio as being beside Sacsahuaman (AHD/Colegio Ciencias: Leg. 10, c. 9, f. 1), and another of 1624 notes that Calispuquio was close to the Suchuna, near the trail that leads from Cusco to Omasbamba (Cornejo Bouroncle 1957:202).

There is a plain with several springs in the Sacsahuaman area northeast of the Suchuna and the Chincana (Photo 5.5). Near the center of this flat area is a carved outcrop (Photo 5.6), and the trail to Omasbamba is a hundred meters to the north. It is possible that this sculpted rock represents Ch. 3:6 (Mollaguanca)[22] and that the springs that feed the flat area were once called Calispuquio (Ch. 3:8).[23] If this is the case, then the so-called house of Topa Inca (Ch. 3:7) may have been nearby, perhaps in an area of terraces above the plain.[24] The final two shrines of this ceque—Cugiguaman (Ch. 3:9), a stone in the shape of a falcon, and Quinoapuquio (Ch. 3:10), a small spring—remain to be identified (Map 5.1 and Map 5.2).

Photo 5.6. This carved outcrop east of Sacsahuaman may be Mollaguanca (Ch. 3:6).

The Fourth Ceque of Chinchaysuyu

The first of the eight huacas of Ch. 4 is recorded as a group of Pururauca stones called Araytampu (Ch. 4:1), next to Benito de la Peña's house; however, neither the location of these stones nor that of Peña's house is known. The second shrine, Puñui (Ch. 4:2), which was associated with sleep, is mentioned as being in a small flat place near Diego Maldonado's house. Although this house is thought to have been somewhere south of the cathedral—based on information provided by Garcilaso de la Vega (1966:424 [1609:Vol. 1, Bk. 7, Ch. 9])—the exact location of Ch. 4:2 is not known.[25]

The entry for the third shrine of this ceque, Curiocllo (Ch. 4:3), is especially interesting. It reads:

> The third guaca was named Curiocllo. It was a house of Curiollo [*sic;* for Curi Ocllo], who had been the wife of Amaro Topa Inca, which was in Colcapata; and they worshipped also a fountain which was next to it. (Cobo 1980:21 [1653:Bk. 13, Ch. 13])[26]

My reading of this entry suggests that two separate huacas (a house *and* a spring) were accidentally classified as a single shrine. If this is the case, then this ceque held a minimum of nine shrines, rather than eight.

Colcapata is a famous terraced area between Cusco and Sacsahuaman with extensive Inca ruins (Photo 5.7).[27] Nevertheless, neither the exact location of the third huaca, the house of Cori Ocllo (Ch. 4:3), nor that of the worshipped spring has been identified. The fourth shrine, Colcapata (Ch. 4:4), is described as a stone idol that was worshipped by the Andasaya in Paullu Inca's house.[28] Paullu Inca ruled Cusco in collaboration with the Spaniards from 1538 to 1549. His house is a famous landmark in Colcapata (Photo 5.8).[29]

The location of the fifth huaca of this ceque, Guamancancha (Ch. 4:5), reported by Cobo to be an enclosure on a small hill near the fortress, is not known.[30] The next huaca, Collaconcho (Ch. 4:6), is listed as a large stone in the fortress. Cobo relates a myth about the stone, saying it fell three times, killing a number of people, and then refused to be moved any farther. Guaman Poma de Ayala (1980:138–139 [1615:159 (161)]) provides a stylized drawing of this stone being transported by Inca Urcon, son of Topa Inca, from Huánuco to Cusco (Figure 5.1). A number of other chroniclers also mention this stone (i.e., *la piedra cansada* [the tired stone]) and its mythical origin (Cieza de León 1985 [1553]; Betanzos 1987:170 [1557:Pt. 1, Ch. 37]; Gutiérrez de Santa Clara 1963 [ca. 1600]). Garcilaso de la Vega, who as a child played in the ruins of Sacsahuaman, includes additional information on this stone as he describes the master builders of the fortress:

> The fourth and last of the masters was called Calla Cúnchuy. It was in his time that the Weary Stone was brought, to which the master mason gave his own name

Photo 5.7. The area of Colcapata, between Cusco and Sacsahuaman, held several shrines. (Courtesy of The Latin American Library, Tulane University. Photograph by Squier, ca. 1865.)

Photo 5.8. The house of Paullu Inca is a famous landmark in Colcapata. A huaca (Ch. 4:4) once stood inside this dwelling. (Courtesy of The Latin American Library, Tulane University. Photograph by Squier, ca. 1865.)

in order to preserve its fame; its size, like that of other similar rocks, is incredible. I should be glad to be able to set down its exact circumference and height, but I have not been able to find precise information: I can only refer the matter to those who have seen it. It stands on a level space in front of the fortress, and the Indians said that after the great labors it experienced on the way there, it grew weary and wept blood, and could not reach the building. (Garcilaso de la Vega 1966:470 [1609: Vol. 1, Bk. 7, Ch. 29])[31]

Both Zuidema (1980:341) and Van de Guchte (1984, 1990: 130–138), in discussions of *piedras cansadas* in Andean mythology, suggest that an elaborately carved outcrop behind Sacsahuaman is the shrine of Collaconcho (Ch. 4:6) (Photos 5.9 and 5.10).

No additional information was found on the penultimate shrine of this ceque, Chachacomacaja (Ch. 4:7), which is described as certain trees next to a stone. The ceque terminated, according to Cobo, at three stones on a high hill called Chuquipalta (Ch. 4:8), next to the fortress of Sacsahuaman, which were representations of the Pachayachachic (the Creator), Inti Illapa (Thunder), and Punchau (the Sun). A hill behind the fortress still retains the name Chuquipalta (Van de Guchte 1984:549; 1990:524), and survey work identified a field near its summit called Huaca Rumiyoc (Huaca Stone), which may be the area where the stones of Ch. 4:8 once stood (Maps 5.3 and 5.4).

The Fifth Ceque of Chinchaysuyu

Possible areas for most of the ten shrines of Ch. 5 have been identified, and the course of the ceque is relatively well understood. It is possible that this ceque was the responsibility of Pachacuti Inca Yupanqui's panaca, Iñaca, since Cobo states that members of this group made sacrifices at its initial shrine. This first huaca was called Cusicancha (Ch. 5:1), and is presented in the *Relación de las huacas* as being opposite the Coricancha. A place labeled Cusicancha is shown on Guaman Poma de Ayala's (1980:970 [1615:1051(1059)]) map of Cusco, and Albornoz (1984:204 [ca. 1582]) mentions a shrine called Cusicancha Pachamama as the house where Topa Inca Yupanqui was born.

Pucamarca (Ch. 5:2), a temple where the idol of Thunder called Chucuylla was kept, is described as located in the house of Licentiate [Antonio] de la Gama. Based on information provided by Garcilaso de la Vega (1966:197, 424, 427 [1609:Vol. 1, Bk. 4, Ch. 2; Vol. 1, Bk. 7, Ch. 9]), it is tra-

tionally thought that Pucamarca (Squier 1877; Agurto Calvo 1980, 1987; Zárate 1921) and Antonio de la Gama's house were located south of Hatun Cancha along Maruri Street.

The third huaca, Cuzcocalla (Ch. 5:3), was apparently between Pucamarca and the Plaza de Armas, since it is characterized by Cobo as a group of Pururauca stones on the street leading to the plaza.[32] The avenue mentioned may be Loreto—famous for its fine Inca stonework—which runs from the central plaza of Cusco toward the Temple of the

Figure 5.1. Piedra Cansada (Tired Stone). Guaman Poma de Ayala (1980:138–139 [1615:159 (161)]) portrays the Piedra Cansada being transported by Inca Urco from Huánuco to Cusco. The caption reads, "The ninth captain, Inca Uron." In the drawing, Inca Uron shouts to the workers, "Keep moving sheep," and on the rock one reads, "The rock cried blood." At the bottom of the figure is written "from Huánuco, Guayllas."

Photo 5.9. Carved rock thought to be the Piedra Cansada (Tired Stone). This stone was included in the Cusco ceque system as Ch. 4:6. (Courtesy of The Latin American Library, Tulane University. Photograph by Squier, ca. 1865.)

Photo 5.10. Another view of the carved rock thought to be the Piedra Cansada (Tired Stone); photograph taken in 1991.

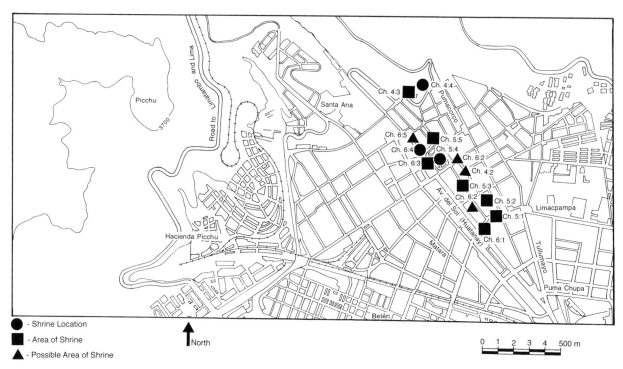

Map. 5.3. Possible locations of Ch. 4, Ch. 5, and Ch. 6 shrines in the city of Cusco.

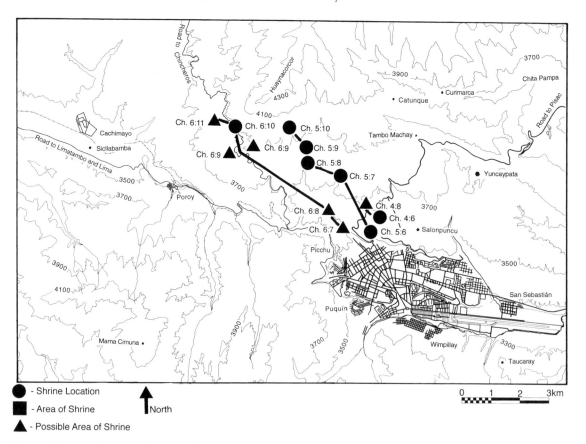

Map. 5.4. Suggested courses of ceques Ch. 4, Ch. 5, and Ch. 6.

Photo 5.11. The central plaza of Cusco, Haucaypata (now called the Plaza de Armas), was a shrine (Ch. 5:4) on the system.

Photo 5.12. The magnificently carved "Throne of the Inca," located in Sacsahuaman, most certainly was Sabacurinca (Ch. 5:6).

Sun, or it may have been that of Arequipa, one block further east.[33]

Aucaypata (Haucaypata), or what is now the Plaza de Armas (Ch. 5:4), is presented in the ceque document as the next shrine (Photo 5.11). The fifth huaca, Coracora (Ch. 5:5), is reported to be where the Cabildo, or Town Hall, stood.[34]

While Betanzos (1987:281 [1557:Pt. 2, Ch. 25]) briefly mentions the structure of Coracora, Garcilaso de la Vega (1966: 425 [1609:Vol. 1, Bk. 7, Ch. 10]) states that it was a large stone building on the north side of the plaza. He also indicates that it was destroyed soon after the Spaniards arrived in Cusco.

From these closely spaced huacas, the fifth ceque of Chinchaysuyu crossed over Sacsahuaman to the Suchuna. Near the middle of this smooth outcrop is the famous "Throne of the Inca," a series of magnificently carved horizontal and vertical planes resembling seats (Photo 5.12), which most certainly represents Ch. 5:6 (Sabacurinca), described as a well-carved seat near Sacsahuaman.[35]

The seventh shrine is registered as a hill called Chacaguanacauri (Ch. 5:7) where the initiates to manhood gathered a special grass for their lances. Elsewhere in his chronicle, Cobo gives a detailed explanation of the importance of this hill during the opening days of the Capac Raymi festival and the concurrent Warachikoy ritual:

> Far in advance preparations were started. Clothing was made, adornments were made, and everything else necessary for this solemn festival. Before anything else, they gathered a goodly number of noble maidens from twelve to thirteen or fourteen years of age, who, richly dressed, would serve on the occasion. Some days before, these girls would be at the hill called Chacaguanacauri spinning the thread for the fringe of the *guaras* [loincloth] which the boys would have to put on as they were made *orejones* or knights. The boys would also go to the same hill to get a certain kind of straw which they had to carry on their staffs, and the straw that was left over from what they had brought was divided up among their relatives. Moreover, all during the time that the maidens spent on their task at the hill, the *guaca* or idol of Guanacauri was left on the said hill. The rest of what was needed for this solemn occasion was provided by the parents and relatives of the boys. (Cobo 1990:127 [1653:Bk. 14, Ch. 25]).[36]

Albornoz (1984:204 [ca. 1582]) writes that the shrine of Chaca guanacauri was "a stone above the fortress." To the northwest of Cusco stands an archaeological complex known as Chacan, which contains an important canal system, a huge outcrop spanning the upper Saphi (or Chacan) River (Photo 5.13), several large outcrops with platforms on their summits, a number of carved stones, and many terraces. Sherbondy (1982:81), Zuidema (1986b:192–193), and Van de Guchte (1990:108–110, 371) each suggest that the archaeological complex of Chacan should be associated with

Photo 5.13. The Saphi River flows beneath the massive outcrop of Chacan. This outcrop was dressed with fine Inca stonework and contains a nature overlook. It may have been Ch. 5:7.

Photo 5.14. Guamanguachanca (Ch. 5:8) is still a well-known outcrop.

Ch. 5:7. A 1578 land document supports their suggestions by referring to a landmark in this area as Chacan-Guanacaure (AGN/Títulos de Propiedad: Leg. 19, c. 387, f. 75).

The eighth shrine of this ceque, Guamanguachanca (Ch. 5:8), is presented as a small tomb at the side of the fortress. The earliest reference found to Guamanguachanca dates to 1578 (AGN/Títulos de Propiedad: Leg. 19, c. 387, f. 75). It is also mentioned in a 1595 document (AHD/Justiciales Civiles: Leg. 73, f. 4v). This huaca is most certainly associated with a large, isolated outcrop of the same name two kilometers northwest of Chacan (Photo 5.14). Today this rock marks the intersection point for the lands of three different communities, and it appears to have been an important landmark in the past.[37]

Traditionally, Andean peoples believed that the ancestral founders of kin groups (ayllus) emerged from sacred locations in the landscape called *paqarinas* (Bauer 1991). Two such origin places, Cinca (Ch. 5:9) and Autviturco (An. 1:4), are listed in the *Relación de las huacas* as shrines on the ceque system. Cinca (Ch. 5:9) is described as a hill on which there was an important stone that the Ayamaca Indians worshipped as their origin place, and Autviturco (An. 1:4) was a cave where the Goalla (Hualla) were born. The area of Cinca must have been important in the Inca and post-conquest periods because it is noted on two of Guaman Poma de Ayala's drawings (1980:288, 970 [1615:316 (318), 1051 (1059)]) and is mentioned by Sarmiento de Gamboa (1906: 69 [1572:Ch. 31]) as one of six important mountain shrines in the Cusco region:

> In addition to that house, there were several huacas around the town, that of Huanacauri [Co. 6:7], and another one called Anahuarque [Cu. 1:7], and another called Yauira [Ch. 9:6] and another called Cinca [Ch. 5:9] and another Picol [An. 8:11?] and another called Pachatusan, ...[38]

Cobo (1979:113, 155 [1653:Bk. 12, Chs. 5 and 16]) mentions the hill of Cinca in two other passages in his chronicle. The mountain of Singa (Cinca) is also listed in a 1592 document (AGN/Títulos de Propiedad: Leg. 19, c. 387) and in one dating to 1595 (AHD/Justiciales Civiles: Leg. 73, f. 4v).

The large ridge of Cinca, located just beyond Guamanguachanca, contains an impressive outcrop called Mamaguachanca (Photo 5.15), whose name can be glossed as "Mama = mother" and "guachanca = birthing place." The outcrop of Mamaguachanca dominates the bottom of a small ravine, and the remains of terraces and Inca pottery

Photo 5.15. The outcrop of Mamaguachanca is a good candidate for Cinca (Ch. 5:9), the *paqarina* (origin place) of the Ayamaca people.

Photo 5.16. The spring of Corcorpuquiu (Ch. 5:10) marked the end of the fifth ceque of Chinchaysuyu.

can be found along its base. The location, the prominent nature, and the name of this outcrop make it a good candidate for Ch. 5:9.

The final shrine of Ch. 5 was a spring called Corcorpuquiu (Ch. 5:10). The ridge of Cinca descends from the mountain of Huaynacorcor, one of the tallest in the immediate Cusco region. Fieldwork between the ridge of Cinca and the summit of Huaynacorcor, beyond Mamaguachanca, has identified a spring named Corcorpuquiu, which may well be the terminus huaca of Ch. 5 (Photo 5.16; Maps 5.3 and 5.4).

The Sixth Ceque of Chinchaysuyu

The projection of the sixth ceque across Chinchaysuyu was defined by eleven huacas. Aveni (1980, 1981a) and Zuidema (1981c), working on the assumption that the ceques formed straight lines, suggest that Ch. 6 projected out from Cusco, up the Saphy River valley, and terminated in an area called La Fortaleza (the fortress). Our survey work provides an alternative interpretation.

The first huaca, Catonge (Ch. 6:1), was one of the many boulders of the Cusco area believed to have helped Pachacuti Inca Yupanqui to defend the city against the Chanca. This Pururauca was in a window close to the Temple of the Sun.[39]

A house or a temple called Pucamarca (Ch. 6:2), the site for sacrifices for the Pachayachachic (the Creator), is recorded by Cobo as the second shrine of Ch. 6. Because the palace of Pucamarca, a temple where the idol of Thunder was kept, is also listed in the *Relación de las huacas* as the location for Ch. 5:2, it is possible that this complex was large enough to hold two shrines on adjacent ceques. Albornoz (1984:204 [ca. 1582]) supports the idea that Ch. 5:2 and Ch. 6:2 were two closely spaced shrines, since he describes a huaca called Pucamarca quisuarcancha as a house of the Creator and Thunder.[40]

The third huaca carried the simple name of *road*, or Ñan (Ch. 6:3), and is characterized as the beginning of the Chinchaysuyu road. Although it is known that this road led out of the northwest corner of the central plaza of Cusco, the exact position of Ch. 6:3 has not been determined. The following two shrines also seem to have been near this same corner of the plaza. The fifth huaca is described as the palace of Huayna Capac, called the Cajana (Cassana, Ch. 6:5), in which there was a lake named Ticcicocha,[41] and the fourth, Guayra (Ch. 6:4), was the doorway of this palace where sacrifices were made to the wind. Albornoz (1984:205 [ca. 1582]) describes the shrine of Guairaguaca as "a hole in the fortress from where they say the wind leaves." Brief descriptions of the Cassana and its location are presented in several chronicles,[42] but it is Garcilaso de la Vega who provides the fullest description of this palace:

> In my time the Spaniards built a street which divided the schools from the palace. I saw in my time a great part of the walls of the buildings called Cassana, which were of finely worked masonry, showing that it had been a royal dwelling, as also a splendid hall which the Incas used for festivals and dances in rainy weather. It was so large that sixty mounted men could easily joust with canes in it. I saw the convent of St. Francis established in this hall, for it was moved from the ward of Tococachi, where it had formerly been, owing to the great distance of the latter from the houses of the Spaniards. . . . I also saw the hall destroyed, and the modern shops with doorways for merchants and craftsmen built in the ward of Cassana. (Garcilaso de la Vega 1966:426 [1609: Vol. 1, Bk. 7, Ch. 10])[43]

True to Garcilaso de la Vega's description, the punctured walls of the Cassana still stand on the northwestern corner of the Plaza de Armas and now serve as entrances to restaurants and shops (Photo 5.17).[44]

The next three shrines of Ch. 6—Capipacchan (Ch. 6:6), Capi (Ch. 6:7), and Quisco (Ch. 6:8)—are associated in the *Relación de las huacas* with the Saphi River, which enters Cusco at a place traditionally called Huancapuncu and divides the modern city in half. The exact location of Ch. 6:6 (Capipacchan), a spring and a bath, is not known.[45] The next shrine is listed as a very large tree named Capi (Ch. 6:7). This shrine is also among those described by Albornoz (1984:205 [ca. 1582]), who writes, "Capa was a large tree and they dressed it and offered it much." One possible location can be suggested for this huaca: a conical hill, called Muyu Urco, in the center of the Saphi Ravine about one and one-half kilometers upstream from Cusco (Photo 5.18). Its summit, which offers a clear view of the city straight down the Saphi Ravine, has been cut in half by looters.[46] The distinct conical shape of this hill, its prominent location, its view of Cusco, and the evidence of looting on it indicate that it may once have held a huaca. It is possible, albeit speculative, that the "tree" of Saphi once stood on this remarkable location.[47]

The eighth huaca of this ceque, Quisco (Ch. 6:8), is presented as a place on top of the hill of Saphi where universal sacrifices were made. The hill of Quisco is mentioned in

Photo 5.17. The northwest corner of the Plaza de Armas where the Cassana (Ch. 6.5) once stood.

Photo 5.18. The distinct conical shape of Muyu Urco (center), its prominent location, its view of Cusco, and the evidence of looting on it indicate that it may once have held a huaca.

a number of late-seventeenth-century documents as being in the parish of Santa Ana (AHD/Corregimiento, Causas Ordinarias: Leg. 23, c. 17, 1684–1686; Corregimiento, Pedimentos: Leg. 82, 1600–1669c). One possibility for this shrine, proposed by Aveni (1981a) and Zuidema (1981c), is a large hill on the slope of Cinca that overlooks the Saphi River.

The ninth huaca of Ch. 6, one of the most widely discussed shrines of the system, is portrayed by Cobo as a hill called Quiangalla (Quiancalla, Ch. 6:9) on the Yucay road,

Photo 5.19. La Fortaleza aqueduct.

Photo 5.20. The outcrop of Congoña, possibly Illacamarca (Ch. 6:11).

where there were two pillars marking the sunset at the beginning of the summer (i.e., the June solstice). Guaman Poma de Ayala (1980:289 [1615:316 (318)]) includes a hill called Quean calla in one of his drawings, and we have found two early references to this important feature of the Cusco landscape.[48] Although it is generally believed that these pillars were in the Cinca area, which dominates the western horizon of the Cusco Valley, the exact position of the huaca is being debated (Zuidema 1977c, 1981b, 1981c; Aveni 1980, 1981a; Bauer and Dearborn 1995:80–90).

The tenth shrine, Guarguaillapuquiu (Ch. 6:10), is registered as a small fountain next to Quiangalla (Ch. 6:9). One possible candidate for this huaca, suggested by Aveni (1981a) and Zuidema (1981c), is a small stream northwest of the Cinca ridge, notable for an impressive aqueduct, commonly called La Fortaleza, that is built over it (Photo 5.19). I, however, favor an alternate location for Guarguaillapuquiu (Ch. 6:10): a spring just above the community of Huara Huaylla, approximately one-half kilometer west of the aqueduct, which serves as the village's principal water source.

The final huaca, Illacamarca (Ch. 6:11), of this ceque is described by Cobo (1979:25 [1653:Bk. 13, Ch. 13]) as "in a fort called Illaca Marca which the Inca built on a steep rock on the way to Yucay."[49] Zuidema and Aveni suggest that a steep hill called Balconjoc, behind the stone aqueduct, represents Ch. 6:11.[50] However, another possibility for Ch. 6:11, a large isolated outcrop currently called Congoña (Photo 5.20), is located approximately one kilometer downslope from Huara Huaylla and the Yucay road. Along the southwest base of this steep rock are the remains of a large stone struc-

Photo 5.21. Carved caves at the base of Congoña.

ture that appears to be built on prehistoric foundations. There is also a series of carved caves and rocks, and a petroglyph in the shape of an elaborate cross, along its southwest base (Photo 5.21). Congoña's location and its prominent size, as well as the carved caves and rocks found at its base, suggest that it may represent the terminus of Ch. 6 (Maps 5.3 and 5.4).

The Seventh Ceque of Chinchaysuyu

The first of the eight shrines of Ch. 7 is said to be a long stone called Omanamaro (Ch. 7:1), one of the Pururaucas. It was located in the doorway of [Juan de] Figueroa's house. Albornoz (1984:204 [ca. 1582]) writes that a shrine called Uman amaro was "a stone in the figure of a skittle which was in the plaza." In contrast, following Garcilaso de la Vega (1966:424 [1609:Vol. 1, Bk. 7, Ch. 9]), Figueroa's house was located between the Temple of the Sun and Hatun Cancha. Accordingly, the exact location of this huaca is unknown.

The second shrine of this ceque is described as two small structures called Sanca Cancha and Hurin Sanca (Ch. 7:2) that were used as prisons (*sanca*). These buildings may be mentioned by other early writers. For example, a place labeled as Sancay Uaci is shown on Guaman Poma de Ayala's map of Cusco (1980:970 [1615:1051 (1059)]). A Cusco prison called Sanzahuaci is discussed by Loarte (1882:234 [1572]), and one called Cangaguase is described by Betanzos (1987: 95 [1557:Pt. 1, Ch. 19]), while both Cabello de Balboa (1951: 353 [1586:Ch. 20]) and Albornoz (1984:204 [ca. 1582]) mention a prison called Sanca. Despite these numerous references, the location of Ch. 7:2 is not known.[51]

The following huaca, Marcatampu (Ch. 7:3), is described by Cobo as a set of round stones in the Carmenga (Carmenca) area where the parish church of Santa Ana was built. Albornoz (1984:204 [ca. 1582]) includes a shrine called Marcatambo, "a steep rock which was in Carmenca," in his list of Cusco shrines. The church of Santa Ana still stands, and it is possible that many of the carved Inca stone blocks used in the church's foundation came from this huaca (Photo 5.22).

The fourth shrine, Taxanamaro (Ch. 7:4), and the fifth, Urcoslla Amaro (Ch. 7:5), are mentioned as standing on small hills above Carmenca. A comparison of the names of Ch. 7:5 (Urcos[ca]lla Amaro) and Ch. 8:9 (Urcoscalla) suggests that Cobo left out several letters in the name of the former. Albornoz's (1984:204 [ca. 1582]) shrine list contains a reference to Tucanamaro, describing it as a stone that was in Carmenca. No evidence of these shrines has survived the urbanization of the Santa Ana area.

Callancapuquiu (Ch. 7:6) is listed as the spring of Ticutica (Ticatica). The area of Ticatica is above Santa Ana, and the spring of Callanca, now capped with cement, is beside the Inca road to Chinchaysuyu.[52] The next-to-last shrine on this ceque is reported to be a round hill called Churuncana (Ch. 7:7), above Carmenca at a fork in the royal road. Albornoz (1984:204 [ca. 1582]) also describes this shrine: "Churucani guanacauri, large stone and around it [were] many little stone guacas which they call cachauis." The *Relación de las huacas,* however, specifically states that this shrine was located where the royal road to Chinchero leaves that to Yucay. This road reference is not, in fact, especially helpful because the road to Chinchero is the *same* road that leads to Yucay. A 1594 document clarifies the confusion by locating the hill of Churucana at the juntion of the royal road to Chinchaysuyu that led to Los Reyes (now Lima) and

Photo 5.22. The parish church of Santa Ana marks the area where the shrine of Marcatampu (Ch. 7:3) once stood.

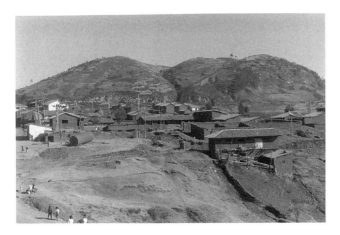

Photo 5.23. A prominent round hill above Santa Ana is a good candidate for Churuncana (Ch. 7:7). It is still considered a special place by many of the residents who live near it.

the road to Yucay (AGN/Títulos de Propiedad: Leg. 1, c. 3, f. 132, 1557 [1594]). A good candidate for Ch. 7:7 is a prominent round hill above Santa Ana now called Curaca (Lord). This hill is a major apu of the region, and it is at the fork of the Yucay and Chinchaysuyu roads (Photo 5.23). The eighth and final huaca on this ceque is cataloged as a spring called Muchayllapuquiu (Ch. 7:8) near Guarguaylla (Huara

Huaylla). Although the community of this name is well known, survey work found no spring with the name of Muchaylla near it (Maps 5.5 and 5.6).

The Eighth Ceque of Chinchaysuyu

The eighth ceque of Chinchaysuyu is described as containing thirteen shrines.[53] The ceque began with a huaca called Illanguarque (Ch. 8:1), which is said to have been a small house next to the Temple of the Sun. Albornoz (1984: 204 [ca. 1582]) includes a huaca called Yllanquaiqui in his list of Cusco shrines, and states that it was a house in the plaza of Santo Domingo where the festival of Raymi was celebrated.

The location of the second shrine, a field of Huanacauri called Mancochuqui (Ch. 8:2), is not known. The third huaca, Aucaypata (Haucaypata [Paccha], Ch. 8:3), is described as a spring next to the Cabildo. López de Velasco (1894:479 [1571–1574]) writes that there was a fountain of good water in the center of Cusco, and Albornoz (1984:204 [ca. 1582]) includes Haucaypata Pacha on his list of Cusco shrines. It is widely known that the central plaza of Cusco was called Haucaypata, and Garcilaso de la Vega (1966:425

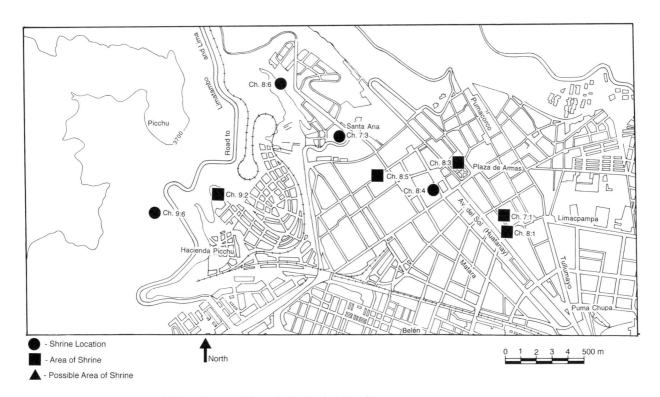

Map. 5.5. Possible locations of Ch. 7, Ch. 8, and Ch. 9 shrines in the city of Cusco.

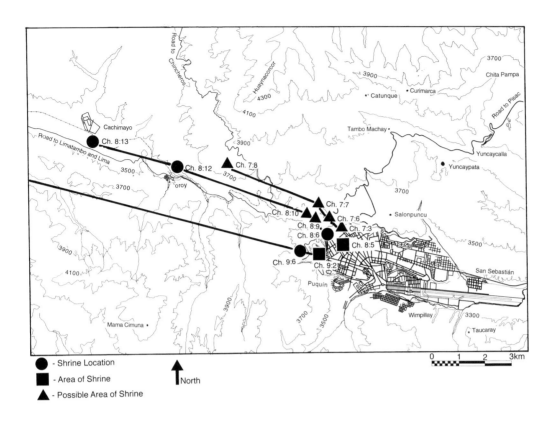

Map 5.6. Suggested courses of ceques Ch. 7, Ch. 8, and Ch. 9.

[1609:Vol. 1, Bk. 7, Ch. 10]) indicates that the house of the Cabildo was situated on its north side.[54] Accordingly, it is logical to suggest that this spring was near the northern end of the plaza. This location for Ch. 8:3 is problematic, however, because the rest of Ch. 8 appears to run west of the plaza.

Cugitalis (Ch. 8:4), the fourth shrine, is presented as being where Garcilaso's house was built. There is a large building in Cusco along one side of the Regocijo Plaza that is traditionally thought to be the house of Garcilaso de la Vega (Photo 5.24). If this is true, then Ch. 8:4 was located there.

The next shrine, a field of Amaro Topa Inca called Chacuaytapara (Ch. 8:5), is described as being in Carmenca. A 1643 map of Cusco indicates that an area called Chaguaytapra was near the street called Nueva Alta (Rowe 1990).[55] Several other documents also place Chaguaytapra (Chanaytapra, Chaquaitapra) near this street as well (AHD/Protocolos Notariales, Domingo de Oro: Prot. 255, f. 477, 1627; Beltran Lucero Alonso: Prot. 3, f. 347, 1634). The following huaca, the spring of Orocotopuquiu (Ch. 8:6), is also

Photo 5.24. The house of Garcilaso de la Vega stands on the site of Cugitalis (Ch. 8:4).

said to have been in Carmenca. The exact position of Ch. 8:6 is currently unknown, although there seems to have been a spring called Cotopuquiu in Santa Ana (Zuidema 1982a:437).

The location of Ch. 8:7 (Sucanca), has been the subject

of considerable research (Aveni 1981a; Zuidema 1982c, 1988b; Bauer and Dearborn 1995:69–76). It is registered as a hill, crossed by the Chinchero canal, on which there were two solar markers. The site of this huaca is of special interest because Cobo states that when the sun arrived at the markers it was time to begin planting maize. It is generally assumed that this huaca was on the north slope of Picchu Hill, which contained the Chinchero canal. It is also believed that the pillars marked a late-August or early-September date because the maize fields of Cusco are plowed and sowed during these months. These pillars must have been prominent features of the landscape, since they are also mentioned by several other chroniclers (Aveni 1981a: 309–316; Bauer and Dearborn 1995:67–76). Nevertheless, their exact positions are still open to debate.

Mamararoy (Ch. 8:8) is described by Cobo as a group of stones thought to be the wives of Ticci Viracocha. Albornoz (1984:204 [ca. 1582]) mentions this same shrine in the following way: "Mararoray, which was a figure of a woman made of stone, where they sacrificed women." Its location has not been determined.

The next huaca, Urcoscalla (Ch. 8:9), is said to be where the city of Cusco was lost from sight on the Chinchaysuyu road. Albornoz (1984:204 [ca. 1582]) relates Ch. 8:8 with Ch.

Photo 5.25. The pass of Arco Punco and its modern aqueduct offer a final view of the Cusco Valley.

8:9, writing that the huaca of Urcos calla uiracocha was a small hill close to the shrine of Mararoray. Aveni (1981a) and Zuidema (1982a) suggest that Urcoscalla is the pass of Arco Punco, which offers a final view of the Cusco Valley (Photo 5.25). However, because the *Relación de las huacas* notes that this shrine was where the *city* is lost from view, an alternative location several hundred meters farther down the slope, closer to Cusco where the urban center is seen for the last time, seems a more likely location for Urcoscalla (Ch. 8:9). This suggestion is supported by a series of pho-

Photo 5.26. Hiram Bingham took a series of photographs between 1914 and 1915 of people praying along the road to Cusco. He may have recorded the location of Urcoscalla (Ch. 8:9). (Hiram Bingham, Yale Peabody Museum/Courtesy National Geographic Society, negative 11304.)

tographs taken by Hiram Bingham between 1914 and 1915 that show various individuals praying at a spot along the road where Cusco is first seen (Photo 5.26). One of the photographs is labeled "July 3, 1915 9:50 a.m. The praying place on the road. The name of it is said to be Apunches Manacuna [Place of Supplication to our Lord]."

Catachillay (Ch. 8:10) and Aspadquiri (Ch. 8:11), the tenth and eleventh shrines of Ch. 8, are both listed as being on the first flat area after leaving Cusco. The name Catachillay is presented by Polo de Ondegardo (1916c:4 [1585]) as a major Inca star constellation related to a female llama and her offspring (Zuidema and Urton 1976; Zuidema 1982b; Bauer and Dearborn 1995:105–108, 139–140). There is a spring called Llama Ñahuin (Llama Eye), on the first flat area outside of Cusco (Photo 5.27), that may represent the huaca of Catachillay (Ch. 8:10). If the spring of Llama Ñahuin is the shrine of Catachillay, then Aspadquiri (Ch. 8:11) was somewhere on this same flat area.

The penultimate huaca of this ceque is recorded as Poroypuquiu (Ch. 8:12), a spring next to the mill of Juan Julio [de Hojeda]. A spring called Poroypuquiu, along with the remains of a mill, can be found in the community of the same name some seven kilometers from Cusco (Aveni 1981a; Zuidema 1982a). The final shrine, Collanasayba (Ch. 8:13),

Photo 5.27. The spring of Llama Ñahuin may be Ch. 8:10.

is mentioned as a marker on a hill near Sicllabamba. As noted by Aveni (1981a) and Zuidema (1982a), there is a small hill with evidence of Inca structures, approximately four kilometers northwest of Poroy, beside the community of Sicllabamba, which in all likelihood marks the terminus of Ch. 8 (Maps 5.5 and 5.6).

The Ninth Ceque of Chinchaysuyu

The course of the ninth ceque of Chinchaysuyu is poorly understood despite the fact that it contained a total of twelve shrines. The first huaca was a spring called Aypanospacha (Ch. 9:1) on Pedro Alonso Carrasco's street, which Garcilaso de la Vega (1966:430 [1609:Vol. 1, Bk. 7, Ch. 11]) indicates was near the base of Carmenca. Cobo does not record the name of the second shrine, mentioning only that it was a small house on a farm of the Society of Jesus called Picchu. It can be assumed that Ch. 9:2 was in the area of Hacienda Picchu, west of Cusco, because this farm was owned by the Jesuits.[56] The positions of the third shrine, Quinoacalla (Ch. 9:3), a hill in Carmenca; the fourth, Pomacucho (Ch. 9:4), which Cobo notes was a spring situated somewhat separate from this ceque; and the fifth, Vicaribi (Ch. 9:5), a tomb of a lord of Maras Ayllu in Picchu, have not been identified.

The sixth huaca, a stone called Apuyauira (Ch. 9:6), was of considerable importance to the Inca. Cobo notes that the Inca believed that this stone was a person who emerged with Huanacauri and that the ayllus of Cusco went to it during the festival of [Capac] Ramyi.[57] This shrine is also mentioned by Cieza de León (1976:35 [1554:Pt. 2, Ch. 6]), Molina (1989:106 [ca. 1575]), and Albornoz (1984:204 [ca. 1582]), who all indicate that the youths participating in the Warachikoy initiation rites gathered at it several days after their ascents of Huanacauri and Anaguarque.[58] Betanzos (1987:67 [1557:Pt. 1, Ch. 14]) provides the following description of the ritual activities that took place at the huaca during the male initiation rites:

> The next day they will leave the city for a place where I will point out another *guaca* tomorrow. It will be called Yavira and will be the idol of the favors. When they are there they will have a big fire built and offer to the *guaca* and to the Sun sheep and lambs, beheading them first. With the blood of these animals they will draw a line with much reverence across their faces, from ear to ear. They will also sacrifice in this fire much maize and coca.

All of this will be done with great reverence and obeisance in making the offering to the Sun. (Betanzos 1996:62 [1557:Pt. 1, Ch. 14])[59]

Because the shrine of Huanacauri was thought to be a brother of Manco Capac, it can be suggested that this stone represented another royal sibling who emerged with him from the cave of Tambo Toco.[60]

Less than a kilometer from Hacienda Picchu stands an outcrop called the Ñusta (Princess). The stone is located in a small terracelike area that offers an outstanding view of the imperial capital (Photo 5.28).[61] Surveyors were repeatedly told by informants that this stone had been a sister of Manco Capac who walked up the mountain slope with a baby on her back and was transformed into stone. Given the similarities between the myth associated with the Ñusta and that presented in Cobo's document for Apuyauira, as well as its location on the side of Picchu, this site is a good candidate for Ch. 9:6.

The succeeding three shrines of Ch. 9 are related to the mythohistoric war between the Inca and the Chanca. Cutirsaspampa (Ch. 9:7) is cataloged as a flat place where the Inca won a victory, and Queachili (Ch. 9:8) is registered as a flat, gatewaylike area between two hills where the battle finished.[62] After the battle, the Inca warriors are thought to have drunk at Quishuarpuquiu (Ch. 9:9). Albornoz (1984: 204 [ca. 1582]) also describes Ch. 9:8: "Oma chilligues, a

Photo 5.28. The Ñusta (Princess), said to be a sister of the mythical Manco Capac, is a good possibility for Apuyauira (Ch. 9:6).

plain where the Incas had a battle with the Chanca and they defeated them; and the Chanca fled, and they say that they turned into condors and escaped. And thus most Chanca ayllus are called condor guachos."

While most of the chroniclers mention the Chanca War, Miguel Cabello de Balboa (1951:299 [1586:Pt. 3, Ch. 14]) provides especially important information, noting that the land of Quiachilli, where the last battle took place, was "behind" a place called Ayavira.[63] The small village of Ayaviri lies on one side of what is now called the Huillque Pass, formerly called Vilcaconga,[64] some forty-five kilometers west of Cusco and ten kilometers east of Limatambo (Photo 5.29). This pass, which marks the watershed between the Apurimac and Urubamba Rivers, was the site of a series of battles in the Conquest and Early Colonial periods. Although the name Quiachilli is no longer used in the pass area, it and other associated toponyms are mentioned in local land documents dating from 1566 to 1809 (AGN/Real Hacienda, Tribunal de Cuentas, Composición de tierras de indígenas: Leg. 5, 1643–1717; AHD/Cajas de Censos: Leg. 4, 1687–1697; AHD/Cajas de Censos: Leg. 20, 1802–1809).

The locations of the tenth, Yuyotuyro (Ch. 9:10), and eleventh, Pillolliri (Ch. 9:11), huacas, both said to be stones, and that of the twelfth, a spring called Totorguaylla (Ch. 9:12), are unknown (Maps 5.5 and 5.6).

The Additional Shrines of Chinchaysuyu

After presenting the shrines of Cuntisuyu, and before beginning a new chapter of his chronicle—on the coastal temple of Pachacamac, Cobo (1980:61 [1653:Bk. 2, Ch. 16]) describes four additional huacas, which in his words, ". . . belong to various ceques but were not set down in the order that the rest [were], when the investigation was made." The presence of these four shrines at the end of the ceque descriptions suggests that the author of the *Relación de las huacas* continued to find shrines after his initial investigation was completed.

All four of these "extra" huacas appear to have been in Chinchaysuyu. The precise position of the first extra shrine, described as a lake called Mamacocha (Ch. Extra:1) above the fortress (i.e., Sacsahuaman), is not known. The second extra huaca, Tocoripuquiu (Ch. Extra:2), is said to be the source of the stream that passes through the city of Cusco.[65] Elsewhere in his chronicle, Cobo describes the rituals that took place at this huaca to ensure irrigation water:

The eighth month was named Chahua Huarquis. During this month, one hundred brown sheep were burned, just like the ones of the previous month. In addition, they took two more on the first day of the month to burn at the *guaca* of Tocori. One was taken to where they started to irrigate the valley and the other to where they ended their irrigation. This was done to preserve the water. This sacrifice was established by Inca Roca, and the Indians tell this fable about him. Very little water used to come out of that spring, but after making certain sacrifices, Inca Roca thrust his arm into the spring, and this made the water gush out as abundantly as it does now. This they considered to be such an established fact that the members of his family unit and lineage used it as justification for laying claim to that water for their own use exclusively, and during the time of the Incas, they succeeded in getting it. (Cobo 1990:143 [1653:Bk. 13, Ch. 28]).[66]

There were two large streams that passed through ancient Cusco: Saphi and Choquechaca. It can be deduced, however, that the spring of Tocori was located at or near the headwaters of the Saphi because this river was used to irrigate a much larger percentage of land than that of the Choquechaca River. Nevertheless, the exact location of

Tocoripuquiu (Ch. Extra:2) has not been determined, since the Saphi River does not originate at a single point, but is formed by the union of three small streams high on Huaynacorcor Mountain. The third and fourth huacas included at the end of the *Relación de las huacas* were two hills called Chinchacuay (Ch. Extra:3), which was opposite the fortress, and Quiquijana (Ch. Extra:4), which was behind Chinchacuay. Neither of these hills has been identified.

Summary and Discussion

Possible courses for the Chinchaysuyu ceques as documented by field research are shown on Map 5.7. According to Cobo, the ceques of the Cusco system radiated from the Coricancha. This seems to have been true for the ceques of Chinchaysuyu because the first shrines of most of these lines are described as being in or near the Temple of the Sun. Although many of the huacas of this suyu have yet to be found, the available data suggest that the ceques did not overlap, and that most of the Chinchaysuyu ceques formed relatively straight lines. The average length of the ceques in this suyu is difficult to discuss because many of the final ceque huacas have not been identified with certainty.

Photo 5.29. The last battle of the Chanca War took place near this plain. The Inca road traveled to the left of the distant hill, and Ch. 9:8 may have stood at this pass, now called Huillque Pass.

The first ceque of Chinchaysuyu (Ch. 1) ran from near the center of Cusco toward the ruins of Kenko Grande and may have ended in the Tambomachay area. The ninth ceque (Ch. 9) projected out from Cusco in the direction of Hacienda Picchu and may have terminated more than forty-five kilometers from Cusco. If the positioning of these huacas is correct, then Ch. 9 was certainly the longest ceque of the system. The best-charted line among the nine Chinchaysuyu ceques is that of Ch. 5, which begins at the birthplace of Pachacuti Inca Yupanqui, Cusicancha (Ch. 5:1), across from the Temple of the Sun. This line then ran through the center of Cusco (Ch. 5:2, Ch. 5:3), the Plaza de Armas (Ch. 5:4, Ch. 5:5), and up to the "Throne of the Inca" in Sacsahuaman (Ch. 5:6). From this carved stone the ceque continued to the natural outcrops of Chacaguanacauri (Ch. 5:7), Guamanguachanca (Ch. 5:8), and Cinca (Mama Guachanca, Ch. 5:9). The line terminated at the small spring of Corcorpuquiu (Ch. 5:9), on the slope of Huaynacorcor some six kilometers from Cusco.

At the end of Cobo's account of the shrines of Cuntisuyu, he includes an appendix of four additional shrines that were not included in the ceque list at the time of the original investigation. Since each of these four extra huacas appear to be located in Chinchaysuyu, they have been discussed in this chapter. Although field research did not identify the exact location of any of these extra shrines, their appearance at the end of the *Relación de las huacas* has important implications for the study of the Cusco ceque system as a whole. Cobo specifically notes that these four shrines belong to various ceques within the system, but that they were not recorded when the list was made. This suggests that the system had more than the 328 shrines frequently credited to it. This is noted by Cobo himself, who states that with the inclusion of the Temple of the Sun and the four extra shrines presented at the conclusion of the *Relación de las huacas,* there was a total of 333 huacas distributed across forty ceques.[67] Furthermore, he may have miscounted the number of huacas on Ch. 4, leaving one out of the list. As will be discussed in Chapter 9, an account of 37 shrines by Albornoz indicates that there may have been many more shrines in Chinchaysuyu than those preserved in Cobo's chronicle. Given this information, it is reasonable to suggest that there were various shrines in the other three suyus of the system that were also not recorded when Cobo's source document was made.

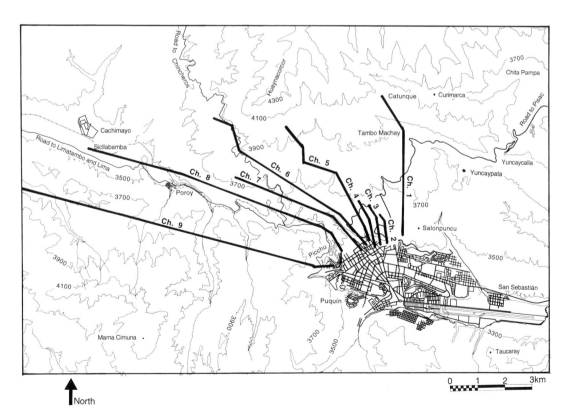

Map. 5.7. Suggested courses of Chinchaysuyu ceques Ch.1–Ch. 9.

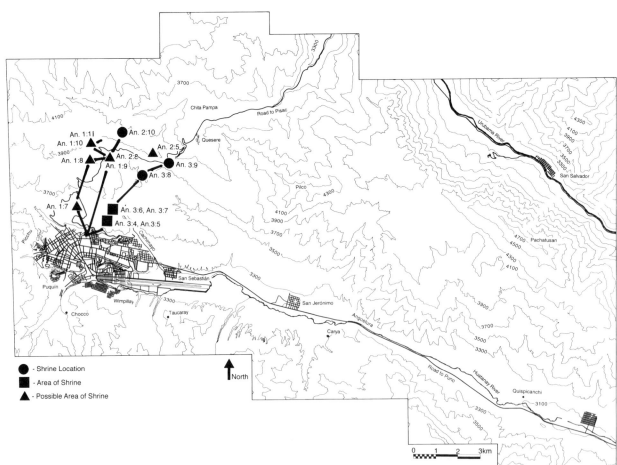

Map 6.1. Suggested courses of Antisuyu ceques An. 1, An. 2, and An. 3.

6

The Huacas and Ceques of Antisuyu

Antisuyu was the northeast quarter of the Cusco region. The division between Chinchaysuyu and Antisuyu was just west of the Inca road that ran from Cusco to Tambomachay (Map 6.1). The demarcation between Antisuyu and Collasuyu was the Huatanay River, which flows through the city and out the eastern end of the valley. This river also marked the moiety division between Hanan and Hurin Cusco. Antisuyu is described by Cobo as containing a total of nine ceques and seventy-eight huacas.

The locations of various huacas and the projection of certain ceques in Antisuyu have been examined by other researchers. Zuidema (1977c, 1982b, 1982c, 1986b, 1990b), Sherbondy (1982, 1986), and Van de Guchte (1990) suggest that the ceques of Antisuyu traveled out from Cusco in straight lines. Niles (1987), on the other hand, proposes that the ceques of this suyu were less straight than previously predicted. The data collected during the course of this project support Niles's findings.

The First Ceque of Antisuyu

The first ceque of Antisuyu is characterized as having eleven shrines under the care of Cubcu [Suscu] Panaca, the descendents of Viracocha Inca, the eighth king of Cusco. Its first two huacas, an enclosure called Chiquinapampa (An. 1:1) and a nearly round stone named Turuca (An 1:2), are described as being next to the Temple of the Sun. The third shrine, a large stone called Chiripacha (An. 1:3), was at the beginning of the Collasuyu road.[1] Since the road to Collasuyu left Cusco via the plaza of Limac Pampa Grande, this shrine may have been between this plaza and the Temple of the Sun.

The fourth, fifth, and sixth huacas of An. 1 are reported to be near Patallacta (Ch. 1:2), a locality that is mentioned in the descriptions of Ch. 1:2 and Ch. 1:3. Autviturco (An. 1:4) is characterized as a large cave down the ravine from Patallacta, from which the Goalla [Hualla] Indians were

born. The Hualla are traditionally believed to be one of several groups indigenous to Cusco before the arrival of Manco Capac (Loarte 1882 [1572]; Sarmiento de Gamboa 1906 [1572]). There are several caves in the Chunchul Ravine below Hacienda Patallacta that may represent their origin place (Photo 6.1).[2] Although road construction has partially destroyed the Chunchul Ravine, a series of waterfalls may still be found beside its caves. These waterfalls are good candidates for An. 1:5, which is recorded as a spring called Pacha in the ravine of Patallacta.[3] The sixth huaca, Corcorchaca (An. 1:6), is said to be a spring in the same ravine as Autviturco (An. 1:4) and Pacha (An. 1:5). Since *chaca* can be translated as "bridge," the name of this shrine suggests that there was once a bridge in the Chunchul Ravine. After analyzing historical references to Corcorchaca, Sherbondy (1982:192–193 n. 85) suggests that this shrine was near the above-mentioned caves.

Amaromarcaguaci (An. 1:7), a house of Amaro Topa Inca

Photo 6.1. The Hualla are thought to be one of several tribes who lived in the Cusco Valley before Manco Capac arrived. Caves in the Chunchul Ravine may represent Autviturco (An. 1:4), the origin place of this indigenous group.

on the road to the Andes, was the seventh shrine of this ceque.[4] Amaro Topa Inca was the eldest son of Pachacuti Inca Yupanqui, the ninth king of Cusco, and the older brother of Topa Inca, the tenth king (Cabello de Balboa 1951:334 [1586:Pt. 3, Ch. 18]; Sarmiento de Gamboa 1906:84 [1572:Ch. 42]). According to the mythic history of the Inca, Pachacuti Inca Yupanqui selected Topa Inca as his successor rather than Amaro Topa Inca, and it is reported that Amaro Topa Inca remained in Cusco to help his younger brother rule the empire. It is also said that Amaro Topa Inca was responsible for the adoption and veneration of the major Inca huacas, and for the destruction of non-Inca shrines, in all parts of the empire (Sarmiento de Gamboa 1906:77 [1572:Ch. 37]). Research conducted by Sherbondy (1982:83–84, 193–194 n.86) and Van de Guchte (1990:72, 152–165) indicates that the area north of Kenko was called Amaro. The area of Amarumarca is listed in a 1636 document as near the Curimarca road (BN/Virreynato, Real Audiencia, Asuntos Judiciales, B701). This road leads from Kenko to Curimarca via Tambomachay. Sherbondy and Van de Guchte suggest that a site in this area currently called Llanllakuyoc—an extensively sculpted, cavernous outcrop with adjacent buildings—situated just off the road to Curimarca, may represent Amaromarcaguaci (An. 1:7) (Photo 6.2).[5]

The *Relación de las huacas* states that the shrine following Amaromarcaguaci (An. 1:7) was a boiling spring near Tambomachay called Tipc (Ti[n]p[u]c) Puquiu (An. 1:8). There are, however, two separate springs called Timpuc Puquiu (Boiling Spring) in this area. The first is a small spring about one and one-half kilometers upstream from Tambomachay on the northern bank of the Timpuc River. The second is a spring near the community of Huaylla Cocha, approximately one kilometer south of Tambomachay. This second spring churns and bubbles as the water rises to its surface, and the poorly preserved remains of a number of well-crafted Inca structures border it (Photo 6.3). The presence of these Inca remains, and the distinct manner in which the water rises to its surface, suggests the second spring is the best candidate for the eighth shrine of An. 1.

The ninth huaca of An. 1 is characterized as a house of Pachacuti Inca Yupanqui called Tambomachay (An. 1:9), set on a hill along the road to the Andes. Rowe (1980:12) and Niles (1987:180) propose that the Inca site of Puca Pucara, on a small hill beside the Inca road to Corimarca, is this huaca (Photo 6.4).

A fountain with two springs near Tambomachay, called Quinoapuquiu (An. 1:10), is registered as the tenth shrine of this ceque. There are two extraordinary stone fountains

Photo 6.2. This extensively sculpted cavernous outcrop with adjacent buildings may represent Amaromarcaguaci (An. 1:7).

Photo 6.3. A "boiling" spring, surrounded by the foundations of Inca buildings, near the community of Huaylla Cocha is the best candidate for Tipc (Ti[n]p[u]c) Puquiu (An. 1:8).

Photo 6.4. The Inca site of Puca Pucara may have been a house of Pachacuti Inca Yupanqui on the road to the Andes (An. 1:9).

Photo 6.6. A dual-channel fountain beside Puca Pucara could be An. 1:10 or An 2:8.

Photo 6.5. The elaborate, dual-channel fountain of Tambomachay is a good candidate for Quinoapuquiu (An. 1:10). (Courtesy Fototeca Andina—Centro Bartolomé de las Casas. Photograph by Miguel Chani, ca. 1915.)

with dual channels in this area. One is the elaborate fountain of Tambomachay, located approximately half a kilometer from Puca Pucara, which includes an area of monumental terraces with large niches and a dual-channel fountain at its base (Photo 6.5). The other dual-channel fountain is situated beside Puca Pucara (Photo 6.6).[6] While either of these fountains could represent Quinoapuquiu, the location of the final huaca of this ceque, close to the terraces of Tambomachay, suggests that the Tambomachay fountain may be the best candidate for An. 1:10.

The concluding huaca on this ceque, Quiscourco (An.

1:11), is recorded as a round, but not very large, stone. There is a remarkably round boulder (Photo 6.7) across the ravine from the fountain area of Tambomachay—still used as a landmark in the region—which may represent the ultimate shrine of An. 1 (Maps 6.1 and 6.2).[7]

The Second Ceque of Antisuyu

The second ceque of Antisuyu, like the first, projected from Cusco to the Chunchul Ravine and then continued toward Tambomachay. The ceque began at a place called Vilcacona

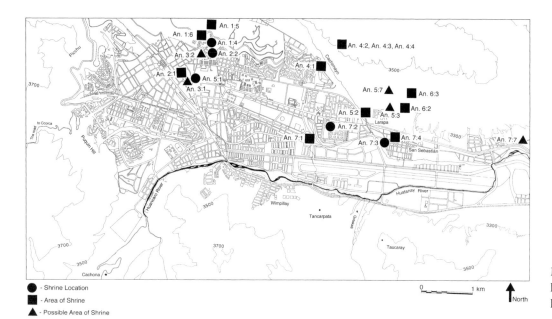

- ● - Shrine Location
- ■ - Area of Shrine
- ▲ - Possible Area of Shrine

0   1 km

↑
North

Map 6.2. Suggested locations of Antisuyu huacas in Cusco.

Photo 6.7. A remarkably round boulder near the fountain of Tambomachay (background) may represent Quiscourco (An. 1:11), the ultimate shrine of An. 1.

(An. 2:1), where the house of Juan de Salas was later built. Cobo indicates that once a year the Inca gathered together and made offerings to all the Cusco shrines at this place:

> To this shrine they brought at a certain time of the year all the guacas and idols of the city of Cuzco, and they sacrificed to them there, all together, and then they returned them to their places. It was a very solemn guaca; they offered it very small cestos [bags] of coca. (Cobo 1980:31 [1653:Bk. 13, Ch. 14])[8]

Guaman Poma de Ayala (1980:235 [1615:261 (263)]) depicts an analogous gathering of huacas in his chronicle, suggesting that Topa Inca called these shrines together to determine which of them caused a drought and the destruction of crops by frost and hail (Figure 3.1). The approximate position of Vilcacona is suggested by Garcilaso de la Vega (1966:423 [1609:Vol. 1, Bk. 7, Ch. 9]), who indicates that the house of Juan de Salas was near the lower end of San Agustín Street. Accordingly, An. 2:1 may have been the small plaza area at the beginning of San Agustín Street currently called Limacpampa Chica.

A large stone called Pachatosa (Pachatusan), next to Diego Cayo's house, on top of which sacrifices were burned, is listed as An. 2:2. The location of this stone is indicated by Loarte (1882:240 [1572]) in a reference to the town of the Huallas:

> ... they are the descendents and origins of the Hualla Indians of the town of Payatusan [Pachatusan], that is at the back of San Blas, in this city, to the east, near the terraces that leave San Blas towards Salinas.[9]

The area of Pachatusan thus corresponds to the zone of Cusco currently called Lucrepata, which is behind and to the east of the San Blas neighborhood at the base of several terraces. The area of Lucrepata is also notable because it is cut by the Chunchul Ravine, which may hold Autviturco (An. 1:4), the cave from which the Hualla are thought to have emerged. In addition, there is a large flat rock known as Mesa Redonda (Round Table) and a sculpted outcrop called Cinca (Nose) in Lucrepata at the base of the Chunchul Ravine, which together may well represent An. 2:2 (Photo 6.8).

The locations of the third huaca, Chusacachi (An. 2:3), stones on a large hill on the way to the Andes, and of the fourth, a quarry called Curovilca (An 2:4), are problematic because there are many outcrops and quarries northeast of Cusco. Possible candidates for An. 2:3 include a cluster of carved stones on top of the first hill away from Cusco east

Photo 6.8. A large flat rock known as Mesa Redonda and a sculpted outcrop called Cinca in Lucrepata are likely candidates for Pachatosa (An. 2:2).

of Kenko Grande, as well as an elaborately carved outcrop in the middle of the nearby field; and a possibility for An. 2:4 is a large quarry approximately one kilometer north of these carved rocks.

Sunchupuquiu (An 2:5), the fifth huaca of this ceque, is characterized as a shrine next to the slope of a hill so named [Sunchu]. Fieldwork northeast of Cusco identified a sector of land called Sunchu Qata north of the community of Yuncaypata (An. 3:8) and west of Yuncaycalla (An. 3:9).[10] The location of this slope is problematic, however, because it is far off the apparent course of this ceque.

The position of the sixth shrine of An. 2, Aucapapirqui (An. 2:6), a spring along the road to the Andes, and that of the seventh, Caynaconga (An. 2:7), a resting place near Tambomachay, remain to be identified. The eighth huaca, simply called Puquiu (An. 2:8), or Spring, is said to be at the

Photo 6.9. A mountain pass, currently called Queser Qasa, stands above the ruins of Puca Pucara. The pass may formerly have been called Macaycalla (An. 2:10).

end of Tambomachay. There is a dual-channel fountain beside the ruins of Puca Pucara that should be considered as a possible candidate for this shrine (see Photo 6.6).[11]

The ninth huaca, Cascasayba (An. 2:9), is listed as certain stones on the hill of Quisco. In the discussion of An. 1:11, it was suggested that a round stone near the fountain area of Tambomachay may represent the shrine of Quisco. If this is the case, then An. 2:9 may have been on the mountain slope near this boulder.

The concluding shrine of An. 2 is described in the *Relación de las huacas* as a flat place called Macaycalla (An. 2:10) between two hills, where the view of one side is lost and the other revealed.[12] Sherbondy (1982:173, 187 n.75) found a number of historic references to the pass of Macaycalla. She suggests that the high pass that separates the Tambomachay area from the Chita Pampa, currently called Queser Qasa, was formerly called Macaycalla (Photo 6.9).[13] If this is the case, then the remains of a small platform beside the road at the height of the pass may mark where offerings were made to the shrine (Maps 6.1 and 6.2).

The Third Ceque of Antisuyu

The probable projection of An. 3 has been discussed by several researchers (Aveni 1981a; Dearborn and Schreiber 1986; Zuidema 1986b), since some of the most important huacas of the Cusco ceque system are among its ten shrines. The initial shrine of An. 3, Guarupuncu (An. 3:1), is presented as

a bridge that passed from the Temple of the Sun to a place the Spaniards called the plaza of Peces.[14] Sherbondy (1982: 192 n.84) and Azevedo (1982:52) suggest that this bridge was in Cusco near the small plaza now called Limacpampa Chico.

Cobo does not provide a name for the second shrine of this ceque, but he describes it as a wall with an outward bulge near the field of Hernando Bachicao. An early land sale dating to 1557 describes the fields of Bachicao as on the edge of the city (AGN/Real Audiencia, Causas Civiles: Leg. 6, 35v), and they are mentioned in other documents as well

Photo 6.10. The *Relación de las huacas* provides no name for An. 3:2, but describes it as a wall with an outward bulge near the field of Hernando Bachicao. This unusual building corner, on the edge of ancient Cusco, may represent this shrine.

(BN/Virreynato, Cacicazgo, B561, f. 29, 35v). A possible, although highly speculative, candidate for this anonymous shrine has been found on Totora Paccha Street—one of the roads leading from the center of Cusco to the Chunchul Ravine—where the street's straight course is abruptly interrupted by the corner of an Inca building (Photo 6.10). If this unusual corner represents An. 3:2, then the succeeding huaca, Ayacho (An. 3:3), described as a spring in the same field as the wall, was nearby.

A temple of the sun called Chuquimarca (An. 3:4), on the hill of Mantocalla, is listed as the fourth shrine of this ceque. Cobo notes that sacrifices were offered to this huaca because the sun descended there many times to sleep, a statement that led Zuidema (1977a, 1982c, 1986b) and Aveni (1981a) to propose that the Inca observed the June solstice sunset from this huaca. These researchers suggest that Chuquimarca is an enormous outcrop two kilometers northeast of Cusco currently called Salonpuncu (or Lacco). While this is certainly a possibility, it should also be noted that the major trail from Cusco to Pisac and the jungle passes an extensively carved outcrop with adjacent Inca buildings, currently called Cusilluchayoc, approximately two hundred meters before reaching Salonpuncu (Photo 6.11). The position of this outcrop along the Inca road and its proximity to other possible huaca locations to be presented below indicate that Cusilluchayoc should also be considered a possible candidate for Chuquimarca.

The fifth shrine of this ceque, Mantocallaspa (An. 3:5), is described as a spring on the hill of Mantocalla near Chuquimarca. Because Cobo notes that this shrine was a

Photo 6.11. Cusilluchayoc, an extensively carved outcrop with adjacent Inca buildings, is a possible candidate for Chuquimarca (An. 3:4).

spring, we can suggest that the last three letters of the name were deleted at some time (Mantocallaspa[cha]). There are a number of canals, springs, and reservoirs in the area surrounding the ruins of Cusilluchayoc and Salonpuncu. Three possible candidates for An. 3:5 are: (1) a well-crafted stone fountain less than fifty meters from Cusilluchayoc, (2) a large spring approximately seventy-five meters north of Cusilluchayoc, and (3) a possible Inca reservoir at the base of Salonpuncu.

The next huaca, An. 3:6, the hill of Mantocallas (Mantocalla), was an especially important shrine where the Inca offered elaborate offerings during the shelling of maize.[15] Cobo recorded additional information elsewhere in his chronicle on the elaborate rituals that took place at Mantocalla during the month of Inti Raymi:[16]

> The seventh month corresponded to June, and it was called Aucay Cuzqui. During this month the most important festival of the Sun was performed; it was called Inti Raymi. On the first day, an offering was made of one hundred brown sheep of the Sun. It was made in the way that has been described above. They performed this festival and sacrifice on the hill of Manturcalla, where the Inca would go and remain until the festival was over, drinking and enjoying himself. This festival was performed only by the Incas of royal blood, and not even their wives participated in it; instead the wives stayed away in a patio. The *mamaconas,* wives of the Sun, would give drink to the Incas, and all of the vessels from which they ate or drank were made of gold. An offering was made to the said statues on behalf of the Incas. It included thirty sheep: ten to Viracocha, ten to the Sun, and ten more to the Thunder, and thirty articles of clothing made of very colorful *cumbi* [fine cloth]. Moreover, on that same hill they made a large number of statues from carved *quishuar* wood. These statues were dressed in rich clothing and were there from the beginning of the festival. At the end of it, they set fire to the statues and burned them. They also took to the said hill six *aporucos* [male llamas] that were burned with everything else. After all the many sacrifices were concluded, in order to start the dance called *cayo,* which was performed four times a day, all of the Indians divided up. Half of them remained there dancing and drinking. Of the other half, part of them went to Chuquichanca [An. 6:3], and part of them went to Paucarcancha. On these hills six more *aporucos* were distributed, and these animals were sacrificed with great solemnity.
>
> During this festival the Sun would send, on behalf of his statues and with those who cared for them, two little lambs, one silver and the other gold, to Paucarcancha,

and two others made of seashells to Pilcocancha, and two others to the hill of Manturcalla. All of them were buried in these hills after an offering had been made of the lambs. As they finished performing the said dance called *cayo,* the statues of the Sun would send large sheep made of certain materials and two lambs to the hill of Manturcalla. These animals were carried on a litter with a large retinue. The litter was held on the shoulders of important lords who were richly dressed. Leading the way were the royal insignia of the *sunturpaucar* [royal staff] and the white sheep in a red tunic with gold ear ornaments. On reaching the said hill, an offering was made of the animals to Viracocha, and they were burned with many ceremonies. (Cobo 1990:142–143 [1653:Bk. 13, Ch. 28])[17]

Less than half a kilometer from the sculpted outcrop of Cusilluchayoc is an enormous rock formation called Salonpuncu (Photos 6.12 and 6.13). This impressive feature of the landscape is famous for the elaborately carved chambers, niches, and stairs at its base and for its extensively sculpted summit. A major canal, which originates at Ucu Ucu approximately three kilometers away, runs along the southern base of the outcrop, and the Inca road to Pisac passes just south of it. Rather than representing Chuquimarca (An. 3:4), as suggested by Zuidema (1977a, 1982c, 1986b) and Aveni (1981a), I propose that this outcrop is Mantocalla (An. 3:6). This proposition is supported by a 1649 account that describes the area of Mantocalla as being crossed by the Uru Uru canal as well as by the road to Pisac (AHD/Cajas de Censos: Leg. 2, 1656–1675]).

Photo 6.13. Salonpuncu (facing south).

Photo 6.14. A small spring on the northern slope of Salonpuncu is a possibility for Caripuquiu (An. 3:7).

Photo 6.12. The impressive carved-rock formation now referred to as Salonpuncu (facing north) was called Mantocalla (An. 3:6) by the Inca. It was here that elaborate offerings were made at the time of maize shelling.

The seventh huaca, a spring called Caripuquiu (An. 3:7), is said to be on the slope of Mantocalla. The identification of this shrine is difficult because there are a number of springs in the Salonpuncu area. There is, however, one especially interesting possibility for An. 3:7: a small spring on the northern slope of Salonpuncu that is reached by means of a stone stairway (Photo 6.14).

Approximately three kilometers from Cusilluchayoc and Salonpuncu, along the Inca road to Pisac, is the community of Yuncaypata (Photo 6.15). Sherbondy (1982:92), citing

Photo 6.15. The community of Yuncaypata marks the location of Yuncaypampa (An. 3:8).

Rostworowski (1964:27), indicates that this community was used as "a watering place for llama trains on the main route from Cusco to the jungle." This community, with all certainty, marks the location of Yuncaypampa (An. 3:8), which Cobo presents as a flat place with a spring on the road to the Andes.[18]

The trail from Cusco to Pisac leads from Yuncaypata across a pass called Yuncaycalla.[19] The pass, now marked with a cross, provides a clear view of the Cusco Valley to the south and the plain of Chita to the north (Photo 6.16). Modern offerings are still placed near the cross, and a light scatter of Inca pottery can be found on the pass as well. There can be little doubt that this pass is An. 3:9, which is described by Cobo as a gateway called Yancaycalla (Yuncaycalla) where the plain of Chita is seen and Cusco is lost from view.

The terminus of the third ceque, a spring called Urcomilpo (An. 3:10) on the plain of Chita, has not been identified (Maps 6.1 and 6.2).[20]

The Fourth Ceque of Antisuyu

The seven huacas of An. 4 were the responsibility of Aucailli Panaca, the descendents of the seventh Inca king, Yahuar Huacac. Possible locations for six of these shrines have been proposed by Niles (1987:181–190) in a study of An. 4, An. 5, and An. 6. Fieldwork conducted under the auspices of

Photo 6.16. The pass of Yuncaycalla (An. 3:9) provides a view of the Cusco Valley to the south and the plain of Chita to the north. This pass was a shrine during Inca times, and the modern cross that has been set there suggests that it has retained some of its religious importance.

this project supports Niles's identifications, with some emendations.

The initial huaca of An. 4, Cariurco (An. 4:1), is listed as certain stones on a hill near Mantocalla.[21] Both Sherbondy (1982:77, 80) and Niles (1987:180) suggest that the hill of Cariurco was near the mouth of the Cachimayo (Salt River), somewhere above the Hacienda Cari Grande. The next four shrines may have been closely spaced. Chuquiquirao Puquiu (An. 4:2) is described as a spring in a ravine on the slope of Cariurco. The third shrine, Callachaca (An. 4:3), is presented as certain stones placed on the same hill; and the fourth, Viracocha (An. 4:4), was a nearby quarry. The fifth shrine, Aucanpuquiu (An. 4:5), was a spring near the ravine of Yancacalla (Yuncaycalla; An. 3:9).[22] The area of Callachaca is on the eastern slope of the Cachimayo, upstream from the Cari Grande region. There is a cluster of Inca architectural works in the Callachaca area called Chuquiquirao consisting of several buildings, an elaborate stone passageway lined with fine Inca masonry, two terraced conical hills, and a small quarry (Photos 6.17 and 6.18).[23] There is also a large spring beside these ruins and a series of small pools on the slope below them. Niles (1987:181–190) suggests that Chuquiquirao Puquiu (An. 4:2) was one of the small pools below the ruins of Chuqui-

quirao. She also indicates that the largest of the two terraced conical hills may be Callachaca (An. 4:3), and that the adjacent quarry is the shrine of Viracocha (An. 4:4). In addition, Niles proposes that the large spring beside the ruins of Chuquiquirao may be Aucanpuquiu (An. 4:5).

While my data do not contradict Niles's findings for Callachaca (An. 4:3) or Viracocha (An. 4:4), I offer different interpretations for Chuquiquirao Puquiu (An. 4:2) and Aucanpuquiu (An. 4:5). Cobo writes that the shrine of Aucanpuq iu (An. 4:5) was located *near* the ravine of Yuncaycalla. Aucapuquio is also listed within the lands of Pumamarca in a document dating to 1570 (Guevara Gil 1993:389). In addition, it is known that the fields of Aucanpuquiu marked the northern limits of the Hacienda Pumamarca in 1897 (PA/Chávez Ballón: Document 1, f. 1).[24] This spring and field area has been located between the Callachaca area and Yuncaycalla. In light of this information, it is reasonable to conclude that the prominent spring of the Chuquiquirao area is not the Aucanpuquiu (An. 4:5) described by Cobo, but may instead be Chuquiquirao Puquiu (An. 4:3).

A group of stones on a hill called Illansayba, where people who entered the province of the Andes made sacrifices for their health, is registered as An. 4:6. While no hill was

Photo 6.17. Within the terraced area of Chuquiquirao are several Inca buildings, an elaborate stone passageway lined with fine Inca masonry, two conical hills, and a quarry.

Photo 6.18. The quarry at Chuquiquirao may be the shrine of Viracocha (An. 4:4).

identified with this name during survey work northeast of Cusco, a looted area on a ridge immediately east of the Yuncaycalla Pass was found (Photo 6.19). It is possible, albeit very speculative, that this looted ridgetop represents the area of Illansayba (An. 4:6).

The final shrine of this ceque, Maycha-guanacauri (An. 4:7), is described as a stone shaped like the hill of Huanacauri on the Antisuyu road. Near the end of Chita Pampa, the Inca road to Antisuyu passed between two mountains called Huanacauri and Maycha.[25] Until additional information is found, it seems reasonable to suggest that the huaca of Maychaguanacauri was located beside the Inca road between these two mountains (Maps 6.2 and 6.3).

Photo 6.19. A looted area on a ridge east of Yuncaycalla Pass could represent Illansayba (An. 4:6).

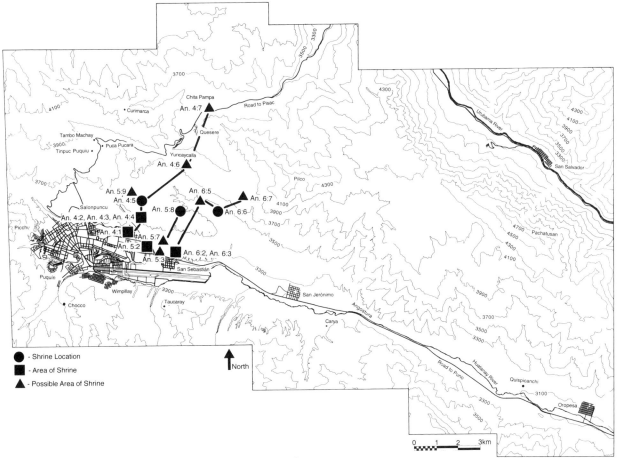

Map 6.3. Suggested courses of Antisuyu ceques An. 4, An. 5, and An. 6.

The Fifth Ceque of Antisuyu

The fifth ceque of Antisuyu contained ten huacas. Possible positions for a number of these have been offered by Zuidema (1977b, 1982b, 1990b) and Niles (1987:190–198); however, the course of the ceque is still poorly understood and additional research is needed to confirm many of the suggested shrine locations.

The ceque began with An. 5:1, a stone in the plaza of Hurin Aucaypata (Hurin Haucaypata) called Usno.[26] Zuidema (1977b, 1980:321), using information from Molina (1989:72 [ca. 1575]), suggests that Hurin Haucaypata was located at the plaza of Limacpampa Grande, east of the Temple of the Sun.[27] The second huaca, Cachipuquiu (An. 5:2 [Salt Spring]), is reported to be a spring in Las Salinas, an area of former salt pans near the mouth of the Cachimayo. Although there are numerous salt springs in this area, one spring, approximately five hundred meters up the Cachimayo from the Cusco–San Sebastián road, is widely known as Cachipuquiu, and thus may represent An. 5:2 (Photo 6.20). Nevertheless, since a large percentage of the Las Salinas area has been destroyed by urban growth, this huaca identification should be considered tentative.

The third shrine, a round stone called Sabaraura (An. 5:3), is reported to be an ancient shrine in the town of Ya-

Photo 6.21. This large, elaborately sculpted outcrop in Yacanora may once have been called Sabaraura (An. 5:3).

canora. An area above San Sebastián, east of the Cachimayo, that contains an abundance of Inca-style buildings retains the name Yacanora. Within the Yacanora area is a large sculpted outcrop (Photo 6.21) that Niles (1987:193, 196, 197) proposes to be the stone of Sabaraura.

The next three huacas, Pachayaconora (An. 5:4), Oyaraypuquiu (An. 5:5), and Arosayapuquiu (An. 5:6), are all described as springs. The first two are listed as being in Yacanora, while the third is said to be in Callachaca. While our survey in the areas of Yacanora and Callachaca found numerous springs, none have retained the names provided in the *Relación de las huacas* for An. 5:4, An. 5:5, or An. 5:6.[28]

Cobo states that the seventh shrine of this ceque, Aquarsayba (An. 5:7), was a greatly venerated huaca and that the Inca believed that whatever they offered to it was received by all the huacas. Approximately three hundred meters above the Yacanora outcrop thought to represent An. 5:3 is a second set of archaeological remains. Niles (1987:106–114) refers to this area as "the T-shaped plaza complex," and notes that it contains an elaborately carved rock, a plaza area, several Inca buildings, and an isolated outcrop that has been topped with masonry. In the absence of any more likely locations, Niles proposes that this complex is related to An. 5:7.

The eighth shrine of An. 5 was a spring called Susumarca

Photo 6.20. An area of former salt pans lies directly east of Cusco. One of the many springs in this area was called Cachipuquiu ([Salt Spring] An. 5:2).

(An 5:8) in Callachaca. This huaca may be related to a famous spring called Susurpuquiu mentioned in several chronicles. For example, Sarmiento de Gamboa (1906:62 [1571:Ch. 27]) states that Pachacuti Inca Yupanqui had a vision at Susurpuquiu on the eve of the Chanca War:

And as he found himself one day at Susurpuquio, in great distress and debating the best way to oppose his enemies, in the air in front of him appeared a being in the image of the Sun, who comforted him and encouraged him to give battle. And he showed him [Pachacuti] a mirror in which were revealed the provinces that he was to conquer; and [he told Pachacuti] that he would surpass all his ancestors; and that he should harbor no doubt [and] return to the city, for he would defeat the Chancas, who were moving against Cusco.[29]

Juan de Santa Cruz Pachacuti Yamqui Salcamayhua (1950:237 [1613]) indicates that Pachacuti Inca Yupanqui had this vision near Callachaca.[30] Molina (1989:60 [ca. 1575])[31] provides another reference to Susurpuquiu, describing what seems to be the same mythical vision:

They say that before he [Pachacuti] became ruler, he was on his way to visit his father Viracocha Inca in Sacsahuana, five leagues from Cusco, [and] just as he came upon a spring called Susurpuquio, he saw a crystal tablet fall into the spring, within which he saw a figure of an Indian. . . .[32]

Photo 6.22. It is said that Pachacuti Inca Yupanqui had a vision at Susurpuquiu on the eve of the Chanca War. This spring may have been located in the heavily terraced area now called Susurmarca (An. 5:8).

A well-known area called Susurmarca near Callachaca and Yacanora contains an elaborate set of Inca terraces and a complex irrigation system (Photo 6.22).[33] The spring that feeds this irrigation system, located just above the Susurmarca terraces, is a good candidate for An. 5:8.[34]

The shrine following Susurmarca is described as a set of stones on a hill called Rondoya (An. 5:9).[35] While survey work in the Antisuyu area of Cusco found no hill with this name, a hill was found that is called Runtuyan. Its location is problematic, however, since it is situated some two kilometers due east of the Susurmarca area, well off the apparent projection of this ceque and in the general area of An. 4:5.

The final shrine of this ceque, Poma Urco (An. 5:10), is simply described as a stone. Although this place-name is recorded several times in land documents (BN/Virreynato, Real Audiencia, Asuntos Judiciales, B701; AHD/Corregimiento, Causas Ordinarias: Leg. 28, c. 20, 1700–1711), its exact position remains unknown (Maps 6.2 and 6.3).

The Sixth Ceque of Antisuyu

The *Relación de las huacas* indicates that seven huacas defined the course of the sixth ceque of Antisuyu. Even though the course of this ceque has been researched by both Niles (1987) and Zuidema (1990b), it is still not well understood.

The first shrine, Auriauca (An. 6:1), is listed as a portico or arbor next to the Temple of the Sun.[36] The second shrine, Comovilca (An. 6:2), was a curved rock near Callachaca, and the third, Chuquicancha (An. 6:3), is presented as a house of the Sun on a well-known hill. Comovilca is mentioned in a document dating to 1687, and there is an 1897 reference to a rocky place (*peñascal*) called Kumu-ccacca west of Hacienda Pumamarca that may be related to this shrine (PA/Chávez Ballón: Document 1). A number of Spanish chronicles mention Chuquicancha (An. 6:3). For example, Cobo (1990:142 [1653:Bk. 13, Ch. 28]) specifically states that large celebrations were held at Chuquicancha during the June festival of Inti Raymi.[37] Molina (1989:123–125 [ca. 1575]) describes elaborate activities that occurred there during the Ccapacocha festival and indicates that Chuquicancha was up the slope from San Sebastián:

. . . and thus they buried the bodies together with all the other sacrifices, in a place called Chuquicancha, which is a small hill above San Sebastián, about half a league from the town, as was said before. And then the priests of the Sun, in the same order, would receive those who were dedicated to the Sun, and at the same place they made the sacrifice to the Sun, . . .

And likewise, on behalf of Thunder, which was called Chuqueylla, the priests in charge of its image, which has been described earlier, would receive the children and other sacrifices dedicated to it, and bury them in the same order in the same place, called Chuquicancha; and in the same order in the same place, they buried the sacrifices for the Moon, to whom they prayed for the health and prosperity of the Inca, and that he should always defeat his enemies.[38]

Niles (1987:59–92) suggests that an area uphill from San Sebastián called Rumi Huasi, which contains two clusters of archaeological remains, held An. 6:2 (Comovilca) and An. 6:3 (Chuquicancha). The ruins of Rumi Huasi Bajo include four well-preserved structures, a large sculpted outcrop, and several high terraces (Niles 1987:61). The sculpted outcrop is of special interest because it has a series of unusual niches ringing its semicircular base, and a nine-meter-long passageway has been carved through it (Photo 6.23). Several hundred meters uphill from this site is a second outcrop and another set of elaborate Inca structures called Rumi Huasi Alto (Photo 6.24). Two large Inca buildings stand on the summit of the outcrop, and a series of smaller buildings flank its sides (Niles 1987:86–91). A carved rock and several small structures can also be found along the hill slope between these two Inca complexes. Niles (1987:192–202) proposes that the stone of Comovilca (An. 6:2) may have been this small carved rock. Since the Inca structures at Rumi Huasi Bajo are built on a large semicircular outcrop, a feature that has been enhanced by a series of niches and a carved tunnel, it should be noted that this site is also a strong possibility for An. 6:2, which is described by Cobo as a curved stone. Niles (1987:192–202) also propounds that the so-called House of the Sun, Chuquicancha (An. 6:3), is represented by Rumi Huasi Alto.

Alternatively, Sherbondy (1982:47, 184 n. 50) and Zuidema (1990b:631, 635) suggest that An. 6:2 and An. 6:3 may have been in an area called Cusicallanca, a hundred meters

Photo 6.23. A nine-meter-long passageway has been carved through a stone outcrop at Rumi Huasi Bajo. This site may be Comovilca (An. 6:2).

Photo 6.24. Rumi Huasi Alto may represent Chuquicancha (An. 6:3).

Photo 6.25. This hacienda four kilometers northeast of San Sebastián is built on top of an Inca complex called Pumamarca (An. 6:6). Several fine Inca doorways and walls can still be seen at the site.

east of the Rumi Huasi area, across a small ravine. Within this heavily terraced area there is an isolated outcrop with a single "seat" carved into it that could represent Comovilca. Furthermore, as noted by Sherbondy and Zuidema, there are the remains of several large Inca structures in the Cusicallanca area west of a small reservoir called Cochapata that may mark the location of Chuquicancha. Additional field and archival research is needed to further evaluate these possible shrine locations in this archaeologically complex region.

A stone on a small hill called Sanotuiron (An. 6:4) was the fourth shrine on this ceque. Cobo notes that offerings were made to this huaca for the health of the crown prince, and that a special offering was made the year that his ears were pierced. Despite the importance of this huaca, it remains to be found, although a place called Sanoctuyro is listed as being within the lands of Pumamarca in 1570 (Guevara Gil 1993:389).

The fifth, Viracochapuquiu (An. 6:5), and sixth, Pomamarca (An. 6:6), shrines of the ceque are described respectively as a fountain and a house on a flat place on the way to Chita. Cobo also notes that the mummy of Pachacuti Inca Yupanqui's wife was kept in Pumamarca. Santa Cruz Pachacuti Yamqui Salcamayhua (1950:239 [1613]) states that

after the Chanca War, Viracocha Inca remained at Pumamarca until his death. Local landownership documents dating to 1570 also suggest that Pumamarca was owned by Viracocha Inca (Guevara Gil 1993:385). An intricate complex of Inca structures called Pumamarca is located approximately four kilometers northeast of San Sebastián (Photo 6.25). A spring (Photo 6.26) called Pilcopuquiu emerges from a cave behind the buildings of Pumamarca, and a complicated canal system funnels water from this spring across the site. Pilcopuquiu is listed, along with Viracocha Cancha (i.e., the ruins of Pumamarca), in a 1570 document (Guevara Gil 1993:389). It has been suggested (Zuidema 1977b, 1983c; Niles 1987) that the ruins of Pumamarca and its adjacent spring represent Pomamarca (An. 6:6) and Viracochapuquiu (An. 6:5), respectively. While the identification of Pomamarca is certain, that of the spring is less so. If the spring of Pilcopuquiu does represent the spring of Viracochapuquiu (An. 6:5), then it should be noted that the order of these two shrines in the *Relación de las huacas* is incorrect, because the buildings of Pumamarca are closer to Cusco than its spring. However, field researchers found a small spring called Virapuquiu at the base of a large rock, between Susurmarca and Pumamarca, that is also listed in the same 1570 document that mentions Pilcopuquio and

Photo 6.26. The large spring of Pilcopuquiu, located behind the ruins of Pumamarca, is believed by some researchers to represent Viracochapuquiu (An. 6:5).

Viracochacancha (Guevara Gil 1993:389). Since the name of this spring resembles that of Viracochapuquiu, and it is located closer to Cusco than Pomamarca (An. 6:6), this spring represents an alternative candidate for An. 6:5.

The final shrine of this ceque, Curauacaja (An. 6:7), is presented as a knoll on the way to Chita where the city is lost from sight. There are three prominent passes from the Cusco Valley to Chita. The first is Quesere Qasa, formerly known as Macaycalla (An 2:10). It leads to Chita Pampa via the communities of Corimarca and Quesere. The second pass, Yuncaycalla (An. 3:9), leads to the community of Corao on Chita Pampa. The third pass from the Cusco Valley to Chita, like the second, leads to Corao. This pass, a likely location for the huaca that Cobo refers to as Curauacaja (An. 6:7), is immediately east of Pumamarca (Maps 6.2 and 6.3).

The Seventh Ceque of Antisuyu

The seventh ceque of Antisuyu was called Yacanora, the name of a town north of San Sebastián and of an ethnic group. The *Relación de las huacas* registers seven huacas along the course of An. 7; tentative locations can be suggested for most of these shrines.[39]

The first huaca, Ayllipampa (An. 7:1), was a flat area in the field of Alonso de Mesa. An extensive plain southeast of the Cusco suburb of Santa Mónica still retains this name.[40] The following shrine, Guamantanta (An. 7:2), is listed as a small spring next to the field of Ayllipampa. Several hundred meters west of Ayllipampa is a well-known spring called Guamantiana, which most certainly represents An. 7:2.[41]

The third shrine of this ceque, Pacaypuquiu (An. 7:3), is on the outskirts of San Sebastián behind the Colegio Delago Ttito Quispe, along the Cachimayo.[42] Cobo writes that Colcapampa (An. 7:4), the fourth shrine on this ceque, was

Photo 6.27. Near the plaza of San Sebastián, formerly called Colcapampa (An. 7:4), was an important stone idol.

a large plaza where the parish church of the Martyrs was constructed, and at one end of the plaza was a stone that was an important idol.[43] Colcapampa is also mentioned by Sarmiento de Gamboa (1906:30 [1572:Ch. 13]), who spells it Colcabamba, and by Cabello de Balboa (1951:269 [1586: Pt. 3, Ch. 10]), who writes Cullca Bomba. The most intriguing, although somewhat confusing, description of the huaca of Colcapampa is provided by Santa Cruz Pachacuti Yamqui Salcamayhua (1951:214–215 [1613]).[44] A reading of his text suggests that the stone idol mentioned by Cobo was thought to be a brother and a sister of Manco Capac who were transformed into stone as these mythical Incas descended from the mountain of Huanacauri and made their way toward Cusco. Cobo indicates that the plaza of Colcapampa, and its adjacent idol, were located where the church of the Martyrs was later constructed. Since this

parish church is also known as San Sebastián, it can be concluded that An. 7:4 was on or near the central plaza of this community (Photo 6.27).[45]

The fifth huaca, Cuillorpuquiu (An. 7:5), is described as a spring further down from Colcapampa. Archival information dating to 1690 indicates that Coyllorpuquio was beside the royal road of San Sebastián (AHD/Corregimiento, Pedimentos: Leg. 82, 1600–1669) and that the name was in use as late as 1757 (AHD/Corregimiento, Pedimentos: Leg. 85, 1753–1765). The urban growth between San Sebastián and San Jerónimo has destroyed this shrine.

The sixth huaca, Unugualpa (An. 7:6), a stone that resembled a figure, has not been identified. Cobo states that An. 7 terminated at Cucacache (An. 7:7 [Salt Pans]), a spring that contained small salt pans. There were two areas of salt pans in the Cusco Valley. The largest was Las Salinas, north-

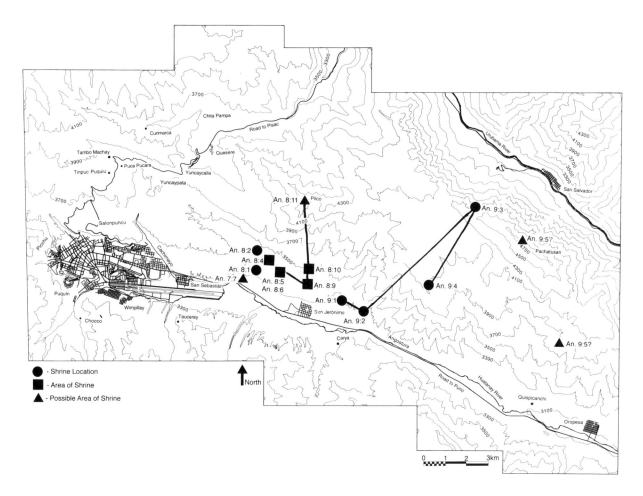

Map 6.4. Suggested courses of Antisuyu ceques An. 7, An. 8, and An. 9. Ground documentation of the shrines does not support the suggestion that the last three ceques of Antisuyu formed a single straight line.

Photo 6.28. The spring of Sacasguaylla (An. 8:1).

west of San Sebastián (see An. 5:2), and the second, smaller area was near the Hacienda Santutis, east of San Sebastián. The final huaca of An. 7 may have been near this second area (Maps 6.2 and 6.4).

The Eighth Ceque of Antisuyu

The penultimate ceque of Antisuyu was called Ayarmaca, a name derived from a large ethnic group that inhabited much of the area north and east of Cusco (Rostworowski 1970). Our field research located a number of shrines along An. 8, and its course is depicted as running along the base of Picol Mountain and then climbing to its summit. This proposed course for An. 8 is markedly different from those suggested in other studies (Zuidema 1977a, 1982b, 1982c, 1986b, 1990b; Sherbondy 1982; Aveni 1990b:59).

A spring called Sacas[gu]ayllapuquiu (An. 8:1) is listed as the first of eleven shrines on this ceque.[46] This spring is near the hacienda of the same name and is marked by the emergence of a host of small outlets (Photo 6.28). The second and third shrines are described as a spring named Pirquipuquiu (An. 8:2) and some nearby stones called Cuipanamaro (An. 8:3). Pirquipuquiu is a well-known spring that emerges north of Sacasguaylla at the base of

Picol Mountain, and there is a dry, steep riverbed called Collpayo above it that may represent Cuipanamaro.[47]

The succeeding huaca was a spring named Auacospuquiu (An 8:4). There is a set of terraces east of Pirquipuquiu called Aguacuyoc. Given the name and location of these terraces, it seems reasonable to suggest that one of the small springs that feeds them represents An. 8:4.[48]

The fifth and sixth shrines of An. 8, Sabaraura (An. 8:5) and Urcopuquiu (An. 8:6), are said to be near the town of Larapa. This community is known in the chronicles as the place where Polo de Ondegardo found the mummified body of Inca Roca, the sixth ruler of Cusco (Sarmiento de Gamboa (1906:50 [1572:Ch. 19]). It is northeast of Sacasguaylla near the base of Picol Mountain.[49] An. 8:5 (Sabaraura) is described as three stones in that town. One of the major ayllus of Larapa is called Raurau, and there is an area associated with this group to the east of the community that may be related to An. 8:5.[50]

An. 8:6 (Urcopuquiu) is characterized as a square stone in a corner of Larapa. The river of Urcopuquiu, one of the largest of this area, begins near the summit of Picol Mountain and passes near the community of Larapa before entering the Huatanay River. A document dated 1616 notes that there was a set of worked-stone walls near the river of

Photo 6.29. Huayna Picol is now extensively looted, but it may once have held Inca offerings related to An. 8:11.

Urcopuquiu (AGN/Archivo Agrario, Miscelánea: Hacienda Larapa, Venta de 27/1/1616, f. 413). It seems logical to suggest that An. 8:5 was located somewhere along the course of this river.

The position of Pilco Puquio (An. 8:7), described as being near an unidentified town called Corcora, and that of Cuipan (An. 8:8), said to be a group of stones on a hill, have not been found. A spring named Chora (An. 8:9), near a place called Andamacha[y], is listed as the ninth shrine of this ceque. The location of Andamachay is important because Cobo also refers to it in his discussion of An. 9:1.[51] Andamachay was one of several large ayllus resettled into San Jerónimo soon after the Spanish conquest, and there is a large terraced area associated with Andamachay Ayllu just north of San Jerónimo, with an adjacent set of Inca remains currently called Racay-Racayniyoc.[52] A map (AMAC/Fundo file for Lirca y Andamachay) based on 1662, 1722, and 1724 land titles specifically labels Racay-Racayniyoc as "the old town of Andamachay." This being the case, then the spring of Chora (An. 8:9) was most likely situated somewhere in the general area of these ruins.

The tenth shrine, Picas (An. 8:10), is described as a small stone, a protector against hail, on the hill above Larapa. A review of land documents reveals that Picas continued to be used as a boundary marker during the seventeenth and eighteenth centuries (AMAC/Fundo file for Larapa; AMAC/

Community file for San Jerónimo),[53] and surveyors were informed that a rock called Picas is situated in the ravine that passes along the eastern side of Racay-Racayniyoc.

The last shrine of this ceque, Pilcourco (An. 8:11), is listed as a stone on a large hill near Larapa. The shrine must have been of considerable importance, since Cobo also notes that young girls were sacrificed to it when there was a new Inca. Directly behind the community of Larapa is the mountain of Picol. This mountain, with its twin peaks of Huayna Picol ([Young Picol] 4451 masl) and Machu Picol ([Old Picol] 4448 masl), is a dominant feature of the Cusco landscape (Photo 6.29). Its peaks may once have held Inca offerings, because they are now extensively looted.[54] Given the importance of this mountain to Cusco, its location behind Larapa, and the extensive evidence of looting at its summits, it is possible to suggest that one of its peaks once marked the terminus of An. 8 (Maps 6.2 and 6.4).

The Ninth Ceque of Antisuyu

The final ceque of Antisuyu, which contained five huacas, was the responsibility of the little-known ayllu called Cari. The ceque started east of San Jerónimo, some twelve kilometers from Cusco and the Temple of the Sun, at the spring of Lampapuquiu (An. 9:1).[55] Suramapuquiu (An. 9:2), the second shrine, is in the Surama Ravine on the northern slope of the Angostura, the narrow terminus of the Cusco Valley.[56] The third shrine, Corcorpuquiu (An. 9:3), is listed as a spring in the puna above the Angostura. There is still a well-known spring with this name on the San Salvador side of Pachatusan Mountain, high above the Angostura.

Churucana (An. 9:4), the fourth shrine, is mentioned as a group of stones on a hill down from Corcorpuquiu. There is a ridge called Churucana that descends from the Pachatusan puna into the Angostura.[57] The lower end of this ridge is marked by a small bluff that offers a clear view down the valley toward the city of Cusco, fourteen kilometers away. It appears from Zuidema's drawings that he (1982b, 1982c, 1990a) selects this bluff as An. 9:4. There is, however, an impressive 12 m × 28 m, two-terraced platform, with a staircase in the center of its northern side, at the summit of Churucana Ridge that provides an alternative candidate (Photo 6.30). The platform offers a magnificent overview of the Cusco Valley, and fragments of Inca pottery were found in the looters' pits that have disturbed its surface.

The last huaca of this ceque (An. 9:5), the final shrine of Antisuyu, is called Ataguanacauri. It is characterized as an ancient shrine composed of certain stones placed next to a hill. There are two possible locations for this huaca, although both are highly speculative. The first is the summit of a steep hill, currently called Cruz Moco, above the archaeological site of Tipón (also called Quispicanchi), which contains more then a dozen petroglyphs. The second possible location for Ataguanacauri is the summit of Pachatusan.[58] As the highest mountain immediately adjacent to the Cusco Valley, Pachatusan (4842 masl) is a major apu, and reconnaissance work found evidence of Inca offerings at its summit.[59] This suggestion is supported by the fact that the mountain of Pachatusan is also called Atas (Sallnow 1987: 129).[60] Additional research is needed to determine which of these two possible locations represents An 9:5 (Maps 6.2 and 6.4).

Summary and Discussion

Possible courses for the Antisuyu ceques are presented on Map 6.5. The first three ceques of this suyu projected from near the center of Cusco into the area between Tambomachay and the Yuncaycalla Pass. The next three ceques ran east of the Cachimayo, covering much of the region north of San Sebastián. The orientations of An. 7, An. 8, and An. 9,

Photo 6.30. A terraced platform at the summit of Churucana Ridge may mark the location of An. 9:4.

the last three ceques of this suyu, varied from the generally evenly spaced projections of the other ceques of this suyu. Both Zuidema (1982b, 1982c, 1990a) and Sherbondy (1982:89) have noted this unusual feature of Antisuyu and suggest that its last three ceques formed one continuous line.[61] Sherbondy writes:

> Ideally, all lines diverge from one central point, the Coricancha, but when one plots the ceques on a map of Cuzco using the locations of each huaca listed in the description of the Ceque System, we find that some ceques do not begin at Coricancha . . . , although they always go in the direction from Coricancha.
>
> There is one interesting case where this happens that we will consider, that of the last two ceques of Antisuyu (III 3b,c [An. 8 and An. 9]). The pattern of these ceques extends the preceding ceque (III 3a [An. 7]) farther east in roughly linear fashion of one line following on the other until the last one reaches beyond the limits of the Cuzco valley. Actually, the three ceques form one line. (Sherbondy 1982:86)

Zuidema (1983:252b) has further proposed that these three ceques form a line that correlates with the sunrise and sunset positions, as seen from central Cusco, on the zenith passage dates for the Cusco region (cf. Bauer and Dearborn 1995). The data collected during this project allow for a different interpretation of the projections of An. 7, An. 8, and An. 9. While Zuidema (1982b, 1982c, 1983, 1990a), Sherbondy

(1982), and I have each concluded that the last three ceques of Antisuyu begin progressively farther from Cusco, my alternative plotting of these ceques suggests that they did not form a continuous line.

The projections of An. 7, An. 8, and An. 9 are interesting because they appear to have been constrained by the narrow eastern end of the Cusco Valley. Each of these ceques began at a shrine that was progressively farther from Cusco. Ground documentation of the shrine locations and archival research indicate that the seventh ceque of Antisuyu started just outside the city and ended in the area of salt pans near Hacienda Santutis. The eighth ceque began near the termination of the seventh at the well-known spring of Sacasguayllapuquiu (An. 8:1). It is clear that this ceque then trav-

eled north to the springs of Pirquipuquiu (An. 8:2) and Auacospuquiu (An. 8:4), and then passed through or near the towns of Larapa and Andamachay (now called Racay-Racayniyoc). This course of An. 8 is very different from that proposed by Zuidema (1982b, 1982c, 1990a) and Sherbondy (1982), who have the ceque begin at Sacasguayllapuquiu (An. 8:1) and pass through the center of the modern community of San Jerónimo, for an unspecified reason. Similarly, these authors have An. 9 commence near San Jerónimo and then run straight down the valley. While data recovered during this project support the suggestion that the ninth ceque of Antisuyu began near San Jerónimo, they indicate that the course of An. 9 was far from straight.

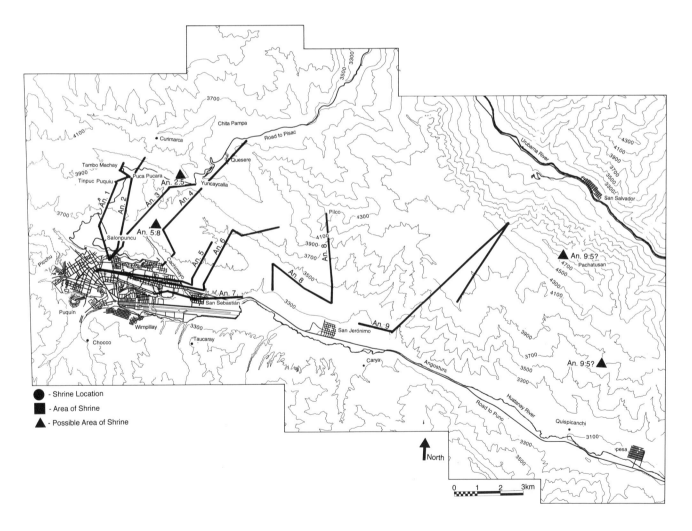

Map 6.5. Suggested courses of Antisuyu ceques An. 1–An. 9.

7

The Huacas and Ceques of Collasuyu

COLLASUYU represents the southeast quarter of the Cusco region, including the area south of the Huatanay River and east of the ridge of Anaguarque.[1] The *Relación de las huacas* notes that the area of Collasuyu contained at least eighty-five shrines that were organized along nine ceques. The system in Collasuyu included one of the most famous huacas of the Cusco region, the mountain shrine of Huanacauri. Although the location of Huanacauri has been known since the early 1900s (Aguilar 1913), and various other archaeological sites in Collasuyu have been studied, no previous work on the ceques of this region had been conducted before this project.

The First Ceque of Collasuyu

The huacas along the first ceque of Collasuyu were, according to Cobo, the concern of Aguini Ayllu. Because this ayllu is not mentioned by any other chronicler, its position in the Cusco social hierarchy is not known. Both Zuidema (1964:8) and Rowe (1985:53) suggest that Aguini Ayllu may be synonymous with Cuycussa Ayllu. Alternatively, it is possible that Aguini is a misspelling for Hahuanina (also spelled Aguanin, Aguayni, Ahuani, and Haguayni) Ayllu. If this is the case, then there may be some confusion about what kin group was responsible for the huacas on this ceque, because Hahuanina Ayllu is listed as the caretaker for Co. 2. In light of these uncertainties, I have classified Aguini as an unidentified ayllu until more documentation becomes available.

The first of the nine shrines of this ceque is described as one of the many Pururaucas (Co 1:1), or stone warriors, of the Chanca War. According to Cobo, this particular stone was near Mancio Serra de Leguizamo's house. In his description of the homes of prominent Spaniards in central Cusco, Garcilaso de la Vega (1966:427 [1609:Vol. 1, Bk. 7, Ch. 10]) indicates that Serra de Leguizamo's house was in the area of Amaru Cancha on the south side of the Plaza de

Armas where the church of the Compañía de Jesús was constructed (Hyslop 1990, Rowe 1991). According to the distribution of other shrines in the ceque system, this area of Cusco was in Chinchaysuyu, not Collasuyu.

Mudcapuquiu (Co 1:2), the second shrine, is reported to be a spring below the houses of Antón Ruiz Guevara.[2] Because the lower end of Tullumayu Street was formerly called Mudcapuquiu (Wiener 1880; Valcárcel Vizquerra 1935; Azevedo 1982), it can be assumed that Co 1:2 was situated somewhere along this street.[3]

A group of stones called Churucana (Co. 1:3) on top of a small round hill next to San Lázaro is listed as the next huaca.[4] A 1544 document also describes a place called Churucana as being next to San Lázaro (Guevara Gil 1993:361). The chapel of San Lázaro, built in 1538 to commemorate the Spaniards killed in the battle of Las Salinas (Garcilaso de la Vega 1966:857 [1609:Vol. 2, Bk. 2, Ch. 38]), is on the south side of the plaza of San Sebastián (Photo 7.1). A little more than two kilometers east of San Lázaro is a prominent hill on the valley floor called Churucana, which is still considered by some Cusco residents to be hallowed ground (Photo 7.2). The foundation of the Hacienda Santutis Grande house, situated at the base of this hill, is made of large Inca stone blocks, suggesting that an Inca structure, perhaps related to the shrine, once stood there.[5]

The fourth huaca of Co. 1, Caribamba (Co. 1:4), is presented as a flat area in the town of Cacra.[6] The location of Cacra is important to the study of the Cusco ceque system because it is mentioned in Cobo's discussions of Co. 1:4, Co. 2:6, Co. 2:7, Co. 4:6, Co. 5:8, and Co. 6:10, as well as in his description of where members of Ahuani (Hahuanina) Ayllu lived (Cobo 1979:117 [1653:Bk. 12, Ch. 6]). There are, however, no historical references to a community named Cacra outside of Cobo's work. Nevertheless, there is a town with a similar name, Cayra, at the east end of the Cusco Valley, in the area suggested by Cobo for Cacra, and there are numerous early colonial documents that mention this com-

Photo 7.1. The chapel of San Lázaro was built in 1538 to commemorate the Spaniards killed in the battle of Las Salinas. The chapel is mentioned in relation to Churucana (Co. 1:3).

Photo 7.2. The hill of Churucana (Co. 1:3) stands near Hacienda Santutis Grande. This is still considered a sacred place by some residents of Cusco.

munity.[7] For example, Cayra is referred to as both an encomienda and a *pueblo* with a population of 293 in Toledo's (1975:161 [1571]) *Tasa de la visita general . . .* of Peru. It is likely that Cobo's town of Cacra is a systematic error for Cayra. Because Cobo states that Caribamba (Co. 1:4) was in the town of Cacra, we can assume that this plain was near Cayra.

The huaca following Caribamba, Micaya Puquiu (Co. 1:5), is reported to be a spring on the slope of Huanacauri. There is a well-known spring named Micay Puquiu on the northeast slope of Huanacauri.[8] This large spring emerges at the base of a cliff and serves as a principal water source for the region (Photo 7.3). Given the large size and regional importance of Micay Puquiu, and its location on the slope of Huanacauri, it is a good candidate for Co. 1:5. The location of the spring is problematic, however, because it is well away from the general course of this ceque, close to the sug-

Photo 7.3. The spring of Micay Puquiu is a good candidate for both Micaya Puquiu (Co. 1:5) and Micaypuquiu (Co. 6:8).

gested direction of the sixth (Co. 6) or seventh (Co. 7) ceque of this suyu.

The sixth shrine, Atpitan (Co. 1:6), is listed as a group of stones in a ravine where Huanacauri is lost from sight. A myth fragment preserved in the *Relación de las huacas* indicates that the stones of Atpitan had formerly been the sons of Huanacauri. This seems to be a reference to the Pacariqtambo Origin Myth of the Inca, in which several brothers of Manco Capac were converted into stone during their journey to Cusco (Urbano 1981; Bauer 1991). Murúa (1946:51 [1590:Pt. 1, Ch. 2]) also refers to this myth, stating that the eldest brother of Manco Capac died at a place called Apitay, near Huanacauri. There is a small village named Acpita in a narrow, rocky ravine at the base of Huanacauri one and one-half kilometers south of Micay Puquiu. The similarity between the words "Acpita" and "Atpitan" has been considered by Rowe:

> The Classic Inca dialect permitted a *t* at the end of a syllable: at-pi-tan. There has been a sound change, however, and in the modern Cuzco dialect, syllable-final *t* became a spirant, usually spirant *c*. Thus, Acpita is just the form we should expect for a modern name derived from Atpitan (Rowe, pers. com. 1991).

In addition, a 1595 document describing lands of Sucso Ayllu indicates that a ravine called Atpian was in the same general area as the community currently called Acpita (AHD/Corregimiento, Causas Ordinarias: Leg. 26, c. 8, f. 53v, 1691–1692).[9] On the basis of this information, the ravine and community of Acpita represent good possibilities for the sixth shrine of Co. 1. Like Micaya Puquiu (Co. 1:5), the probable location of this huaca is problematic because it is located well away from the general course of this ceque.

The seventh huaca, a large stone on top of a hill next to the Angostura, was called Guamansaui (Co. 1:7). The Angostura is the Spanish name for the narrow east entrance to the Cusco Valley, an area traditionally known as Acoya Punco. This shrine appears to have been of some importance, because Cobo reports that miniature garments, silver, and gold were offered there for the strength of the Inca. Its exact location near the Angostura remains unknown.[10]

The final two shrines of Co. 1 were called Guayra and Mayu. Cobo writes that sacrifices were made at the huaca of Guayra (Co. 1:8 [Wind]), characterized as a ravine, when strong winds blew. He also notes that sacrifices were offered to the huaca Mayu (Co. 1:9 [River]), a river in the Angostura, because it flowed through the city of Cusco. The An-

Photo 7.4. The first ceque of Collasuyu ended in the Angostura at the Huatanay River.

gostura ravine is still venerated in August, when winds in the Cusco Valley are strongest, so it seems likely that Co. 1:8 was this same ravine. Similarly, the shrine called Mayu is in all likelihood the Huatanay River (Photo 7.4), which runs through the city of Cusco and the Angostura (Maps 7.1 and 7.2).

The Second Ceque of Collasuyu

The eight shrines of Co. 2 were the responsibility of Haguayni (Hahuanina) Ayllu, the kin group of Lloque Yupanqui, the third ruler of Cusco. The route of this relatively well understood ceque began with the huaca of Limapampa ([Limacpampa] Co. 2:1), a flat place where, according to Cobo, the Inca maize-harvest festival was held. Molina (1989:72 [ca. 1575]) indicates that Limacpampa was also important in the maize-sowing festival:

> . . . they [the common people] came to drink and dance at Aucaypacta, where the Spaniards now call Limacpampa, which is below Santo Domingo; and there in the morning, the priests of the Maker burnt a white llama and corn and coca and bird feathers the color of mullu (i.e., pink), which is a sea shell, as has been said, requesting the Maker to give a good year, . . .[11]

Garcilaso de la Vega also specifically mentions this small plaza in his description of Cusco:

> Further toward the south follows another large ward called Rimacpampa, "the talking square," for it was there that some of the decrees issued for the government of

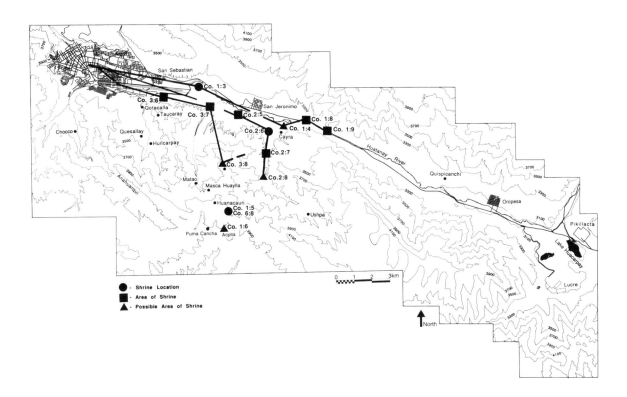

Map 7.1. Suggested courses of Collasuyu ceques Co. 1, Co. 2, and Co. 3.

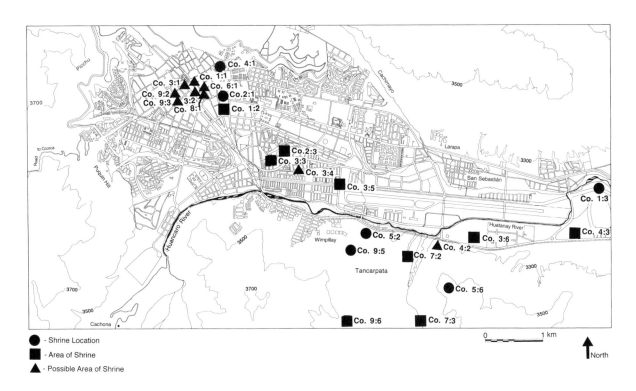

Map 7.2. Suggested locations of Collasuyu huacas in Cusco.

the republic were announced. They were proclaimed from time to time so that the inhabitants might hear them and present themselves to carry out whatever obligations they entailed. As the square was in this ward, its name was given to the ward: from the square the royal highway leads out to Collasuyu. (Garcilaso de la Vega 1966:420 [1609:Vol. 1, Bk. 7, Ch. 8])[12]

The well-known area of Limacpampa is east of the Temple of the Sun on the far bank of the Tullumayu (Photo 7.5).[13]

A small hill called Raquiancalla (Co. 2:2), where the idols of the four suyus were kept and where a large celebration was held, was somewhere near Limacpampa. The third shrine, Sausero (Co. 2:3), was a maize field that the royal Incas plowed (Bauer 1996). Information concerning the location of Sausero and the maize rituals held there is contained in a number of different chronicles. For example, Guaman Poma de Ayala stresses the importance that offerings and communal work, accompanied by song and dance, held during the planting ritual at Sausero:

During this month they begin to work. They plow and break the earth simply to plant maize. In this month the poor of this kingdom sacrifice to the idols and the huacas, whatever they can: *cues* [guinea pigs] and *mullu* [spondylus shells] and *zanco* [a pottage containing blood] and *chicha* [corn beer] and llamas. . . .

In this month, the Inca and everyone in the kingdom perform *haylle* [songs of triumph] and celebrations of labor, and drink during the *minga* [collective labor presentation to an authority] and eat and sing *haylli* and *aymaran* [songs of breaking the earth], each one with the

Photo 7.5. The plaza of Limacpampa (Co. 2:1). Large celebrations were held here by the Inca during the planting and harvest of maize.

haylli of his group. And they offer each other food and drink instead of payment.

And they start to sow the maize until the month of January, in accordance with the time and the movement of the sun and the condition of the earth. If it is *yunga* [warm Andean zone] later, if it is in highlands, early, as is convenient this month.[14]

Two of Guaman Poma de Ayala's (1980:224, 1050 [1615:250 (252), 1153 (1163)]) drawings illustrate the ruling Inca tilling a field along with three other men. Perhaps these figures depict the ritual breaking of the earth by the royal Inca and other nobles at Sausero.

Cobo also describes the maize-planting and -harvest rituals that took place at Sausero. Like Guaman Poma de Ayala, he stresses that a large number of sacrifices were made at Sausero before the maize planting could begin:

During the ninth month, called Yapaquis, one hundred chestnut sheep without any blemishes were burned with the ceremonies described above, and they had a festival called *guayara* in which they asked for a good and abundant year. Fifteen sheep were distributed for all of the *guacas* of the area surrounding Cuzco. These sheep were from the livestock of the Sun, and with this sacrifice the *chacara* [field] called Saucero was sown. This job of seeding was done with great solemnity because this *chacara* belonged to the Sun.[15] What was harvested from it was for the ordinary sacrifices made in addition to the ones described above. All during the time that the seeding was done, in the middle of the field there was a white sheep with its ears of gold, and with this sheep there were numerous Indians and *mamaconas* [holy women] of the Sun pouring out much *chicha* [corn beer] in the name of this sheep. Since they were finishing the sowing, a thousand *cuis* [guinea pigs] were brought by shares from all the provinces. Each province brought a designated amount, according to the distribution that was established. With great solemnity they slit the throats of the animals and burned them at this *chacara,* except a certain number of them that were distributed among the *guacas* and shrines of the city in the name of the Sun. This sacrifice was made to the Frost, the Wind, and the Sun, and to all things that seemed to them capable of making their sown fields grow or capable of harming them. The Tarpuntay priests fasted by not eating anything other than cooked maize and herbs without salt, and the only thing they drank was dark *chicha* which they called *concho.* They continued this fast until the maize grew up one finger above the ground. (Cobo 1990:143–144 [1653:Bk. 13, Ch. 28])[16]

Apparently the harvest at Sausero was ceremonially begun by men who had recently been initiated into adulthood. In addition, it seems that once the harvest was completed, the field was ritually plowed. Cobo writes:

> Those who had been knighted appeared at a certain *chacara* [field] named Sausero, which is located along the road to San Sebastian, to bring the maize that had been harvested. They carried it in small sacks, singing a song called *aravi*. On the first day, the said new knights, handsomely dressed, brought it alone. On the rest of the days, all of the people of Cuzco came to do the same. A little later, all of the lords and important people of Cuzco, accompanied by a large number of other people, went to the same chacara with their plows, and they plowed the field. After this was finished, they returned with great rejoicing to the main square, wearing the tunics that they had won in war. (Cobo 1990:140 [1653:Bk. 13, Ch. 27])[17]

Furthermore, information contained in Molina's chronicle indicates that the maize-planting and -harvest ceremonies took place in this particular field because it was believed to be the place where the legendary founders of Cusco, Manco Capac and Mama Huaco, first planted maize. The crops from the field were, according to Molina (1989:118 [ca. 1575]), specifically used to support the cult of Mama Huaco:

> They called the month of April Ayrihuay. In it they harvested the fields, and also brought in and stored the grain, which is what they called Aymoray. And those who had been knighted, would go to the field of Sausiro to bring in the corn that had been harvested there, which is below the arch where they say Mama Huaco, sister of Manco Capac, the first Inca, sowed the first maize. They cultivated that field every year for the mummy of Mama Huaco, producing from it the chicha necessary for the service of her mummy.[18]

The arch to which Molina refers in this quote is that of Arco Punco (also called Arco de la Plata). Although the arch has been destroyed, a street in Cusco east of Limacpampa still retains its name, and its location is indicated in Wiener's (1880) map of Cusco. The area "below" the arch corresponds to the sector of Cusco near the end of the old airport. Molina's description of the location of Sausero is supported by older citizens of Cusco who still remember the area by this name.[19] Furthermore, Agurto Calvo (1980), Sherbondy (1982:198–199), and Ardiles Nieves (1986) each suggest that Sausero was in this region.

The exact location of Co. 2:4, a field with a spring called Omatalispacha, is unknown. The fifth huaca is listed as a flat place called Oscollo (Co. 2:5), which belonged to Capitán Garcilaso de la Vega, the father of the famed chronicler. The owership of this area by Garcilaso de la Vega is confirmed in a 1559 document (Guevara Gil 1993:392). There is a broad plain on the south bank of the Huatanay River, between San Sebastián and San Jerónimo, called Oscollopampa, which most certainly represents this shrine (Photo 7.6).[20]

A set of stones called Tuino Urco (Co. 2:6) in a corner of the town of Cacra (Cayra) is said by Cobo to be the sixth shrine. Less than a kilometer west of the community of Cayra is a small, steep ridge that juts out into the Cusco Valley (Photo 7.7). The slopes of the ridge contain Inca, Killke, and pre-Inca pottery fragments, and looters' trenches have

Photo 7.6. The area of Oscollopampa (Co. 2:5) was once owned by Captain Garcilaso de la Vega, father of the famous chronicler.

Photo 7.7. The looted ridge of Tuino Urco (Co. 2:6).

all but destroyed its northern end. This ridge, still revered by many as a sacred place, is called Tuino Urco, and the looted area may mark the location of the huaca itself.[21]

Palpancay Puquiu (Co. 2:7), the next shrine on this ceque, is characterized as a spring on a hill near Cacra (Cayra). Approximately one kilometer south of Cayra is a small, well-cultivated plain called Palpancay Pampa.[22] There are three springs on the slopes adjacent to this pampa called Sipas, Mama Tunya, and Calis. While none of these springs presently carries the name of Palpancay Puquiu, it may be tentatively assumed that the region of Palpancay Pampa, and perhaps one of its springs, was associated with Co. 2:7 during the Inca period (Photo 7.8).

The identification of the last huaca of this ceque is tenuous. The shrine was known as Collocalla (Co. 2:8) and is listed as a ravine.[23] According to Cobo, there was a marker along a road near this ravine where offerings were made. A location called Ccollo Huaycco is mentioned in a 1595 document discussing landholdings in the southeastern end of the Cusco Valley (AMAC/Community File for Collana Chahuancuzco 1656, f. 98v), but this place-name is no longer used. If the road that Cobo refers to is the royal road of Cuntisuyu, then it is possible that the marker of Collocalla was located in one of the ravines crossed by the road as it approached the Angostura. However, another important trail, leading from the community of Cayra to a pass

near Huanacauri, has a narrow spit of land called Collollacta (Photo 7.9) along it, three kilometers up the valley from Palpancay Pampa, which also represents a possible location for the shrine (Maps 7.1 and 7.2).

The Third Ceque of Collasuyu

Research in the Cusco region has found possible locations for most of the nine huacas along the course of Co. 3. The first and second shrines, Tampucancha (Co. 3:1) and Pampasona (Co. 3:2), are described in the *Relación de las huacas* as being part of, or near, the house of Mancio Serra de Leguizamo. Co. 3:1 and Co. 3:2 appear to have been relatively close to Co. 1:1, because all three of these shrines are associated with the house of Serra de Leguizamo. As noted in the discussion of Co. 1:1, Garcilaso de la Vega (1966:427 [1609:Vol. 1, Bk. 7, Ch. 10]) suggests that Serra de Leguizamo's house stood somewhere south of the Plaza de Armas, in what seems to be Chinchaysuyu rather than in Collasuyu. The succeeding huaca (Co. 3:3) was a spring called Pirpoyopacha (Lirpuypacha).[24] The Hacienda Lirpuy and its adjacent spring of the same name once stood in the area now called El Progreso, west of Sausero (Agurto Calvo 1980; Sherbondy 1982). Sherbondy (1982:50) reports that the spring of Lirpuy "continued to be a religious site of importance in the colonial period because of a miraculous ap-

Photo 7.8. Palpancay Puquiu (Co. 2:7) was most certainly near Palpancay Pampa.

Photo 7.9. The ridge of Collollacta is a possible location for Collocalla (Co.2:8).

pearance of a painting of the Virgin on a wall there in the seventeenth century."

The fourth huaca, Co. 3:4, is characterized as a field called Guanipata (Huanaypata). This field is mentioned several times in Sarmiento de Gamboa's account of Manco Capac's conquest of the Cusco Valley. For example, Sarmiento de Gamboa (1906:38 [1572:Bk. 13]) describes Huanaypata as a fertile area near Cusco where Manco Capac's golden staff first sank into the ground:

> After this, they stayed in Matagua for two years, intending to cross on the upper valley above in search of good fertile land. Mama Guaca, who was very strong and dexterous, took two staffs of gold and hurled them towards the north. One landed about the length of two arquebus shots away in a fallow field called Colcabamba, but it did not pitch itself into the ground because the soil was shallow and not terraced; that is how they knew the land was not fertile. And the other reached further, near Cuzco, and planted itself in the place called Guanaypata, where they knew the land was fertile. Others say that this test was made by Manco Capac with the golden staff he carried with him, and thus they knew the fertility of the land, when he planted it in one go, into the land called Huanay Pata, two arquebus shots from Cuzco, ...[25]

Sarmiento de Gamboa (1906:39 [1572:Bk. 13]) indicates that the area of Huanaypata was near the Arco de la Plata (or Arco Punco). Combining this information with that provided in the *Relación de las huacas* (i.e., Huanaypata was "further down" from Lirpuypacha), it may be suggested that Co. 3:4 was established somewhere within the eastern sector of El Progreso.[26]

A field called Anaypampa (Añaypampa, Co. 3:5), said to have belonged to Mama Ocllo, the principal wife of Huayna Capac, was the fifth huaca of this ceque. A large expanse of flat land where the Cusco suburbs of Ttio and Kennedy intersect with the west end of the airport is still called Añaypampa.[27] The area of the sixth huaca, Suriguaylla (Co. 3:6), is also known. Suriguaylla is characterized by Cobo as a spring in a flat place that shares this name. Garcilaso de la Vega (1966:261 [1609:Vol. 1, Bk. 5, Ch. 10]) mentions this field in his chronicle as being about a league south of Cusco.[28] The ruins of the Hacienda Suriguaylla, and several springs, may be found beside Huatanay River, about two kilometers east of the airport.[29]

The next two huacas are called Sinopampa (Sañupampa, Co. 3:7) and Sanopuquiu (Sañupuquiu, Co. 3:8).[30] Zuidema (1979:239) suggests that Sañu was the preconquest name for

San Sebastián, and he speculates that the huacas of Sañupampa and Sañupuquiu were located near this community. Multiple early references to Sañupampa are contained within the land titles of Hacienda Santutis (Guevara Gil 1993:340, 364, 356), and they indicate that it was located east of the hill of Churucana (Co. 1:3) more than two kilometers from San Sebastián. Approximately one kilometer east of Churucana, on the south side of the Huatanay River, is a large plain called Pillao, which may be the site of Co. 3:7. There is a spring called Sañupuquiu above this plain in the community of Quicas, which may represent Co. 3:8.

The concluding shrine of this ceque, Llulpacturo (Co. 3:9), is characterized as a small hill opposite the Angostura dedicated to Viracocha, the Creator god of the Inca. Many small hills near the entrance to the Angostura contain archaeological remains and show evidence of looting. Furthermore, there is a platform on the slope of the Angostura, and farther above this, a small set of Inca terraces and structures. However, none of these sites retains the name Llulpacturo. Thus, it can only be suggested that Co. 3 terminated near the east end of the Cusco Valley somewhere near the Angostura (Maps 7.1 and 7.2).

The Fourth Ceque of Collasuyu

The fourth ceque of Collasuyu was the responsibility of Apu Mayta, the kin group of Capac Yupanqui, the fifth ruler of Cusco. Pomapacha (Co. 4:1), a spring where the Incas bathed, is presented as the first of its ten huacas. Sherbondy (1982:192) suggests an approximate location for this shrine, a street with the same name as the huaca, beside the market of San Blas. This possible location of Co. 4:1, north of Limacpampa and east of the Plaza de Armas, is problematic because it places Pomapacha in Antisuyu, far from the initial shrines of the other Collasuyu ceques.

The following two huacas were on agricultural property belonging to Diego Maldonado. The second shrine, Taucaray (Co. 4:2), is described as a tomb in a field of Maldonado's where the Inca believed that the dead assembled at a certain time. A well-known hill called Taucaray lies south of the Cusco airport, and it seems logical to assume that Co. 4:2 was near it.[31] At the base of Taucaray Hill are the remains of Hacienda Quispiquilla (Photo 7.10), which was once owned by Diego Maldonado and was inherited by his grandson (AHD/Cabildo: Leg. 1, 1569–1605).[32] There are two large springs close to the hacienda, either of which

Photo 7.10. Hacienda Quispiquilla is in the foreground of this photograph. Co. 4:3 was somewhere near this building.

Photo 7.11. The hills of Huchuy Ayavillay and Hatun Ayavillay, with Cayra in foreground. Two shrines, Co. 4:5 and Co. 4:6, both called Ayavillay, were near these hills.

could represent Co. 4:3, described by Cobo as the spring of Quispiquilla.[33]

The position of the fourth huaca on this line, five stones referred to as Cuipan (Co. 4:4), remains to be identified.[34] According to Cobo, Co. 4:5 and Co. 4:6 shared the same name of Ayavillay. The fifth huaca was a tomb where the lords of Ayavillay Ayllu were buried, and the sixth was certain stones on a hill opposite Carca (Cayra). Ayavillay Ayllu is mentioned by Sarmiento de Gamboa (1906:57 [1572:Bk. 24]) in his discussion of the wives and sons of the eighth ruler of Cusco, Viracocha Inca:

> And from another beautiful Indian called Cori Chulpa, of the Ayavilla nation of the Cusco Valley, he had two male children, one called Inca Urcon and the other Inca Socso.[35]

The name of Viracocha Inca's wife, Cori Chulpa, may be glossed as "Golden Burial Tower," and the names of the hills behind Cayra—Ayavillay—may be glossed as "to communicate with the dead," or "the sacred dead." These names are intriguing because they hint that an association existed between Viracocha Inca, his wife, the Ayavillay ethnic group, tombs, and the hills behind Cayra. The location of the first huaca called Ayavillay (Co. 4:5) may be marked by a series of rectangular structures that appear to be the remains of burial towers (or *chulpas*) east of the community of Cayra on the hill of Huchuy Ayavillay (Photo 7.11). The sixth shrine of Co. 4, the second shrine called Ayavillay, may have been on the hill behind the burial towers, which is called Hatun Ayavillay.[36]

The *Relación de las huacas* lists Raurao Quiran (Co. 4:7), a large hill worshipped because of its size, and Guancarcalla (Co. 4:8), a gatewaylike ravine next to the hill, as the seventh and eighth shrines of Co. 4. One of the largest mountains in the Cusco area, Cori Huayrachina (4188 masl), is located directly behind the hills of Ayavillay. On its summit is a circular platform measuring approximately twenty meters in diameter and one meter high (Photo 7.12). Fragments of Inca pottery were recovered on the surface of the platform, which is riddled with looters' pits. In addition, the major trail of the region passes between two unusual sets of stepped Inca platforms or terraces, several hundred yards from its summit. These structures are extensively looted, but could be said to define a gateway. Their locations, on either side of the trail, suggest that these structures mark the location of Co. 4:8, while the summit of Cori Huayrachina, with its circular stone platform, may be Co. 4:7.

The ninth huaca, Sinayba (Co. 4:9), is described as a large hill at the far end of Quispicanche. A possible location for Co. 4:9 is a high mountain peak called Sayhua across the valley from Quispicanche (Photo 7.13). The final shrine of this ceque, Sumeurco (Co. 4:10), described as a hill located near Sinayba (Co. 4:9), has not been identified (Maps 7.1 and 7.3).[37]

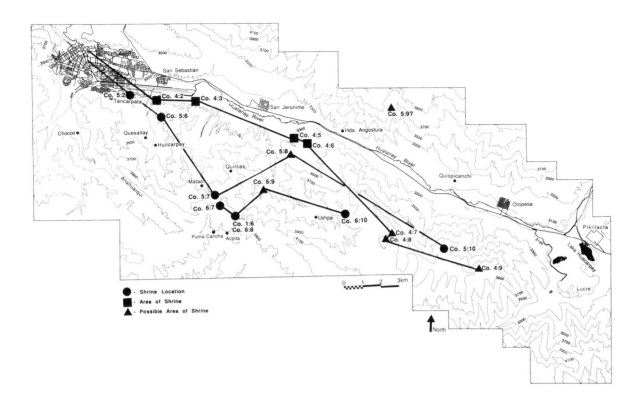

Map 7.3. Suggested courses of Collasuyu ceques Co. 4, Co. 5, and Co. 6.

Photo 7.12. A circular platform on the summit of Cori Huayrachina may mark Raurao Quiran (Co. 4:7).

Photo 7.13. The mountain of Sayhua may be Sinayba (Co. 4:9).

The Fifth Ceque of Collasuyu

According to Cobo, the first of the ten huacas on Co. 5, Catonge [Cluster], was a stone near Juan Sona's house. Neither the location of this house nor that of the shrine is known. Membilla Puquiu (Co. 5:2), the second shrine, is described as the spring of the inhabitants of Membilla. Membilla is the name once used by the Spaniards for the community now called Wimpillay. It is best known in the chronicles as the village where Polo de Ondegardo discovered the mummies of the Inca rulers of Hurin Cusco, including Sinchi Roca, Lloque Yupanqui, Mayta Capac, and Capac Yupanqui. A spring near the former center of the community is a good possibility for Co. 5:2 (Photo 7.14).[38]

The third, fourth, and fifth shrines on this ceque—Quintiamaro (Co. 5:3), Cicacalla (Co. 5:4), and Ancasamaro (Co. 5:5)[39]—are characterized as groups of stones in or near the town of Quijalla (also spelled Quicalla, Quiçala, and Quisalla). While the locations of these shrines are not known, there are two possibilities for the town of Quijalla. The location of Quijalla is of particular importance because it is used as a reference point in the *Relación de las huacas* for a number of shrines, including Co. 5:6, Co. 6:4, Co. 6:5, Co. 6:6, and Co. 7:2, as well as Co. 5:3, Co. 5:4, and Co. 5:5. Rowe (1980:11–12) suggests that the archaeological site of Qotakalli, across the Huatanay River from the Cusco airport, can be associated with the village of Quijalla:

Photo 7.14. The spring of Wimpillay is located upslope from this building. It is a good possibility for Membilla Puquiu (Co. 5:2).

The archaeological site corresponding to Quisalla is the one now called Qotakalli (Cz6–37) in the jurisdiction of San Sebastián. The identification is based partly on indications of location implicit in the organization of the list, and partly on the statement that the hill still called Taucaray ("Tocacaray" in Cobo) faced "Quijalla" (Co-5:6). The equivalence becomes even more convincing when one notes that one of the Pururaucas "near the town of Quicalla" was named Cotacalla (Co-7:2). (Rowe 1980:11)

Our survey work in the Cusco Valley suggests another possibility for the ancient community of Quijalla: the village of Quesallay, one and one-half kilometers south of Qotacalla.[40] Inca pottery was found in this village, indicating that it, like the ruins of Qotakalli, was occupied during the Inca period, and the orthographic similarities between the names of Quijalla and Quesallay suggest that it may be related to the town described by Cobo as containing a number of huacas. Because the ruins of Qotakalli stand on the eastern end of a large plain currently called Tancarpata, and the village of Quesallay is on its southern edge, it seems reasonable to assume that the third, fourth, and fifth shrines of Co. 5 were on or near this plain.[41]

The fieldwork in the Cusco region recovered more definitive information on the whereabouts of the last five shrines of Co. 5 than of the first five. Tocacaray (Taucaray, Co. 5:6), a hill facing the town of Quijalla, may be identified as the prominent hill called Taucaray north of Quesallay and east of Qotakalli (Photo 7.15).[42] The seventh huaca, Mascaguaylla (Co. 5:7), a spring on the road to Huanacauri, is in all likelihood a spring at the base of Huanacauri in a small village called Mascaguaylla (Photo 7.16).[43] The eighth shrine was named Intipampa (Co. 5:8) and is said to be near Cacra. Two separate documents dating to 1595 provide insights into the location of this shrine. The first mentions the ravine of Intipampa in the region of Cayra (AMAC/Community File for Collana Chahuancuzco: 1656, f. 100), while the second notes the presence of "terraced lands of the sun" in the adjacent Palpancay area (AHD/Corregimiento, Causas Ordinarias: Leg. 26, c. 8, f. 42, 1691–1692). A large plain with an adjacent set of elaborate stone terraces, currently called Intipata (Sun Terrace), less than a kilometer from the village of Cayra, above the Palpancay region, is most certainly this huaca (Photo 7.17).[44]

The penultimate shrine, Co. 5:9, is problematic. Cobo suggests that the huaca following Intipampa was called Rondao, a flat place facing Cacra next to the royal road of

Photo 7.16. The village of Mascaguaylla (Co. 5:7) with Huanacauri (Co. 6:7) in background.

Photo 7.15. The hill of Taucaray still contains remains of Inca buildings halfway up its slope. The shrine of Co. 4:2, where the Inca believed the dead assembled once a year, may have been near this hill, and the shrine of Co. 5:6 was most likely on its summit.

Photo 7.17. The plain of Intipata (Co. 5:8) with the hill of Hatun Ayavillay (Co. 4:6) in the background.

Collasuyu. When surveyors inquired about an area called Rondao, they were repeatedly referred to a small community called Rondobamba, more than five kilometers from Cayra, above the royal road of Collasuyu, in an area traditionally associated with Antisuyu.[45] Because *bamba* may be translated as "flat area," there is a similarity between the name of this community and the name and description of Co. 5:9. The problem is that Rondobamba is a considerable distance from Cayra and well off the general course of this ceque.

The final huaca on this ceque, Omotourco (Co. 5:10), is characterized as a set of stones on a small hill in the puna or opposite the village of Quispicanche. Molina (1989:68 [ca. 1575]) also mentions this mountain, calling it Omoto Yanacauri, in his description of the annual Inca pilgrimage to Vilcanota (Zuidema 1982a). Interviews with the inhabitants of Quispicanche and survey work in the puna region south of this community found that the slope of one of the highest mountain peaks in the region is called Motourco, which seems a likely candidate for Co. 5:10. (Maps 7.1 and 7.3)[46]

The Sixth Ceque of Collasuyu

The sixth ceque of Collasuyu is said to have contained ten shrines. The location of the first huaca, Tampucancha (Co. 6:1), like those of the initial shrines of Co. 1 and Co. 3, is described as near Serra de Leguizamo's house.[47] Following information provided by Garcilaso de la Vega (1966:427 [1609: Vol. 1, Bk. 7, Ch. 10]), it is believed that this house was situated south of the Plaza de Armas in an area thought to be in Chinchaysuyu. The second shrine, Mamacolca (Co. 6:2), is reported to be in the community of Membilla; however, its exact location is not known. The third huaca, Acoyguaci (Co. 6:3), was said to be a house in Membilla in which the body of Cinchi Roca, the second Inca, was kept. Its location is also not known. Similarly, fieldwork south of Cusco yielded no additional information on the locations of Co. 6:4 (Quirarcoma), Co. 6:5 (Viracochacancha), or Co. 6:6 (Cuipan). It can only be suggested, based on the information provided in the *Relación de las huacas,* that these three shrines were on the large plain of Tancarpata, which is delineated by Wimpillay, Qotakalli, and Quesallay.

The well-known shrine of Huanacauri (Co. 6:7) was the seventh huaca of this ceque (Photo 7.18). Its location on a high ridge some eleven kilometers from the imperial capital and its pivotal role in numerous Inca ceremonies are described in several chronicles. However, the most detailed description of Huanacauri is provided in the text of the *Relación de las huacas.* This is also the longest description of a huaca provided in the ceque system document and is well worth quoting:

> The seventh was named Huanacauri; it was among the most important shrines of the whole kingdom, the oldest which the Incas had after the window [cave] of Pacaritampu, and where the most sacrifices were made. This is a hill which is about two and a half leagues distant from Cuzco by this Road of Collasuyu we are following. On it they say that one of the brothers of the first Inca turned to stone, for reasons which they give. They had the said stone hidden. It was of moderate size, without [representational] shape, and somewhat tapering. It was on top of the said hill until the coming of the Spanish and they [i.e., the Incas] held many festivals for it. After the Spanish arrived, they [i.e., the Spaniards] removed a great quantity of gold and silver from this shrine but paid no attention to the idol, because it was, as I have said, a rough stone. This situation gave the Indians an opportunity to hide it until Paullu Inca, on his return from Chile, built a house for it next to his own. From that time on, the festival of Raymi was held there until the Christians found out about the stone and took it away from him. With it was found a quantity of offerings, small garments /f. 239/ for little idols, and an abundance of ear spools for the young men who are knighted. They very commonly took this idol to war with them, particularly when the king went in person. Guayna Capac took it to Quito, whence they brought it back again with his body. The Incas, indeed, were convinced that it had a large share in their victories. For the festival of the Raymi, they placed it on the hill of Huanacauri, dressed richly and adorned with many feathers. (Cobo 1980:47 [1653:Bk. 13, Ch. 15])[48]

Romualdo Aguilar (1913) identified a small set of Inca remains near the summit of Huanacauri that were studied in more detail by Rowe (1944). The actual huaca of Huanacauri, a moderately sized, somewhat tapering rock, was situated above these ruins. The mountain continues to be of religious importance for many residents of the valley, and offerings are still made to it (see Photo 3:10).

The succeeding huaca, Micaypuquiu (Co. 6:8), described as a spring on the road to Pacariqtambo, is problematic be-

Photo 7.18. Huanacauri (Co. 6:7) was one of the most important shrines in the Cusco Valley. The ruins of a small set of buildings stand near its summit.

cause its name is similar to that of Micayapuquiu (Co. 1:5). As noted in the discussion of Co. 1:5, there is a large spring called Micaypuquiu on the northern slope of Huanacauri, and the road from Cayra to Pacariqtambo passes near it (see Photo 7.3). This spring is one of the largest in the area, and a 1595 document places it within the territory of Sucso Panaca (AHD/Corregimiento, Causas Ordinarias: Leg. 26, c. 8, f. 55v, 1691–1692). It is unclear whether this spring represents Co. 1:5 or Co. 6:8, or both of these huacas.

The *Relación de las huacas* lists the ninth shrine of Co. 6 as a set of stones on a small hill called Quiquijana (Co. 6:9). Survey work between the mountain of Huanacauri and the community of Cayra found a small section of the Cayra River valley called Quiquijana—a name that dates to at least 1595 (AHD/Corregimiento, Causas Ordinarias: Leg. 26, c. 8, f. 55v, 1691–1692)—that may be related to Co. 6:9.

The final shrine of this ceque, Quizquipuquiu (Co. 6:10), is characterized as a flat place near Cacra (Cayra). Approximately five kilometers southeast of Cayra, past Quiquijana (Co. 6:9) and Hacienda Ushpa (Co. 7:7), is a mountain slope called Quizqui with a spring (Photo 7.19) that may well mark the terminus for Co. 6 (Maps 7.1 and 7.3).[49]

Photo 7.19. The sixth ceque of Collasuyu (Co. 6) may have ended on this mountain slope at the spring of Quizqui (Co. 6:10).

The Seventh Ceque of Collasuyu

Cobo indicates that the maintenance of the eight huacas of Co. 7 was the responsibility of Usca Mayta Panaca: the descendants of the fourth Inca, Mayta Capac. The ceque began at an unidentified shrine called Santocollo (Co. 7:1). The second shrine, Cotacalla (Co. 7:2), is described as a stone on the royal road near the town of Quicalla. The archaeological site of Qotakalli is south of the Cusco airport along a major Inca road that led from Cusco to the mountain of Huanacauri (Photo 7.20). The name, location, and age of these ruins suggest that they are related to Co. 7:2.[50]

A stone called Chachaquiray (Co. 7:3), not far from Qotacalla, is listed as the next shrine. Although survey work in the Cusco Valley did not identify a specific stone called Chachaquiray, a deep ravine one kilometer south of Qotakalli carries this name (Photo 7.21).[51] The fourth huaca is described in the *Relación de las huacas* as a flat area where the Chachapoya Indians settled, called Vircaypay (Huilcarpay, Co. 7:4).[52] Because the community and plain of Huilcarpay are beside the Chachaquiray Ravine, it is reasonable to assume that the fourth huaca of Co. 7 was somewhere nearby.

The fifth shrine of this ceque, Matoro (Co. 7:5), is characterized as a mountain slope near Huanacauri containing ancient buildings. Rowe (1944:43) suggests that Matoro is related to the legendary Matagua, where Manco Capac is said to have stopped for an extended period on his descent from Huanacauri to the Cusco Valley.[53] For example, Sarmiento de Gamboa (1906:38 [1572:Bk. 13]) writes:

> . . . they descended to the foot of the hill, where they began to enter the Cusco Valley, and arrived at a site called Matagua, where they settled and made huts to stay some time.[54]

Photo 7.20. The ruins of Qotakalli (Co. 7:2) are in the foreground. The hill of Muyu Urco is at the upper left and the village of Wimpillay at the center right.

Cobo also associates the town of Matagua with Manco Capac's mythical journey to Cusco, suggesting that Manco Capac's first son, Cinchi Roca, was born there. Furthermore, Cobo states that Cinchi Roca's first haircutting (*rutuchicoy*) took place at Matagua and that a large Warachikoy celebration was held there when he was initiated into manhood:

Before the Inca went into Cuzco, his wife, Mama Huaco, bore him a son in a town called Matagua, which was one league from Cuzco; he named his son Cinchi Roca, and he raised him with great care, as the one who would succeed him as ruler of the kingdom he founded. So that this son would be acknowledged as his heir and be respected, the Inca commanded his most important subjects to gather together on a certain day in the same town of Matagua to celebrate the Rutuchico, a new ceremony never held before; the Inca invented it on this occasion to celebrate his son's first haircutting; from then on it was an accepted practice.

This fiesta was held with stately display before a large gathering of nobles who came forward in sequence according to their rank within the nobility; each one cut part of the prince's hair, offering him at the same time magnificent gifts of fine clothing and jewels of gold and silver, and venerating him as the grandchild of the Sun himself, whom they worshiped for their god. In order to make this fiesta more solemn, new music, songs, and dances were invented; and between the music and the eating and drinking, the festivities lasted ten days.

It was with no less a royal, stately, and solemn display that they celebrated on the day that the young Inca Cinchi Roca was knighted and given the insignia of the nobility. For this fiesta, which was held in the afore-

Photo 7.21. The ravine of Chachaquiray (Co. 7:3) in the center, with the plains of Quijallay to the right and Huilcarpay (Co. 7:4) to the left.

mentioned town of Matagua, a much larger group of people was gathered together than for the previous fiesta; the road from Cuzco to Matagua was adorned with meticulously constructed floral arches; and diverse inventions of dances and festivities were performed on this day. The assemblage included the young Inca, very richly dressed, and the king and queen, his parents, and along with them the priest who was to knight the young Inca; these four rode in litters and the rest went on foot. Upon arriving at the designated place, first the priest delivered a brief discourse which he had prepared for the prince; then the priest dressed him in the royal clothing and gave him the other insignia that from then on were used by the successors to the throne. (Cobo 1979:109 [1653:Bk. 12, Ch. 4])[55]

Like Cobo, Molina (1989:100–101 [ca. 1575]) mentions Matagua in his description of the Warachikoy ritual of the Inca, during which the young nobles of Cusco were initiated into manhood:

Each of the (youths) who were to be knighted had already prepared a llama to be sacrificed, and they went with them and those of their lineage to the hill called Guanacauri. And they slept this day at the bottom of the hill in a place that is called Matagua; and the following day, that is the tenth day [of the festival], they did not eat because they all fasted on this day, at sunrise they ascended the hill above to arrive at the *guaca* Guanacauri. They left the llama that they had carried for the sacrifice at the foot of the hill in Matagua . . .[56]

There is a small settlement called Matao, near the community of Mascaguaylla on the northern slope of Huanacauri, that has been associated in the literature with Matagua since the 1940s (Rowe 1944:43). On a mountain summit above this community there is evidence of Inca and Killke remains. This archaeological site may mark the location of ancient Matoro (Co. 7:5).

The sixth huaca, Vilcaraypuquiu (Co. 7:6), is said to be a spring on the same slope as Matao. This shrine may be related to the Huilcarpay River, which flows between the slope of Matao and the Huilcarpay plain. If this is the case, then Matoro (Co. 7:5) and Vilcaraypuquiu (Co. 7:6) appear in the *Relación de las huacas* in incorrect order. Additional research is needed to clarify this ambiguous situation.

The final two shrines of this ceque are characterized as Uspa (Co. 7:7), a large flat area near Huanacauri, and Guamancapuquiu (Co. 7:8), a spring in a ravine. Approximately four kilometers east of Huanacauri is a large plain, with

Photo 7.22. Uspa (Co. 7:7) once stood near Hacienda Ushpabamba.

Killke and Inca pottery, still referred to as Ushpa (Photo 7.22). There is a spring called Guancapuquiu beyond Ushpa on the southern slope of the valley, which may be the ultimate shrine of Co. 7 (Maps 7.1 and 7.4).

The Eighth Ceque of Collasuyu

The eighth ceque of Collasuyu radiated from Cusco toward the mountain of Huanacauri. The course of this ceque remains highly speculative, however, because few of its eight shrines have been identified. The first huaca, Sancacancha (Co. 8:1), is registered as a prison that was on a house lot belonging to Juan de Figueroa.[57] Garcilaso de la Vega (1966: 424 [1609:Vol. 1, Bk. 7, Ch. 9]) suggests that Figueroa's house was between Coricancha and Pucamarca.[58] This location is problematic because it is in Chinchaysuyu. One could suggest that Figueroa owned more than one house lot, except that Ch. 7:1 is described as a stone in the door of Figueroa's house, and the following huaca, Ch. 7:2, is also listed as Sanca Cancha. The writer of the original ceque system manuscript may have confused a Sanca Cancha in Collasuyu with one in Chinchaysuyu (Rowe, pers. com. 1991), or there may have been some other kind of transcription error in recording the location of Co. 8:1.

Only general locations can be suggested for the second, third, and fourth huacas of Co. 8. The second shrine, a field

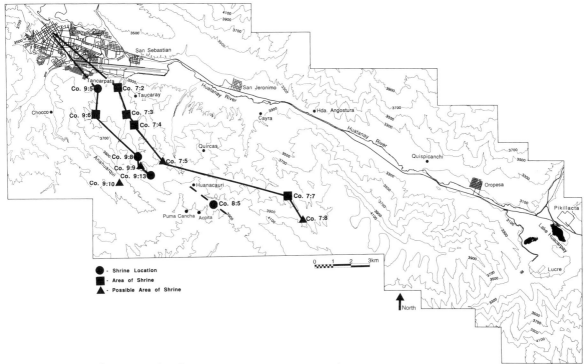

Map 7.4. Suggested courses of Collasuyu ceques Co. 7, Co. 8, and Co. 9.

called Guanchapacha (Co. 8:2), may have been in the sector of Cusco called Huanchac. The third huaca, Mudca (Co. 8:3), is listed as a stone pillar near Membilla (Wimpillay), and the fourth, Chuquimarca (Co. 8:4), is described as a small hill next to Huanacauri.

A hill near Huanacauri called Cuicosa (Co. 8:5) is presented as the fifth shrine on this ceque.[59] There is a rocky hill named Cuicus immediately southeast of Huanacauri, and an Inca road crosses this hill near its summit (Photo 7.23). This hill (also spelled as cuycuisa) is listed as a marker in a 1595 document discussing the territory of Sucso Panaca (AHD/Corregimiento, Causas Ordinarias: Leg. 26, c. 8, f. 54, 1691–1692). It is a likely candidate for Co. 8:5. The sixth huaca is listed as Coapapuquiu (Co. 8:6), a spring next to the hill of Huanacauri. While fieldwork yielded no additional data on this shrine, a 1595 reference to a spring called Cuapacha in this general area was found (AMAC/Community File for Collana Chahuancuzco, 1656, f. 101). Accordingly, it is possible that the *Relación de las huacas* contains a transcription error and that the name of the huaca should be Cuapa[cha]puquiu.

Cobo provides little information on the final two huacas

of this ceque, except that they were close to Huanacauri. He calls the seventh shrine Puquin (Co. 8:7), which may simply mean "spring" (puquiu), and he does not give a name for the last huaca (Co. 8:8), describing it only as a ravine. Their locations remain unknown (Maps 7.1 and 7.4).

Photo 7.23. An Inca road leads through this mountain pass of Cuicus. The shrine of Cuicosa (Co. 8:5) may have been near this summit.

The Ninth Ceque of Collasuyu

The ninth and final ceque of Collasuyu contained thirteen huacas, the most of any ceque in this suyu. Its first shrine is reported to be a seat called Tampucancha (Co. 9:1), next to the Temple of the Sun, where Mayta Capac planned a battle against the Alcaviza.[60] Its exact location remains unknown.[61] The second shrine, Tancarvilca (Co. 9:2), is described as a small round stone, one of the Pururaucas, in a house lot of Antonio Pereira. Garcilaso de la Vega (1966:430 [1609:Vol. 1, Bk. 7, Ch. 11]) indicates that Pereira's house was south of his own father's house, and that Alonso de Toro's house stood near that of Pereira's. The location of Toro's house is noteworthy because Cobo writes that the third shrine of this ceque, Pactaguañui (Co. 9:3), was a much-venerated flat place belonging to Alonso Toro where sacrifices were made to prevent sudden death. Gutiérrez (1981: 178, 180) has found archival evidence suggesting that Toro's house was in central Cusco near the corner of San Bernardo and Marqués Streets, and that Pereira's house stood next to it. Although it is unclear in Cobo's description whether Co. 9:3 was on a house lot or on another piece of land owned by Toro, the proximity of Pereira's and Toro's houses suggests that Co. 9:2 and Co. 9:3 were in Cusco near the homes of these conquistadors. The tentative positions of these huacas are surprising because they are northwest of the Temple of the Sun, in Chinchaysuyu. Alternatively, it may be noted that the huaca list does not specifically mention the houses of either of these men. Tancarvilca (Co. 9:2) is said to be in a house lot owned by Pereira, while Pactaquañui (Co. 9:3) is listed as being in a flat placed belonging to Toro. Accordingly, these huacas and landholdings could have been located elsewhere in Collasuyu (Rowe, pers. com. 1991).

Cobo's ceque account contains two consecutive shrines referred to as Co. 9:5: Quicapuquiu and Tampuvilca, and no huaca for Co. 9:4. This is a recording error; Quicapuquiu should be Co. 9:4, and Tampuvilca should be Co. 9:5. Quicapuquiu (Co. 9:5 [*sic* Co. 9:4]) is presented as a spring on the Cusco side of Membilla. Field and archival research found no additional information on this huaca. The following shrine, Tampuvilca (Co. 9:5), is described as a group of stones on a round hill next to Membilla. A 1595 document mentions a round hill called Tamburque in this same area (AHD/Corregimiento, Causas Ordinarias: Leg. 55, c. 17, f. 1v, 1773–1774). There is a distinctly round hill, currently called Muyu Urco (Round Hill), beside the community of Wimpillay (Photo 7.24).[62] The hill, a prominent feature of the landscape that can be seen from Cusco, is a likely location for Co. 9:5.[63]

The next shrine is characterized as a flat place at the end of Membilla called Chacapa (Co. 9:6). Approximately three kilometers south of Wimpillay, near the end of a small branch of the Tancarpata River, is a terraced area called

Photo 7.24. The round hill of Muyu Urco is a likely location for Tampuvilca (Co. 9:5).

Photo 7.25. The area of Chacapahua (Co. 9:6).

Photo 7.26. The abutment of Guarmichaca can be seen in the foreground. The shrine of Guarmichaca Puquiu (Co. 9:8) was near this bridge.

Chacapahua (Photo 7.25). It appears that Cobo mistranscribed the name of this huaca, leaving off the last three letters of its name: Chacapa[hua].[64]

The seventh (Chinchaypuquiu), eighth (Guarmichaca Puquiu), and ninth (Cupaychangiri Puquiu) huacas of this ceque are all characterized as springs. Survey work southeast of Cusco found no evidence of a spring called Chinchaypuquiu (Co. 9:7). Guarmichaca Puquiu (Co. 9:8) is said to be in a ravine near Huanacauri. Additional references to this huaca have been found (AHD/Corregimiento, Causas Ordinarias: Leg. 19, c. 15, f. 52v, 1672–1675), and there is a set of twin bridges, known as Guarmichaca, in the Huilcarpay Ravine along an Inca road that leads from Wimpillay to Huanacauri (Photo 7.26).[65] A spring located less than fifty meters from the two bridges may represent the shrine of Co. 9:8.[66]

The ninth huaca, Cupaychangiri Puquiu (Co. 9:9), is described as being beside the eighth.[67] Approximately half a kilometer upstream from Guarmichaca is a set of Inca structures called Inca Racay (Photo 7.27) and a florescence of springs (Aguilar 1913; Rowe 1944:42–43). The appearance of these springs is especially striking because the ravine is completely dry above them and they form the headwaters for one of the major rivers descending from Huanacauri. On the basis of these observations and Cobo's descriptions, this area of springs is a possibility for Co. 9:9.

The tenth shrine of this ceque, Quillo (Co. 9:10), is characterized as a set of stones on a hill near Huanacauri.[68] Approximately four kilometers to the southwest of Hua-

Photo 7.27. The ruins of Inca Racay and its adjacent spring. The trail from Huanacauri to Cusco runs beside these Inca structures.

nacauri, on the southern slope of Anaguarque Mountain, stands a towering outcrop called Quello (Photo 7.28). This rock measures more than one hundred meters wide and nearly forty meters high, and it contains a large, natural platform area at its base. The outcrop is well known in the region as a shrine and is a candidate for Co. 9:10. Its location is problematic, however, because Quello is several kilometers "off" the suggested course of this ceque, in an area traditionally associated with Cuntisuyu rather than Collasuyu.

Survey work in this region of Collasuyu found no clear evidence of the eleventh shrine of this ceque, a set of stones called Cachaocachiri (Co. 9:11). Nor was information re-

Photo 7.28. The outcrop of Quello is more than one hundred meters wide and nearly forty meters high. (Note the person standing near its base.) The outcrop may represent Quillo (Co. 9:10).

Photo 7.29. This pass (Puncu, Co. 9:13) was the last shrine of Collasuyu.

covered concerning the location of the twelfth shrine, Quiropiray (Co. 9:12), described as a large stone. The thirteenth shrine, the last of this ceque, was called Puncu (Co. 9:13). The Inca road that leads from Cusco to Pumacancha and the site of Huanacauri runs through a well-known pass a short distance from the ruins of Inca Racay (Photo 7.29). This impressive opening between the edge of the ravine and a large outcrop is a good possibility for Co. 9:13, the final shrine of Collasuyu (Maps 7.1 and 7.4).

Summary and Discussion

The approximate projections of the nine ceques of Collasuyu, as defined by the locations of their respective shrines, are illustrated on Map 7.5. This map shows a series of lines radiating from various locations near the center of Cusco. The first ceque, Co. 1, appears to have traveled down the Cusco Valley toward the Angostura, while the ninth ceque ran along the base of the ridge of Anaguarque. The seven other ceques of Collasuyu filled the territory between these two lines. The courses of the Collasuyu ceques seem to have been more erratic than those recorded in the other suyus of the system. This is particularly true in the area south of Cayra and north of Acpita ([Atpitan]Co. 1:6), where the ceques currently appear to cross over one another.

Several huacas seem to be situated a considerable distance from the general orientation of the ceques on which they are listed. These shrines present complicating factors in the study of the system. For example, the spring of Micaypuquiu may be the shrine of Micaya Puquiu (Co. 1:5), and the village of Acpita may be related to the huaca Cobo calls Atpitan (Co. 1:6). However, these two possible shrines are located six to eight kilometers south of the Cusco Valley, well away from the general course of Co. 1. Other problematic huacas include the area of Rondobamba, which may be related to the shrine of Rondao (Co. 5:9), and the large outcrop of Quello, which is a good candidate for Quillo (Co. 9:10). There are several possible explanations for these unusual observations. If these are the correct locations, then the individual ceques may have curved or doubled back to include them on their course. It is also possible, however, that these loci do not represent the huacas described in the *Relación de las huacas* as Co. 1:5, Co. 1:6, Co. 5:9, and Co. 9:10, and that four other shrines with similar names, perhaps now destroyed, were located along the general orientation of the respective ceques. A third explanation is that the identified places were indeed shrines in the ceque system, but they are listed on the wrong ceques.

A number of shrines in the city of Cusco described in this section of Cobo's report seem to have been located in suyus other than Collasuyu. Pumapacha (Co. 4:1) may have been in Antisuyu. The second and third shrines of Co. 9, Tancarvilca (Co. 9:2) and Pactaguañui (Co. 9:3), seem to have been on house lots in Chinchaysuyu. Several huacas (Co.

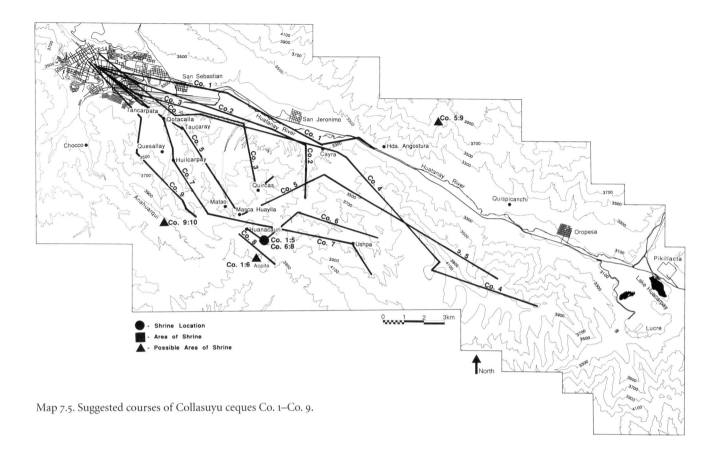

Map 7.5. Suggested courses of Collasuyu ceques Co. 1–Co. 9.

1:1, Co. 3:1, Co. 3:2, and Co. 6:1) are described as being near the house of Mancio Serra de Leguizamo. According to information provided by Garcilaso de la Vega (1966:427 [1609: Vol. 1, Bk. 7, Ch. 10]), this house was south of the central plaza in Chinchaysuyu. These shrines, like those mentioned above (Co. 1:5, Co. 1:6, Co. 5:9, and Co. 9:10), are problematic in the study of the system.

Field and archival research has found a number of other recording errors in the ceque system document. One shrine, Micaypuquiu, appears to be listed on two widely separate ceques: Co. 1:5 (Micaya Puquiu) and Co. 6:8 (Micaypuquiu). In the case of Chacapa (Co. 9:5), Cobo may have mistranscribed the name of the huaca, leaving off the last three letters of the huaca's name: Chacapa[hua]. Quicapuquiu (Co. 9:5 [*sic* Co. 9:4]) and Tampuvilca (Co. 9:5) are both listed as the fifth shrine of Co. 9. In addition, it seems possible that the original author of the *Relación de las huacas* may have confused a Sancacancha (Co. 8:1) in Collasuyu with a second Sanca Cancha in Chinchaysuyu (Ch. 7:2). It is also

worth mentioning that three huacas, Co. 3:1, Co. 6:1, and Co. 9:1, all share the same name of Tambocancha. However, because each of these three shrines was the first shrine on the first ceque of separate ceque clusters, this may not have been a recording error.

Finally, it should be noted that Cobo describes the third shrine of the first ceque, Churucana (Co. 1:3), as "a small and round hill, which is next to San Lázaro, on top of which were three stones regarded as idols." The hill of Churucana has been found beside the Santutis Hacienda house, some two kilometers from the chapel of San Lázaro. In other words, despite the fact that Cobo describes Churucana as *next to* San Lázaro, ground variation of the system reveals that they are separated by a considerable distance. This demonstrates the importance of fieldwork in the study of the system and emphasizes the fact that extreme care must be taken when attempting to reconstruct it directly from Cobo's account.

8

The Huacas and Ceques of Cuntisuyu

THE FOURTH SUYU described in the *Relación de las huacas* is Cuntisuyu, which lies to the south and southwest of the imperial city. Anaguarque Mountain was the division between Collasuyu and Cuntisuyu, and the first ceque of Cuntisuyu runs along its crest. The Cuntisuyu and Chinchaysuyu division, which also marked the separation between Hanan and Hurin Cusco, is less well defined. It appears to have been somewhere south of Cusco between the shrine of Pantanaya (Cu. 14:4) and the slope of Picchu.

The names and approximate locations of eighty Cuntisuyu shrines have been preserved in the *Relación de las huacas*. This is comparable to the number of shrines found in the other suyus of the region. Cuntisuyu is unique, however, in the number of ceques it contained. Unlike the other three suyus, which held nine ceques each, the shrines of Cuntisuyu were distributed across fourteen or fifteen ceques. The exact number of ceques in Cuntisuyu is open to debate, since one series of fifteen huacas, said to form Cu. 8, defined two separate lines radiating from Cusco. This ambiguity is recognized by Cobo because he states that the first eight huacas of Cu. 8 were called cayao and the last seven shrines were referred to as collana.

The First Ceque of Cuntisuyu

The first ceque of Cuntisuyu contained fifteen shrines, more than any other ceque in the suyu. It was called Anaguarque, a name associated in the chronicles with the wife of Pachacuti Inca Yupanqui, as well as with a mountain near Huanacauri.[1] The ceque of Anaguarque projected from Cusco toward this mountain, and many of the huacas are found along its slopes.

The first shrine of Cu. 1, a stone called Sabaraura (Cu. 1:1),[2] is reported to have been one of the Pururaucas and was beneath the belvedere of Santo Domingo (see Photo 1.1).[3] Gasparini and Margolies (1980:240), Zuidema (1982c: 100), and Hyslop (1990:47) all state that the famous curved wall of the Temple of the Sun is the belvedere mentioned in the ceque system document, and they propose that the stone of Sabaraura stood in a large niche on the upper course of this wall (Photo 8.1).

The exact location of Cu. 1:2 (Quingil), another stone in a wall next to the Coricancha, remains to be identified. However, the position of the third huaca, a flat place in the precinct of Poma Chupa (Cu. 1:3) where offerings were made to the two rivers flowing through Cusco, is well known. A place labeled Poma Chupan is shown on Guaman Poma de Ayala's (1980:970 [1615:1051 (1059)]) map of Cusco, and it is also mentioned by Betanzos (1987:60, 77 [1557:Pt. 1, Chs. 13 and 16]). Cobo (1983:123 [1653:Bk. 11, Ch. 8]) notes in a separate section of his chronicle that the area of Pumachupa was below the convent of Santo Domingo. This same area is described in more detail by Garcilaso de la Vega:

> Beyond the ward of Rimacpampa lies another to the south of the city, called Pumapchupan, "lion's tail," for the ward tapers to a point between two streams that unite at a right angle. (Garcilaso de la Vega 1966:420 [1609:Vol. 1, Bk. 7, Ch. 8])[4]

The chronicle of Molina contains an unusually detailed description of ritual activities taking place at Pumachupa during the month of Camay (approximately January). Molina explains how elaborate offerings, which included the ashes and other burnt remains from all the sacrifices that had taken place in Cusco during the previous year, were made at Pumachupa, and how the Saphi River was dammed and then released, creating a surge of water to carry away these materials. Molina (1989:114–115 [ca. 1575]) reports:

> And the following day, which was the nineteenth of the said month, they went to the square of Cusco called Haucaypata, as is said, the Inca and all the other people, and they also brought out all the other *huacas* and the embalmed bodies of the dead. Having made the accustomed obeisances, they began to make the sacrifice called *mojucata,* in the following manner:

Photo 8.1. The stone of Sabaraura (Cu. 1:2) may have stood in this large niche on the belvedere of Santo Domingo.

A small river passes through the middle of Cusco called Saphi Mayo [Root River] and Huaca Puncu Mayo [Shrine Opening River]. It comes down from some ravines which are in the heights above Cusco. They made in it some dams to block the water, although it was winter, so that it would carry away the sacrifices that they were about to make with greater force.

And thus for this day they had prepared kinds and sorts of food which they used, all sorts of hot peppers, great quantities of coca baskets, all sorts of colored clothes that they used, and footwear that they used, *llautus* [headbands] and feathers that they placed on the head; livestock, flowers, gold, silver, and all the things that they used, all the ashes and cinders that they had saved from the sacrifices that they had offered during the whole year; all of which they threw in the river, and opening the first dam so that the water rushed down with such force that it went breaking the others and carrying away the sacrifices.

They burnt a lamb this day in sacrifice, throwing the ashes and cinders of it, with the others, into the river. There were many people on one side and on the other (of the river) on the outskirts of the city of Cuzco, at a place called Pumachupa, where they made these sacrifices. They were made a little less than an hour before sunset and the Indians who were on one side of the river and on the other, making the sacrifices in the river, were sent by the Lord Inca, who was present, with these sacrifices to Ollantaytambo.[5]

Cobo provides a similar description of Inca ceremonies at Pumachupa, which included the simultaneous drinking and offering of chicha to the huaca, a symbolic act that was, and still is, a common practice in the Andes:

Six days after the full moon, having made some dams at intervals on the stream that passed by the square, they took out the ashes and cinders that they had kept from what was left over of the bones from the sacrifices of the whole year. They ground them up with two bundles of coca, many flowers of diverse colors, hot peppers, salt, and burned peanuts, and all together made into powder, they took out a certain amount and put it into the storehouse. They would take the rest [of the powder] to a place below the district of Pumachupa where the said stream joins another stream. Accompanying this sacrifice were the statues of the Sun and the rest of the gods that they usually placed out in the square for the important festivals, and the Inca himself with the whole court. All went to the place mentioned above, including two hundred men with staffs in their hands. On arriving at the said confluence of the streams, the Indians carrying staffs put them aside and each one took two tumblers of *chicha*. They offered one to the water of the stream and they drank the other tumbler of *chicha* themselves. After dancing around the statues for a while with great rejoicing, a little before nightfall, they threw all of that ash into the stream, cleaning thoroughly the vessels in which it was brought so that none of it would remain. Then they took up their staffs and stationed themselves on either side of the river. The Inca ordered them to go with that sacrifice down the river to the town of Tambo . . . (Cobo 1990:136–137 [1653:Bk. 13, Ch. 26])[6]

The two rivers mentioned by Cobo, Molina, and Garcilaso de la Vega as those defining the Pumachupa area are the Saphi and Tullumayu. The confluence of these rivers is now covered by a small municipal park.

The fourth shrine, Uxi (Cu. 1:4), is recorded as the beginning of a road that led to Tampu (i.e., Pacariqtambo). Because one of the major roads to Pacariqtambo and the rest of Cuntisuyu departed Cusco approximately two hundred meters below the area of Pumachupa, it is reasonable to suggest that Cu. 1:4 was near this point (AHD/Colegio Ciencias: Leg 10, c. 18, f. 1v, 1642). The fifth shrine, Guaman (Cu. 1:5), a small round stone in a ravine, remains unidentified. A ravine or spring on the Membilla road called Curipoxapuquiu is presented as Cu. 1:6. The word "Curipoxa" may be an orthographic error for Coripata, an area of Cusco with a large number of springs, approximately half a kilometer south of Pumachupa.

The succeeding shrine, Anaguarque (Cu. 1:7), is characterized as a large hill next to Huanacauri. Several writers indicate that this huaca was visited by young men during the first days of the Warachicoy celebration, soon after they began initiation rites at Huanacauri (Cieza de León 1976: 35–36 [1554:Pt. 2, Ch. 7]; Tito Cusi Yupanqui 1988:184 [1570]). For example, Betanzos describes the youths' trip to Anaguarque as follows:

> From there they will go to a *guaca* that I will point out tomorrow, which will be called Anaguarque. On arrival there, they will make their sacrifice, offering a *chicha* and making a fire before it. In the fire they will make offerings of maize, coca, and fat. When they are there, the relatives of this neophyte, who are almost like godfathers, will carry some long halberds of gold and silver. After making the sacrifice, they tie that straw they carry in their hands to the heads of the halberds and hang from the heads of the halberds that wool that was hung on the straw. Having tied the straw on, they will put one of these halberds in the hands of each of the neophytes. Then all of the neophytes there will be brought together and they will all be ordered to leave there all running together with the halberds in their hands as if they were chasing their enemies. This run will be from the *guaca* to a hill where the city comes into view. (Betanzos 1996: 61–62 [1557:Pt. 1, Ch. 14])[7]

Molina (1989:105 [ca. 1575]) also writes of the youths' pilgrimage to the huaca of Anaguarque and of the rituals that took place there:

> . . . and thus they went walking until they arrived at the hill called Anaguarque, which will be two leagues from Cuzco, to give to the *huaca,* of the same name, which was on the summit of the hill. It was the *huaca* of the Indians of the village[s] of Chocco and Cachona. The reason why they went to this *huaca* to make this sacrifice was because on this day they had to run a race, to prove which was the best runner, hence they had this ceremony. They say that this shrine, at the time of the flood, became so swift that it ran as fast as a hawk could fly. Having arrived, the youths offered to this *huaca* a little of the wool which they carried in their hands and the priests of the Sun (not the principal priest and those of the other *huacas,* called Tarpuntays, sacrificed five lambs, burning them to the Creator, Sun, and Thunder, and Moon, and for the Inca, to each of them for their own already mentioned reasons. Their families once more whipped the youths who were now knighted, with the same *huaracas* [woven slings], urging them value their own bravery and endurance. After this, the people sat down and performed the *taqui* [dance] called *haurita*

with the *huaylla quepas* and shells. The knights stood, holding in their hands the staff called *yauri,* which were the weapons given to them and their (. . .) which were in the staff; some were of gold and others of copper, each according to their means.[8]

Molina suggests that Anaguarque was the principal shrine of the villages of Cachona and Chocco. It is interesting to note in this regard that the inhabitants of these two communities, located approximately five kilometers south of Cusco, still regard Anaguarque as a sacred place.[9] A private archive in Cusco retains copies of reports, dating from 1555 to 1591, on the boundaries of Chocco. These reports, which collectively will be called the Chocco Document, indicate that the mountain of Anaguarque was a major land boundary in the region and that the people of Chocco were the descendants of Mama Anaguarque (PA/Bauer, Chocco Document 1589: f. 4). Because several chroniclers provide similar information, there appears to be an association between the name of this ceque, the community that controlled much of the territory through which it passed, and the huacas along its course.

Anaguarque Mountain stands between Huanacauri and Cusco. At the mountain summit there is a small plain with a clear view of Cusco. The plain contains the remains of a poorly preserved structure and fragments of Inca pottery (Photo 8.2). There can be little doubt that the initiates to manhood gathered in this area during the Warachicoy ceremony and that offerings to the mountain, Cu. 1:7, were once made there.[10]

Photo 8.2. This plain on the summit of Anaguarque marks the area of Cu. 1:7, where the initiates to manhood gathered during the Warachicoy ceremony.

Photo 8.3. This spring on the slope of Anaguarque may be Achatarque Puquiu (Cu. 1:9).

Photo 8.4. These stones near Anaguarque are candidates for Anahuarque Guaman (Cu. 1:10).

The next three shrines were all on or near the ridge of Anaguarque. A stone called Chataguarque (Cu. 1:8) is said to be on a small hill near Anaguarque. This shrine may have been just above the plain on the rocky crest of Anaguarque. The following huaca, a spring named Achatarque Puquiu (Cu. 1:9), is most likely related to a spring on the southeastern slope of Anaguarque (Photo 8.3), the only water source near the summit. Approximately three hundred meters from this spring is a row of large stones (Photo 8.4) that are good candidates for Cu. 1:10, a stone called Anahuarque Guaman.

The eleventh and twelfth shrines of this ceque are characterized as two springs: Yamarpuquiu and Chicapuquiu. Yamarpuquiu (Cu. 1:11) is said to be in a ravine on the slope of Anaguarque. As noted in the discussion of Collasuyu, two communities, called Quesallay and Huilcarpay, are separated by the Chachaquiray Ravine (Co. 7:3) at the northern base of Anaguarque. The water of this ravine flows from a cluster of springs below the row of stones thought to be Cu. 1:10.[11] One of these springs, which flows out of the ground with such force that it churns, is called Yanapuquiu. Based on its location and its distinct appearance, this spring is a possibility for Cu. 1:11. A good candidate for the shrine of Chicapuquiu (Cu. 1:12) is a large spring, currently called Chillapuquiu, that emerges several hundred meters above Yanapuquiu and that forms the headwater for the Chachaquiray Ravine (Photo 8.5).[12] This identification is supported by a 1595 document that places Chicapuquiu at the beginning of a ravine above Huilcarpay (AHD/Corregimiento, Causas Ordinarias: Leg. 19, c. 15, f. 51, 1672–1675).

Photo 8.5. The spring of Chillapuquiu may be Chicapuquiu (Cu. 1:12).

Photo 8.6. This cave beyond Anaguarque may be Incaroca (Cu. 1:13).

Photo 8.7. A set of large outcrops, which stand over twenty meters high on the summit of Pintu, is a good possibility for Puntuguanca (Cu. 1:14).

A possibility for the next shrine along this ceque, a cave called Incaroca (Cu. 1:13), exists near the summit of Pintu (or Pitu) Ridge, which is a continuation of Anaguarque. Near the top of Pintu is a well-known cave simply called Tocco (window or cave). The cave is over five meters deep and is formed by the interdigitating of several large, oval boulders (Photo 8.6). Its entrance offers an impressive view of Cusco.

The penultimate shrine of Cu. 1 is registered as a stone called Puntuguanca (Cu. 1:14) on the top of a hill near Anaguarque. The most likely candidate for this huaca is an enormous outcrop on the summit of Pintu referred to as Pinturumiyoc (Photo 8.7). The largest stone of the outcrop is twenty meters high. There is also a very large, circular looter's pit, measuring fourteen meters across and six meters deep, at the base of these rocks. The Pinturumiyoc outcrop is large enough to be seen from Cusco, and it stands less then one hundred meters above the cave believed to be Cu. 1:13.

The final shrine of this first ceque, Quiguan (Cu. 1:15), is described as three stones in a small pass on the way to Poma-cancha (Pumacancha). The community of Pumacancha is on the southern slope of Huanacauri, and the major Inca road from Cusco to it travels through a pass between Huanacauri and Pintu. Although numerous boulders are scattered along the pass, three large rocks called the Kinsa Huacacuna (three huacas) are singled out by the local residents as qualitatively different from the others. A legend of Pumacancha suggests that these stones were once three giant frogs from the province of Paruro that were on their way to consume Cusco (Photo 8.8). As the frogs began to descend to Cusco, the mountain of Huanacauri transformed them into stones and saved the city. These three stones, which lie about two hundred meters from the pass of Puncu (the last huaca of Co. 9), may be the final shrine of Cu. 1 (Maps 8.1 and 8.2).

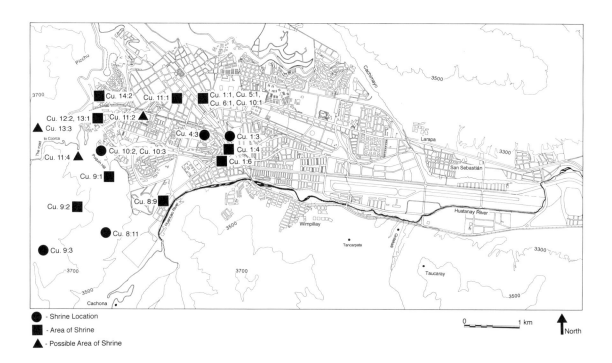

Map 8.1. Suggested locations of Cuntisuyu huacas in Cusco.

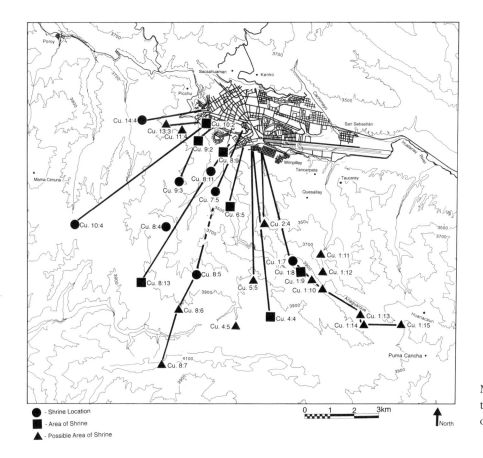

Map 8.2. Suggested locations of Cuntisuyu huacas outside Cusco.

Photo 8.8. A legend suggests that three stones in this valley were once giant frogs. They may be the three stones of Quiguan (Cu. 1:15).

The Second Ceque of Cuntisuyu

The four shrines of Cu. 2 are said to be the responsibility of Quisco Ayllu, a nonroyal kin group mentioned by Molina and Sarmiento de Gamboa. The course of Cu. 2, like those of many of the short ceques of the system, is poorly understood. The first two shrines, Cotocari (Cu. 2:1) and Pillo Lluri (Cu. 2:2), a flat place in a field of Antonio Altamirano and a long stone that was in a ravine on the way to Tampu (Pacariqtambo), remain to be identified. Cobo explains that the third huaca, a cave called Paylla Llanto (Cu. 2:3), was worshiped because a lady of the same name, the mother of an important lord called Apu Curimaya, disappeared into it. Survey work south of Cusco identified a ridge beside Anaguarque called Paylla Ranto, which is a good candidate for Cu. 2:3.

The fourth and final shrine of this ceque, Rauaraya (Cu. 2:4), is described as a small hill where Inca youths finished a race. Betanzos (1987:67 [1557:Pt. 1, Ch. 14]) is a little more specific, describing it as a hill where the city comes into view. It is known from Molina as well as other writers (Cieza de León 1976:35 [1554:Pt. 2, Ch. 7]; Santa Cruz Pachacuti Yamqui Salcamayhua 1950:221 [1613]) that this race took place toward the end of the Warachicoy celebration, which was itself part of the larger December festival of Capac Raymi (Rowe 1946:283). Molina (1989:104 [ca. 1575]) indicates that the initiated youths left Cusco with various members of their families to spend the night at Rauaraya the day before the race. The next morning, after ascending Anaguarque and offering sacrifices to its huaca, the young men ran back to Rauaraya. Because the ridge of Paylla Ranto (Cu. 2:3) represents the northern end of Anaguarque, it seems likely that the huaca of Rauaraya (Cu. 2:4) was located somewhere between the northern shoulder of this mountain and its summit, where the race began (Maps 8.1 and 8.2).

The Third Ceque of Cuntisuyu

According to the *Relación de las huacas,* there were four shrines along the third ceque of Cuntisuyu. The initial huaca is listed as a spring called Chuquimatero (Cu. 3:1) where the Indians of Cayocache (Cayaocache) drank, and the second, Caquia Sabaraura (Cu. 3:2), was a group of stones on top of a hill opposite Cayaocache.[13] The location of Cayaocache is important because it is mentioned by Cobo in relation to a number of other shrines of the Cusco ceque system, including Cayaopuquiu (Cu. 4:3), Tiucalla (Cu. 5:2), Guaman (Cu. 6:2), Orcopacla (Cu. 6:3), Caruinca Cancha (Cu. 7:3), Quiacas Amaro (Cu. 8:8), Puquincancha (Cu. 10:2), and Matarapacha (Cu. 11:1).

Cayaocache is also mentioned by a number of other early colonial writers. Sarmiento de Gamboa (1906:41 [1572: Ch. 14]) provides information on the mythic history of the people living in Cayaocache, and the place is mentioned in Cobo's description of Ahuani Ayllu and Usca Mayta (Cobo 1979:117, 120 [1653:Bk. 12: Chs. 6 and 7]), as well as by Betanzos (1987:67, 79 [1557:Pt. 1, Chs. 14 and 16]), Santillán (1950:44 [ca. 1564]), and Tito Cussi Yupanqui (1988:195 [1570]). Garcilaso de la Vega describes it as a settlement of approximately three hundred inhabitants, a thousand paces from the ancient limits of Cusco:

> At a distance to the west of this ward [Pumachupa] there was a village of over three hundred inhabitants called Cayaucache. It stood more than a thousand paces

from the last houses in the city. This was in 1560. As I write this, in 1602, I am told that it is already within the limits of Cuzco, the population of which has so multiplied that the city has surrounded the village on all sides. (Garcilaso de la Vega 1966:420 [1609:Vol. 1, Bk. 7, Ch. 8])[14]

Sarmiento de Gamboa (1906:35 [1572:Ch. 11]) is even more specific, writing that Cayaocache was the area near Cusco that the Spaniards called Belén. López de Velasco (1894:479 [1571–1574]) concurs with Sarmiento de Gamboa, stating that the community of Cayaocache was called Belén. He also states that Cayaocache was one arquebus shot from Cusco and that it had a population of 1,400 in the early 1570s.[15]

The modern church of Belén is on the end of a low ridge about one kilometer south of Cusco. The church of Belén was, however, originally built in another location and was moved after the great 1650 earthquake that destroyed much of colonial Cusco (AHD/Corregimiento, Causas Ordinarias: Leg. 19, c. 15, 1672–1675; Rowe, pers. com. 1992). The town of Cayaocache and the former site of the church appear to have been located approximately half a kilometer east of the modern church where there is a large archaeological site called Coripata.

Although it seems likely that Cayaocache was located in the area now called Coripata, the positions of most of the shrines that Cobo lists as being in this community, including those of Chuquimatero (Cu. 3:1) and Caquia Sabaraura (Cu. 3:2), have not been determined. This is not surprising because Cusco was already encroaching on Cayaocache in 1602 (Garcilaso de la Vega 1966:421 [1609:Vol. 1, Bk. 7, Ch. 8]).

The location of the third huaca, Cayascas Guaman (Cu 3:3), reported to be a long stone in a town of the same name, is not known. The terminus point of this ceque was a spring called Chucuracay Puquiu (Cu. 3:4), which was in a ravine where one loses sight of the Cusco Valley on the way to Tampo (Pacariqtambo).[16] Two major trails from Cusco to Pacariqtambo run near Chocco. The first, the royal road of Cuntisuyu, travels through Cachona and crosses a high ridge above Chocco. The second road to Pacariqtambo branches off from the royal road of Cuntisuyu after crossing the Huancaro River. It travels through the community of Chocco and then crosses the puna near Churucana (Cu. 4:4), where it again intercepts the royal road of Cuntisuyu. The last shrine of Cu. 3 may have been along either of these roads (Maps 8.1 and 8.2).

The Fourth Ceque of Cuntisuyu

The first of the five shrines on Cu. 4 is described as a Pururauca (Cu. 4:1) on a stone bench next to the Temple of the Sun. The second huaca of this ceque, Amarocti (Cu. 4:2), is listed as a group of stones in a small town called Aytocari. A 1698 document indicates that this shrine was located in the parish of Belén (AGN/Derecho Indígena, c. 180, 1698); however, its exact location is not known.

A spring called Cayaopuquiu (Cu. 4:3), said to be opposite Cayaocache, is presented as the third shrine along Cu. 4. Despite the urban growth that has occurred in the Cusco area since the writing of the ceque system document, this spring can still be found along the Avenida del Ejército. The fourth shrine, Churucana (Churucalla, Cu. 4:4), is characterized as a large stone on a hill next to Anaguarque. This same shrine is also listed in the Chocco Document as a landmark beside the royal road of Cuntisuyu. It is also included in Molina's chronicle (1989:75 [ca. 1575]) as a point two leagues from Cusco where Inca runners passed their loads to natives from the province of Paruro during the Cusco Citua ceremony. Based on Molina's writings, it is possible to suggest that Cu. 4:4 marked the boundary between the territory controlled by the Inca and that under the jurisdiction of other groups, or what have been called elsewhere "Incas of Privilege" (Zuidema 1983a; Bauer 1992b: 18–35). There is a prominent area in the puna called Churucalla, above the community of Chocco near the provincial border of Cusco and Paruro and beside the Cuntisuyu road, that most certainly marks the area of Cu. 4:4.[17]

The final huaca of Cu. 4 is presented in the *Relación de las huacas* as a ravine called Cuipancalla (Cu. 4:5) on the way to Tambo (Pacariqtambo). Survey work south of Cusco found one possible location for Cu. 4:5, but it remains highly speculative because it is off the general course of this line. The possible site, a well-known sacred place, is a pass called Collpan two kilometers west of Churucalla (Maps 8.1 and 8.2).

The Fifth Ceque of Cuntisuyu

Chima Panaca, composed of people believed to be the descendants of the first mythical ruler of Cusco, was responsible for the five shrines of Cu. 5. Cobo indicates that this line began in a small plaza called Caritampucancha (Cu. 5:1) inside the monastery of Santo Domingo, the first place settled by Manco Capac. The location of the second huaca,

Tiucalla (Cu. 5:2), an assemblage of stone warriors in Cayaocache, and that of the third shrine, Cayallacta (Cu. 5:3), a group of stones on a hill near Chocco, remain to be identified, as does that of the fourth, a spring called Churupuquiu (Cu. 5:4) above Chocco.

The final shrine of this ceque, Cumpu Guanacauri (Cu. 5:5), is described as a group of stones on top of a hill in line with Chocco. There is a large hill between Chocco and Churucalla called Cunu, which is a possibility for Cu. 5:5. Its summit contains a light scatter of Inca pottery and offers a view straight down the Chocco Valley into the center of Cusco (Maps 8.1 and 8.2).[18]

The Sixth Ceque of Cuntisuyu

The sixth ceque of Cuntisuyu contained five huacas. Its course is poorly understood. The initial shrine, a round stone called Apian (Cu. 6:1), one of the Pururaucas, is described as being on the site of Santo Domingo. The second huaca, a stone called Guaman (Cu. 6:2), and the third, an assemblage of Pururaucas called Orcopacla (Cu. 6:3),[19] are recorded as being in Cayaocache. The fourth shrine, a spring named Pachapuquiu (Cu. 6:4), is listed as being in the direction of a place called Pomapampa. A 1544 document indicates that a son of Topa Inca Yupanqui held lands at Pomabamba (AHD/Corregimiento, Causas Ordinarias: Leg. 27, c. 12, f. 23, 1693–1699).[20] Nevertheless, the exact location of Pomapampa and the shrine remain unknown.

The concluding huaca of this ceque is reported to be a hut called Intirpucancha (Cu. 6:5) in the middle of Chocco. The modern community of Chocco is at the base of a low ridge covered with Inca pottery. It is reasonable to assume that the final shrine of Cu. 6 was somewhere on this ridge because these archaeological remains mark the location of the village before the arrival of the Spaniards (Maps 8.1 and 8.2).[21]

The Seventh Ceque of Cuntisuyu

The seventh ceque of Cuntisuyu contained five shrines. Like Cu. 6, this ceque began in or near the Temple of the Sun and terminated near Chocco. The first huaca, a small house called Inticancha (Cu. 7:1), was thought to be a structure where the sisters of Manco Capac had lived. This shrine seems to be related to the house of Manco Capac, Cari-

Photo 8.9. The plain of Cutacuta (Cu. 7:5), situated between the villages of Chocco and Ccachona, marks the area where a *tinku* (ritual battle) took place.

tampucancha (Cu. 5:1), and it may have been in the monastery of Santo Domingo.[22] The exact location of the second huaca, a large rock named Rocromuca (Cu. 7:2) said to be next to the Temple of the Sun, is not known, although a 1569 reference to it has been found (Rowe 1986:204). The position of the third shrine, a house of an important lord of Cayaocache called Caruinca Cancha (Cu. 7:3), and that of the fourth, a hill called Sutirmarca (Cu. 7:4), are not known.

The closing huaca of this ceque, Cotacotabamba (Cu. 7:5), was a flat place between the villages of Chocco and Cachona. Cobo notes that a festival was held on certain days on this plain when the inhabitants of these two villages would stone one another. This is a reference to a ritual battle, or *tinku*.[23] There is a large plain between Chocco and Cachona called Cutacuta (Photo 8.9), which is mentioned in various documents as bordering these two communities (PA/Bauer, Chocco Document [1555–1591]; Chávez Ballón, Document 3 [1613]). There can be little doubt that the plain of Cutacuta marks the location of the final huaca of Cu. 7 because it contains a light scatter of Inca pottery and is remembered by older members of these two communities as the site of annual boundary festivals a half century ago (Maps 8.1 and 8.2).

The Eighth Ceque of Cuntisuyu

Cobo begins his description of Cu. 8 with an unusual statement indicating that half of this ceque was named cayao and the other half collana. This ceque, said to be composed of fifteen huacas, was actually two separate lines, both of which radiated from Cusco. The first ceque, hereafter called Cu. 8(cayao), began at an unidentified location and terminated at the pass of Cachicalla (Cu. 8[cayao]:7), southwest of Cusco. The second line, Cu. 8(collana), began with Quiacas Amaro (Cu. 8[collana]:8) and ran northwest of the first (Maps 8.1 and 8.2).[24]

Cu. 8(cayao)

The first huaca of this unusual ceque was a stone named Tanancuricota (Cu. 8[cayao]:1), which Cobo explains had been a woman (Chañan Cori Coca) who came with the Pururaucas.[25] While the exact location of this monument remains to be identified, references to the heroic actions of Chañan Cori Coca (Valiant Gold Coca) and her affiliation with Chocco and Cachona are found in Santa Cruz Pachacuti Yamqui Salcamayhua's account (1950:238 [1613]) as well as in Sarmiento de Gamboa's chronicle (1906:63 [1572:Ch. 27]). The latter of these authors writes:

> And those (Chancas) that entered through the sector of Cuzco called Chocco (and) Cachona were valorously rebutted by those of that sector, where they recount that a woman called Chañan Cori Coca fought like a man, . . . against the Chanca that had assaulted there, that she made them withdraw.[26]

Photo 8.10. A canal from Chinchay Puquiu (Cu. 8[cayao]:5) waters the nearby fields.

The location of the second huaca, Cutimanco (Cu. 8 [cayao]:2), the tomb of a principal lord, is not known. The next shrine, Cauas (Cu. 8[cayao]:3), was also a tomb. This may have been the burial place of Mama Cava (or Cachua), who is said to have been the wife of Capac Yupanqui (Murúa 1946:91 [1590:Bk. 1, Ch. 20]) or Lloque Yupanqui (Sarmiento de Gamboa 1906:45 [1572:Ch. 17]; Garcilaso de la Vega 1966:113 [1609:Bk. 2, Ch. 20]; Cobo 1979:116 [1654:Bk. 13, Ch. 6]). The location of the tomb has not been found.

Candidates for the fourth and fifth shrines, two springs named E Con Con Puquiu and Chinchay Puquiu, have been identified on separate slopes in the territory of Huamancharpa, a small village above Cachona.[27] Chinchay Puquiu (Cu. 8[cayao]:5) is southeast of Huamancharpa on the west side of the Chinchay Ravine (Photo 8.10). E Con Con Puquiu may be the spring of Cor Cor Puquiu (Cu. 8 [cayao]:4), which can be found to the southwest of Huamancharpa beside a small cluster of houses called Muyucancha (Photo 8.11).[28] This location for Cor Cor Puquiu is

Photo 8.11. The spring of Cor Cor Puquiu may be the shrine listed as E Con Con Puquiu (Cu. 8[cayao]:4).

problematic, however, because it is off the apparent course of the ceque.

The sixth shrine on this ceque, Mascata Urco (Cu. 8 [cayao]:6), is described as a hill where one loses sight of Cusco.[29] Although no hill with this name was identified, a possibility for the huaca does exist: a pass currently called Llaulli above Huamancharpa on a trail to the village of Cachicalla (Photo 8.12). There is a two-tiered Inca platform, measuring approximately 9 m × 8 m × 2 m, in the middle of the pass, which provides a clear and final view of the imperial city some ten kilometers in the distance. The location of this pass, the stone platform built in its center, and its view of Cusco provide circumstantial evidence that it may have been a shrine, perhaps that of Cu. 8(cayao):6.[30]

The seventh shrine, Cachicalla (Cu. 8[cayao]:7), a ravine between two hills resembling a gateway, marked the end point of the first, or cayao, half of the ceque. The settlement of Cachicalla is in the puna area above Cachona.[31] A major trail heading south from the village leads through a narrow opening in an outcrop known as Huacaracalla.[32] From the physical appearance of this passageway and its location close to Cachicalla, it is suggested as a possible area for Cu. 8(cayao):7.

Cu. 8(collana)

The first seven huacas on this ceque form a relatively straight line—with the exception of Cor Cor Puquiu (Cu. 8 [cayao]:4)—projecting out of Cusco to the southwest. Field research indicates that the seventh shrine of this ceque may have been a pass some twelve kilometers from the Inca capital. The eighth shrine defined the beginning of a new line radiating from Cusco. This second line of huacas most certainly corresponds to what Cobo described as the collana half of Cu. 8.

The exact location of Cu. 8(collana):8 (Quiacas Amaro), described as certain stones on top of a hill beyond Cayaocache, is unknown. Cobo indicates that the ninth huaca of this ceque, Cu. 8(collana):9 (Managuanunca Guaci), was a house of one of the Inca in an area owned by the Mercedarian order. The Mercedarians held large tracts of land south of Cusco along the Huancaro River. A portion of their land on the west side of this river is still known as Managuañunca and is mentioned in a number of documents, the earliest dating to 1540 (PA/Chávez Ballón, Document 3).

The site of Cu. 8(collana):10 (Cicui), a tomb on the slope of Cachona, was not found, but a 1666 document also places it (Sicuy) near this town (ADH/Protocolos Notariales, Varios escribanos, 1683–1720 [Antonio Moreno Notario #313, f. 889]). The location of the next shrine, listed as a large hill called Cumpi (Cu. 8[collana]:11) on the way to Cachona, was identified on the west side of the Huancaro River (Photo 8.13). This hill, still considered to be a sacred place, towers above the village.[33]

The next two shrines, Pachachiri (Cu. 8[collana]:12) and Pitopuquiu (Cu. 8[collana]:13), are both springs. Although the exact location of Pachachiri has not been pinpointed, there is a river called Chirimayo near the base of Cumpi.

Photo 8.12. A rectangular, two-tiered stone platform in the middle of Llaulli Pass may be the shrine of Mascata Urco (Cu. 8[cayao]:6).

Photo 8.13. Cumpi Hill (Cu. 8[collana]:11), still considered a sacred place, is visible from Cusco and towers above the village of Ccachona.

The spring of Pitopuquiu seems to have been in the puna above Cachona near a large hill called Cimón because an area beside this hill is called Pitocancha and several documents dating to the late 1500s list Pitopuquiu as near Cimón (AGN/Títulos de Propiedad: Leg. 34, c. 660, f. 170, 1620; PA/Chávez Ballón, Document 3) or above Cachona (AHD/Corregimiento, Causas Ordinarias: Leg. 53, c. 3, 1771–1772).[34]

The final two huacas of the ceque, Cauadcalla (Cu. 8 [collana]:14), a gateway between two hills, and Lluquiriui (Cu. 8[collana]:15), a large hill near Cauadcalla, are listed as being in the direction of Guacachaca, a famous Inca bridge over the Apurimac River approximately thirty aerial kilometers from Cusco. Although fieldwork between Cusco and this bridge did identify a number of impressive passes and large mountains, none were found with the names of Cauadcalla or Lluquiriui.

The Ninth Ceque of Cuntisuyu

The ninth ceque of Cuntisuyu is described as containing only three huacas. The first, Collquemachacuay (Cu. 9:1), was a well-known spring on the slope of Puquín Hill near Cusco. A place labeled Collque Machacuay is also on one of Guaman Poma de Ayala's drawings (1980:288 [1615:316 (318)]), and it is mentioned in numerous local land documents. Two maps of Cusco, published by Zárate (1921), show two springs called Colquemachacuay (Silver Snake) and Corimachacuay (Gold Snake) southwest of the Almodena cemetery. These springs are apparently the same ones that Garcilaso de la Vega mentions as being near a district of Cusco known as Chaquilla Chaca[35] and the royal road of Cuntisuyu:

Near the road there are two streams of excellent water which are channeled underground. The Indians do not know where the water comes from, for the work is a very ancient one and traditions about these things are being forgotten. The channels are called *collquemachác-huay*, silver snakes, for the water is as white as silver and the channels wind like snakes through the earth. (Garcilaso de la Vega 1966:420–421 [1609:Vol. 1, Bk. 7, Ch. 8])[36]

The spring of Corimachacuay can still be visited, but the spring of Colquemachacuay has been destroyed by city growth.

A large hill above Puquín called Micayurco (Cu. 9:2) is listed as the second shrine of this ceque. Puquín is a well-known sector of Cusco at the base of a large hill of the same

name. Fieldwork on the summit of Puquín Hill identified two possible areas for Cu. 9:2. The first is a large looters' pit on the summit's southeast edge containing Inca pottery fragments and the remains of a juvenile skull (Photo 3.6).[37] The second possible area, situated several hundred meters to the west of the first, contains two looters' pits. Although no ancient artifacts were found on the surface of this disturbed area, a recent burnt offering was found inside one of the pits.

The third and final shrine of this ceque, Chaquira (Cu. 9:3), is listed as a group of stones on a hill near the Alca road.[38] The community of Haquira is behind the hill of Puquín, and an Inca road to Chumbivilcas, formerly called Alca, passes near it.[39] A large hill beside the community may well have marked the end of this short ceque (Maps 8.1 and 8.2).

The Tenth Ceque of Cuntisuyu

Pilcopuquiu (Cu. 10:1), a fountain in the garden of Santo Domingo, is the first of four huacas along Cu. 10, and there is a well-crafted stone fountain with two canals directly south of the Temple of the Sun that may be this initial shrine (Photo 8.14). The second huaca, Puquincancha (Cu. 10:2), was a house of the Sun above Cayaocache, and the third, simply called Cancha (Cu. 10:3), was an enclosure wall of Puquincancha.[40] Cobo describes the ceremonies that took place at Puquincancha to mark the end of the month of Capac Raymi and the Inca ear-piercing celebrations:

On the last day of the month, they would go to the square on the hill of Puquin. They took two big sheep, one made of silver and the other of gold, six lambs, and the same number of *aporucos* [male llamas] which were dressed, along with six lambs of gold and silver, seashells, thirty white sheep, and the same number of articles of clothing. They burned everything, except the articles of silver and gold, on the said hill. And with this they ended the festival of Capac Raymi, which was the most serious and solemn festival of the whole year. (Cobo 1990:134 [1653:Bk. 13, Ch. 25])[41]

Molina (1989:110 [ca. 1575]) provides a second, similar description of activities at Puquincancha in the closing days of Capac Raymi:[42]

On the 23rd day of this month, they carried the statue of the Sun called *Huayna Punchao* [young day] to the

Photo 8.14. This well-crafted stone fountain with two canals near the Temple of the Sun could be Pilcopuquiu (Cu. 10:1).

Photo 8.15. Excavations on Puquín Hill revealed a large number of carved stone blocks, a foundation wall, and burnt Inca offerings. These may well be the remains of the Inca Sun temple called Puquincancha (Cu. 10:2).

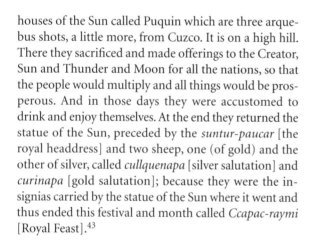

houses of the Sun called Puquin which are three arquebus shots, a little more, from Cuzco. It is on a high hill. There they sacrificed and made offerings to the Creator, Sun and Thunder and Moon for all the nations, so that the people would multiply and all things would be prosperous. And in those days they were accustomed to drink and enjoy themselves. At the end they returned the statue of the Sun, preceded by the *suntur-paucar* [the royal headdress] and two sheep, one (of gold) and the other of silver, called *cullquenapa* [silver salutation] and *curinapa* [gold salutation]; because they were the insignias carried by the statue of the Sun where it went and thus ended this festival and month called *Ccapac-raymi* [Royal Feast].[43]

In 1990, construction work on Puquín Hill unearthed several finely worked Inca stone blocks at a depth of more than two meters in an area traditionally known as Inticancha. Excavations were conducted at this site by the Instituto Nacional de Cultura in 1990 and 1991 (Photo 8.15). These excavations revealed a large number of carved stone blocks, a foundation wall, and burnt Inca offerings (Justo Torres, pers. com. 1991). The construction of a large Inca structure on the slope of Puquín is unusual, and given the quantity of remains at this site, it is reasonable to suggest that it represents the second and third shrines of Cu. 10.

The final huaca of this ceque, Viracochaurco (Cu. 10:4), is described as a hill above Puquín. There is a well-known mountain by this name (Photo 8.16) beyond Puquín near the community of Huancabamba that may mark the terminus for Cu. 10 (Maps 8.1 and 8.2).[44]

The Eleventh Ceque of Cuntisuyu

A spring named Matarapacha (Cu. 11:1) on the way to Cayaocache is listed as the first of four huacas on Cu. 11. This spring has been destroyed by urban growth, but there is a street called Matara, near the center of Cusco, marking its approximate location. The second shrine was a flat place below Matarapacha called Cuchiguayla (Cu. 11:2). One possible location for this shrine would be in the lower region of Matara Street. A second, more likely, location is an area called Cuchiriguaylla on the south bank of the Chinchul River, near the Almudena Bridge.[45] The third shrine was a spring, Puquinpuquiu (Cu. 11:3), on the slope of Puquín Hill. Although the exact position of this shrine has not been identified, it can be assumed to have been in the sector of Puquín.[46]

The final shrine, Tampu Vrco (Cu. 11:4), is characterized as a hill to one side of Puquín. While the generality of this

Photo 8.16. The summit of Viracochaurco (Cu. 10:4) may mark the terminus for Cu. 10.

Photo 8.17. The hill of Pucapuca offers the last view of the imperial city on the Inca road to Ccorca.

description makes a definitive identification difficult, a possibility has been found in a small but distant hill called Pucapuca on the eastern slope of Puquín that is covered with a light scatter of Inca and Killke pottery (Photo 8.17).[47] The Inca road to Ccorca enters a deep ravine after reaching Pucapuca, and inhabitants of Ccorca report that offerings were made there for a safe journey because the hill offers the last view of the imperial city (Maps 8.1 and 8.2).

The Twelfth Ceque of Cuntisuyu

The twelfth ceque of Cuntisuyu may have contained only three shrines. This short line began with Cunturpata (Cu. 12:1), described in the *Relación de las huacas* as a seat where the Inca rested when he went to the festival of Capac Raymi. Since much of this festival took place in Puquincancha (Cu. 10:2), it is possible that this huaca was between the center of Cusco and the slope of Puquín. The second shrine, Quilca (Cu. 12:2), is reported to be the tomb of a lord. The area of Cusco to the west of Puquín is called Killke. If the name Quilca is synonymous with that of Killke, then the huaca of Cu. 12:2 was most likely situated in this ward.

The final huaca of this ceque, Llipiquiliscacho (Cu. 12:3), described in the document as "another tomb behind Chocco," represents an interesting anomaly because the vil-

lage of Chocco is located southwest of Cusco, well off the apparent course of Cu. 12. The reference to this community appears to be an error, and the location of this shrine remains be to identified (Maps 8.1 and 8.2).

The Thirteenth Ceque of Cuntisuyu

The course of the thirteenth ceque of Cuntisuyu, defined by four huacas, is poorly understood. The first shrine was a spring called Chilquichaca (Cu. 13:1). A similar name, Chaquillchaca, appears in the chronicle of Garcilaso de la Vega (1966:420–421 [1609:Vol. 1, Bk. 7, Ch. 10]) as he described an area "a thousand paces west of Cayaocachi"; this places the shrine near the area of Killke. The second huaca, Colcapuquiu (Cu. 13:2), a spring in the ravine that descends from Chilquichaca, remains to be identified.

The ceque system document indicates that the third shrine, Chinchincalla (Cu. 13:3), was a large hill where there were two markers.[48] The document also states that when the sun reached these two markers it was time for the Inca to plant. Aveni (1981a) proposes that the Chinchincalla pillars marked the December solstice sunset, and he has identified a region on the west slope of Killke where the December solstice sun sets as viewed from Coricancha. My fieldwork found a small stone terrace, a light scatter of Inca

Photo 8.18. Killke Hill as seen from the Coricancha. Fieldwork in 1990 identified looted burials on Killke near where the sun sets on the December solstice as seen from the Coricancha.

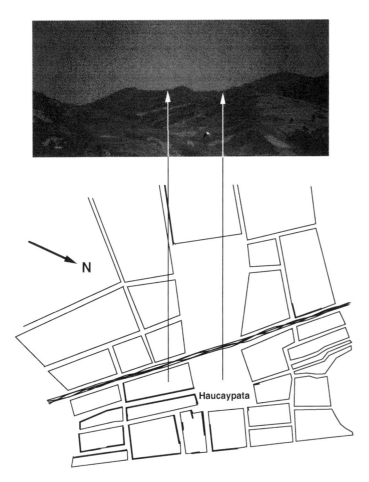

Figure 8.1. The location of the December solstice sunset as seen from the Plaza de Armas (Haucaypata). At this time, the sun sets over the area of Llamacancha.

Photo 8.19. Hacienda Picchu was a farm of the Jesuits, and Otcuropuquiu (Cu. 14:2) was near it.

Photo 8.20. The last huaca of Cuntisuyu was Pantanaya (Cu. 14:4). This cleft hill is still a sacred place.

pottery, and the remains of looted burials on the western shoulder of Killke.

As viewed from the center of the Coricancha, these burials mark a date in early December (Photo 8.18). From the small plaza in front of the temple traditionally called Intipata (Terrace of the Sun), they mark the December solstice sunset. It is possible, however, that the December solstice sunset was watched from the Cusco plaza, from which the sun can be seen to set to the southwest along the hill above Llamacancha (Figure 8.1). This hill is in the region that contained the thirteenth ceque of Cuntisuyu, and it marks an alternative location for Chinchincalla (Cu. 13:3).

The location of the final shrine of this line, a small hill called Pomaguaci (Cu. 13:4), is not known (Maps 8.1 and 8.2).

The Fourteenth Ceque of Cuntisuyu

The final ceque of Cuntisuyu contained four shrines.[49] The first huaca, a stone called Oznuro (Cu. 14:1) in a field of the Gualparocas, has yet to be identified.[50] Cobo explains that the second huaca, Otcuropuquiu (Cu. 14:2), was near Picchu, a farm of the Jesuits. This shrine is mentioned by Murúa (1987:332 [ca. 1615:Bk. 1, Ch. 91]), who writes, "another [spring], towards the north, was called Ocorura Puquiu, Watercress Spring, which is in Cuntisuyu . . ."[51] It may be presumed that this shrine was near the Jesuit hacienda of Picchu (Photo 8.19). The third shrine, Rauaypampa (Cu. 14:3), a terrace on the slope of the hill of Chinchincalla where the Inca lodged, has not been found.[52]

Pantanaya (Cu. 14:4), a hill cleft in the middle where the roads of Chinchaysuyu and Cuntisuyu divide, is characterized as the last shrine of the ceque. A well-known outcrop called Pantanaya, where the trail from Cusco diverges, with one branch leading northwest in the direction of Chinchaysuyu and the other heading southwest toward Cuntisuyu, is located five kilometers west of Cusco (Photo 8.20).[53] Pantanaya is still considered to be a special space, and some travelers will recite short prayers as they pass through it. There is a large looters' pit near the center of this outcrop, beside the fork in the road, which almost certainly marks the location where offerings were once made (Maps 8.1 and 8.2).

Summary and Discussion

Possible courses for the ceques of Cuntisuyu are presented on Map 8.3. From the data currently available, the Cuntisuyu ceques seem relatively straight, with the possible exceptions of Cu. 1 and Cu. 4. It should be noted that several of the initial shrines of the Cuntisuyu ceques are described as being in the Temple of the Sun. These include Cu. 1:1 (Sabarauva), Cu. 5:1 (Caritampucancha), Cu. 6:1 (Apian), Cu. 10:1 (Pilcopuquiu), and perhaps Cu. 7:1 (Inticancha). The location of the shrines on two ceques (Cu. 3 and Cu. 11) are so poorly defined that they cannot be plotted, and four of the ceques were exceptionally short (Cu. 6, Cu. 7, Cu. 11, and Cu. 12).

The best-charted ceque in Cuntisuyu is Cu. 1. It began with a Pururauca stone (Cu. 1:1) beneath the belvedere of Santo Domingo. From central Cusco the ceque crossed through the precincts of Pumachupa and Coripata (Cu. 1:3,

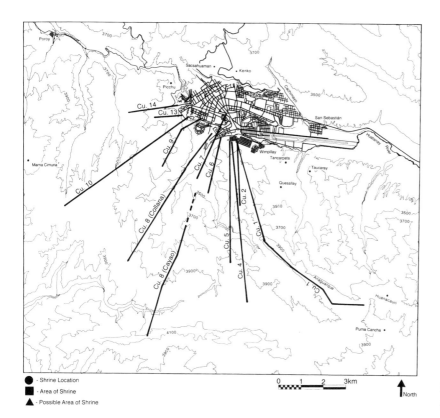

- ● - Shrine Location
- ■ - Area of Shrine
- ▲ - Possible Area of Shrine

0 1 2 3km

North

Map 8.3. Suggested courses of Cuntisuyu
ceques Cu. 1–Cu. 14.

Cu. 1:4, and Cu. 1:6). This line then ran along the ridge of Anaguarque (Cu. 1:7) to a series of closely spaced shrines (Cu. 1:8–Cu. 1:14) and ended with three stones in a mountain pass (Cu. 1:15), some eleven kilometers from Cusco.

The course of the eighth ceque is also noteworthy. Ground documentation of the system indicates that Cu. 8 was composed of two separate lines, both of which traveled to the southwest of Cusco. The first half, Cu. 8(cayao), began in Cusco and ended at the pass of Cachicalla (Cu. 8[cayao]:7) ten kilometers from the city. The second half, Cu. 8(collana), started just outside of Cusco and ran to the west of Cu. 8(cayao). Of the fifteen shrines that formed the two parts of Cu. 8, there is one particularly problematic huaca. The shrine of Cor Cor Puquiu (Cu. 8[cayao]:4) is found several kilometers west of the general course of Cu. 8(cayao), in approximate alignment with the course of Cu. 8(collana). I offer three possible explanations for this irregularity. First, it is possible that the ceque of Cu. 8(cayao) curved from the town of Cachona (Cu. 8[cayao]:3) to the spring of Cor Cor and then back to Chinchay Puquiu (Cu. 8[cayao]:5). It is also possible that there is a second, unidentified, spring called Cor Cor nearer Cachona, which repre-

sents the shrine mentioned in the *Relación de las huacas*. The third possibility is that the location of this spring has been incorrectly recorded in the ceque system document and that it belongs on the second half of this ceque, where it seems to fit better.

A recording error was found in the description of Cu. 12. The third shine of this line, Llipiquiliscacho (Cu. 12:3), is recorded as "another tomb behind Chocco." The village of Chocco is located some four kilometers east of this line and is associated with Cu. 6. Because the second shrine of Cu. 12 is described as "Quilca . . . a very ancient tomb," it is possible that Cu. 12:3 should read as "another tomb behind Quilca."

This chapter concludes the archaeological and archival documentation of the shrines of the Cusco ceque system as recorded in the *History of the New World*. Cobo was not, however, the only writer to record the existence of a system of huacas in the imperial valley. In the next chapter, the shrines of Cusco as described by Cristóbal de Albornoz will be discussed, and the information that he preserved will be compared to that found within Cobo's work.

9

Albornoz and the Cusco Ceque System

ONE OF THE most difficult aspects of studying Andean ceque systems is that there are few detailed data sources on these indigenous ritual complexes.[1] This dearth of information is in many ways surprising, since several literate Spaniards were aware of the Cusco ceques and of analogous systems in other communities. As noted in Chapter 2, José de Acosta (1954:560–561, 562 [1580:Bk. 5, Chs. 9 and 10]) and Cristóbal de Molina (1989:126 [ca. 1575]), as well as Pedro Córdoba Mexía (1900:396 [ca. 1572]) and Viceroy Toledo (1924:394 [1572]), each obliquely mentions Andean ceque systems, but provides no substantive information on their internal organization. Similarly, we know that Juan Polo de Ondegardo's (1916c:55–57 [1571]; 1916a:43 [1585]; 1940:183–184 [1561]) report on the Cusco shrines was widely circulated among the religious leaders of that city, and that he investigated a large number of other systems in the highlands, yet few specific details on the internal arrangement of these systems have survived.

Apart from Cobo and Polo de Ondegardo, it seems that only one Spaniard, Cristóbal de Albornoz, systematically recorded the huacas he encountered. Albornoz (1984:218 [ca. 1582]) was aware of various ceque systems throughout the Andes and, like Polo de Ondegardo, implored other Spaniards to destroy them and their shrines. He writes:

> It needs to be cautioned that, around the other huacas located in the mountains and in the plains, there are some marks that are called ceques or cachauis, which are marks of the offerings that were made to these huacas. These are made and those signs immortalize the names of those who offered there a child or a sheep of gold, (or of) silver, or (of) mollo [shell]. You will find the offerings in those ceques or cachauis. It is necessary to destroy them together with the huacas, and with great care.[2]

Albornoz indicates that huacas and certain marks called ceques occurred together. He also suggests that each of the ceques was named for the people who maintained the hua-cas along them. Because he offers advice on how to discover and destroy the ceques themselves, it seems that some may have been more than imaginary lines, possibly forming marks or trails that could be physically obliterated.[3]

Albornoz became one of the most effective extirpators of idolatries of the Early Colonial period.[4] After leading a series of brutal campaigns against native religious practices in the Huamanga region, Albornoz wrote his treatise *Instrucción para descubrir . . .*, encouraging his fellow countrymen to continue the destruction of Andean shrines.[5] In this work, Albornoz describes various types of huacas that he identified during his extirpation campaigns, and he presents lists of shrines between Cusco and Quito. Within this information, Albornoz provides the names of thirty-seven shrines in the confines of Cusco, the majority of which also appear in the *Relación de las huacas*.

Albornoz's description of the shrines near Cusco is short, poorly written, and in places difficult to understand. Some researchers suggest that the surviving manuscript is an incomplete summation of the information collected by this extirpator of idolatry. For example, Rowe (1980:72) notes that Albornoz's account "is known to us only in a very poor copy with many omissions and spelling errors. It is quite possible that the copy we have is only a summary of the original, and that the original listed many more shrines." Despite these many shortcomings, because Albornoz's huaca list is the only known description of the Cusco ceque system outside the writings of Bernabé Cobo, his *Instrucción para descubrir . . .* is critical to the study of the ceques. As an alternative and independent source, Albornoz's account furnishes a wealth of locational, descriptional, and mythological information on individual huacas of the Cusco system that is not preserved by Cobo. It also provides comparative data to analyze (1) the number of shrines in the Cusco ceque system, (2) the internal organization of the system, and (3) the overall accuracy of Cobo's document.

Albornoz and the Huacas of Chinchaysuyu

A section of Albornoz's *Instrucción para descubrir . . .* describes various huacas situated between Cusco and the northern frontier of the Inca Empire, as well as a few on the coast. The catalogue begins with shrines in the Chinchaysuyu region of Cusco. The huacas of other areas are then described in relation to their distance from Cusco. After discussing the highland Chinchaysuyu huacas, Albornoz presents brief discussions of coastal shrines in the Lima, Pisco, Ica, Chincha, and Pachacamac areas. The apparent purpose of these shrine lists was to illustrate that a large number and a great diversity of huacas were still being worshipped a generation after the Spanish conquest (Bauer and Barrionuevo Orosco 1998).

The form of Albornoz's Cusco shrine list varies distinctly from that included in Cobo's chronicle. Cobo begins by stating that the Cusco shrines were organized in lines that radiated out from the center of the city, and that the huacas along each ceque were the responsibility of different kin groups. He then presents systematic descriptions of 328 shrines in accordance with their positions along forty-two ceques. Furthermore, before discussing the individual huacas of a ceque, Cobo notes the number of shrines on that line and whether the ceque was classified as collana, payan, or cayao. Albornoz's account is less complex, because he simply presents a list of 37 shrines. However, as will be seen in the conclusion of this chapter, the order of Albornoz's shrines is consistent with information presented by Cobo concerning the organization of the system as a whole.

The Cusco huacas recorded by Albornoz are presented below in Table 9.1. Like Rowe (1980:72–76), I include short commentaries after each shrine description (pp. 137–141), noting if the shrine is mentioned in the *Relación de las huacas* or by other chroniclers.

Table 9.1. List of Huacas in the Chinchaysuyu Region of Cusco from Albornoz [ca. 1582]

(1) La primera guaca fue Curicancha, que quiere dezir casa de oro y era casa del Sol.
(2) Quillcai cancha, que era en la plaça ques agora de Santo Domingo.
(3) Yllanguaiqui, que era otra casa en la dicha plaça donde se celebrava la fiesta del raimi.
(4) Uman amaro, piedra de figura de un bolo questava en la plaça.
(5) Sanca que era casa y carcel y la mochauan mucho.
(6) Margauiche, piedra pequeña questava en la dicha plaça.
(7) Agmoasca, que era un altar questava en la dicha plaça donde sacrificavan.
(8) Haucaypata pacha ques una fuente questá en la ciudad.
(9) Marcatambo, una peña questava en Carmenga.
(10) Tucanamaro, que era una piedra questava en Carmenga.
(11) Cacchacuchui, que eran unas piedras redondas en la dicha Carmenga.
(12) Yauirac, que eran unas piedras juntas, hazían muchos sacrificios en ellas de indios.
(13) Mararoray, que era un bulto de mujer hecha de piedra, donde sacrificavan mujers.
(14) Urcos calla uiracocha, ques un cerro pequeño junto a la guaca Mamoray.
(15) Oma chilligues, un llano adonde los yngas tubieron batalla con los changas y los vencieron; e huyeron los changas, y dizen que se volvieron cóndores y se escaparon. Y ansí los más ayllos de los chancas se llaman condor guachos.
(16) Suchique era un altar donde sacrificavan personas, animales y otros animales en la dicha pampa.
(17) Churucani guanacauri, piedra grande y al rededor muchas guaquillas de piedras que llaman cachauis.
(18) Guaman cancha era un montón de piedras encima de Carmenga.
(19) Cusicancha pachamama, que era una casa donde nasció Tupa Ynga Yupangui.
(20) Quicasunto, que era una piedra como bola,[1] que tenían en lugar público para mocharla.
(21) Pucamarca quisuarcancha, que era la casa del hazedor y de los truenos.
(22) Catungui, que era un escuadrón de piedras como gentes de guerra, camino de Alca.
(23 & 24) Hanan chaca y hurinchaca, dos nacimientos de fuentes.
(25) Uscucalla, que eran piedras en el río del Cuzco, redondas.
(26) Usno era un pilar de oro donde bevían al Sol en la plaça.
(27) Capa era un árbol grande y lo bestian y ofrescíanle mucho.
(28) Guairaguaca, agujero en la fortaleza de donde dizen sale el biento.
(29) Chaca guanacauri, piedra sobre la fortaleza.
(30) Anca, un cerro encima del Cuzco y en él muchas piedras guacas.
(31) Piuni guaca, piedra en la ladera del cerro.
(32) Nina era un bezerro que siempre ardía.
(33) Guaracinci, una piedra labrada a la puerta del Sol.
(34) Luchus amaro era una piedra en Tococache.
(35) Ancas pata es un peñon donde estava la casa de Uiracocha Ynga.
(36) Pilco puquio es una fuente.
(37) Sico cayan, guaca cueva de donde dizen salió el granizo.

Source: Albornoz (1984:204–205 [ca. 1582]).
1. Rowe (1980:74) notes that the original document might have read "bolo" (ninepin).

(#1) "The first huaca was Coricancha, which means 'House of Gold,' and was the house of the Sun." Although Cobo states that the ceques radiated from the Coricancha, he does not include it on a specific line.

(#2) "Quillcai cancha, which was on the plaza that now is the plaza of Santo Domingo." No additional information is available on this shrine.

(#3) "Yllanguaiqui, which was another house on the said plaza where the Raymi festival was celebrated." Cobo (1980:27 [1653:Bk. 13, Ch. 13]) writes that Ch. 8:1 was "a small house next to the Temple of the Sun named Illanguarque, in which were kept certain weapons which they said the sun had given to Inca Yupanqui, [and] with which he conquered his enemies."

(#4) "Uman amaro, stone in the figure of a skittle that was in the plaza." Cobo (1980:25 [1653:Bk. 13, Ch. 13]) describes Ch. 7:1, Omanamaro, as "a long stone which they said was [one] of the Pururaucas and which was in the doorway of the house which belonged to [Juan de] Figueroa." Garcilaso de la Vega indicates that Figueroa's house was somewhere north of the Temple of the Sun and south of the Plaza de Armas.

(#5) "Sanca, which was a house and prison, and they revered it very much." Cobo (1980:27, 49 [1653:Bk. 13, Chs. 13 and 15]) provides two descriptions of shrines called Sanca. The first description is of Sanca Cancha and Hurin Sanca (Ch. 7:2), which is said by Cobo to be "two small *buhios* (huts) . . . where they had a quantity of lions [i.e., pumas], tigers [i.e., jaguars], serpents, and all the other evil vermin that were available." The second is Sancacancha (Co. 8:1), which is registered as "a prison . . . , which Mayta Capac made; it was on the house lot which belonged to [Juan de] Figueroa." This prison of Sanca must have been an important building in Cusco because it is also mentioned by Guaman Poma de Ayala (Sancay Uaci), Loarte (Sanzahuaci), and Cabello de Balboa (Sanca). Since Garcilaso de la Vega indicates that Juan de Figueroa lived between the Coricancha and Pucamarca, it can be proposed that this shrine was located north of the Temple of the Sun.

(#6) "Margauiche, a small stone that was in the said plaza." No additional information is available on this shrine.

(#7) "Agmoasca, which was an altar that was in the said plaza where they made sacrifices." No additional information is available on this shrine.

(#8) "Haucaypata pacha, which is a spring that is in the city." Cobo (1980:27 [1653:Bk. 13, Ch. 13]) describes Ch. 8:3 as a spring called Aucaypata [Paccha], "which was next to where the house of the cabildo [municipal council] is now. In it the priests of Chucuilla said that the Thunder bathed, and they made up a thousand other absurdities." Because the plaza of Cusco was called Haucaypata and Garcilaso de la Vega states that the Cabildo was situated on its northern side, this shrine may have been somewhere near the northern end of the plaza.

(#9) "Marcatambo, a cliff that was in Carmenca." Cobo (1980:25 [1653:Bk. 13, Ch. 13]) suggests that this shrine was located in Carmenca, near the church of Santa Ana, because he describes Marcatampu (Ch. 7:3) as "some round stones which were in Carmenga, where the parish church of Santa Ana is now, which [stones] Inca Yupanqui designated as an important shrine."

(#10) "Tucanamaro, which was a stone that was in Carmenca." According to Cobo (1980:27 [1653:Bk. 13, Ch. 13]), the shrine that followed Marcatampu (Ch. 7:3) was called Taxanamaro (Ch. 7:4), and "it consisted of five round stones which Viracocha Inca ordered placed on the hill of Toxan [*sic*] which is above Carmenga. . . . This guaca was prayed to for the victory of the Inca." The exact location of this shrine remains to be identified.

(#11) "Cacchacuchui, which were some round stones in the said Carmenca." No additional information is available on this shrine.

(#12) "Yauirac, which was a group of stones; they made many sacrifices of Indians to them." For this shrine (Ch. 9:6) Cobo (1980:29 [1653:Bk. 13, Ch. 13]) writes, "a stone called Apuyauira which was on the hill of Picho [Picchu]. They believed that it was one of those who emerged from the earth with Huanacauri, and that after having lived for a long time he climbed up there and turned to stone. All the ayllos went to worship at it in the festival of Raymi." Betanzos and Cieza de León both mention this shrine, as does Molina, who indicates that part of the male initiation rites, held during the Capac Raymi festival, took place there. Survey work on the south slope of Picchu identified an outcrop called the Ñusta (Princess), which most likely represents this shrine.

(#13) "Mararoray, which was a figure of a woman made of stone, where they sacrificed women [or, where women made sacrifices]." Cobo (1980:27 [1653:Bk. 13, Ch. 13]) indicates that there was a shrine called Mamararoy (Ch. 8:8), which he describes as "a house . . . in which were venerated certain stones which they said were women [or wives] of Ticci Viracocha, and that, walking at night, they had turned to stone. Finding them in that place, they made that temple for them." The location of this shrine has not been determined.

(#14) "Urcos calla uiracocha, which is a small hill beside the huaca of Mamoray [*sic*; i.e., the one just mentioned]." Cobo (1980:27 [1653:Bk. 13, Ch. 13]) writes that the shrine following Mamararoy (Ch. 8:8) was called Urcoscalla (Ch. 8:9), and he describes it as "the place where those who traveled to Chinchaysuyu lost sight of the city of Cuzco." This shrine may have been the pass of Arco Punco, the north entrance to the Cusco Valley (Aveni 1981a; Zuidema 1982a), or it may have been located several hundred meters downslope where the city is last seen (see Photo 5.26).

(#15) "Oma chilligues, a plain where the Incas had a battle with the Chanca and they defeated them; and the Chanca fled, and they say that they turned into condors and escaped. And thus most Chanca ayllus are called condor guachos." A similar shrine is recorded by Cobo (1980:29 [1653:Bk. 13, Ch. 13]) as Ch. 9:8: "The eighth was another flat place . . . named Queachili, which is between two hills like a gateway; in it the said victory was completed, and for that [reason] it was venerated." This battleground is also mentioned by Cabello de Balboa and by Santa Cruz Pachacuti Yamqui Salcamayhua (Rowe 1980:9). Archival research suggests that this shrine was a pass near the end of the Anta plain, some forty-five kilometers west of Cusco.

(#16) "Suchique was an altar where they sacrificed people, animals, and other animals (sic) in the said pampa." No additional information is available on this shrine.

(#17) "Churucani guanacauri, a large stone and around it were many little stone guacas which they call cachauis." A shrine called Churuncana (Ch. 7:7) is presented by Cobo (1980: 25 [1653:Bk. 13, Ch. 13]) as "a round hill which is above Carmenga where the royal road of Chinchero leaves that of Yucay. From this hill the sacrifices to Ticci Viracocha were made, asking him that the Inca be victorious throughout the land to the limits of the sea." This shrine may be a prominent round hill above Santa Ana currently called Curcaca.

(#18) "Guaman cancha was a pile of stones above Carmenca." Within the *Relación de las huacas*, a shrine named Guamancancha (Ch. 4:5) is described as "near the fortress on a small hill of this name. It was an enclosure inside of which there were two small buhios designated for fasting when orejones were made." Molina also writes that young men spent the night at a place called Guamancancha before ascending to the shrine of Yauira (Ch. 9:6). However, the exact location of this shrine remains to be identified. The proposed locations of these shrines, #18 in Carmenca and Ch. 4:5 on the slope of Sacsahuaman, suggest that there may have been two separate shrines named Guamancancha.

(#19) "Cusicancha pachamama, which was a house where Tupa Inca Yupangui was born." Cobo (1980:21 [1653:Bk. 13, Ch. 13]) also includes a place called Cusichanca (Ch. 5:1) in his list of huacas, stating that it "was the place where Inca Yupanqui was born, opposite the temple of Coricancha; for this reason the members of the ayllo Inacapanaca sacrificed there." A place labeled Cusicancha is also shown on Guaman Poma de Ayala's map of Cusco.

(#20) "Quicasunto, which was a stone like a ball, which they had in a public place to revere it."[6] No additional information is available on this shrine.

(#21) "Pucamarca quisuarcancha, which was the house of the Creator and of the Thunders." There are two shrines in the *Relación de las huacas* called Pucamarca. The first, Ch. 5:2, fol-lows Cusichanca (Ch. 5:1) and is described as "a temple . . . which was in the houses which belonged to Licentiate [Antonio] de la Gama; in it was an idol of the Thunder called Chucuylla." The second, Ch. 6:2, is presented as "a house or temple designated for the sacrifices of the Pachayachachi [Creator] in which children were sacrificed and everything else." Rowe (1980:23), using information from Molina, who states that the temple of the Creator was called Quishuarcancha, suggests that Ch. 6:2 (Pucamarca) is misnamed in the *Relación de las huacas*.[7]

Pucamarca, based on information provided by Garcilaso de la Vega, is thought to have been south of Hatun Cancha, along Maruri Street (Squier 1877; Zárate 1921; Agurto Calvo 1980, 1987). Quishuarcancha is believed to have been beneath the Cusco Cathedral or the Triunfo Church (Molina 1989:59 [ca. 1575]; Urbano and Duviols 1989:59 n. 17; Hyslop 1990; Rowe 1990:86–87). Given this mix of information, it is difficult to suggest which of these two locations is the better possibility for Albornoz's shrine Pucamarca Quisuarcancha.

(#22) "Catungui, which was a squadron of stones like men of war, [on the] trail to Alca." This is an interesting entry because Cobo (1980:23, 59 [1653:Bk. 13, Chs. 13 and 15]) describes Ch. 6:1, Catonge, as "a stone of the Pururaucas, which was in a window next to the Temple of the Sun"; however, he also presents Cu. 9:3, Chaquira (Haquira), as "a hill which is near the Alca road, on top of which there were ten stones held to be idols." Haquira is, as suggested by Cobo, near the road to Alca, or what is now known as Chumbivilcas. It seems that Albornoz mistakenly included a description of Cu. 9:3, Haquira, under the listing for Ch. 6:1, Catunqui. This suggests that Albornoz may have known about, or had access to, additional information on the other shrines of the Cusco region.

(#23) and (#24) "Hanan chaca [Upper Bridge] and hurinchaca [Lower Bridge], two sources of springs." Although Cobo does not list these two shrines in his discussion of the Cusco ceque system, the springs of Hananchaca and Hurinchaca must have been well-known features of the Cusco landscape because they are described in detail by a number of other writers (Santa Cruz Pachacuti Yamqui Salcamayhua 1950 [1613]; Villanueva and Sherbondy 1978). The accounts associate Hananchaca and Hurinchaca with the sixth king of Cusco, Inca Roca, in that they recount the mythical establishment of an irrigation system in Hanan Cusco (Van de Guchte 1990: 112–115). For example, Sarmiento de Gamboa (1906:49 [1572: Ch. 19]) writes:

> And he also conquered to Caytomarca four leagues from Cuzco, and discovered and canalized the waters of Hurinchacan and those of Hananchacan, which is to say the "waters of upper" and the "waters of lower" Cusco, which up to the present irrigate the fields of Cusco; and thus his sons and descendants have and possess them now.[8]

Similar information is provided by Cabello de Balboa, who had access to Sarmiento de Gamboa's manuscript or used a shared source:

> . . . and vassals agreed to create order by putting canals of water in that valley so that the land[s] could be used, which because of lack of irrigation were not worked, and untilled, and thus he chose those that today are called Hananchaca and Hurinchaca, which have been and will be a work of much importance for all that community.[9]

Cieza de León also describes the mythical origin of irrigation in the Cusco Valley. Although he does not mention Hananchaca and Hurinchaca by name, it is clear that the events that he describes were believed to have taken place at these shrines:

> These Indians tell that at the time this Inca's [Inca Roca] ears were pierced for the earrings the *Orejones* wear to this very day, one of them hurt him very much, and that with this annoyance he left the city and went to a very high nearby hill, called Chaca, where he sent for his wives and the Coya, his sister Micay Cuca, whom he had received as his wife during the life of his father, to keep him company. At this point they tell of a fabulous mystery that occurred. In those days no brook or river ran through the city. . . . Now when the Inca was at this hill, withdrawing from this people, he began to pray to the great Tici-Viracocha, and to Huana-cauri, and to the sun, and to the Incas, his father and grandfathers, to make known to him how and in what way, by human means, he could bring a river or canal of water to the city; and while he was praying, a great clap of thunder was heard which frightened all who were there, and the Inca himself, from the great fright he received, lowered his head until his left ear touched the ground, from which blood began to gush, and suddenly he heard a great rushing of water beneath that spot. When he perceived this wonder, he joyously ordered many Indians to come from the city, who quickly set about digging until they reached the stream of water which had made a channel through the bowels of the earth and was flowing without doing any good. (Cieza de León 1976:202–203 [1554:Pt. 2, Ch. 35])[10]

Despite these references, the exact locations of the springs of Hananchaca and Hurinchaca remain unknown. It should be noted, however, that this shrine may be related to Ch. Extra:2, Tocoripuquiu, which Cobo (1980:60 [1653:Bk. 13, Ch. 28]) describes as the spring "from which issues a stream which passes through the city," and which Cobo also associates with Inca Roca and the irrigation of Hanan Cusco.

(#25) "Uscucalla, which were round stones in the river of Cusco." The name of the shrine is similar to that of Cuzcocalla (Ch. 5:3). However, the description of this huaca presented by Cobo is markedly different, since he suggests that Cuzcocalla

was a group of stones, which were all Pururaucas, on the street that leads to the plaza.

(#26) "Usno was a pillar of gold where they drank to the Sun in the plaza." While Cobo does include the central plaza of Cusco, otherwise called Haucaypata (Ch. 5:4), in his shrine list, and an usnu in a lower plaza called Hurin Haucaypata (An. 5:1), he does not specifically mention a pillar called Usnu in the central plaza. Nevertheless, the central usnu of Cusco was a prominent feature of the plaza, and it is mentioned by a number of different writers (Rowe 1980:75). Cieza de León (1985:109 [1554:Pt. 2, Ch. 36]) describes it as a cone-shaped stone covered with gold, and the Anonymous Chronicler (1906:158 [ca. 1570]) supports Cieza de León, writing that a stone pillar and a platform called "osno" stood in the main plaza of Cusco. Betanzos (1987:52 [1557:Pt. 1, Ch. 11]) indicates that it was a pointed rock covered with gold, and Segovia (1943:22 [1553]) states that it was "a high, square platform with a very high stairway."[11]

(#27) "Capa was a large tree and they dressed it and offered it much." This shrine is included in Cobo's list of huacas as Ch. 6:7. He writes that Capi means root, and describes the shrine as "a very large quinua [tree] root which the sorcerers said was the root from which Cuzco issued and by means of which it was preserved" (Cobo 1980:25 [1653:Bk. 13, Ch. 13]). This shrine was most certainly in the ravine of Saphi, perhaps at the summit of a hill now called Muyu Urco, which has been heavily damaged by looters.

(#28) "Guairaguaca, a hole in the fortress from where they say the wind leaves." Cobo (1980:23 [1653:Bk. 13, Ch. 13]) presents this shrine (Ch. 6:4) as "Guayra . . . in the doorway of Cajana. At it sacrifice was made to the wind, so that it would not do damage, and a pit had been made here in which sacrifices were buried." The Cassana, the palace of Huayna Capac, was on the northwest corner of the plaza.

(#29) "Chaca guanacauri, a stone above the fortress." Chacaguanacauri (Ch. 5:7) is described by Cobo (1980:23 [1653: Bk. 13, Ch. 13]) as "a small hill which is on the way to Yucay, where the young men who were preparing themselves to be orejones went for a certain grass which they carried on their lances." Researchers (Sherbondy 1982:81; Zuidema 1986: 192–193; Van de Guchte 1990:108–110, 371) suggest that this shrine is related to a large archaeological complex called Chacan along the upper Saphi River.

(#30) "Anca, a hill above Cusco and on it many stone huacas." No additional information is available on this shrine.

(#31) "Piuni guaca, a stone on the slope of the hill." No additional information is available on this shrine.

(#32) "Nina was a brazier that always burned." Cobo (1980:19 [1653:Bk. 13, Ch. 13]) describes this shrine (Ch. 3:1) as "Nina, which was a brazier made of a stone where the fire for sacrifices was lit, and they could not take it from anywhere else. It

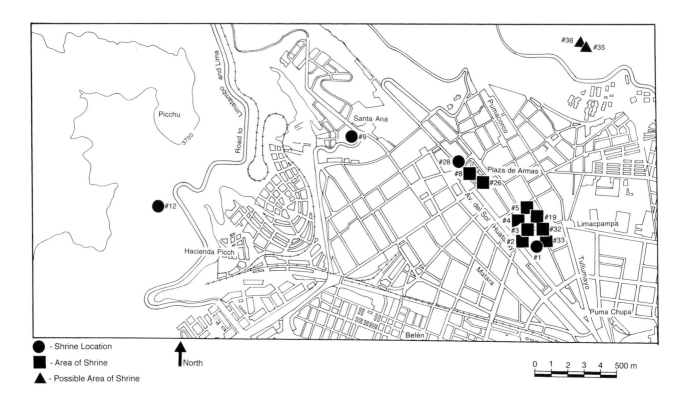

Map 9.1. Possible locations of shrines in the city of Cusco as described by Albornoz.

was next to the Temple of the Sun; it was held in great veneration, and solemn sacrifices were made to it." This shrine must have been a prominent feature of ancient Cusco, since it is further described by Cobo as well as by Murúa.

(#33) "Guaracinci, a worked stone in the door of the Sun." Cobo (1980:17 [1653:Bk. 13, Ch. 13]), suggesting that this shrine (Ch. 2:1) was in the Coricancha complex, writes, "Guaracince, which was in the plaza of the Temple of the Sun, [a plaza] called Chuquipampa (it means 'plain of gold'). It was a bit of flat ground which was there, in which they said that the earthquake was formed."

(#34) "Luchus amaro was a stone in Tococache." Cobo (1980: 15 [1653:Bk. 13, Ch. 13]) provides an extended discussion of this shrine (Ch. 1:1), calling it Michosamaro: "It was located up against the slope of the hill of Totocache, and they said it was one of those who they fancied had emerged with the first Inca Manco Capac from the cave of Pacaritampu. They relate that one of the women who came out of the cave with them killed him because of an act of disrespect towards her which he committed. He turned to stone, and his spirit appeared in this same place and ordered that they make sacrifices to him there. Thus the sacrifice at this guaca was very ancient. It always consisted of gold, clothing, sea shells, and other things, and it used

to be made for good rains." Although the general area of Totocache is known, the location of this shrine has not been identified.

(#35) "Ancas pata is a cliff where the house of Viracocha Inca was." Cobo calls this shrine Patallacta (Ch. 1:2) and describes it as "a house which Inca Yupanqui designated for his sacrifices, and he died in it" (Cobo 1980:17 [1653:Bk. 13, Ch. 13]). Other chroniclers who mention Patallacta include Acosta and Sarmiento de Gamboa. Sherbondy suggests that the most likely position for this famous Inca palace is the area of Kenko (Grande and Chico), which is beside an area still called Patallacta.

(#36) "Pilco puquio is a spring." The shrine, which follows Patallacta (Ch. 1:2) in the *Relación de las huacas*, is a spring called Pilcopuquio (Ch. 1:3). A small stream once flowed between the ruins of Kenko Grande and Kenko Chico and may have represented this shrine.

(#37) "Sico cayan, a cave guaca from which they say the hail came out." Cobo (1980:23 [1653:Bk. 13, Ch. 13]) provides a similar description for the shrine following Pilcopuquio (Ch. 1:3), writing that Cirocaya (Ch. 1:4) was "a cave of stone from which they believed that hail issued. Hence, at the season when they were afraid of it, all went to sacrifice in the cave, so that it

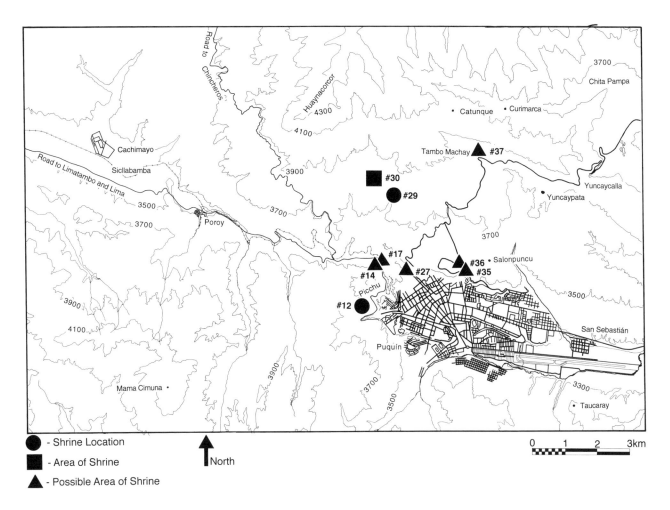

Map 9.2. Possible locations of shrines outside Cusco as described by Albornoz.

should not come out and destroy their crops." The likely candidate for this huaca is the famous cave of Tambomachay, situated at the northeastern corner of the Cusco Valley.

Summary and Discussion

Albornoz's shrine list for Chinchaysuyu was recorded around 1582, twenty-three years after the proposed 1559 drafting of the *Relación de las huacas,* and nearly fifty years after the Spaniards gained control of Cusco. Nevertheless, this account contains information not preserved in Cobo's chronicle that can be used in the advancement of Andean ceque system studies (Maps 9.1 and 9.2).

Perhaps as many as twenty-four of the thirty-seven shrines described by Albornoz as being in Chinchaysuyu are also represented in Cobo, although, as noted by Rowe

(1980:76), "the information given about them is sometimes quite different and in one case [#35] the name is different." Thirteen of the shrines named by Albornoz do not seem to appear in the *Relación de las huacas.* Huacas close to Cusco are more likely to appear on both lists than are those at a distance from the imperial city. The end section of Albornoz's list presents the area of greatest consistency, because Albornoz's shrines 32, 33, 34, 35, 36, and 37 all appear in Cobo's account. There is considerable overlap between the two authors for the shrines of the first ceque of Chinchaysuyu (Ch. 1), which Cobo indicates contained a total of five huacas. Albornoz provides the names of the first four shrines of Ch. 1. The area of least consistency is the middle of Albornoz's account, because shrines 20, 22, 23, 24, and 26 are absent from the *Relación de las huacas.*

Cobo's representation of the system begins in the northeast and moves to the northwest. Albornoz's list moves in the opposite direction. Nevertheless, Albornoz's account of Chinchaysuyu shrines supports Cobo's suggestion that certain huacas of Cusco were organized along lines that were enumerated into sequences of three (Rowe 1980:76). The first seventeen shrines of Albornoz's list appear to have been along ceques Ch. 7, Ch. 8, and Ch. 9; the next fourteen were on ceques Ch. 4, Ch. 5, and Ch. 6; and the final six were on ceques Ch. 3, Ch. 2, and Ch. 1. It also supports the belief that the shrines were counted outward from the center of Cusco. This ordering is especially clear in Albornoz's presentation of shrines 34, 35, 36, and 37.

Juan Polo de Ondegardo may have continued finding shrines in the Cusco region after writing the *Relación de las huacas* around 1559, since he noted in 1561 that there were some four hundred shrines in the Cusco area. The nonin- clusive nature of the *Relación de las huacas* is also suggested by a parenthetical remark, near the end of the document, which indicates that at least four huacas of the system were not recorded when the initial investigation was made. The recovery of Albornoz's list, which, while partially overlap- ping with the *Relación de las huacas,* provides the names and descriptions of thirteen Chinchaysuyu shrines not found in Cobo's account, lends considerable strength to the argument that the total number of shrines in Chinchaysuyu was far greater than that reported by Cobo (Rowe 1980:76). Furthermore, given this information, it is reasonable to sug- gest that there were various shrines in the other three suyus of the system not recorded when Cobo's source document was made. The recognition that the *Relación de las huacas* may be incomplete limits the quality and quantity of con- clusions that can responsibly be derived from it.

10

Systems of Huacas and Ceques: Past and Present

THE CUSCO CEQUE SYSTEM has long held a prominent position in ethnohistorical research on Inca ritual complexes. This is a result of the extraordinary information presented within the *Relación de las huacas* and of Zuidema's explorations of the system. The review of early colonial references to Andean ceque systems presented in Chapter 2 indicates, however, that the imperial city of the Inca was not unique among Andean communities in containing such a shrine network. Albornoz states that Andean shrines were frequently organized along lines, and Polo de Ondegardo investigated more than one hundred systems during his travels across the Andes. Around 1571, the bishop of Charcas, who doubted that ceque systems were universal, was shown one in Pocona (Bolivia) by Polo de Ondegardo.

The goal of this chapter is to examine the archaeological, historical, and ethnographical evidence for radial lines of shrines outside the Cusco Valley.[1] In the first and second sections, I discuss various Inca and pre-Inca remains that provide strong circumstantial evidence that these systems can be found beyond the Inca heartland. In the third section, I present ethnographic information indicating that complex systems of shrines in remote areas of Bolivia and Chile endured into the twentieth century, with some practices continuing today.

Evidence of Other Inca Ceques

Various colonial documents and Inca archaeological remains have been examined by researchers for evidence of huaca worship and radial pathways. Some of the results suggest that there were ceque systems, or at least ceque-like systems, in other parts of the Andes during Inca times. The most convincing cases are those of the Capac Cocha ritual and the Cusco–Vilcanota ceque (Zuidema 1982a). Others, including those of Anta (Bauer and Barrionuevo Orosco 1997), Huánuco Pampa (Morris and Thompson 1985), and Inkawasi (Hyslop 1985), are more speculative.

The Capac Cocha

It has frequently been suggested that there is a relationship between the Capac Cocha rituals of the Inca and the Cusco ceque system. Indeed, Molina (1989:126 [ca. 1575]) indicates that during a Capac Cocha event, the shrines of the Cusco ceque system were visited first, and then priests were sent to the other huacas of the empire. Capac Cocha rituals involved the transportation of offerings from the city of Cusco to the most important shrines of the Inca Empire. The objects presented to the shrines differed according to the importance of the huacas, but the range of offerings (e.g., coca, llama blood, shells, cloth, silver, gold, children) was similar to that listed in the *Relación de las huacas* for the Cusco ceque system. According to Molina (1989:120–128 [ca. 1575]) and Cobo (1990:154–157 [1653:Bk. 13, Ch. 32]) the Capac Cocha ritual was an elaborate ceremony held on the rarest of occasions. It was performed only when a new Inca ascended to power or at times of great need. Other writers, principally Cieza de León (1976:151–152, 190–193 [1554:Pt. 2, Chs. 28 and 29]), suggest that Capac Cocha rituals were annual celebrations.[2] Whether held yearly or occasionally, the process of huaca adoration in this ritual was similar to what Cobo describes for the huacas of the Cusco region.

A Capac Cocha event began in the central plaza of Cusco with the collection of an immense amount of sacrificial material from all the provinces of Tahuantinsuyu. Huaca experts then left Cusco with the offerings to visit the major shrines of the empire. Molina wrote that on their departure from Cusco, the priests did not follow roads, but walked in straight lines, through ravines and over hills, to each of the selected shrines. Cobo, who had a copy of Molina's report, provides an even more detailed account of the route taken by the Capac Cocha priests. He suggests that all the huacas of the Cusco Valley were visited first, and then the attendants traveled toward those located in the provinces:

Once the sacrifices for all the *guacas* of Cuzco were concluded, the Inca ordered the provincial priests to take what had been allotted to the *guacas* of their lands in the distribution that had been made and offer it to them. The priests left at once to carry out the order, walking according to the following arrangement. The livestock went alone along the royal road, and the throng of people carrying the other sacrifices, off the road in parties somewhat separated and lined up in single file with the sacrifices ahead. They went straight toward the place where they were going without turning anywhere, going over hills and through ravines until each one reached his land. The children who could walk went on foot, but they carried the very tiny ones on their backs, along with the gold and other things. From time to time they raised their voices in a loud shout, starting with one person who was designated for this purpose, . . . (Cobo 1990:156 [1653:Bk. 13, Ch. 32])[3]

Molina (1989:127–128 [ca. 1575]) explained that the priests continued to travel, visiting huaca after huaca, until they reached the edge of the empire. The orchestration of such a complex ritual required considerable oversight from Cusco. Molina explains:

And they walked in that way throughout the land that the Inca had conquered, in the four quadrants, and made the said sacrifices until traveling along the road each one reached the outer limits [of the empire] and markers that the Inca had placed there.

They had such efficient information about that and left Cusco so precisely fanned out that although the said sacrifice was enormous and the sites where sacrifice had to be performed were numerous, there was never a mistake, and they never erred or confused one site for another. To that effect, the Inca kept in Cusco Indians of the four suyus or quarters, and each of them kept precise account of all the huacas, no matter how small, that were to be found in the quarter of which he was the *quipucamayoc* or accountant; whom they call *vilcacamayoc*. Some of these Indians were responsible for the information relating to as much as five hundred leagues of territory. They kept the record of everything that had to be sacrificed at each huaca . . . [4]

The Capac Cocha ritual is often discussed in the literature in the context of Inca child sacrifice. Confirmation that child sacrifice did take place during a Capac Cocha is provided by other chroniclers (e.g., Betanzos 1987:50, 84, 142 [1551:Chs. 11, 17, and 30]; Sarmiento de Gamboa 1906:39, 69, 83, 84 [1572:Chs. 13, 31, 40, and 42]) and by provincial documents describing Capac Cocha sacrifices at individual villages (Duviols 1968, 1986; Zuidema 1973; Hernández Príncipe 1986 [1621]), as well as by the remains of sacrificed children on mountain summits (Reinhard 1983, 1985b, 1996; Beorchia 1987; Schobinger 1991; McEwan and Van de Guchte 1992). According to the *Relación de las huacas*, children were also occasionally offered to important shrines in the Cusco ceque system. For example, Cobo provides the following description of Pilcourco (An. 8:11):

The eleventh and last guaca of this ceque was named Pilcourco; it was another stone to which they did great reverence, which was on a big hill near Larapa. When there was a new Inca, in addition to the usual things they sacrificed to it a girl twelve years old or less. (Cobo 1980:39 [1653:Bk. 13, Ch. 14])[5]

This entry not only mentions child sacrifices at a Cusco huaca, but places them within a Capac Cocha event.

Although the practice of child sacrifice has often highlighted discussions of the Capac Cocha ceremony, a recently recovered document concerning the ownership of coca fields in the coastal foothills of the Andes adds new information on the role of huacas as land markers in these rituals. In a lawsuit lasting from 1558 to 1567, two groups, the Canta and the Chaclla, struggled to control a small area of coca fields in the Chillón Valley. The text indicates that certain land markers of the region received Capac Cocha offerings during the rule of Huayna Capac and of Huascar. At the heart of the dispute was a claim by the Canta that the Chaclla had *altered* offering locations in order to gain more land. Rostworowski de Diez Canseco (1988:66), finder and transcriber of the document, explains, "The Canta maintained that on different occasions the Chaclla took advantage of the fact that they were transporting the [Capac Cocha] offerings in order to trespass beyond boundary markers, placing themselves inside the lands of the Canta in Quivi (folio 245v). While they were carrying the gourds of blood they went along saying 'get out of the way, get out of the way, *capacocha, capacocha* . . . up to here has arrived my *capacocha*, up to here are my lands . . .'" (folio 250r).

Although there may have been different kinds of Capac Cocha rituals, annual and unscheduled, descriptions of Capac Cocha events provided in various documents share strong similarities with those supplied by Cobo for the adoration of shrines in the Cusco region, except that they occur on a much larger geographical scale. The paths that the Capac Cocha priests walked as they traveled from Cusco to the remote edges of the empire followed a course defined by the locations of particular huacas, just as the members of specific kin groups of Cusco walked from huaca to huaca along specific ceques within the Cusco region. Similarly, while the ultimate huacas of the Capac Cocha marked the frontiers of the Inca Empire, the last huaca on some of the Cusco ceques demarcated the area in which the Cusco kin groups held their greatest influence. Furthermore, Sherbondy (1982) and the archival research conducted in this project have found that some of the shrines of the Cusco ceque system also served as land markers between various groups, just as Rostworowski de Diez Canseco has documented that boundary markers were visited in the Chillón Valley during a Capac Cocha event.

The Cusco–Vilcanota Ceque

Zuidema (1982a), working primarily with Molina's text (1989:68–70 [ca. 1575]), has documented a long-distance ceque that ran from near Cusco to the mountain shrine of Vilcanota.[6] Priests walked the Cusco–Vilcanota pilgrimage near the time of the June solstice because, as noted by Molina, the sun was believed to have been born in that di-

rection. The Vilcanota huaca stood near the pass, now called La Raya, that separates the Vilcanota (or Cusco) watershed from that of Lake Titicaca (Fig. 10.1). This shrine, located approximately 150 aerial km from Cusco, was one of the most respected huacas of the Andes. It is mentioned by numerous chroniclers, including Polo de Ondegardo (1916c:50–51 [1571]) and Guaman Poma de Ayala (1980:244, 248, 1006 [1615:270 (272), 275 (277), 1091 (1101)]) as well as by early explorers (Squier 1877:399–401; Bingham 1922: 117–121; Means 1925: 448–449). Today the pass of Vilcanota marks the boundary between the departments of Cusco and Puno. It may have served a similar function in the past, because it is traditionally interpreted as the boundary between the Inca of Cusco and the Colla of the Lake Titicaca region (Lizárraga 1909:82–83 [1605]; Murúa 1946:214–215 [1590:Bk. 3, Ch. 21]).

The huaca of Vilcanota is specifically mentioned by Santa Cruz Pachacuti Yamqui Salcamayhua (1950:233 [1613]) as a Capac Cocha offering place. This is confirmed by Cieza de León (1976:151 [1554:Pt. 2, Ch. 28]), who notes that *annual* Capac Cocha rituals were conducted between Cusco and

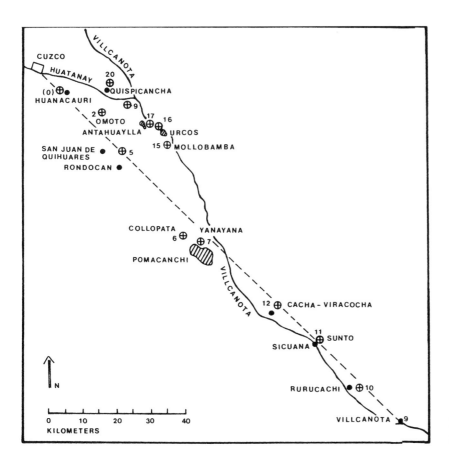

Figure 10.1. Course of the Cusco–Vilcanota Ceque (based on Zuidema 1982a:441).

the Vilcanota Pass. Molina is, however, the only writer who provides detailed notes on the route that the priests took from Cusco to the Vilcanota shrine. In brief, the priests left the imperial valley and traveled to nine sequential huacas distributed between Cusco and the Vilcanota Pass. After visiting the Vilcanota huaca, they returned to Cusco following the Vilcanota River, making offerings at another twelve huacas. Zuidema (1982a) has tentatively identified many of these shrines and provides a plan of the route the priests took to and from the huaca of Vilcanota (Fig. 10.1). This case serves as an example of what Capac Cocha ceques and other long-distance ritual lines may have been like.

Evidence of Other Possible Inca Ceques and Shrine Systems

Several studies have been undertaken to identify ceques and shrine systems outside the Cusco Valley. The most recent study was conducted in the area of Anta by Barrionuevo Orosco and the author, following information provided by Albornoz (1984 [ca. 1582]). Other studies include those directed by Morris and Thompson (1985) at the site of Huánuco Pampa and that of Hyslop (1985, 1990) at Inkawasi. Although the findings of these studies are conjectural, they are worth reviewing because they present alternative methods of studying Inca remains for evidence of shrines and ceques.

The Shrines of Anta (Xaquixaguana)

Albornoz's *Instrucción para descubrir . . .* describes various shrines situated between Cusco and the northern frontier of the Inca Empire, as well as those of the central south coast. His catalog begins with a list of thirty-seven shrines in the Chinchaysuyu region of Cusco, the majority of which also appeared in the Chinchaysuyu section of Cobo's ceque system description. Given that Albornoz understood that Andean shrines were frequently organized along lines, and that his Cusco list records the huacas of Chinchaysuyu along their ceques, we proposed that his other huaca lists may preserve evidence of other ceque systems (Bauer and Barrionuevo Orosco 1998). In other words, we suggested that the order of shrines in Albornoz's regional shrine lists may reflect indigenous systems of shrine organization, as they have been shown to do for Cusco.

Field research was conducted in the Anta (also known as Xaquixaguana) region in 1991, some thirty kilometers northwest of Cusco, to determine whether or not Albornoz's huaca list for this area is organized around similar princi-

ples to his Cusco account. The Anta area was selected for investigation because Albornoz provides the names of twenty-two Anta shrines, a number second only to that of his Cusco list.

Through fieldwork in the region, possible areas were suggested for eighteen of the twenty-two recorded shrines. These shrines circled around the plain of Anta. Although the limited number of shrines presented by Albornoz for the Anta region makes the definitive identification of ceques difficult, an argument can be made for the existence of two possible lines. The locations of shrines #5, #6, and #7 as well as those of shrines #16, #17, and #18 extend out of the western end of the Anta Valley along the general course of the royal road of Chinchaysuyu (Fig. 10.2). It is possible that the locations of these two sets of three shrines mark the courses of two separate ceques. In short, while there appears to have been an Anta shrine system (i.e., a set of recognized shrines that surrounded the region), there is also marginal evidence that the shrines of this system were organized along lines, similar to those of the nearby Cusco area.

It is apparent from the information presented by Albornoz that there was a small-scale system of shrines surrounding the plain of Anta during the postconquest period. While the worship of these shrines was largely localized to the inhabitants of the immediate region, this is not to say that the system functioned completely independent of the Cusco system or those of other nearby areas. There is even some evidence indicating that there may have been a series of overlapping shrine systems throughout the Andes. For example, at the end of his description of the Anta shrines, Albornoz states that people of Yucay, Calca, and Lamay also worshiped the shrines of the Anta area as well as those of their own regions. Another example of overlapping ritual systems can be inferred from the presence of Macra Huaci (#18) on Albornoz's Anta list. This large Inca site is mentioned by Molina (1989:74–75 [ca. 1575]) within his description of the Cusco Citua ceremony, when the city of Cusco was ritually cleaned. The runners of Chinchaysuyu passed through the Anta area on their way to Tilca, which is above Marca Huaci, and then deposited the sacrificial ashes into the Apurimac River.

There is also evidence to suggest that at least one of the Cusco ceques crossed into the Anta area and thus overlapped with its smaller, apparently less complex system. While the exact course of the ninth ceque of Chinchaysuyu (Ch. 9) is poorly understood, the eighth shrine of this line stood near the western end of the Anta plain. This shrine,

Queachili (Ch. 9:8), is registered by Cobo (1980:29 [1653:Bk. 13, Ch. 13]) as a flat place "which is between two hills like a gateway; in it the said victory [over the Chancas] was completed...." Albornoz (1984:204 [ca. 1582]) also includes this shrine within his Cusco list, writing, "Oma chilligues, a plain where the Incas had a battle with the Chanca and they defeated them; and the Chanca fled, ..."

Other associations between the Anta shrines and those of the Cusco area are reflected in the names of some huacas. For example, Albornoz specifically states that three of the shrines in the Anta region (Guanacauri [#12], Anaguarque [#13], and Auiraca [#14]) were named after shrines in Cusco. Furthermore one of the shrines (#15) was called Curicancha (Coricancha), a named derived from the famous Temple of the Sun in Cusco that was the focal point of the Cusco ceque system.

Radial Patterns at Huánuco Pampa

A very different kind of study concerning the organization of Inca installations has been conducted by Morris and Thompson in the ruins of Huánuco Pampa. This immense city, located on the high plains of the north-central Andes, is one of the best-preserved Inca administrative centers. It contains more than 3,500 structures around a large (520 m × 360 m) rectangular plaza. As Morris and Thompson (1985:72) note, "Radiating out from that center are a series of streets, open spaces and walls. These essentially form 'lines,' some clearer than others, that divide the site into several discrete zones." For example, the major road of the region, the *qhapaq ñan* (royal road), crossed diagonally through the center of the city from southeast to northwest, dividing it in half. Morris and Thompson (1985:72) also note that there are other divisions within the plan of this great city: "Other lines extending from near the northeast and southwest corners of the plaza combine with the *qhapaq ñan* to divide the city plan into four parts ... other walls and streets further divide each of the four divisions into three parts, creating a total of twelve sectors."

Influenced by Zuidema's (1964) work on the Cusco ceque system, which emphasizes the bipartition (Hanan and Hurin), tripartition (collana, payan, and cayao), and quadripartition (Chinchaysuyu, Antisuyu, Cuntisuyu, and Collasuyu) of the ceque system, Morris and Thompson believe that the architectural layout of Huánuco Pampa reflects fundamental Andean concepts of space. They suggest that the royal road divided the city into Hanan and Hurin divisions. Each of these halves was further divided by the northeast and southwest corners of the plaza to form four suyu-like zones. Each these four zones was further divided into three distinct architectural units (Map 10.1a). This representation of the city is similar to the division of Cusco into moieties and suyus, and the codification of ceques into clusters of three, as described in the *Relación de las huacas*. Morris and Thompson (1985:73) write, "We do not imply that the twelve divisions of the plan of Huánuco Pampa are necessarily related to shrines, only that the city was laid out in accordance with principles of structure and organization that are analogous to those that govern the system of lines...."

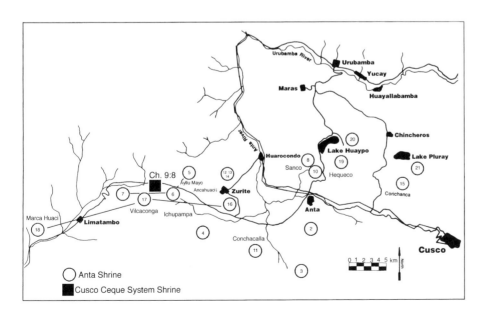

Figure 10.2. Possible locations of shrines in the Anta region. The positions of shrines #5, #6, and #7 as well as those of shrines #16, #17, and #18 suggest that two ceques may have run out of the Anta region to the west. The presence of Ch. 9:8 in the region indicates that the Cusco ceque system overlapped with the huacas of the Anta area.

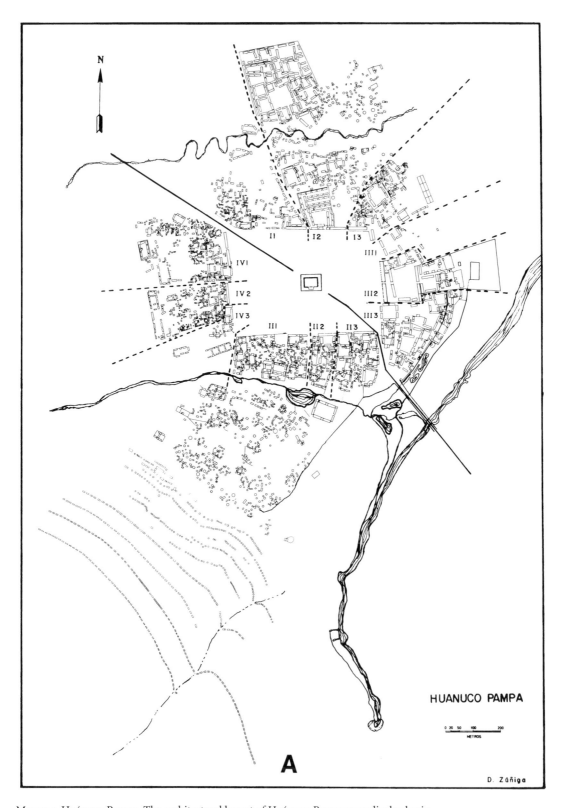

Map 10.1. Huánuco Pampa. The architectural layout of Huánuco Pampa may display basic Andean concepts of space. Here are two alternative representations of the organization of Huánuco Pampa. Map 1A shows the diagonal division of the city by the royal road.

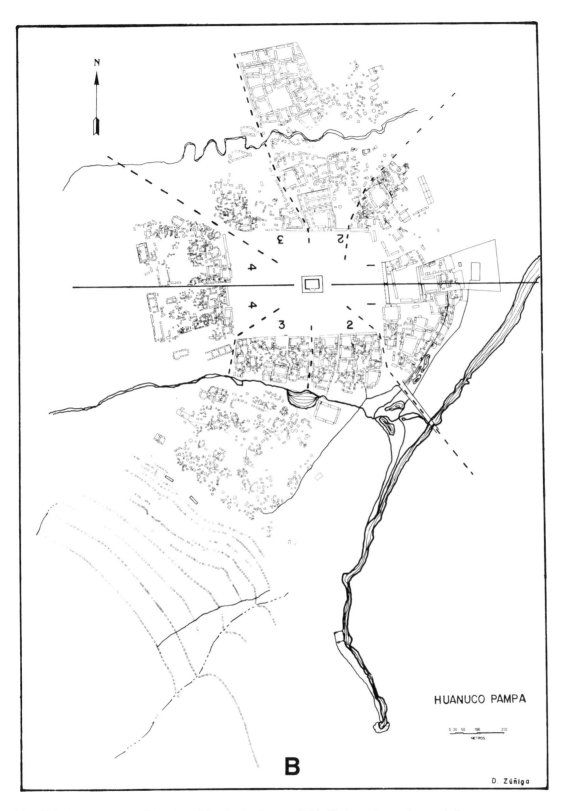

Map 1B depicts an east-west bisection of the city. Both maps divide Huánuco Pampa into moieties and into a number of smaller subdivisions. (Courtesy of Craig Morris and the American Museum of Natural History. Drawing by Delfín Zúñiga.)

Continuing this course of exploration, Morris (1990) has suggested a second possible divisional system for the ruins of Huánuco Pampa. He notes that a straight east-west line through the center of the plaza divides the ruins into two symmetrical halves. Both of these partitions can, on the basis of architectural remains, be subdivided into four sectors (Map 10.1b).

Radial Patterns at Inkawasi

Hyslop (1985, 1990), building on Morris's and Thompson's work at Huánuco Pampa, as well as his own intensive study of the site of Inkawasi in the Cañete Valley and extensive travels across the former empire, has documented that radial architectural patterns are present in several Inca sites, including Huánuco Pampa, Pumpu, Chucuito, Maucallacta, and Inkawasi. Hyslop (1990:202–222) believes that a number of these sites display the spatial relationships found in the Cusco ceque system, including broadly defined bipartitions, tripartitions, and quadripartitions. He also indicates that some sites may even show evidence of ceque systems along similar patterns as described by Cobo for Cusco. For example, at the site of Inkawasi, Hyslop found a radial architectural sector with fourteen units. He suggests that this may be an architectural representation of Cuntisuyu in the Cusco ceque system, with its described fourteen ceques.[7] Although speculative, his models of space and architecture are intriguing and may be worthy of further consideration.

Possible Evidence of Pre-Inca Ceques:
The Nazca Lines

Few topics in archaeology have borne the burden of speculative interpretation as much as the Nazca Lines.[8] First observed by Julio Tello, Toribio Mejía Xesspe, and Alfred Kroeber in the 1920s, and later brought to prominence by Paul Kosok (1965) and Maria Reiche (1968), the Nazca Lines have been the topic of considerable speculation. Forming a complex matrix of lines, and more rarely spirals, trapezoids, triangles, and animal figures, these marks on the arid coastal plain of Peru defy simple explanation. Recent research (Clarkson 1990; Dorn et al. 1992) suggests that most of the desert drawings date to the Early Intermediate period (400 B.C.–A.D. 550).

Toribio Mejía Xesspe (1940), the first author to describe the Nazca Lines, called them "ceques," suggesting that they were somehow related to the shrine system of Cusco. Most researchers working on the Nazca Lines today have also made this same association (Morrison 1978; Reinhard 1985a; Hadingham 1987; Aveni 1990b; 1990c; Aveni and Silverman 1991). Indeed, despite the vast time and distance that separate the Cusco ceque system from the marks on the Nazca plain, there are some unmistakable parallels between them. Perhaps most important is that, like the Cusco ceque system, many of the Nazca Lines radiate from central points. These radial "line centers" have been the topic of extensive research by Aveni (1990a) and his colleagues. Furthermore, fieldwork by Aveni (1990c) and Clarkson (1990) suggest that many of the lines end at small stone cairns. Although the age of these cairns is not known with any certainty, they are reminiscent of huacas along the Cusco ceque system.

There are, however, significant differences between the lines of Nazca and the ceques of Cusco. For example, the Cusco ceque system had one center, the Coricancha. In Nazca, there is no single point from which all lines emerge. Instead, Aveni (1990a) and his team have identified more than sixty separate line centers across the plain from which some 750 lines radiate. Furthermore, the courses of the Cusco ceques were determined by a series of shrines. Some ceques held as few as three huacas, while others contained up to fifteen shrines along their projections. Although most of the lines in Nazca have clear beginning and end points, only a few display significant features along their course. Nevertheless, many researchers now accept the proposition that the Nazca Lines were ritual pathways or markings.

Modern Ritual Lines in the Andes

In the late 1970s, journalist Tony Morrison (1978:154–178) reported a series of lines crossing the altiplano in the Sajama region of northwestern Bolivia. These lines radiate from village chapels to small shrines on hills or in the center of isolated plains. As part of this project, I visited the Sajama region in 1992 and found that the lines are still readily visible (Bauer 1992c). Some of the chapels have only one line extending from them, others have multiple lines radiating in different directions (Photos 10.1–10.4). The lines vary in length from less than half a kilometer to more than ten. Many of the termination shrines are miniature chapels (Photo 10.5), while others are simple cairns (Photo 10.6). Although these lines are now abandoned, informants indicate that as late as the 1950s villagers walked on them from

Photo 10.1. Aerial photograph of radial lines near the village of Cosapa in the Sajama region of Bolivia. (Courtesy Instituto Geográfico Militar, Bolivia.)

Photo 10.2. Small chapels frequently form the terminus of line systems in the Sajama region of Bolivia.

Photo 10.3. A line near the village of Sajama in Bolivia.

Photo 10.4. A line near the village of Cosapa in the Sajama region of Bolivia.

Photo 10.5. A small shrine at the end of a line near the village of Cosapa.

Photo 10.6. A cairn at the end of a line near the village of Sajama.

the chapels to the shrines on specific ritual days (Morrison 1978; Bauer 1992c).

It is now known that these systems of ritual lines are widespread in the altiplano region of Bolivia and Chile, and Morrison proposes that they are related to the Nazca Lines and the Cusco ceque system. Strengthening his argument, Morrison cites the work of French anthropologist Alfred Métraux, who wrote in the 1930s on the Chipaya, an Aymara-speaking group inhabiting areas of highland Bolivia. Métraux (1935:328, 342) and La Barre (1947:583–585, Plate 119), in their discussions of Chipaya religion, describe earth and stone cairns that stood between 1.20 m and 1.70 m high called *mal'kus*. These cairns were worshipped and received sacrifices because of their association with organic forces. Straight trails, at times over fifteen kilometers in length, radiated from villages to these shrines. The cairns, each said to have its own name, were visited during specific rituals by villagers walking the paths. Nathan Wachtel (1990), in a more recent study, documents that such practices continue and suggests that some of the mal'kus also function as land markers.

Other researchers working in highland communities, such as Thomas S. Barthel (1959) in the area of Soairce and Javier Albó (1972) in the community of Jesús de Machaca, also stress the importance of radial systems of social and ritual organization in Bolivia and Chile. Perhaps most notable has been the work of Johan Reinhard (1988), who has followed Morrison's initial observations of the shrines and lines of the altiplano with more extensive research. Reinhard has visited several villages where the lines are still walked and where offerings are made to the shrines that now mark their terminus. Although the organization and antiquity of these modern radial ritual systems remain to be fully documented and analyzed, they may be cognitively related to the shrine system that once surrounded the imperial city of the Inca.

Faint vestiges of such systems may even exist in the Cusco region today during the Feast of the Holy Cross. Each year on 3 May representatives from different villages climb the mountain peaks along specific routes to visit the crosses that watch over their communities (Zuidema 1973:30). At other times of the year, ceremonies are held during which village members run along the boundaries of the community, stopping to make offerings to the markers that separate their lands from those of adjacent villages. Many of the markers are outcrops, passes, and hilltops that may have been huacas before the arrival of the Europeans.

Summary and Discussion

The identification of ancient and modern ceque systems in the Andes is understandably difficult because the Spaniards initiated a series of eradication campaigns against indigenous religious practices throughout the sixteenth and seventeenth centuries. Furthermore, the Catholic and Protestant churches that dominate the highland areas today adamantly discourage huaca veneration. Nevertheless, tantalizing evidence recovered by several scholars suggests that over the past several millennia systems of radial lines have represented a core concept in indigenous religious practices.

At the time of the Inca Empire, systems of radial worship took on a number of forms. For example, the Capac Cocha ceremony, during which offerings were taken from the central plaza of Cusco to all the huacas of the empire, was a large-scale expression of radial rituality. It was, in both form and function, a logical extension of the Cusco ceque system. Similarly, the Cusco–Vilcanota ceque, which stretched some 150 aerial km from the imperial capital to the pass of La Raya, provides an example of a long-distance ceque with multiple huacas along its course. In addition, several archaeologists suggest that generalized notions of radial organization can be used to interpret the layout of Inca occupations (Hyslop 1985, 1990; Morris and Thompson 1985; Morris 1990) and the regional distribution of shrines outside the Cusco Valley (Bauer and Barrionuevo Orosco 1998).

The famous Nazca plain may provide another, more ancient, example of radial ritual organization, since recent research has revealed that many of its lines radiated from line centers (Aveni 1990a). This is not to conclude, however, that the Nazca Lines functioned like the much later Cusco ceques. There are clear differences between these two cultural phenomena. Nevertheless, they both reflect radiality as a basic organizing principle.

Perhaps the most striking research on possible, non-Inca ceques has been that of Métraux (1935), Morrison (1978), Reinhard (1988), and Wachtel (1990). Each of these scholars documents the use of ritual lines and shrines in Bolivia and Chile. Lines, some kilometers long, still cross the high arid region between these two countries. They serve as ritual pathways leading from small village churches to isolated cairns and shrines. They may represent the last vestiges of a radial ritual tradition that reached its last full expression during the rule of the Inca.

11

An Overview of the Cusco Ceque System

THE ANDEAN LANDSCAPE is embossed with innumerable sacred features and locations. For millennia these shrines (huacas) have served as essential elements in the modeling of social space and interaction (Sallnow 1987:267). They vary in size and significance from universally recognized shrines to localities venerated by a single family. The better-known shrines are incorporated into, and help define, the ritual systems of nearby communities. The numerous huacas of the Andes are embued with supernatural powers. Through their worship, and the related ritual responsibilities of various groups, the powers of the shrines can be directed, the future affected, and the social and political organization of the participating communities reproduced. In this book, I have provided ground documentation of huacas in the Cusco region and have explored various aspects of the ritual system that tied them to the imperial city of the Inca. This chapter provides a summary of the research findings.

At the time of the European invasion of the Andes (A.D. 1532), many of the shrines around Cusco were organized in lines of ritual pathways (ceques) that are described as radiating from the Temple of the Sun at the heart of the city. According to the few descriptions we have about this ritual system, there were more than 328 huacas, perhaps as many as 400, and they were conceptually organized along forty-two paths. The shrines were represented by a wide range of natural features, such as caves, boulders, springs, mountaintops, as well as by artificial features, such as houses, fountains, and canals. Each of the shrines required prayers and offerings. Responsibility for maintenance of the shrines along each ceque was divided among the various kin groups of the city. Frequently called "the Cusco ceque system," this network of shrines and lines represents the most complex ritual system yet identified in the ancient New World.

Detailed historical information on the Cusco ceque system is found in the works of two early colonial religious scholars: Bernabé Cobo and Cristóbal de Albornoz. Cobo's 1653 work, *Historia del Nuevo Mundo,* is the more important of these sources. In his book, Cobo devotes four chapters to describing the Cusco ceques and the individual huacas that defined their projections. Each chapter presents systematic information on the huacas and ceques in a separate quarter of the imperial valley. The quantity and quality of information on the shrines vary from account to account, and decrease as the four chapters progress. Nevertheless, within these densely written lists of shrines and lines, Cobo also records, among other things, the offerings made to the huacas, and the kin groups who maintained them.

Cobo's four chapters, called the *Relación de las huacas,* are the most comprehensive account of Andean shrine worship to survive. Cobo was not, however, the original author of this ceque system description. Analysis of information contained within the *Relación de las huacas* suggests that the original ceque system manuscript, which Cobo copied into his chronicle, was written in Cusco between 1559 and 1572. A review of existing Spanish sources indicates that a number of prominent Spaniards who inhabited or visited Cusco during this thirteen-year period were familiar with indigenous huaca worship. They include Cristóbal de Albornoz, Cristóbal de Molina, Juan Polo de Ondegardo, Pedro Córdoba Mexía, Juan de Matienzo, José de Acosta, Martín de Murúa, and Viceroy Francisco de Toledo. Most of these men not only were aware of huacas, they led active field campaigns to destroy them. Among these individuals, Polo de Ondegardo, twice chief magistrate of Cusco, stands out as the most likely author of the original ceque system manuscript. It is known that Polo de Ondegardo, after interviewing the recordkeepers (quipucamayocs) of Cusco, wrote a report in 1559 on the religious activities of the Inca, and that years later Cobo came to possess the original copy of his account. It was most certainly this 1559 report that was incorporated into Cobo's *Historia del Nuevo Mundo.*

The second source containing detailed information on the Cusco ceque system comes from an unlikely contributor to native American studies. Its author, Albornoz, who was a zealous persecutor of idolatry in the second half of the sixteenth century, destroyed thousands of shrines in a series of campaigns across the north-central Andes. To inspire other Christians to follow his lead, Albornoz wrote a small treatise around 1582 listing various shrines of the Chinchaysuyu region, northwest of Cusco. In this work, Albornoz specifically states that many Andean shrines were organized along lines, and he encouraged fellow "extirpators of idolatry" to record the order and location of the shrines so that they might be inspected in the future for evidence of continued worship. In his account of one quarter of the Cusco region, Albornoz lists a total of thirty-seven shrines, thirteen of which do not seem to be listed by Cobo. Albornoz's account provides independent confirmation of the Cusco ceque system and indicates that the system was even more complex than was suggested in Cobo's work.

Evidence of Other Shrine and Ceque Systems

Cusco was not the only Andean community to contain a ceque system, and it is becoming increasingly clear that such systems represented a core concept in indigenous religious practices. Both Albornoz and Polo de Ondegardo indicate that such systems were present in all highland communities, and the latter writer showed the bishop of Charcas a system in the village of Pocona (Bolivia). In addition, Matienzo and Córdoba Mexía provide general instructions for inspectors of indigenous communities to record the "order" of huacas, suggesting that ceque systems were widely present in the Andes.

Recent work in the Anta plain, some thirty kilometers northwest of Cusco, suggests that some of the huacas within its shrine system may have been organized along lines. In addition, several of the huacas within this localized system were named after those of the capital city, and there is evidence to suggest that the Anta system was overlapped by the larger Cusco system. Furthermore, it has been documented that a long-distance ceque, with multiple huacas along its course, stretched some 150 aerial kilometers from Cusco to the mountain pass of La Raya, and that in a logical extension of the Cusco ceque system, offerings were taken from the central plaza of Cusco to all the major shrines of the empire during a ceremony called Capac Cocha. There is

also evidence suggesting that despite centuries of systematic persecution, some shrine and line complexes continue to operate in isolated regions of Bolivia and Chile today.

Cusco was unusual, however, in its large number of huacas. This is not surprising because Cusco was the capital of the largest empire of the New World. Although currently untested, my suggestion is that as Cusco grew from a small mountain community to the center of an expansionistic empire, its shrine system developed with it. Based on pre-existing patterns of shrine veneration and grounded in pan-Andean worship of sacred objects and places, the Cusco ceques developed from a village system into the most elaborate manifestations of huaca adoration known.

Social Organization of the Cusco Ceque System

The Cusco Valley was conceptually divided by the Inca into two parts (moieties): Upper Cusco and Lower Cusco. Each of these moieties was further divided into two divisions (suyus). Chinchaysuyu and Antisuyu formed the upper section and Collasuyu and Cuntisuyu the lower. These four quarters converged at the Temple of the Sun. Cobo's work uses these divisions to organize the ceque and huaca materials. We are told that the first three quarters, Chinchaysuyu, Antisuyu, and Collasuyu, each contained nine ceques. Although these three suyus held the same number of ceques, they contained different numbers of shrines: Chinchaysuyu had at least eighty-five shrines, Antisuyu had seventy-eight, and Collasuyu had eighty-five. The last quarter, Cuntisuyu, is more complex. Rather than containing nine ceques like the other three suyus, this suyu held fourteen ceques, according to Cobo. Yet, within his text, Cobo notes that one of the ceques (Cu. 8) was called by two different names, and field research indicates that this ceque actually formed two separate lines. It seems, then, that Cuntisuyu held fifteen ceques and a minimum of eighty shrines.

The exact number of shrines in the system as a whole is not known. In the main section of his text, Cobo describes 328 huacas, but then adds an addendum of 4 additional shrines, writing that "these belonged to various ceques but were not set down in the order that the rest [were]." Soon after this, Cobo suggests that there were at least 350 public shrines in the valley, but he does not say if they were all in the ceque system or not. Other writers provide estimates of 340 (Polo de Ondegardo), 360 (Acosta), 400 (Polo de Ondegardo), and 450 (Murúa) shrines. Most importantly,

Albornoz's shrine list, which describes 13 shrines in the Chinchaysuyu region not named by Cobo, provides evidence that the Cusco ceque system included a host of additional huacas beyond those included within the *Relación de las huacas.*

The ceques of each suyu were grouped into sets of three. Chinchaysuyu, Antisuyu, and Collasuyu each contained three ceque clusters, while Cuntisuyu held five. The ceques within each cluster were characterized as being either "collana," "payan," or "cayao." Various Conquest- and Colonial-period documents indicate that these are prestige-ranking terms that begin with collana and end with cayao.

Cobo indicates that certain Cusco kin groups held the responsibility of maintaining the huacas along particular ceques. Determining which kin group was in charge of which ceque is difficult because there were a large number of lines in the system and various kin groups in the city. This task is also complicated by the fact that we have only fragmentary information on the system. The most conservative model that can be reconstructed from the *Relación de las huacas* suggests that each of the ten panacas (or royal ayllus) maintained the huacas along separate ceques. It is also evident that no two panacas maintained ceques within the same ceque cluster, and that the relative standing of a panaca in the Cusco social order determined which ceque that group maintained. The panacas of the first five Incas (traditionally associated with Hurin Cusco) held responsibility for ceques in Lower Cusco, while the panacas of the second five Incas (conventionally linked to Hanan Cusco) maintained lines in Upper Cusco.

Besides containing ten royal ayllus, the city of Cusco also held ten nonroyal kin groups. A second, more speculative and complex, model of the Cusco ceque system proposes that each of these nonroyal ayllus was conceptually paired with a particular panaca, and that they maintained a line within the same ceque cluster as their panaca. It should be noted, however, that even if this highly tentative reconstruction of ritual obligations is accepted, we still do not know which groups maintained nearly half of the lines in the system.

Ground Documentation of the Cusco Ceque System

The sacred landscape of Cusco was highly centralized and ritualized, and it has long been the topic of intellectual speculation. One of the major research goals of this study was to examine the relationship between the concrete form of the system on the ground and its idealized representations as expressed in the *Relación de las huacas.* Extensive archaeological fieldwork was conducted in the Cusco area and intensive archival research in Cusco, Lima, and Seville to address this goal. Gradually, likely candidates or the approximate positions for more than half of the huacas mentioned in Cobo's document were identified. Detailed discussions, photographs, and historical references for these potential shrines have been presented in this work. The identification of possible shrines allows tentative courses for most of the forty-two ceques of the system to be presented. This ground documentation of the shrines and ceques can be used to analyze the accuracy of Cobo's document and to examine differing theories concerning the physical nature of the system (Map 11.1).

The radial form of the Cusco ceque system reflects the importance that Cusco held as the nucleus of Tahuantinsuyu and as the center of power for the dynastic order that ruled over it. As Sherbondy (1982:95) notes, "Radial distribution of space is a conceptual scheme that is particularly well adapted to expressing the viewpoint of an elite from a central point, such as the capital." Since the imperial city of Cusco was visualized as the center of Andean cosmological order by the Inca, it is only appropriate that the idealized divisions of the heartland were seen as radiating out from it. Map 11.1 illustrates the approximate projections of the Cusco ceques as defined by the location of shrines. While several huacas were identified along most of the lines, the positions of the shrines along three ceques (Cu. 3, Cu. 11, and Cu. 12) are so poorly defined that these ceques cannot be plotted with confidence. The courses of the Collasuyu ceques are more erratic than those of the other suyus. This is particularly true in the area south of Cayra and north of Acpita (Co. 1:6), where the ceques appear to cross over one another. Other unusually curving ceques include the final ceques of Antisuyu (An. 7, An. 8, and An. 9). Nevertheless, the overall ground documentation of the system suggests that the Cusco ceques were directions or paths that radiated from the city. In their idealized form, the ceques may have been envisioned as running in straight lines from the center of the city toward the horizon, but in more practical terms, their zigzagging routes appear to have defined, or to have been confined within, pie-shaped segments of the countryside.

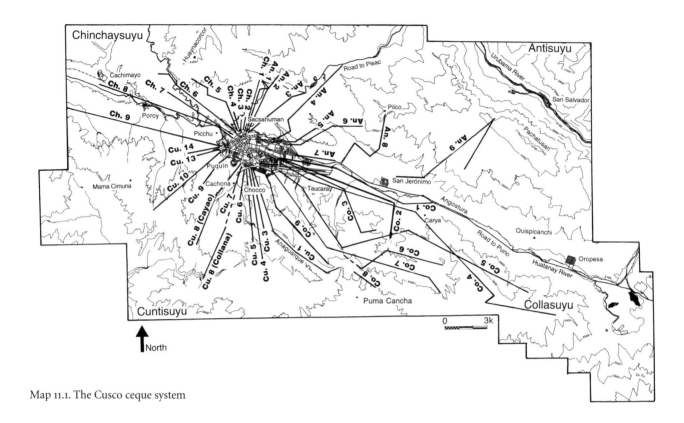

Map 11.1. The Cusco ceque system

The Number of Shrines and the Lengths of the Ceques

In his introduction to the *Relación de las huacas,* Cobo writes that the ceques radiated from the Coricancha. Many subsequent studies of the system have uncritically accepted this statement and have illustrated the ceques as projecting, like the spokes of a wheel, from this temple. Field data indicate that this is true for most but not all of the ceques, because the initial shrines of several lines are located at some distance from this temple. As noted by both Zuidema and Sherbondy, the final three ceques of Antisuyu (An. 7, An. 8, and An. 9) began progressively farther from the city.

Following Cobo's description, the ceques contained varying numbers of shrines. The largest number of huacas, fifteen, is recorded on Cu. 9, while several ceques held only three shrines. The average number of huacas on the forty-two ceques of the system is eight. The lengths of the ceques also varied greatly. Not surprisingly, the longer ceques have a larger number of huacas than the shorter ones. Although not all the terminal huacas have been identified, there appear to have been several exceptionally long lines, including Co. 4 and Co. 5, which were over twenty kilometers in

length. The longest documented ceque extended more than forty-five kilometers from Cusco to the shrine of Quiachilli (Ch. 9:8), situated near the pass of Huillque, and then continued to the currently unidentified huacas of Quishuarpuquiu (Ch. 9.9), Yuyotuyro (Ch. 9:10), Pillolliri (Ch. 9:11), and Totorgoaylla (Ch. 9:12). Four of the ceques were exceptionally short (Cu. 6, Cu. 7, Cu. 11, and Cu. 12). These ceques contained only three shrines each and are less than five kilometers long. More typically, however, the ceques ended near, or at, the valley ridges, and varied in length between five and eleven kilometers.

Problematic Huaca Locations

The Coricancha represented the junction of the four great suyus of the Inca Empire. The initial shrines of Cuntisuyu seem to have had a special relationship with the Coricancha, because the starting points of most of these lines—including Cu. 4:1 (Pururauca), Cu. 5:1 (Caritampucancha), Cu 6:1 (Apian), Cu. 10:1 (Pilcopuquiu), and perhaps Cu. 7:1 (Inticancha)—were located within the temple complex. In contrast, the initial huacas of some ceques, particularly those of Collasuyu, appear not to be located in the appropriate suyu. These include, among others, Co. 1:1 (Puru-rauca), Co. 3:1 (Tampucancha), Co. 3:2 (Pampasona), Co. 6:1 (Tampucancha), and Co. 8:1 (Sancacancha). These "Collasuyu" shrines are situated between the Temple of the Sun and the Plaza de Armas in an area that, according to the distribution of other huacas in the system, was in Chinchaysuyu. In addition, it is possible that Co. 9:2 (Tancarvilca) and Co. 9:3 (Pactaguañui) were located northwest of the temple in Chinchaysuyu, and the shrine of Pomapacha (Co. 4:1) in Antisuyu.

Another problem in reconstructing the Cusco ceque system is that certain shrines appear to be located a significant distance off the general projection of their ceques. Cobo specifically mentions this phenomenon in relation to Pomacucho (Ch. 9:4), which he states was a spring somewhat separated from its ceque. Fieldwork has found other possible examples, including Corcorpuquiu (An. 9:3), E Con Con Puquiu (Cu. 8[cayao]:4), Micaya Puquiu (Co. 1:5), Atpitan (Co. 1:6), Quillo (Co. 9:10), and perhaps Rondao (Co. 5:9).

Three possible explanations are offered for these irregularities. First, it is possible that these loci do not represent the huacas described in the *Relación de las huacas,* and that other, similarly named, locations, now forgotten or destroyed, were closer to the respective ceques. Second, these locations may indeed be the shrines described in the document, but through recording or copying errors, they have been listed on the wrong ceques. Third, if these are the correct locations of the described shrines, then the individual ceques may have curved or doubled back to include them on their course. If this is the case, then the actual routes of the ceques were far more irregular than is currently believed.

These findings demonstrate our imperfect understanding of the system as a whole. Continued ethnographic, historical, and archaeological research is needed to further identify the locations of the huacas and ceques in the Cusco region. The results of these studies will expand the corpus of information on this unique ritual system.

Problematic Huaca Locations and Recording Errors

Recent research has revealed a number of recording errors in the *Relación de las huacas.* One huaca may be recorded on two distant ceques (Co. 1:5 and Co. 6:8). There seems to be a confusion in the document concerning the locations of two shrines (Ch. 7:2 and Co. 8:1) that shared the same name (Sanca Cancha). Furthermore, Cobo may have mis-counted the number of huacas on Ch. 4 by leaving one shrine, a fountain next to the house of Curi Ocollo (Curi-ocllo, Ch. 4:3), nonenumerated in his description.

There are also a number of transcription errors in Cobo's version of the *Relación de las huacas.* For example, in his account of Llipiquiliscacho (Cu. 12:3), Cobo wrote the village name of Chocco when it should have been Quilca. Other examples include the cases of Mantocallaspa (Mantocallaspa[cha], An. 3:5), Sacasayllapuquiu (Sacas[gu]aylla puquiu, An. 8:1), and Urcoslla Amaro (Urcos[ca]lla Amaro, Ch. 7:5), in which Cobo left out letters of the huaca's names. Furthermore, Cobo miscounted the number of ceques in the system, stating that it was composed of forty lines. There are either forty-one or forty-two lines, depending on whether one counts the eighth ceque of Cuntisuyu (Cu. 8) as one or two ceques.

The problematic huaca locations and recording errors indicate that numerous internal inconsistencies exist in Cobo's documentation of the ceques.[1] Future archaeological and historical studies concerning the form and function of the Cusco ceque system should proceed with the idea that Cobo's work is an incomplete, and partially inaccurate, description of the system as a whole.

The Cusco Ceque System and Inca Calendrics

In Zuidema's (1977a) introductory investigation of the Inca calendar, and in others produced since, Zuidema (1980, 1981b, 1982a–c, 1983a–c, 1988b) and Aveni (1981a) have proposed that some ceques are astronomically aligned. They also suggest that the ceque system held astronomical functions beyond those specifically mentioned in Cobo's chronicle. In Zuidema's (1977a:220) elaborate hypothesis, each shrine of the ceque system (totaling 328) represents a day in the year, and some of the ceques were used as sight lines for observing astronomical events on the horizon. Moreover, Zuidema (1981b, 1982b, 1983b) suggests that besides containing markers for the December and June solstices and an August planting date, all of which are noted within the *Relación de las huacas,* various ceques, huacas, and parts of the Temple of the Sun were used to sight the rise or set of the Pleiades, the Southern Cross, Alpha and Beta Centauri, as well as the solar zenith and what Zuidema has termed the "antizenith passage" of the sun. The proposition that some ceques formed sight lines aligned with certain solar and stellar risings and settings, and that the ceque system represented a counting device for the Inca calendar, has become widely accepted and has influenced the findings of other researchers (Sherbondy 1982, 1986, 1987; Hyslop 1985; Anders 1986a, 1986b; Van de Guchte 1990). However, the current calendrical models for the Inca have been tested through the identification of huaca locations and the precise determination of ceque projections across the landscape (Bauer and Dearborn 1995). Although there are many outstanding questions and areas of research that still need extensive investigation, current findings suggest that the application of the ceque system for astronomical observations was limited to those specific references that are presented within the folios of Cobo's manuscript.

The Cusco Ceque System and Resource Tenure in the Region

The general Inca systems of resource control at the time of the Spanish invasion have not been extensively studied, and even less is known about the specific land and water resources controlled by the Cusco kin groups. Principal exceptions to these statements include the works of Rostworowski (1962, 1964), Sherbondy (1982, 1986, 1987), and La Lone (1985). Sherbondy's investigations are especially important to this study, because she has worked in the Cusco Valley and has attempted to integrate her understanding of the Cusco irrigation system and the social organization of the imperial capital with field data on its ceque system.

Since the late 1970s, Sherbondy has studied the relation between the canals of Hanan Cusco and the social organization of the city. She has found that in contrast to the general predictions set forth by Wittfogel (1957), which suggest that specialized managerial bureaucracies develop in complex societies to oversee and administer water rights, kin groups in Cusco continued to control the distribution of water during the periods of imperial growth and expansion. She writes: "The most interesting feature of the social organization of Andean irrigation is that it coincides with the organization of the ayllu, even within a state" (Sherbondy 1982:150). This is not to suggest, however, that the distribution of land and water rights in the Cusco region existed and functioned independently of the social organization of the capital. Each Cusco kin group must be viewed as a unit of the overall social organization of the city. Among many factors, the location, size, and composition of each group could influence its relative position in Cusco's social orga-

nization, and that position affected the territory of the group. Furthermore, the physical demonstration of the groups' relations through rituals, including journeys across the sacred landscape of the Cusco ceque system, most certainly helped to reproduce the social and territorial composition of the imperial capital. In the words of Sallnow (1987:11), "Human groups are identified with their named habitats and vice versa, so social relations become spatial relations and spatial relations social ones."

As has been noted, there were ten royal and ten nonroyal ayllus in Cusco. Each of these groups was responsible for the maintenance of the shrines along a specific ceque. Sherbondy's studies on the irrigation systems of Chinchaysuyu and Antisuyu suggest that certain ceques ran toward or near the resources controlled by the group responsible for their maintenance. She proposes that the ideal intention of the Inca was to use ceques as boundary lines for the lands of each panaca and nonroyal ayllu (Sherbondy 1982:80). While the use of the ceques themselves as boundary lines is speculative, Sherbondy provides clear evidence that some of the huacas in the system did function as land markers. Now that the physical distribution of the shrines and lines in the Cusco region is better understood, I hope that additional studies exploring the relationship between the Cusco ceque system and resource tenure in the region will be conducted.

Final Reflections

Some of the shrines in the Cusco ceque system served as spatial boundaries, others marked the locations where important events of the past occurred, and a few functioned as calendar markers. Furthermore, the ritual passage of the various Cusco kin groups along their separate ceques, and across specific segments of the landscape, was certainly an important component in the continuous redefinition of social power in the region. More broadly stated, the Cusco huacas and ceques served as a means to control space and time, as well as a means through which the social order of the Inca could be reaffirmed.

Previous models of the system suggest that there was a limited number of shrines, 328, and that the ceques were constricted to follow straight lines from the center of the city to specific, astronomically related points on the horizon. However, data presented throughout this work have directly challenged these basic assumptions at a number of levels. The Cusco ceque system, no longer constrained by a set number of shrines or a need for the ceques to run in straight lines, can now be seen as more flexible. It was a system that was able to adapt to social and territorial changes, and it was capable of incorporating those changes into the continually developing ritual order of the region.

The form the Cusco ceque system assumed as it crossed the countryside was a precipitate of the specific social and territorial relationships in the valley at any particular time. We have seen, in a well-documented case of a Capac Cocha ritual, that kin groups actively manipulated rituals to promote their own causes. In this example, carriers of an offering extended their territory into that of another group by altering the offering location. As they exploited their religious obligations and established a new boundary marker in the region, they shouted, "get out of the way, get out of the way, *capacocha, capacocha* . . . up to here has arrived my *capacocha,* up to here are my lands . . ." (Rostworowski de Diez Canseco 1988:66).

Similar practices are likely to have taken place in the Cusco region. Variations in the landholdings and the power of different groups through the centuries may have brought certain markers into prominence and eclipsed the usefulness of others. As the various kin groups of the city manipulated aspects of the ritual system to their own advantage, its physical form, and perhaps even its internal structure, would have been altered. Focusing on the Cusco ceque system as a flexible expression of social and spatial relations, rather than as a rigidly defined system, provides new diachronic possibilities for the system. Within this perspective, the formation, development, and continuation of the system over time can be seen as a product of the relations that existed between the many kin groups of the Inca heartland. By discussing the system within a framework that allows variations to occur in the number and location of the huacas as well as the courses of the ceques, the system becomes dynamic and is able to respond to particular events of history.

Appendix 1

Rowe's (1980) and Zuidema's (1964) Numbering Systems for the Cusco Ceque System

Rowe	Zuidema		Co. 1	II 3 c
Ch. 1	I 3 c		Co. 2	II 3 b
Ch. 2	I 3 b		Co. 3	II 3 a
Ch. 3	I 3 a		Co. 4	II 2 c
Ch. 4	I 2 b		Co. 5	II 2 b
Ch. 5	I 2 c		Co. 6	II 2 a
Ch. 6	I 2 a		Co. 7	II 1 c
Ch. 7	I 1 c		Co. 8	II 1 c
Ch. 8	I 1 b		Co. 9	II 1 a
Ch. 9	I 1 a		Cu. 1	IVb 3 b
An. 1	III 1 a		Cu. 2	IVb 2 c
An. 2	III 1 b		Cu. 3	IVb 2 b
An. 3	III 1 c		Cu. 4	IVb 2 a
An. 4	III 2 a		Cu. 5	IVb 1 c
An. 5	III 2 b		Cu. 6	IVb 1 b
An. 6	III 2 c		Cu. 7	IVb 1 a
An. 7	III 3 a		Cu. 8	IVb 3 a/c
An. 8	III 3 b		Cu. 9	IVa 2 c
An. 9	III 3 c		Cu. 10	IVa 2 b
			Cu. 11	IVa 2 a
			Cu. 12	IVa 1 c
			Cu. 13	IVa 1 b
			Cu. 14	IVa 1 a

Appendix 2

Account of the shrines of Cuzco (Bernabé Cobo, *Historia del Nuevo Mundo*, ms. 1653, Book Thirteen, Chapters 13–16). /f. 223v/ English translation by John H. Rowe.[1]

Chapter 13. The shrines and guacas which there were on the Road of Chinchaysuyu.

From the Temple of the Sun as from the center there went out certain lines which the Indians call ceques; they formed four parts corresponding to the four royal roads which went out from Cuzco. On each one of those ceque were arranged in order the guacas and shrines which there were in Cuzco and its district, like stations of holy places, the veneration of which was common to all. Each ceque was the responsibility of the partialities and families of the city of Cuzco, from within which came the attendants and servants who cared for the guacas of their ceque and saw to offering the established sacrifices at the proper times.

Beginning, then, with the Road of Chinchaysuyu, which leaves the city through the precinct of Carmenga, there were in [the part corresponding to] it nine ceques on which were included eighty-five guacas, in this order.

[Ch. 1:0] The first ceque was called Cayao; it was the responsibility of the partiality and ayllo of Goacaytaqui and had the following five guacas. /f. 224/

[Ch. 1:1] The first was named Michosamaro; it was located up against the slope of the hill of Totocache, and they said it was one of those who they fancied had emerged with the first Inca Manco Capac from the cave of Pacaritampu. They relate that one of the women who came out of the cave with them killed him because of an act of disrespect toward her which he committed. He turned to stone, and his spirit appeared in this same place and ordered that they make sacrifices to him there. Thus the sacrifice at this guaca was very ancient. It always consisted of gold, clothing, sea shells, and other things, and it used to be made for good rains.

[Ch. 1:2] The second guaca of the ceque was called Patallacta. It was a house which Inca Yupanqui designated for his sacrifices, and he died in it. The Incas who succeeded him thereafter made ordinary sacrifice here. In general, all the things which they consumed in sacrifice were offered for the health and prosperity of the Inca.

[Ch. 1:3] The third guaca was named Pilcopuquio. It is a fountain next to the house just mentioned from which an irrigation ditch issues. The Indians relate that when Inca Yupanqui had made that house for the sacrifices, he ordered that water to emerge there and afterward decreed that ordinary sacrifice should be made to it.[Ch. 1:4] The fourth guaca was called Cirocaya. It is a

cave of stone from which they believed that the hail issued. Hence, at the season when they were afraid of it, all went to sacrifice in the cave, so that it should not come out and destroy their crops.

[Ch. 1:5] The fifth and last guaca of this ceque had the name Sonconancay. It is a hill where it was [a] very ancient [custom] to /f. 224v/ offer sacrifices for the health of the Inca.

[Ch. 2:0] The second ceque of this same Road of Chinchaysuyu was called Payan; on it were eight guacas of the ayllo and family of Vicaquirao.

[Ch. 2:1] The first guaca was called Guaracince, which was in the plaza of the Temple of the Sun, [a plaza] called Chuquipampa (it means "plain of gold"). It was a bit of flat ground which was there, in which they said that the earthquake was formed. At it they made sacrifices so that it would not quake, and they were very solemn [ones], because when the earth quaked children were killed, and ordinarily sheep and clothing were burned and gold and silver was buried.

[Ch. 2:2] The second guaca was named Racramirpay; this one was a stone which they had set in a window which was a little way below where the monastery of San Agustín is now; they relate the story of it in this way. In a certain battle which Inca Yupanqui fought against his enemies, an Indian appeared to him in the air and helped him to conquer them. After the victory had been won, he came to Cuzco with the said Inca, sat down in this window, and turned to stone. From that time on they worshipped it and made ordinary sacrifice to it. Particularly solemn sacrifice was made to it when the Inca went to war personally, asking it to aid the king as it had aided Inca Yupanqui in the former war.

[Ch. 2:3] The third guaca was an idol of solid gold named Inti illapa, which means "thunder of the Sun," which was set on a rich litter of gold. Inca Yupanqui made it and took it for his guauque or brother. It had a house in the precinct of Totocache, and they did it great veneration. In the same house or temple was /f. 225/ the body of the said Inca Yupanqui. To this idol they very commonly made sacrifices of children and of everything else, asking it that the strength of the Inca be preserved and his dominion not decrease.

[Ch. 2:4] The fourth guaca was called Viroypacha; it is a conduit of fairly good water which was declared a guaca by Inca Yupanqui. It was prayed to for the tranquillity of the Inca.

[Ch. 2:5] The fifth guaca was a flat place called Chuquibamba which is next to the fortress; they sacrificed to it as to the others.

[Ch. 2:6] The sixth guaca was called Macasayba. It was a large stone which Inca Yupanqui set next to the flat place of Chuquibamba, and he ordered that veneration and sacrifices for the health of the king be made to it.

[Ch. 2:7] The seventh guaca was a quarry named Guayranga-llay, which is above the fortress. In it they made sacrifices for various reasons.

[Ch. 2:8] The eighth and last guaca of this ceque was called Guayllaurcaja. It is a little pass formed in the middle of a hill where Viracocha Inca many times sat down to rest climbing the said hill, and from that time on, by his command, it was considered a shrine.

[Ch. 3:0] The third ceque of this road was called Collana; it had ten guacas.

[Ch. 3:1] The first was named Nina, which was a brazier made of a stone where the fire for sacrifices was lit, and they could not take it from anywhere else. It was next to the Temple of the Sun; it was held in great veneration, and solemn sacrifices were made to it. /f. 225v/

[Ch. 3:2] The second guaca was called Canchapacha. It was a fountain which was in the street of Diego Maldonado, to which they made sacrifice on account of certain stories that the Indians tell.

[Ch. 3:3] The third guaca was another fountain named Tici-cocha, which is inside the house which belonged to the said Diego Maldonado. This fountain belonged to the coya or queen, Mama Ocllo. In it were made very great and ordinary sacrifices, especially when they wanted to ask something of the said Mama Ocllo, who was the most venerated woman there was among these Indians.

[Ch. 3:4] The fourth guaca was called Condorcancha and was the house in which Inca Yupanqui lived.

[Ch. 3:5] The fifth guaca was another house called Pomacorco, and they give no other reason for sacrificing in it, except that it had belonged to Guayna Capac.

[Ch. 3:6] The sixth guaca was named Mollaguanca; it was a certain stone which was in the middle of a flat place which they called Calispuquio. Inca Yupanqui ordered it to be placed there and considered a shrine.

[Ch. 3:7] The seventh guaca was the house which formerly belonged to the king, Tupa Inca, named Calispuquio Guaci, in which sacrifices were offered to the said Tupa Inca.

[Ch. 3:8] The eighth guaca was a fountain which was called Calispuquio which was below the said house of Tupa Inca. All those who were made orejones in the festival of Raymi went to wash in it. The water for the Inca was brought from this fountain with many songs made for this one purpose, and the girls who carried it were maidens. /f. 226/

[Ch. 3:9] The ninth guaca was named Cugiguaman. It was a stone shaped like a falcon which Inca Yupanqui said had appeared to him in a quarry, and he ordered that it be placed on this ceque and that sacrifices be made to it.

[Ch. 3:10] The tenth guaca of this ceque was a small fountain called Quinoapuquio which Inca Yupanqui designated as a shrine. Sacrifices for the health of the Inca were made to it.

[Ch. 4:0] The fourth ceque they named Payao [sic]; it had eight guacas.

[Ch. 4:1] The first of these was called Araytampu. It was a large stone with four other small ones which were next to the house which belonged to Benito de la Peña, and they were Pururaucas.

[Ch. 4:2] The second guaca was named Puñui; it was in a small flat place next to the house of Diego Maldonado. It was a very solemn shrine, because it was held to be the cause of sleep; they offered every kind of sacrifice to it. They went to it with two petitions, one to pray for those who were unable to sleep, and the other that they might not die in their sleep.

[Ch. 4:3] The third guaca was named Curiocllo. It was a house of Curiollo [sic; for Curi Ocllo], who had been the wife of Amaro Topa Inca, which was in Colcapata; and they worshipped also a fountain which was next to it.

[Ch. 4:4] The fourth guaca was named Colcapata and was the house of Paullu Inca, where there was a stone serving as an idol which the ayllo of Andasaya worshipped. The origin it had was that Pachacutic Inca had ordered it worshipped, because he said that /f. 226v/ a certain lord had been transformed into the said stone.

[Ch. 4:5] The fifth guaca was called Guamancancha and was near the fortress on a small hill of this name. It was an enclosure inside of which there were two small buhios designated for fasting when orejones were made.

[Ch. 4:6] The sixth guaca was a large stone named Collaconcho which was in the fortress. They declare that, bringing it for that structure, it fell three times and killed some Indians. The sorcerers, in questions they put to it, said that it had replied that, if they persisted in wanting to put it in the structure, all would have a bad end, apart from the fact that they would not be able to do it. From that time on it was considered a general guaca to which they made offerings for the strength of the Inca.

[Ch. 4:7] The seventh guaca was called Chachacomacaja; it consisted of certain trees set out by hand next to which was a stone to which they made sacrifice so that the Inca would not be wrathful.

[Ch. 4:8] The eighth and last guaca of this ceque was a high hill named Chuquipalta, which is next to the fortress, on which were placed three stones in representation of the Pachayachachic, Inti Illapa and Punchau [i.e., the Creator, the Thunder, and the Sun; particular manifestations of the last two are implied by the terms used]. On this hill, universal sacrifice was made of boys and girls and figurines of the same made of gold; and clothing and sheep were burned, because this was considered to be a very solemn shrine.

[Ch. 5:0] The fifth ceque of this same road and direction of Chinchaysuyu was called Cayao [sic]; it included ten guacas.

[Ch. 5:1] The first, named Cusicancha, was the place where Inca Yupanqui was born, opposite the temple of Coricancha; for this reason /f. 227/ the members of the ayllo Inacapanaca sacrificed there.

[Ch. 5:2] The second guaca was a temple named Pucamarca, which was in the houses which belonged to the Licentiate

[Antonio] de la Gama; in it was an idol of the Thunder called Chucuylla.

[Ch. 5:3] The third guaca was called Cuzcocalla. It was on the street which leads to the plaza following this line or ceque, and it consisted of a fair quantity of stones which they said were all Pururaucas.

[Ch. 5:4] The fourth guaca was the main plaza, named Aucaypata, which it also is [i.e., the main plaza] at the present time. In it was made the universal sacrifice for the Sun and the rest of the guacas, and it [i.e., the sacrifice] was divided and taken to the other parts of the kingdom. It was a very venerated place.

[Ch. 5:5] The fifth guaca was a buhio named Coracora, in which Inca Yupanqui used to sleep, which is where the cabildo [municipal council] houses are now. The said Inca ordered worship of that place and burning of clothing and sheep in it, and so it was done.

[Ch. 5:6] The sixth guaca was named Sabacurinca; it was a well carved seat where the Incas sat. It was very venerated, and solemn sacrifices were made to it. On account of this seat, the whole fortress was worshipped; for it [the seat] must have been inside or next to [the fortress].

[Ch. 5:7] The seventh guaca was named Chacaguanacauri. It is a small hill which is on the way to Yucay, where the young men who were preparing themselves to be orejones went for a certain grass which they carried on the lances.

[Ch. 5:8] The eighth guaca was a small tomb named Guamanguachanca, [the tomb] of a brother of Guayna Capac, which /f. 227v/ was at the side of the fortress. They made a shrine of it because the Inca's brother had died as a small child, and they said that because of the veneration they paid to it, no more [children] of that age would die.

[Ch. 5:9] The ninth guaca was a hill which is on the way to the valley of Yucay named Cinca, on which was a stone which the Indians of Ayamarca worshipped, holding the opinion that they originated from it.

[Ch. 5:10] The tenth guaca was a puquio or spring named Corcorpuquiu at which children were offered and everything else.

[Ch. 6:0] The sixth ceque was called Collana, like the third, and it had eleven guacas.

[Ch. 6:1] The first was called Catonge and was a stone of the Pururaucas, which was in a window next to the Temple of the Sun.

[Ch. 6:2] The second guaca was named Pucamarca [*sic*; probably for Quishuarcancha]; it was a house or temple designated for the sacrifices of the Pachayachachic [Creator] in which children were sacrificed and everything else.

[Ch. 6:3] The third guaca was called Ñan, which means "road." It was in the plaza where one took the road for Chinchaysuyu. Universal sacrifice was made at it for travelers, and so that the road in question would always be whole and would not crumble and fall.

[Ch. 6:4] The fourth guaca had the name of Guayra and was in the doorway of Cajana. At it sacrifice was made to the wind, so that it would not do damage, and a pit had been made there in which the sacrifices were buried. /f. 228/

[Ch. 6:5] The fifth guaca was the palace of Huayna Capac named Cajana, within which was a lake named Ticcicocha which was an important shrine and at which great sacrifices were made.

[Ch. 6:6] The sixth guaca was a fountain named Capipacchan [*sic*; for Çapi Pacchan], which was in Capi [Çapi], in which the Inca used to bathe. Sacrifices were made at it, and they prayed that the water might not carry away his strength or do him harm.

[Ch. 6:7] The seventh guaca was called Capi [Çapi], which means "root." It was a very large quinua [tree] root which the sorcerers said was the root from which Cuzco issued and by means of which it was preserved. They made sacrifices to it for the preservation of the said city.

[Ch. 6:8] The eighth was named Quisco; it was on top of the hill of Capi [Çapi], where universal sacrifice was made for the same reason as to the above mentioned root.

[Ch. 6:9] The ninth guaca was a hill named Quiangalla which is on the Yucay road. On it were two markers or pillars which they regarded as indication that, when the sun reached there, it was the beginning of the summer.

[Ch. 6:10] The tenth was a small fountain which was called Guarguaillapuquiu, and it is next to this hill. In it they threw the dust which was left over from the sacrifices of the guacas of this ceque.

[Ch. 6:11] The eleventh and last guaca was called Illacamarca; it was in a fortress which there was, built on a steep rock /f. 228v/ on the way to Yucay, and at it the guacas of this ceque ended.

[Ch. 7:0] The seventh ceque was called Cayao and was [the responsibility] of the ayllo of Capac Ayllu; it had the following eight guacas.

[Ch. 7:1] The first was named Omanamaro and was a long stone which they said was [one] of the Pururaucas and which was in the doorway of the house which belonged to [Juan de] Figueroa. Universal sacrifice was made there for the health of the Inca.

[Ch. 7:2] The second guaca was two small buhios, one named Sanca Cancha and the other Hurin Sanca, where they had a quantity of lions [i.e., pumas], tigers [i.e., jaguars], serpents, and all the other evil vermin that were available. In these buhios they thrust the prisoners they brought back from war. Whoever died that night, the said wild beasts ate; whoever remained alive, they took out. They took this [survival] as a sign that he had a good heart and intended to serve the Inca.

[Ch. 7:3] The third guaca was called Marcatampu. It consisted of some round stones which were in Carmenga, where the parish of Santa Ana is now, which [stones] Inca Yupanqui designated as an important shrine. Children were offered to it for the health and preservation of the Inca.

[Ch. 7:4] The fourth was named Taxanamaro; it consisted of five round stones which Viracocha Inca ordered placed on the hill of Toxan [*sic*] which is above Carmenga. The offering they gave it was only of cut shells. This guaca was prayed to for the victory of the Inca. /f. 228 bis/

[Ch. 7:5] The fifth guaca of this ceque they named Urcoslla Amaro; it consisted of many stones together placed on a small hill which is above Carmenga. Sacrifices were made to it for the health of the Inca.

[Ch. 7:6] The sixth was called Callancapuquiu; it is the spring of Ticutica [*sic*; for Ticatica] to which they offered shells so that it would always flow.

[Ch. 7:7] The seventh guaca was called Churuncana; it is a round hill which is above Carmenga where the royal road of Chinchero leaves that of Yucay. From this hill the sacrifices to Ticci Viracocha were made, asking him that the Inca be victorious throughout the land to the limits of the sea. They offered him all kinds of things, especially children.

[Ch. 7:8] The eighth and last guaca of this ceque was a fountain named Muchayllapuquiu which is near Guarguaylla. They offered it cut shells for certain purposes.

[Ch. 8:0] The eighth ceque of this road was called Payan, like the second, and there were thirteen guacas on it.

[Ch. 8:1] The first was a small house next to the Temple of the Sun named Illanguarque, in which were kept certain weapons which they said the sun had given to Inca Yupanqui, [and] with which he conquered his enemies. Universal sacrifice was made to this guaca.

[Ch. 8:2] The second was called Mancochuqui. It was a chacara of Huanacauri, and what was harvested from it was sacrificed to him.

[Ch. 8:3] The third guaca was a fountain named Aucaypata [Paccha] which was next to where the house of the cabildo [municipal council] is now. In it the priests of Chucuilla said that the /f. 228 bis v/ Thunder bathed, and they made up a thousand other absurdities.

[Ch. 8:4] The fourth guaca was called Cugitalis; it was a flat place where the house of Garcilaso was built. The origin they tell was that Huayna Capac slept there and dreamed that a certain war was coming. Because it afterward came to pass, he ordered that that place be venerated.

[Ch. 8:5] The fifth guaca was a chacara named Chacuaytapara which was in Carmenga and belonged to Amaro Tupa Inca. They offered it only shells, and they were not supposed to stop to sacrifice but make their offering as they passed by.

[Ch. 8:6] The sixth was a spring named Orocotopuquiu which was in Carmenga, to which were given ground up shells.

[Ch. 8:7] The seventh was called Sucanca. It was a hill by way of which the water channel from Chinchero comes. On it there were two markers as an indication that when the sun arrived there, they had to begin to plant the maize. The sacrifice which was made there was directed to the Sun, asking him to arrive there at the time which would be appropriate for planting, and they sacrificed to him sheep, clothing, and small miniature lambs of gold and silver.

[Ch. 8:8] The eighth guaca was a house called Mamararoy in which were venerated certain stones which they said were women [or wives] of Ticci Viracocha, and that, walking at night, they had turned to stone. Finding them in that place, they made that temple for them.

[Ch. 8:9] The ninth guaca was called Urcoscalla. It was the place where those who traveled to Chinchaysuyu lost sight of the city of Cuzco. /f. 229/

[Ch. 8:10] The tenth guaca was called Catachillay. It is a fountain which is in the first flat place which descends to the Road of Chinchaysuyu.

[Ch. 8:11] The eleventh was another fountain, next to the one above, which is called Aspadquiri, to which Inca Yupanqui ordered sacrifices made, because he said that its water took away fatigue.

[Ch. 8:12] The twelfth was another fountain named Poroypuquiu which is next to the mill which belonged to Juan Julio [de Hojeda]. They offered it finely ground shells.

[Ch. 8:13] The last guaca of this ceque was called Collanasayba; it was a marker which is on a hill at the beginning of Sicllabamba, as the end and limit of the guacas of this ceque.

[Ch. 9:0] The ninth and last ceque of this said road of Chinchaysuyu was named Capac and had twelve guacas.

[Ch. 9:1] The first was a fountain called Aypanospacha, which was on the street of Pedro Alonso Carrasco.

[Ch. 9:2] The second was a small house which was in Piccho, a farm which now belongs to the Society of Jesus, in which Huayna Capac ordered that they make sacrifice, because his mother, Mama Ocllo, used to sleep there.

[Ch. 9:3] The third was a hill named Quinoacalla which is in Carmenga, where it was ordained that the orejones should rest in the festival of Raymi.

[Ch. 9:4] The fourth guaca was a fountain named Pomacucho which was somewhat separated from this ceque. They offered shells to it. /f. 229v/

[Ch. 9:5] The fifth guaca was called Vicaribi; it was a well wrought tomb, which was in Piccho, of an important lord so named of the ayllo of Maras.

[Ch. 9:6] The sixth guaca was a stone named Apuyauira which was on the hill of Picho [Piccho]. They believed that it was one of those who emerged from the earth with Huanacauri, and that after having lived for a long time he climbed up there and turned to stone. All the ayllos went to worship at it in the festival of Raymi.

[Ch. 9:7] The seventh was a flat place called Cutirsaspampa, where the Inca won a certain victory, and for this [reason] alone the place was made a shrine.

[Ch. 9:8] The eighth was another flat place near this one named Queachili, which is between two hills like a gateway; in it the said victory was completed, and for that [reason] it was venerated.

[Ch. 9:9] The ninth guaca was called Quishuarpuquiu; it was a spring at which they said the Inca's men had drunk when the above battle was finished.

[Ch. 9:10] The tenth was named Yuyotuyro; it consisted of five stones together which were next to the hill above mentioned.

[Ch. 9:11] The eleventh was a stone called Pillolliri, which the Indians relate had jumped from another hill to that which is so named, and for this flight of fancy which they had they worshipped it.

[Ch. 9:12] The twelfth and last guaca of this ceque was a fountain named Totorgoaylla; here ended the /f. 230/ guacas of the nine ceques of the Road of Chinchaysuyu, which came to eighty-five.

Chapter 14. The shrines and guacas which there were on the Road of Antisuyu.

The Road of Antisuyu had nine ceques and on them seventy-eight guacas, in this order.

[An. 1:0] The first ceque was named Collana and was under the care of the ayllo of Cubcu [Çubçu] Pañaca Ayllu.

[An. 1:1] The first guaca of it was called Chiquinapampa. It was an enclosure which was next to the Temple of the Sun in which the sacrifice for the universal health of the Indians was made.

[An. 1:2] The second guaca was called Turuca. It was an almost round stone, which was next to the said Temple of the Sun in a window, which they said was [the] guauque of Ticci Viracocha. Universal sacrifice was made to it for all the needs that arose.

[An. 1:3] The third guaca was a large stone named Chiripacha which was at the beginning of the Road of Collasuyu. All those who traveled by the said road made offerings to it, so that the journey would turn out well for them.

[An. 1:4] The fourth was caller Autviturco. It was a large cave which is down the ravine from Patallacta, [and] from which they held the view that the Indians of the town of Goalla had been born. The sacrifice was to sprinkle it with the blood of llamas, which are the sheep of the country. /f. 230v/

[An. 1:5] The fifth was a fountain named Pacha which is in the ravine of Patallacta, in which the Inca washed himself a certain time.

[An. 1:6] The sixth was another fountain called Corcorchaca, which is in the same ravine as the one mentioned above; they offered it finely ground shells.

[An. 1:7] The seventh guaca was called Amaromarcaguaci; this was a house of Amaro Tupa Inca which was on the road of the Andes [i.e., the montaña].

[An. 1:8] The eighth guaca was named Tipcpuquiu; [*sic*; for Tinpuc Puquiu]; it was a fountain which is near Tambo Machay. It is so called because it wells up in such a way that the water boils.

[An. 1:9] The ninth was named Tambomachay; it was a house of Inca Yupanqui where he lodged when he went hunting. It was set on a hill near the road of the Andes. They sacrificed all kinds of things to it except children.

[An. 1:10] The tenth guaca was called Quinoapuquiu; it was a fountain near Tambo Machay which consists of two springs. Universal sacrifice was made to it, except children.

[An. 1:11] The last guaca of this ceque was called Quiscourco; it was a round stone, not very big, which served as the limit and marker of these guacas.

[An. 2:0] The second ceque of the said Road of Antisuyu was called Payan and had ten guacas.

[An. 2:1] The first was a place called Vilcacona, where the house /f. 231/ which belonged to Juan de Salas was built. To this shrine they brought at a certain time of the year all the guacas and idols of the city of Cuzco, and they sacrificed to them there, all together, and then they returned them to their places. It was a very solemn guaca; they offered it very small cestos of coca.

[An. 2:2] The second guaca of this ceque was named Pachatosa; it was a large stone which was next to [Diego] Cayo's house. The sacrifice was burned on top of it, and they said that it ate it.

[An. 2:3] The third guaca was called Chusacachi; it is a large hill on the way to the Andes on top of which were certain stones that were worshipped.

[An. 2:4] The fourth was named Curovilca; it was a quarry from which they extracted stone. They sacrificed to it so that it might not give out, and so that the buildings built [of stone] from it might not fall.

[An. 2:5] The fifth guaca was named Sunchupuquiu; it was a shrine which was next to the slope of a hill so named. They offered it sheep and clothing.

[An. 2:6] The sixth was a spring called Aucapapirqui which is on a flat place near the said road.

[An. 2:7] The seventh was named Caynaconga; it was a resting place of the Inca which was on a flat place near Tambo Machay.

[An. 2:8] The eighth guaca was called Puquiu; it was a fountain which is at that end of Tambo Machay. They offered it sheep, clothing, and shells.

[An. 2:9] The ninth was named Cascasayba; it consisted of certain /f. 231v/ stones which were on the hill of Quisco. It was an important guaca and had a certain long origin [story] which the Indians tell. They offered it all kinds of things and children as well.

[An. 2:10] The tenth was named Macaycalla. It is a flat place between two hills where what is on this side is lost to sight and the other side is revealed, and for this reason alone they worshipped it.

[An. 3:0] The third ceque was named Cayao, and it had ten guacas.

[An. 3:1] The first was a bridge called Guarupuncu which passed from the Temple of the Sun to a plaza which they named [the Plaza] of Peces [i.e., Francisco Peces]. They sacrificed to it for many reasons which they gave, and especially because the sacrifices which were offered at the king's coronation passed over it.

[An. 3:2] The second guaca was a wall next to the chacara of [Hernando] Bachicao, which had an outward bulge in it, the origin of which, they said, was that when the Inca passed that way the wall had gone out to do reverence to him, and from that time on they worshipped it, offering it colored shells.

[An. 3:3] The third was a fountain named Ayacho which is in the same chacara. They offered it shells of all colors, not very [finely] ground.

[An. 3:4] The fourth was called Chuquimarca; it was a temple of the Sun on the hill of Mantocalla, in which they said that the Sun descended many times to sleep. For this reason, in addition to the other things, they offered it children.

[An. 3:5] The fifth guaca was called Mantocallaspa; it was a fountain of good water which is on the above mentioned hill where the Indians bathed. /f. 232/

[An. 3:6] The sixth was called Mantocallas [*sic*] which was a hill held in great veneration, on which, at the time of shelling maize, they made certain sacrifices. For these [sacrifices], they placed on the said hill many bundles of carved firewood dressed as men and women and a great quantity of maize ears made of wood. After great drunken feasts, they burned many sheep with the said firewood and killed some children.

[An. 3:7] The seventh guaca was named Caripuquiu; it was a fountain which is on the slope of the said hill. They offered shells to it.

[An. 3:8] The eighth was called Yuncaypampa; it was a flat place which is on the road to the Andes, and it has a small fountain.

[An. 3:9] The ninth guaca was named Yancaycalla [sic; probably for Yuncaycalla]; it is a sort of gateway where the plain of Chita is seen and Cuzco is lost to sight. There were guards placed there so that no one would carry off anything stolen. Sacrifice was made by the merchants each time they passed, and they prayed that things would go well for them on the journey. Coca was the usual sacrifice.

[An. 3:10] The last guaca of this ceque was a fountain called Urcomilpo which is in the great plain of Chita; they offered it only sheep.

[An. 4:0] The fourth ceque of this road was called Collana; it was [the responsibility] of the ayllo and family of Aucailli Panaca and had seven guacas.

[An. 4:1] The first was named Cariurco, and it was a hill which is near Mantocalla, on top of which there were certain stones which were venerated, and they offered them clothing and /f. 232v/ spotted sheep.

[An. 4:2] The second guaca was named Chuquiquirao Puquiu; it was a fountain which has its source in a ravine on the slope of the hill above mentioned; the sacrifice was of sheep and clothing.

[An. 4:3] The third guaca was called Callachaca; it consisted of certain stones placed on the said hill.

[An. 4:4] The fourth was a quarry which is near there named Viracocha. In it there was a stone which resembled a person. They say that when they were cutting stone from there for a house of the Inca it came out so, and the Inca ordered that it should be a guaca.

[An. 4:5] The fifth was named Aucanpuquiu; it was a fountain which is near the ravine of Yancacalla [sic; see An. 3:9].

[An. 4:6] The sixth guaca was called Illansayba; it was a certain hill on top of which there were some stones to which they sacrificed for the health of those who entered the province of the Andes.

[An. 4:7] The last guaca of this ceque was a stone named Maychaguanacauri, shaped like the hill of Huanacauri, which was ordered placed on this Road of Antisuyu, and they offered all kinds of things to it.

[An. 5:0] The fifth ceque had the name of Payan, and there were ten guacas on it.

[An. 5:1] The first was a stone named Usno which was in the plaza of Hurin Aucaypata; this was the first guaca to which those who were being made orejones made offerings.

[An. 5:2] The second guaca was the spring named Cachipuquiu, which is in Las Salinas [the salt pans]. Much /f. 233/ salt of very fine quality is made from it. They offered it all kinds of things except children.

[An. 5:3] The third was called Subaraura. It was a round stone which was in the town of Yaconora and was a very ancient shrine.

[An. 5:4] The fourth was a fountain called Pachayaconora which was in the said town of Yaconora. They offered it only shells, some whole and others cut in pieces.

[An. 5:5] The fifth guaca was called Oyaraypuquiu; it was a small fountain which is somewhat higher up. They offered it shells of all colors, according to the times.

[An. 5:6] The sixth was another fountain named Arosayapuquiu which is in Callachaca; they offered it only shells.

[An. 5:7] The seventh was called Aquarsayba. It was a greatly venerated guaca, and they had the opinion that whatever they offered to it all the guacas received.

[An. 5:8] The eighth was a spring named Susumarca, which is in Callachaca, and they offered it the usual [things].

[An. 5:9] The ninth was called Rondoya; it consisted of three stones which were on the hill so named. The Inca Pachacutic placed them there and ordered them to be worshipped.

[An. 5:10] The tenth and last guaca of this ceque was another stone named Poma Urco which was set as the end and limit of the guacas of this ceque.

[An. 6:0] The sixth ceque was named Cayao, and on it there were seven guacas.

[An. 6:1] The first was called Auriauca; it was a sort of portico or arbor which was next to the Temple of the Sun, where the Inca and the lords took their places. /f. 233v/

[An. 6:2] The second guaca was a curved stone named Comovilca which was near Callachaca; they offered it only shells.

[An. 6:3] The third was named Chuquicancha; it is a well known hill which they held to be a house of the Sun. On it they made very solemn sacrifice to gladden the Sun.

[An. 6:4] The fourth was a small stone called Sanotuiron which was on a little hill. They made offerings to it for the health of the prince who was supposed to inherit the kingdom, and when they made him an orejón they offered a solemn sacrifice to this guaca.

[An. 6:5] The fifth was called Viracochapuquiu; it was a fountain which is in a flat place on the way to Chita.

[An. 6:6] The sixth was a house called Pomamarca which was on the said flat place. In it was kept the body of the wife of Inca Yupanqui, and children were offered there along with all the other things.

[An. 6:7] The seventh was called Curauacaja; it is a knoll on the way to Chita where sight of the city is lost, and it was designated as the end and marker of the guacas of this ceque. They had a dead lion [i.e., puma] there, and they told [a story of] its origin, which is long.

[An. 7:0] On the seventh ceque, named Yacanora [sic], there were another seven guacas.

[An. 7:1] The first was called Ayllipampa; it was a flat place where the chacara is which belonged to [Alonso de] Mesa. They said that it was the goddess Earth named Pachamama, and they offered her small women's garments.

[An. 7:2] The second guaca was a small fountain next to this field named Guamantanta; the usual things were offered to it. /f. 234/

[An. 7:3] The third was another fountain named Pacaypuquiu which is a little below the one mentioned above. They offered it ground up shells.

[An. 7:4] The fourth was a large plaza named Colcapampa, where the parish of the Martyrs was made, at the end of which there was a stone which was an important idol, to whom children were offered along with other things.

[An. 7:5] The fifth guaca was called Cuillorpuquiu; it was a small spring which is further down. They offered it only shells.

[An. 7:6] The sixth was named Unugualpa; this was a stone which was at Chuquicancha. They relate that when they were taking out stone they found it resembling a human figure, and from then on they worshipped it as a remarkable thing.

[An. 7:7] The seventh and last was a fountain named Cucacache, where some small salt pans are made.

[An. 8:0] The eighth ceque was called Ayarmaca; it had eleven guacas.

[An. 8:1] The first was a spring called Sacasaylla Puquiu which is next to the mill of Pedro Alonso [Carrasco]. They offered it only shells.

[An. 8:2] The second guaca was another spring named Pirquipuquiu, which is in a ravine lower down. They offered it small miniature lambs made of silver.

[An. 8:3] The third was named Cuipanamaro; it consisted of some stones next to this spring, which were regarded as an important guaca. They offered it small garments and little lambs made of shell.

[An. 8:4] The fourth was a spring called Auacospuquiu. They offered it only shells. /f. 234v/

[An. 8:5] The fifth was called Sabaraura; it consisted of three stones which were in the town of Larapa.

[An. 8:6] The sixth was named Urcopuquiu and was a squared stone which was in a corner of the said town. They considered it a guaca of authority and offered it small women's garments and little pieces of gold.

[An. 8:7] The seventh was a fountain called Pilcopuquiu which was near the town of Corcora. Shells and small women's garments were offered to it.

[An. 8:8] The eighth was named Cuipan; it consisted of six stones which were together on the hill so named. They offered to this guaca only red shells for the king's health.

[An. 8:9] The ninth was a spring which they named Chora, which was near Andamacha. They offered it ground up shells and little bits of gold.

[An. 8:10] The tenth was called Picas. It was a little pebble which was on a hill above Larapa, which they held to be an advocate against the hail. They offered it, in addition to the usual things, little round bits of gold.

[An. 8:11] The eleventh and last guaca of this ceque was named Pilcourco; it was another stone to which they did great reverence, which was on a big hill near Larapa. When there was a new Inca, in addition to the usual things they sacrificed to it a girl twelve years old or less.

[An. 9:0] The last ceque of this Road of Antisuyu was called Cayao. It was [the responsibility] of the ayllu and partiality of Cari and had the following five /f. 235/ guacas.

[An. 9:1] The first was called Lampapuquiu; it was a fountain which was in Undamacha [*sic*; for Andamacha; Vndamarca crossed out in the ms.]. They sacrificed to it shells of two colors, yellow and red.

[An. 9:2] The second guaca was another fountain named Suramapuquiu, which was in a ravine in Acoyapuncu. They offered it only shells.

[An. 9:3] The third was called Corcorpuquiu; it was another spring which is in the puna above the Angostura [narrows; Spanish name of Acoyapuncu].

[An. 9:4] The fourth guaca consisted of some stones named Churucana, which were on top of a hill further down.

[An. 9:5] The fifth and last [guaca] of this ceque and road was called Ataguanacauri; it consisted of certain stones placed next to a hill. It was an ancient shrine, and the usual things were offered to it.

Chapter 15. The ceques and guacas of the Road of Collasuyu.

There were in [the part corresponding to] this third road nine ceques and on them eighty-five shrines or guacas.

[Co. 1:0] The first ceque was called Cayao, and the family of Aguini Ayllu was concerned with it; it included nine guacas.

[Co. 1:1] The first was named Pururauca. It was where the house of Manso Serra [Mancio Serra de Leguizamo] was later. This [guaca] was a window which opened onto the street, and in it was a stone of the Pururaucas. They offered the usual things to it, except children.

[Co. 1:2] The second was called Mudcapuquiu. It was a small fountain /f. 235v/ which comes out below the houses which belonged to Anton Ruiz. They offered it only shells.

[Co. 1:3] The third guaca was called Churucana. It is a small and round hill, which is next to San Lázaro, on top of which were three stones regarded as idols. The usual things were offered to it and children as well, for the purpose that the Sun might not lose its strength.

[Co. 1:4] The fourth was a flat place called Caribamba which is in the town of Cacra. Children were usually sacrificed to it.

[Co. 1:5] The fifth was called Micaya Puquiu. It is a fountain which is on the slope of the hill of Guanacauri.

[Co. 1:6] The sixth was named Atpitan. It consisted of certain stones which were in a ravine, where one loses sight of Guanacauri. They relate that these stones were men [who were] sons of that hill, and that in a certain misfortune which befell them they turned into stones.

[Co. 1:7] The seventh, Guamansaui, was a large stone which was on top of a hill next to the Angostura. To this guaca all the families sacrificed for the Inca's strength, and they offered it small garments, gold, and silver.

[Co. 1:8] The eighth, Guayra, is a ravine of the Angostura where they related that the wind went in. They made sacrifice to it when strong winds blew.

[Co. 1:9] The ninth and last [guaca] of this ceque was called Mayu. It is a river which runs through the Angostura. They made sacrifices to it at /f. 236/ certain times of year to give thanks because it came through the city of Cuzco.

[Co. 2:0] The second ceque of this road was named Payan. It was the responsibility of the ayllu of Haguayni and had eight guacas.

[Co. 2:1] The first was a flat place called Limapampa where the chacara of Diego Gil was made; there they held the festival when they harvested the maize so that it would last and not rot.

[Co. 2:2] The second guaca was called Raquiancalla. It is a small hill which is in that chacara, on which there were many idols of all four suyus. Here a celebrated festival was held which lasted ten days, and the usual things were offered.

[Co. 2:3] The third was named Sausero. It is a chacara of the descendants of Paullu Inca to which, at sowing time, the king himself went and plowed a little. What was harvested from it was for sacrifices of the Sun. The day when the Inca went to do this was a solemn festival of all the lords of Cuzco. They made great sacrifices to this flat place, especially of silver, gold, and children.

[Co. 2:4] The fourth was a chacara which was called Omatalispacha, which afterwards belonged to Francisco Moreno. They worshipped a fountain which is in the middle of it.

[Co. 2:5] The fifth was a flat place called Oscollo, which belonged to Garcilaso. They offered it the usual things.

[Co. 2:6] The sixth was named Tuino Orco. It consisted of three stones which were in a corner of the town of Cacra. /f. 236v/

[Co. 2:7] The seventh was a spring, Palpancay Puquiu by name, which is on a hill next to Cacra, and they only offered it finely ground shells.

[Co. 2:8] The eighth and last guaca of this ceque was called Collocalla. It is a ravine where there was a marker beside the road, for the offerings.

[Co. 3:0] The third ceque had the name of Collana, and on it there were nine guacas.

[Co. 3:1] The first was named Tampucancha. It was part of the house of Manso Sierra [sic; see Co. 1:1] in which there were three stones worshipped as idols.

[Co. 3:2] The second guaca was a stone named Pampasona which was next to the house mentioned above. They offered it only ground up shells.

[Co. 3:3] The third was a fountain named Pirpoyopacha which is in the chacara of Diego Maldonado, in which the Incas washed themselves on certain days.

[Co. 3:4] The fourth was named Guanipata. It was a chacara far-

ther down where there was a big wall which they said the Sun had made there. They sacrificed children to it and everything else.

[Co. 3:5] The fifth was named Anaypampa. It was a chacara of the coya Mama Ocllo.

[Co. 3:6] The sixth was called Suriguaylla. It was a fountain which had its source in a flat place so named. They offered it ground up shells.

[Co. 3:7] The seventh, Sinopampa [sic; for Sañopampa], consisted of three round stones which were on a flat place in the middle of the town of Sano [Saño]. /f. 237/ They sacrificed children to it.

[Co. 3:8] The eighth, Sanopuquiu [Sañopuquiu] was a certain fountain which was in a ravine of the said town. They offered it sheep and shells.

[Co. 3:9] The ninth and last guaca of this ceque was a small hill named Llulpacturo, which is opposite the Angostura. It was designated as a place where offerings were made to the Ticci Viracocha. A greater quantity of children was sacrificed here than anywhere else. They also offered it children made of gold and silver and small garments, and it was a usual sacrifice of the Incas.

[Co. 4:0] The fourth ceque of this said road was called Cayao and was [the responsibility] of the ayllu of Apu Mayta; it had ten guacas.

[Co. 4:1] The first they named Pomapacha. It was a fountain where the Incas bathed, with a house next to it into which they retired when they came out of the bath. It was where the houses of [Cristóbal de] Sotelo were afterwards.

[Co. 4:2] The second guaca was named Taucaray. It was a tomb which was in the chacara of Diego Maldonado, where they believed that at a certain time all the dead assembled.

[Co. 4:3] The third was a fountain called Quispiquilla which is in the said farm of Diego Maldonado.

[Co. 4:4] The fourth was a hill, Cuipan by name, which is on the other side of Guanacauri. On top of it there were five stones which were regarded as guacas. They sacrificed all things to them, especially children. /f. 237v/

[Co. 4:5] The fifth was called Ayavillay. It was a tomb where the lords of the ayllu of this name were buried.

[Co. 4:6] The sixth was called by the same name as the one above. It consisted of certain stones together placed on a hill which is opposite Cacra.

[Co. 4:7] The seventh was called Raurao Quiran. It is a large hill which they worshipped for its great size and because it was designated [as a guaca].

[Co. 4:8] The eighth, Guancarcalla, is a ravine like a gateway which is next to the hill above mentioned. It was dedicated to the Sun, and they offered it children in certain festivals which they held there.

[Co. 4:9] The ninth guaca is a large hill named Sinayba which is at the far end of Quispicanche.

[Co. 4:10] The tenth and last was called Sumeurco. It is a hill which they had set as the limit of the guacas of this ceque. It is next to the one above, and they offered it shells.

[Co. 5:0] The fifth ceque was named Payan, and it had ten guacas.

[Co. 5:1] The first they named Catonge. It was a stone which was by the house of Juan Sona. They worshipped it as an important guaca and offered it all kinds of things, especially small figures of men and women of gold and silver.

[Co. 5:2] The second was a fountain named Membilla Puquiu from which those of the town of Membilla drank. They offered it only cut shells.

[Co. 5:3] The third was called Quintiamaro. It consisted of certain round stones which were in the town of Quijalla. /f. 238/

[Co. 5:4] The fourth was called Cicacalla. It consisted of two stones which were in the same town [mentioned] above. Small shells and burned garments were offered to it.

[Co. 5:5] The fifth guaca was named Ancasamaro. It consisted of five stones which were in the same town.

[Co. 5:6] The sixth, Tocacaray, was a hill which is facing Quijalla. There were three venerated stones on it; they sacrificed children to them.

[Co. 5:7] The seventh was a fountain called Mascaguaylla, which is on the Guanacauri road.

[Co. 5:8] The eighth was named Intipampa. It was a flat place next to Cacra, in the middle of which there were three stones. It was an important shrine at which children were sacrificed.

[Co. 5:9] The ninth was another flat place called Rondao which is next to the royal road of Collasuyu, facing Cacra.

[Co. 5:10] The tenth and last [guaca] was a small hill named Omotourco, which is opposite Quispicanche in the puna or páramo. On top of it were three stones to which they offered sacrifices.

[Co. 6:0] The sixth ceque they named Collana and there were ten guacas on it.

[Co. 6:1] The first was a buhio called Tampucancha, which was on the site of the house of Manso Sierra [sic; see Co. 1:1] and which was a residence of Manco Capac Inca. They offered it the usual things, except children.

[Co. 6:2] The second guaca was named Mamacolca. It consisted of certain stones which were in the town of Membilla. /f. 238v/

[Co. 6:3] The third was a house called Acoyguaci, which was in Membilla, in which the body of the Inca Cinchi Roca was kept.

[Co. 6:4] The fourth was called Quiracoma. It was a large stone with four small ones which was in the flat place of Quicalla [Quiçalla].

[Co. 6:5] The fifth was named Viracochacancha. It consisted of five stones which were in the town of Quijalla.

[Co. 6:6] The sixth was called Cuipan and consisted of three stones placed in the flat place of Quicalla [Quiçalla].

[Co. 6:7] The seventh was named Huanacauri; it was among the most important shrines of the whole kingdom, the oldest which the Incas had after the window [cave] of Pacaritampu, and where the most sacrifices were made. This is a hill which is about two and a half leagues distant from Cuzco by this Road of Collasuyu we are following. On it they say that one of the brothers of the first

Inca turned to stone, for reasons which they give. They had the said stone hidden. It was of moderate size, without [representational] shape, and somewhat tapering. It was on top of the said hill until the coming of the Spanish and they [i.e., the Incas] held many festivals for it. After the Spanish arrived, they [i.e., the Spanish] removed a great quantity of gold and silver from this shrine but paid no attention to the idol, because it was, as I have said, a rough stone. This situation gave the Indians an opportunity to hide it until Paullu Inca, on his return from Chile, built a house for it next to his own. From that time on, the festival of Raymi was held there until the Christians found out about the stone and took it away from him. With it was found a quantity of offerings, small garments /f. 239/ for little idols, and an abundance of ear spools for the young men who are knighted. They very commonly took this idol to war with them, particularly when the king went in person. Guayna Capa took it to Quito, whence they brought it back again with his body. The Incas, indeed, were convinced that it had a large share in their victories. For the festival of the Raymi, they placed it on the hill of Huanacauri, dressed richly and adorned with many feathers.

[Co. 6:8] The eighth guaca was a fountain named Micaypuquiu on the road to Tambo.

[Co. 6:9] The ninth was called Quiquijana. It is a very small hill where there were three stones. They offered them only shells and small garments.

[Co. 6:10] The last guaca of this ceque was a small fountain named Quizquipuquiu which was on a flat place near Cacra.

[Co. 7:0] The seventh ceque had the name Cayao, and there were on it eight guacas, the responsibility of the ayllo of Usca Mayta.

[Co. 7:1] The first was named Santocollo. It was a flat place down from the chacara of Francisco Moreno. They offered it very fine painted garments.

[Co. 7:2] The second guaca was a stone called Catocalla, which was on the royal road near the town of Quicalla [Quiçalla]; it was [one] of the Pururaucas.

[Co. 7:3] The third was another stone named Chachaquiray, which was not far from the one above. /f. 239v/

[Co. 7:4] The fourth was a flat place which they named Vircaypay, where afterwards the Chachapoyas Indians settled.

[Co. 7:5] The fifth was called Matoro. It is a slope near Guanacauri where there were some ancient buildings, which they relate was where those who went out from Guanacauri after the flood slept at the end of the first day's journey. In this connection they allude to other absurdities.

[Co. 7:6] The sixth is a fountain named Vilcaraypuquiu, which is near the said slope, where they say that those who left Guanacauri drank.

[Co. 7:7] The seventh is a great flat place near Guanacauri named Uspa.

[Co. 7:8] The eighth and last [guaca] of this ceque was a fountain named Guamancapuquiu, which is in a ravine.

[Co. 8:0] The eighth ceque was called Payan, and it had eight guacas.

[Co. 8:1] The first was a prison named Sancacancha, which Mayta Capac made; it was on the house lot which belonged to [Juan de] Figueroa.

[Co. 8:2] The second guaca was a chacara called Guanchapacha which afterwards belonged to Diego Maldonado. All sorts of things were offered to it, except children.

[Co. 8:3] The third was called Mudca. It was a stone pillar which was on a small hill near Membilla. They offered it only ground up shells.

[Co. 8:4] The fourth was a small hill named Chuquimarca which is next to Guanacauri. They offered it ground up shells. /f. 240/

[Co. 8:5] The fifth was called Cuicosa. It consisted of three round stones which were on a hill so named, next to Guanacauri.

[Co. 8:6] The sixth was a certain fountain named Coapapuquiu which is next to the same hill of Guanacauri.

[Co. 8:7] The seventh was another fountain called Puquin [sic; possibly should read Puquiu], next to the one mentioned above.

[Co. 8:8] The last guaca of this ceque was a ravine which is next to Guanacauri. Everything which was left over after the other [guacas] of this said ceque had been taken care of was offered to it.

[Co. 9:0] The ninth and last ceque of this road we are following was named Collana, and it had thirteen guacas.

[Co. 9:1] The first was a seat named Tampucancha, where they said that Mayta Capac used to sit, and that while he was sitting here he arranged to give battle to the Acabicas [sic; Alcabiças]. Because he defeated them in the battle, they regarded the said seat as a place to be venerated. It was next to the Temple of the Sun.

[Co. 9:2] The second guaca was called Tancarvilca. It was a small round stone which was in the house lot which belonged to Don Antonio [Pereira]; they said that it was [one] of the Pururaucas.

[Co. 9:3] The third was a flat place called Pactaguañui which belonged to Alonso de Toro. It was a much venerated place; they sacrificed to it to be preserved from sudden death.

[Co. 9:4] The fifth [sic; fourth] was called Quicapuquiu. It is a spring which is this side of Membilla. They offered it ground up shells.

[Co. 9:5] The fifth was named Tampuvilca. It was a /f. 240v/ round hill which is next to Membilla, on top of which were five stones which they relate had appeared there, and for that [reason] they venerated them. They offered them the usual [things], especially burned cestos of coca.

[Co. 9:6] The sixth was named Chacapa. It is a flat place on that end of Membilla. They offered it ground up shells.

[Co. 9:7] The seventh was called Chinchaypuquiu. It is a fountain which was in a town of this name.

[Co. 9:8] The eighth, Guarmichaca Puquiu, is another fountain which is farther up in a ravine next to Guanacauri.

[Co. 9:9] The ninth, Cupaychangiri Puquiu, was another fountain next to the one above, and they offered it only shells.

[Co. 9:10] The tenth, Quillo, consisted of five stones placed on top of a hill of this name near Guanacauri.

[Co. 9:11] The eleventh guaca was called Cachaocachiri. It consisted of three stones which were on another small hill so named; it was an ancient shrine in which, and in the one above, children were sacrificed.

[Co. 9:12] The twelfth was a large stone named Quiropiray, which was on top of the hill of this name; they said it was [one] of the Pururaucas.

[Co. 9:13] The last guaca of this road was a hill named Puncu, where they offered what was left over from the guacas of this ceque. /f. 241/

Chapter 16. The ceques and guacas of the Road of Cuntisuyu.

The Road of Cuntisuyu, which we call Condesuyu, had fourteen ceques and eighty guacas, as they are here set forth.

[Cu. 1:0] The first ceque they named Anaguarque, and it had fifteen guacas.

[Cu. 1:1] The first was a stone called Sabaraura, which was where the belvedere of Santo Domingo is now; they believed that it was an officer of the Pururaucas.

[Cu. 1:2] The second guaca was another stone like this one, named Quingil, which was in a wall next to Coricancha.

[Cu. 1:3] The third was called Poma Chupa (it means "lion's [i.e., puma's] tail"). It was a flat place in the precinct so named, and from there offerings were made to the two small rivers which flow through there.

[Cu. 1:4] The fourth was named Uxi. It was the road which goes to Tampu. Sacrifices were made at the beginning of it for certain reasons which the Indians give.

[Cu. 1:5] The fifth, Guaman, is a ravine where there was a small round stone which was an idol.

[Cu. 1:6] The sixth, Curipoxapuquiu, was another ravine next to the one above, on the Membilla road; they offered it the usual [things] and children on certain days.

[Cu. 1:7] The seventh, Anaguarque, was a big hill which is next to Guanacauri, where there were many idols, each of which had its origin [story] and history. Children were usually sacrificed.

[Cu. 1:8] The eighth, Chataguarque, was a certain small stone /f. 241v/ which was on a little hill next to that other one.

[Cu. 1:9] The ninth, Achatarque Puquiu, was a fountain next to the hill above; they offered it only clothing and shells.

[Cu. 1:10] The tenth, Anahuarque Guaman, was a stone which was on a hill next to the one above; they offered it children.

[Cu. 1:11] The eleventh guaca was a fountain named Yamarpuquiu, which was in a ravine on the slope of the above hill.

[Cu. 1:12] The twelfth was another fountain called Chicapuquiu, which comes out near the one above.

[Cu. 1:13] The thirteenth was called Incaroca. It was a cave which was farther along than the fountains named above and was an important shrine. They offered it children.

[Cu. 1:14] The fourteenth was a certain stone named Puntuguanca, which was on top of a hill of the same name near the hill of Anaguarque.

[Cu. 1:15] The last guaca was called Quiguan. It consisted of three stones which were in a small gap on the way to Pomacancha.

[Cu. 2:0] The second ceque of this Road of Cuntisuyu was [the responsibility] of the ayllo of Quisco. It was named Cayao and had four guacas.

[Cu. 2:1] The first was a great flat place called Cotocari, which afterwards was a chacara of [Antonio] Altamirano.

[Cu. 2:2] The second was called Pillo Lluri. It was a ravine on the way to Tambo in which there was a long stone of medium size held in veneration. /f. 242/

[Cu. 2:3] The third, Paylla Llanto, was a certain cave into which they believed that a lady of this name, mother of a great lord, Apu Curimaya by name, entered and never again appeared.

[Cu. 2:4] The fourth was called Rauaraya. It is a small hill where the Indians finished running on the feast of the Raymi, and here a certain punishment was given to those who had not run well.

[Cu. 3:0] The third ceque was named Payan and had another four guacas.

[Cu. 3:1] The first was a fountain named Chuquimatero from which the Indians of Cayocache drink.

[Cu. 3:2] The second was called Caquia Sabaraura. It is a hill opposite Cayocache on top of which were five stones regarded as idols.

[Cu. 3:3] The third, Cayascas Guaman, was a long stone which was in the town of Cayascas.

[Cu. 3:4] The fourth, Chucuracay Puquiu, is a ravine on the way to Tambo where the valley of Cuzco is lost to sight.

[Cu. 4:0] The fourth ceque they named Collana, and it had five guacas.

[Cu. 4:1] The first was called Pururauca. It was one of those stones into which they said that the Pururaucas had changed, and it was on a stone bench next to the Temple of the Sun.

[Cu. 4:2] The second was called Amarocti. It consisted of three stones which were in a small town named Aytocari.

[Cu. 4:3] The third, Cayaopuquiu, was a fountain which was opposite Cayocache, on the slope of the river. /f. 242v/

[Cu. 4:4] The fourth, Churucana, was a certain large stone which was on a hill next to that of Anaguarque; they offered children to it.

[Cu. 4:5] The fifth was named Cuipancalla. It is a ravine which is on the way to Tambo, where they cast what was left over of the offerings of this ceque.

[Cu. 5:0] The fifth ceque was called Cayao. It was the responsibility of the ayllu of Chima Panaca, and it had the same number of guacas as the preceding [one].

[Cu. 5:1] The first they named Caritampucancha. It was a small plaza which is now inside the monastery of Santo Domingo, which

they held to be the first place where Manco Capac settled on the site of Cuzco when he came out of Tampu. Children were offered to it along with everything else.

[Cu. 5:2] The second guaca was called Tiucalla. It consisted of ten stones of the Pururaucas which were in Cayocache.

[Cu. 5:3] The third, Cayallacta, consisted of certain stones which were on a hill near Choco, a town which belonged to Hernando Pizarro.

[Cu. 5:4] The fourth, Churupuquiu, is a fountain which is above the small town of Choco.

[Cu. 5:5] The fifth was called Cumpu Guanacauri. It is a hill in line with Choco on top of which there were ten stones which they believed that the hill of Guanacauri had sent there.

[Cu. 6:0] The sixth ceque of this same road was named Payan, and it had five guacas.

[Cu. 6:1] The first had for [its] name Apian. It was /f. 243/ a round stone of the Pururaucas which was on the site which Santo Domingo has today.

[Cu. 6:2] The second guaca was called Guaman. It was a stone which was in Cayocache.

[Cu. 6:3] The third, Ocropacla, consisted of some stones of the Pururaucas which were in Cayocache.

[Cu. 6:4] The fourth, Pachapuquiu, was a fountain which is toward Pomapampa.

[Cu. 6:5] The fifth was called Intirpucancha. It was a buhio in the middle of the town of Choco and had belonged to its first lord.

[Cu. 7:0] The seventh ceque was named Collana, and it had another five guacas.

[Cu. 7:1] The first was a small house called Inticancha, in which they held the opinion that the sisters of the first Inca, who came out of the window [cave] of Pacaritampu with him, dwelt. They sacrificed children to it.

[Cu. 7:2] The second guaca was named Rocromuca. It was a large stone which was next to the Temple of the Sun.

[Cu. 7:3] The third, Caruinca Cancha, was a small house which was in Cayocache, which had belonged to a great lord.

[Cu. 7:4] The fourth, Sutirmarca; this is a hill from which they say that an Indian came out, and that he reentered it again without having any children. /f. 243v/

[Cu. 7:5] The fifth, Cotacotabamba, was a flat place between Choco and Cachona where a festival was held on certain days of the year in which they stoned one another.

[Cu. 8:0] Half of the eighth ceque was named Cayao and the other half Collana; the whole of it had fifteen guacas.

[Cu. 8:1] The first they named Tanancuricota [*sic;* for Chañan Curi Coca]. It was a stone into which they said that a woman who came with the Pururaucas turned.

[Cu. 8:2] The second was a tomb of a principal lord; [the guaca was] named Cutimanco. They sacrificed children to it.

[Cu. 8:3] The third was called Cauas. It was another tomb which was in Cachona.

[Cu. 8:4] The fourth was named E Con Con Puquiu. It was a fountain which is in Cachona.

[Cu. 8:5] The fifth, Chinchay Puquiu, was another fountain which is on a slope of the puna.

[Cu. 8:6] The sixth, Mascata Urco, is a hill where one loses sight of Cuzco on this ceque.

[Cu. 8:7] The seventh, Cachicalla, is a ravine between two hills like a gateway; they did not offer anything to it except the coca which passers-by cast from the mouth.

[Cu. 8:8] The eighth, Quiacas Amaro, consisted of certain stones which were on top of a hill beyond Cayocache.

[Cu. 8:9] The ninth, Managuanunca Guaci [Managuañunca Guaci], was a house of one of the coyas or queens, which was on the site which /f. 244/ the monastery of La Merced now has.

[Cu. 8:10] The tenth, Cicui, was a tomb which was on the slope of Cachona.

[Cu. 8:11] The eleventh, Cumpi, is a large hill which is on the way to Cachona, on top of which there were ten stones regarded as idols.

[Cu. 8:12] The twelfth, Pachachiri, is a fountain which is in the puna of Cachona.

[Cu. 8:13] The thirteenth, Pitopuquiu, is another small fountain which was next to the one above mentioned.

[Cu. 8:14] The fourteenth, Cauadcalla, was a sort of gateway between two hills, which is toward Guacachaca.

[Cu. 8:15] The last guaca of this ceque was called Lluquiriui. It is a big hill next to the above ravine.

[Cu. 9:0] The ninth ceque had the name Cayao and included three guacas.

[Cu. 9:1] The first was called Colquemachacuay (it means "silver serpent"). It is a fountain of good water, very well known, which is on the slope of the hill of Puquin, next to the city of Cuzco.

[Cu. 9:2] The second was named Micayurco. It is large hill which is above Puquin.

[Cu. 9:3] The third, Chaquira, is a hill which is near the Alca road, on top of which there were ten stones held to be idols.

[Cu. 10:0] The tenth ceque they named Payan, and it had four /f. 244v/ guacas.

[Cu. 10:1] The first was a fountain called Pilcopuquiu, which is in the garden of Santo Domingo.

[Cu. 10:2] The second was called Puquincancha. It was a house of the Sun which was above Cayocache. They sacrificed children to it.

[Cu. 10:3] The third had the name Cancha. It was the enclosure wall of the above house, where they also made offerings.

[Cu. 10:4] The fourth, Viracochaurco, is a hill which is above Puquin.

[Cu. 11:0] The eleventh ceque was named Collana, and in it there were four guacas.

[Cu. 11:1] The first was a fountain called Matarapacha, which is on the way to Cayocache.

[Cu. 11:2] The second was named Cuchiguayla. It is a small flat place which is located below the said fountain.

[Cu. 11:3] The third, Puquinpuquiu, is a fountain which is on the slope of the hill of Puquin.

[Cu. 11:4] The fourth, Tampu Urco, is another hill which is to one side of the one of Puquin.

[Cu. 12:0] The twelfth ceque was named Cayao, and it had three guacas.

[Cu. 12:1] To the first, they gave the name Cunturpata. It was a seat on which the Inca rested when he went to the festival of the Raymi.

[Cu. 12:2] The second was called Quilca. It was a very ancient tomb of a lord who was so named.

[Cu. 12:3] The third, Llipiquiliscacho, was another tomb /f. 245/ which was behind Choco.

[Cu. 13:0] The thirteenth ceque was named Cayao [sic; Payan], and it had four guacas.

[Cu. 13:1] The first was a puquiu or fountain named Chilquichaca.

[Cu. 13:2] The second was called Colcapuquiu. It was another fountain which is in a ravine which descends from Chilquichaca.

[Cu. 13:3] The third, Chinchincalla, is a large hill where there were two markers; when the sun reached them, it was time to plant.

[Cu. 13:4] The fourth, Pomaguaci, is a small hill at the end of this ceque which was [there] as the end and limit of the guacas of it.

[Cu. 14:0] The last ceque of this Road of Contisuyu was called Collana, and it had four guacas.

[Cu. 14:1] The first was a stone of no great size named Oznuro, which was in the chacara of the Gualparocas.

[Cu. 14:2] The second guaca of this ceque was called Otcuropuquiu. It was a fountain near Picho, a farm of the Society of Jesus.

[Cu. 14:3] The third was named Rauaypampa. It was a terrace where the Inca lodged which was on the slope of the hill of Chinchincalla.

[Cu. 14:4] The fourth, Pantanaya, is a large hill cleft in the middle which divides the Roads of Chincha [sic] and Condesuyo, or Cuntisuyu.

The four following guacas belong to various ceques but were not set down in the order that the rest [were], /f. 245v/ when the investigation was made.

[extra 1 (Ch)] The first was called Mamacocha. It is a small lake up above the fortress.

[extra 2 (Ch)] The second is a fountain called Tocoripuquiu, from which issues a stream which passes through the city.

[extra 3 (Ch)] The third was named Chinchacuay. It is a hill which is opposite the fortress.

[extra 4 (Ch)] The fourth and last of all was called Quiquijana. It is another hill which is behind the one above.

These were the guacas and general shrines which there were in Cuzco and its vicinity within four leagues; together with the Temple of Coricancha and the last four which are not listed in the ceques, they come to a total of three hundred thirty-three, distributed in forty ceques. Adding to them the pillars or markers which indicated the months, the total reaches the number of three hundred fifty at least. In addition, there were many other private [guacas], not worshipped by everyone, but by those to whom they belonged, such as those of the provinces subject to the Inca, which were shrines only of their natives, and the dead bodies of each lineage, which were revered only by their descendants. Both kinds had their guardians and attendants who, at the proper times, offered the sacrifices /f. 246/ which were established. For all of them these Indians had their stories and fables of how and for what reasons they were instituted, what sacrifices were made to them, with what rites and ceremonies, when and for what purposes, so that if it were necessary to give a detailed account of everything it would be prolix and tedious; indeed, I very nearly refrained from listing, even in this brief fashion, the guacas named in these four chapters, and I would have done so, except that I judged it necessary to enumerate them to explain more clearly the gullibility of these people and how the Devil took advantage of it to inflict on them such a harsh servitude to so many and such foolish errors with which he had taken possession of them.

Appendix 3

Suggested Glosses of Huaca Names

Margot Beyersdorff

This index contains the names of huacas in the Cusco ceque system as presented by Cobo (1980 [1653]) and Albornoz (1984 [ca. 1582]). Additional shrine information is provided in the endnotes and in the general text of this book. The names are listed in the old alphabetical order used for the Spanish language: *ch* follows *c*, *ll* follows *l*, and *ñ* follows *n*. Margot Beyersdorff carried out the lexicographical research and, with Brian S. Bauer, provided the phonemic transcriptions and glosses of the huaca names. In assuming this task of reconstruction, we have rephonologized the terms in order to present the most likely original morphology of the toponyms. Initial aid was also provided by Inéz Callalli Villafuerte and Olga Villagarcía, both native speakers of Quechua.

The task of translating the huaca names is complicated by the limited alphabet used by the Spaniards to record the wide range of Quechua phonemes unfamiliar to them, and by the half millennium that separates modern Cusco Quechua from that of the Inca. Transcription errors were most likely added by Cobo when he copied information on the Cusco huacas from Polo de Ondegardo's original report. Besides, by the time Cobo wrote his *Relación de las huacas*, drawing upon the local lexicon for placenames, speakers had already transformed two terms into one. Rather than a transcription error (although this cannot be ruled out entirely), speakers may have inserted *n*, *s*, or *o* between each term in a compound name, as in Illanguarque (illa warqi), for ease in enunciation.

The absence of final syllables is apparent in many of the compound names, especially in cases in which speakers would ordinarily employ the genitive particles, *-p/pa* on the first term and *-n* on the second. Thus for names in which the genitive is partially conserved, such as the *c(p)* in Amarocti, (amarup tiyanan), "Seat of the Serpent," we complete the possessive construction. In reconstructing the huaca names, we are guided by the observations of Santa Cruz Pachacuti Yamqui Salcamayhua (1993:98 [1613]) that the Lengua General (Language of the Inca) had promoted abbreviated place-names lacking the genitive markers.[1] We have not attempted to rephonologize names having variant contemporaneous spellings (indicated with a ?), as in Chilquichaca/Chaquillchaca. In cases where Cobo writes a known verb or noun root followed by unidentifiable phonemes or morphemes, we place a hyphen after the word root (qhawa-). In the English Name column, when the nature of the connection between two terms is uncertain, we place a dash. Parentheses indicate words we have added to the name to supply context. Certain names appear to have honored an event or characteristic associated with a great warrior or hunter personage as in Chucuracay puquiu (Split-Helmet Spring) and Lluquiriui (Left[Twisted] Snare)respectively.

Our primary sources in translating the huaca names included Diego González Holguín (1901, 1989 [1608]), Jorge Lira (1982 [1941]), Espinoza Galarza (1973), Antonio Cusihuamán G. (1976), Jesús Lara (1978), and our personal knowledge. These glosses are a starting point for understanding the names of the Cusco huacas, and we encourage others to expand on this effort.

Cobo provides no names for two huacas in the *Relación de las huacas*, An. 3:2 and Co. 8:8. These shrines have been placed at the end of the index. Furthermore, as noted by Rowe (1980:62), it is unclear whether the name of Ch. 9:2 was Picchu.

Huaca Name	Number[2]	Quechua/Spanish	English	English Name
Acoyguaci	Co. 6:3	aquy = infortunio wasi = casa	ill fortune house	Ill Fortune — House
Achatarque puquiu	Cu. 1:9	hacha = indómito[3] añay = exquisito warqi = ondulado[4] puquiu = manantial	indomitable exquisite wavy spring	Indomitable Exquisite Wavy (Feathered Hawk) Spring
Agmoasca[5]	#7	alaymosca = piedra púrpura	purple stone	Purple Stone
Amarocti	Cu. 4:2	amarup = serpiente tiyanan = asiento del	serpent seat of the	Seat of the Serpent
Amaromarcaguaci	An. 1:7	amaru = serpiente marka = pueblo wasi = casa	serpent town house	Serpent Town House

Huaca Name	Number[2]	Quechua/Spanish	English	English Name
Anaguarque	Cu. 1:7	añay = exquisito warqi = ondulado	exquisite wavy	Exquisite Wavy (Feathered Hawk)
Anahuarque guaman	Cu. 1:10	añay = exquisito warqi = ondulado waman = halcón	exquisite wavy hawk	Exquisite Wavy (Feathered) Hawk
Anaypampa	Co. 3:5	añay = exquisito panpa = llano	exquisite plain	Exquisite Plain
Anca	#30	anka = águila	eagle	Eagle
Ancasamaro	Co. 5:5	anka = águila amaru = serpiente	eagle serpent	Eagle — Serpent
Ancas pata	#35	anka = águila pata = andén	eagle terrace	Eagle Terrace
Apian	Cu. 6:1	apu = gran señor tiyana = asiento del	great Lord seat of the	Seat of the Great Lord
Apuyauira[6]	Ch. 9:6	apu = gran señor yawira = ?	great lord ?	Lord Yawira
Aquarsayba	An. 5:7	yawar = sangre saywa = mojón	blood marker	Blood Marker
Araytampu	Ch. 4.1	aray = quinoa silvestre[7] tanpu = albergue	wild quinoa lodge	(Lineage of) Wild Quinoa Lodge
Arosayapuquiu	An. 5:6	aran[8] = arriba saya = sector puquiu = manantial	upper sector spring	Upper Sector Spring
Aspadquiri[9]	Ch. 8:11	aspakay = fiesta con sacrificio quiri = ?	celebration with sacrifice ?	Celebration with Sacrifice — ?
Ataguanacauri	An. 9:5	ataw = ilustre wanap = del escarmiento yawrin = cetro real	illustrious of expiation royal scepter	Illustrious Royal Scepter of Expiation
Atpitan[10]	Co. 1:6	Atipaq = todo poderoso tiyana = asiento	all powerful seat	Seat of the All Powerful
Auacospuquiu	An. 8:4	awakuq = tejedor puquiu = manantial	weaver spring	Weaver Spring
Aucanpuquiu	An. 4:5	awqa = enemigo puquiu = manantial	enemy spring	Enemy Spring
Aucapapirqui[11]	An. 2:6	awqap = enemigo apiriqin = raptor	enemy raptor	Raptor of Enemies
Aucaypata	Ch. 5:4	hawkay = solaz, alegría pata = andén	tranquil, happiness terrace	Terrace of Tranquillity
Aucaypata[12] [paccha]	Ch. 8:3	hawkay = solaz, alegría pata = andén phaqcha = cascada	tranquil, happiness terrace waterfall	Terrace of Tranquillity Waterfall
Auriauca	An. 6:1	yarwi = cetro awqa = enemigo	staff enemy	Enemy — Staff

Huaca Name	Number[2]	Quechua/Spanish	English	English Name
Autviturco[13]	An 1:4	anta = cobre wit'u = corte urqu = cerro, montaña	copper slash hill, mountain	Copper Cave Hill
Ayacho[14]	An. 3:3	haya = picante uchu = ají	piquant chili pepper	Piquant Chili Pepper
Ayavillay	Co. 4:5 & Co. 4:6	aya = muerto willka = sagrado	dead sacred	Sacred Dead
Ayllipampa	An. 7:1	haylliy = canción de victoria en la siembra y cosecha del maíz panpa = llano	victory song for the planting and harvesting of maize plain	Maize Song Plain
Aypanospacha[15]	Ch. 9:1	aypa- = alcanzar lo que se distribuye phaqcha = cascada[16]	distribute offerings waterfall	Distribution of Ceremonial Gifts Waterfall
Cacchacuchui	#11	kacha = ídolos de la batalla[17] k'uchu = rincón	idols of battle corner	Corner of the Idols of Battle
Cachaocachiri	Co. 9:11	cacha-[18] = ? chiri = frío	? cold	? — Cold
Cachicalla	Cu. 8:7	kachi = sal qaylla = cerca	salt near	Near Salt
Cachipuquiu	An. 5:2	kachi = sal puquiu = manantial	salt spring	Salt Spring
Cajana	Ch. 6:5	qasana = lugar del hielo[19]	place of ice	Place of Ice
Calispuquio[20]	Ch. 3:8	qhalli = sano puquiu = manantial	healthy spring	Healthy (Water) Spring
Calispuquio guaci	Ch. 3:7	qhalli = sano puquiu = manantial wasi = casa	healthy spring house	Healthy (Water) Spring — House
Callachaca[21]	An. 4:3	kallanka = sillería chaka = puente	Large cut-stone work bridge	Large Cut-Stone Bridge
Callancapuquiu	Ch. 7:6	kallanka = sillería puquiu = manantial	Large cut-stone work spring	Large Cut-Stone Spring
Cancha	Cu. 10:3	kancha = cercado	enclosure	Enclosure
Canchapacha	Ch. 3:2	kancha = cercado phaqcha = cascada	enclosure waterfall	Waterfall Enclosure
Capa[22]	#27	saphi = raíz	root	Root
Capi[23]	Ch. 6:7	saphi = raíz	root	Root
Capipacchan[24]	Ch. 6:6	saphio = raíz phaqchan = cascada	root waterfall of the	Waterfall of the Root
Caquia sabaraura[25]	Cu. 3:2	kaqiy kaq = herencia sapa = único rawra = llama de fuego	heritage unique flame	Heritage — Unique Flame

Huaca Name	Number[2]	Quechua/Spanish	English	English Name
Caribamba	Co. 1:4	qhari = hombre panpa = llano	man plain	Man — Plain
Caripuquiu	An. 3:7	qhari = hombre puquiu = manantial	man spring	Man — Spring
Caritampucancha	Cu. 5:1	qhari = hombre tanpu = albergue kancha = cercado	man lodge enclosure	Man — Lodge Enclosure
Cariurco	An. 4:1	qhari = hombre urqu = cerro, montaña	man hill, mountain	Man — Mountain
Caruinca cancha[26]	Cu. 7:3	karu = lejano[27] inka = inca kancha = cercado	distant Inca enclosure	Distant (Kindred of the Reigning) Inca Enclosure
Cascasayba	An. 2:9	cascajillo = cascajo[28] saywa = mojón	pebbles marker	Pebbles Marker
Catachillay	Ch. 8:10	qhatiqin = arriero illa = símbolo sagrado[29]	herder sacred symbol	Star Herder
Catonge[30]	Ch. 6:1	qhatu = campamento	encampment	Cluster (of Stone Warriors)
Catonge	Co. 5:1	qhatu = campamento	encampment	Cluster (of Stone Warriors)
Catungui	#22	qhatu = campamento awki = señor inca[31]	encampment lord Inca	Cluster (of Stone Warriors) Lords
Cauadcalla	Cu. 8:14	qhawa- = mirar qaylla = cerca	to look near	Near the Lookout[32]
Cauas[33]	Cu. 8:3	qhawa- = mirar	to look, to care for	(Sepulchre of) Mother Watchful
Cayallacta	Cu. 5:3	kayaw = un sector del Cusco llaqta = pueblo	a sector of Cusco town	Kayaw Town
Cayaopuquiu	Cu. 4:3	kayaw = un sector del Cusco puquiu = manantial	a sector of Cusco spring	Kayaw Spring
Cayascas guaman	Cu. 3:3	saytu = larga[34] waska = soga waman = halcón	long rope hawk	Long Rope (Stone), Hawk
Caynaconga	An. 2:7	waynarikuna = descanso y recreación[35]	rest and recreation	Resting Place
Cicacalla	Co. 5:4	cica = ? qaylla = cerca	? near	Near — ?
Cicui[36]	Cu. 8:10	sikuy = paja brava[37]	bunch grass	Bunch Grass
Cinca	Ch. 5:9	sinqa = nariz	nose	Nose
Cirocaya[38]	Ch. 1:4	ciro = ? qaylla = cerca	? near	Near — ?
Coapapuquiu[39]	Co. 8:6	quya = reina phaqcha = cascada puquiu = manantial	queen waterfall spring	Queen — Waterfall Spring

Huaca Name	Number[2]	Quechua/Spanish	English	English Name
Colcapampa[40]	An. 7:4	qullqa = almacén panpa = llano	storehouse plain	Storehouse — Plain
Colcapata	Ch. 4:4	qullqa = almacén pata = andén	storehouse terrace	Storehouse — Terrace
Colcapuquiu	Cu. 13.2	qullqa = almacén puquiu = manantial	storehouse spring	Storehouse — Spring
Colquemachacuay	Cu. 9:1	qullqi = plata machaqway = culebra	silver snake	Silver Snake
Collaconcho[41]	Ch. 4:6	kallanka = sillería kuchuy = cortar	Large cut-stone work cut	Large Cut-Stone Work
Collanasayba	Ch. 8:13	qullana = principal saywa = mojón	principal marker	Principal Marker
Collocalla	Co. 2:8	qullu = morro qaylla = cerca	round hill near	Near Round Hill
Comovilca	An. 6:2	k'umu = agachado willka = sagrado	bowed sacred	Sacred Bowed (Stone)
Condorcancha	Ch. 3:4	kuntur = cóndor kancha = cercado	condor enclosure	Condor Enclosure
Coracora	Ch. 5:5	qhura qhura = herbazal	plot of herbaceous plants	Field of Weeds
Corcorchaca[42]	An. 1:6	qunqur = arrodillado chaka = puente	kneeling bridge	Kneeling (Stone) Bridge
Corcorpuquiu	Ch. 5:10	qunqur = arrodillado puquiu = manantial	kneeling spring	Kneeling (Stone) Spring
Corcorpuquiu	An. 9:3	qunqur = arrodillado puquiu = manantial	kneeling spring	Kneeling (Stone) Spring
Cotacalla[43]	Co. 7:2	qhatu = asentamiento qaylla = cerca	settlement near	Near Settlement
Cotacotabamba	Cu. 7:5	qutu qutu = montones[44] panpa = llano	piles plain	Piles (of?) Plain
Cotocari	Cu. 2:1	coto = ? qhari = hombre	? man	? — Man
Cucacache	An. 7:7	suka- = camellón kachi = sal	furrow salt	Salt Pans
Cuchiguayla[45]	Cu. 11:2	suchi = dar plata[46] waylla = prado	to exchange silver for employment meadow	Exchange Silver for Employment Meadow
Cugiguaman	Ch 3:9	kusi = alegre waman = halcón	happy hawk	Happy Hawk
Cugitalis	Ch. 8:4	kusi = alegre qhalli = sano	happy healthy	Happy Healthy
Cuicosa[47]	Co. 8:5	cuicosa = ayllu en Hurin Cusco	ayllu in Lower Cusco	Ayllu Cuicosa

Huaca Name	Number[2]	Quechua/Spanish	English	English Name
Cuillorpuquiu	An. 7:5	quyllur = estrella puquiu = manantial	star spring	Star — Spring
Cuipan	An. 8:8	qullpa = salitre[48]	saltpeter	Saltpeter
Cuipan	Co. 4:4	qullpa = salitre	saltpeter	Saltpeter
Cuipan[49]	Co. 6:6	?	?	?
Cuipanamaro	An. 8:3	qullpa = salitre amaru = serpiente	saltpeter serpent	Saltpeter Serpent
Cuipancalla	Cu. 4:5	qullpa = salitre qaylla = cerca	saltpeter near	Near Saltpeter
Cumpi	Cu. 8:11	kunpi = cumbe, tejido fino[50]	fine cloth	Fine Cloth
Cumpu guanacauri	Cu. 5:5	kumpa = derrumbe[51] wanap = del escarmiento yawrin = cetro real	landslide of expiation royal scepter	Landslide — Royal Scepter of Expiation
Cunturpata	Cu. 12:1	kuntur = cóndor pata = andén	condor terrace	Condor Terrace
Cupaychangiri Puquiu	Co. 9:9	supay = diablo ch'anki = cactácea[52] k'iriy = herir puquiu = manantial	devil cactus to hurt spring	Hurting Devil Cactus Spring
Curauacaja	An. 6:7	kurawa = techado de paja q'asa = abra	straw roof pass	Straw Roof Pass
Curicancha	#1	quri = oro kancha = cercado	gold enclosure	Gold Enclosure
Curiocllo	Ch. 4:3	quri = oro uqllu = abrazo	gold embrace	Mother Golden Embrace[53]
Curipoxapuquiu[54]	Cu 1:6	quri = oro pata = andén puquiu = manantial	gold terrace spring	Gold Terrace Spring
Curovilca	An. 2:4	qhuru = piedra maciza redonda[55] willka = sagrado	large round stone sacred	Sacred Large Round Stone
Cusicancha[56]	Ch. 5:1	kusi = alegre kancha = cercado	happy enclosure	Happy Enclosure
Cusicancha pachamama[57]	#19	kusi = alegre kancha = cercado pacha = tierra mama = madre	happy enclosure earth mother	Happy Enclosure, Earth — Mother
Cutimanco	Cu. 8:2	kuti = torcida manku = venda	twisted band	(Sepulchre of) Lord of the Twisted Band
Cutirsaspampa	Ch. 9:7	cutirsas = ? panpa = llano	? plain	— Plain
Cuzcocalla[58]	Ch. 5:3	khuskan = junto qaylla = cerca	in the middle near	Near the Middle (of River)

Huaca Name	Number[2]	Quechua/Spanish	English	English Name
Chacaguana-cauri[59]	Ch. 5:7	chaka = puente wanap = del escarmiento yawrin = cetro real	bridge of expiation royal scepter	Bridge — Royal Scepter of Expiation
Chacanguana-cauri[60]	#29	chaka = puente wanap = del escarmiento yawrin = cetro real	bridge of expiation royal scepter	Bridge — Royal Scepter of Expiation
Chacapa[61]	Co. 9:6	chakapa = tipo de terraza	type of terrace	Lattice-like Terrace
Chacuaytapara[62]	Ch. 8:5	chacuaytapara = ?	?	?
Chachacomacaja	Ch. 4:7	chachakuma = árbol andino[63] q'asa = abra	Andean tree mountain pass	Chachakuma Tree Pass
Chachaquiray	Co. 7:3	chacha = árbol andino[64] k'iraw = cuna	Andean tree cradle	Chacha Trees — Cradle
Chaquira[65]	Cu. 9:3	hacha = indómito k'iraw = cuna	indomitable cradle	Indomitable Cradle
Chataguarque[66]	Cu. 1:8	hacha = indómito añay = exquisito warqi = ondulado	indomitable exquisite wavy	Indomitable Exquisite Wavy (Feathered Hawk)
Chicapuquiu	Cu. 1:12	chiqa = principal puquiu = manantial	principal spring	Principal Spring
Chilquichaca[67]	Cu. 13:1	chilqui = ? chaka = puente	? bridge	? — Bridge
Chinchacuay	Ch. Extra:3	chincha = tigrillo machaqway = culebra	ocelot[68] snake	Ocelot — Snake
Chinchaypuquiu	Co. 9:7	chincha = tigrillo puquiu = manantial	ocelot spring	Ocelot Spring
Chinchay puquiu	Cu. 8:5	chincha = tigrillo puquiu = manantial	ocelot spring	Ocelot Spring
Chinchincalla	Cu. 13:3	chinchin = ? qaylla = cerca	? near	Near — ?
Chiquinapampa[69]	An. 1:1	chikina = el apartar la cría de la madre panpa = llano	weaning an animal plain	Weaning of Animals Plain
Chiripacha	An. 1:3	chiri = frío pacha = tierra	cold earth	Cold Earth
Chora	An. 8:9	ch'uraq = pantano	marsh	Marsh
Chucuracay puquiu	Cu. 3:4	chuku = morrión[70] raqay = hender puquiu = manantial	helmet to cleave in two parts spring	Split-Helmet Spring
Chuquibamba	Ch. 2:5	chuqi = oro[71] panpa = llano	gold plain	Gold Plain
Chuquicancha	An. 6:3	chuqi = oro kancha = cercado	gold enclosure	Gold Enclosure

Huaca Name	Number²	Quechua/Spanish	English	English Name
Chuquimarca	An. 3:4	chuqi = oro marka = pueblo	gold town	Gold Town
Chuquimarca	Co. 8:4	chuqi = oro marka = pueblo	gold town	Gold Town
Chuquimatero	Cu. 3:1	chuqi = oro matero = ?	gold ?	Gold — ?
Chuquipalta	Ch. 4:8	chuqi = oro p´alta = piedra chata⁷²	gold flat stone	Flat Stone — Gold
Chuquiquirao puquiu	An. 4:2	chuqi = oro k'iraw = cuna o lecho puquiu = manantial	gold cradle or lair spring	Gold Cradle Spring
Churucana⁷³	An. 9:4	churucana = ?	?	?
Churucana⁷⁴	Co. 1:3	churucana = ?	?	?
Churucana	Cu. 4:4	churucana = ?	?	?
Churucani⁷⁵ guanacauri	#17	churucani = ? wanap = del escarmiento yawrin = cetro real	? of expiation royal scepter	? — of the Royal Scepter of Expiation
Churuncana⁷⁶	Ch. 7:7	churucana = ?	?	?
Churupuquiu	Cu. 5:4	ch'uru = caracol puquiu = manantial	snail spring	Snail Spring
Chusacachi⁷⁷	An. 2:3	chusaq = liviano, vacío kachi = sal	light, empty salt	Light — Salt
E con con puquiu⁷⁸	Cu. 8:4	E con con⁷⁹ = ? puquiu = manantial	? puquiu = spring	? — Spring
Guairaguaca⁸⁰	#28	wayra = viento waka = adoratorio	wind shrine	Wind Shrine
Guaman	Cu. 1:5	waman = halcón	hawk	Hawk
Guaman	Cu. 6:2	waman = halcón	hawk	Hawk
Guamancancha	Ch. 4:5 and #18	waman = halcón kancha = cercado	hawk enclosure	Hawk Enclosure
Guamancapuquiu	Co. 7:8	wamanqa = halcón puquiu = manantial	hawk spring	Hawk Spring
Guamanguachanca	Ch. 5:8	waman = halcón wachanqa = lugar de parir	hawk birthing place	Hawk Birthing Place
Guamansaui	Co. 1:7	waman = halcón chawa = feroz	hawk ferocious	Ferocious Hawk
Guamantanta⁸¹	An. 7:2	waman = halcón tiyana = asiento	hawk seat	Hawk Seat
Guancarcalla	Co. 4:8	wankar = tambor qaylla = cerca	drum near	Near Drum
Guanchapacha	Co. 8:2	wanchaq = rana pacha = tierra	frog earth	Frog Earth

Huaca Name	Number[2]	Quechua/Spanish	English	English Name
Guanipata	Co. 3:4	wanay = escarmiento pata = andén	expiation terrace	Expiation Terrace
Guaracince[82]	Ch. 2:1	wara = bragas sinchi = fuerza	loin cloth strength	Loin Cloth — Strength
Guaracinci[83]	#33	wara = bragas sinchi = fuerza	loin cloth strength	Loin Cloth — Strength
Guarguailla- puquiu	Ch. 6:10	wara = arreboles de la tarde waylla = prado puquiu = manantial	red sunset meadow spring	Sunset Meadow Spring
Guarmichaca puquiu	Co. 9:8	warmi = mujer chaka = puente puquiu = manantial	woman bridge spring	Woman — Bridge Spring
Guarupuncu	An. 3:1	waru = pedregal[84] punku = portal	rocky place portal	Rocky Place Portal
Guayllaurcaja	Ch. 2:8	waylla = prado urqu = cerro q'asa = abra	meadow mountain pass	Mountain Meadow Pass
Guayra[85]	Ch. 6:4	wayra = viento	wind	Wind
Guayra	Co. 1:8	wayra = viento	wind	Wind
Guayrangallay	Ch. 2:7	wayra = viento qaylla = cerca	wind near	Near Wind
Hanan chaca	#23	hanan = superior chaka = puente	upper bridge	Upper Bridge
Haucaypata pacha[86]	#8	hawkay= solaz, alegría pata = andén phaqcha = cascada	tranquil, happiness terrace waterfall	Terrace of Tranquillity Waterfall
Huanacauri	Co. 6:7	wanap = escarmiento yawrin = cetro real del	escarmiento royal scepter of	Royal Scepter of Expiation
Hurinchaca	#24	hurin = abajo chaka = puente	lower bridge	Lower Bridge
Hurin sanca[87]	Ch. 7:2	hurin = abajo sanq'a = cárcel	lower prison	Lower Prison
Illacamarca[88]	Ch. 6:11	illa- = tesoro marka = pueblo	treasures town	Town of Treasured Things
Illanguarque[89]	Ch. 8:1	illapa = relámpago[90] warqi = ondulado	lightning wavy	Wavy Lightning
Illansayba	An. 4:6	illa = atesorado saywa = hito	treasure marker	Treasure (Hill) Marker
Incaroca[91]	Cu. 1:13	inca = inka ruka = prudente	Inca prudent	Inca — Prudent
Inticancha	Cu. 7:1	inti = sol kancha = cercado	sun enclosure	Enclosure of the Sun
Inti illapa	Ch. 2:3	inti = sol illapa = rayo	sun lightning	Sun — Lightning

Huaca Name	Number[2]	Quechua/Spanish	English	English Name
Intipampa	Co. 5:8	inti = sol panpa = llano	sun plain	Sun — Plain
Intirpucancha	Cu. 6:5	inti = sol llirpu = espejo kancha = cercado	sun mirror enclosure	Sun — Mirror — Enclosure
Lampapuquiu	An. 9:1	llanpa = pala puquiu = manantial	digging stick spring	Digging-Stick Spring
Limapampa	Co. 2:1	rima- = hablar panpa = llano	to speak plain	Plain — Speaker
Luchus amaro[92]	#34	luchus [michuq] = juez amaru = serpiente	judge serpent	Judge — Serpent
Llipiquilis-cacho[93]	Cu. 12:3	lliphi = fugaz q´illi q´illi = cernícalo kacha = mensajero	fleet kestrel messenger	(Lord) Fleet Kestrel Messenger
Llulpacturo	Co. 3:9	llullpaq = limpio t'uru = barro[94]	clean clay	Clean Clay
Lluquiriui	Cu. 8:15	lluqi = izquierdo lliwi = boleadora	left animal snare	Left (Twisted) Snare
Macasayba	Ch. 2:6	mast'a- = extender saywa = hito	to extend marker	Extended (View) Marker
Macaycalla	An. 2:10	mast'a- = extender qaylla = cerca	to extend near	Near Extended (View)
Mamacocha	Ch. Extra:1	mama = madre qucha = lago	mother lake	Mother Lake
Mamacolca	Co. 6:2	mama = madre qullqa = almacén	mother storehouse	Mother Storehouse
Mamararoy[95]	Ch. 8:8	mama = madre ruway = hacer	mother maker	Mother — Maker
Managuanunca guaci	Cu. 8:9	mana wañunqa = no morirá wasi = casa	never will die house	Never Will Die — House
Mancochuqui	Ch. 8:2	manku = venda chuqi = oro	band gold	Gold Band
Mantocallas[96]	An. 3:6	mantur = color bermejo[97] qaylla = cerca	reddish color near	Near Red Paint (Tree)
Mantocallaspa[98]	An. 3:5	mantur = color bermejo qaylla = cerca phaqcha = cascada	reddish color near waterfall	Near Reddish Waterfall
Mararoray[99]	#13	mama = madre ruway = hacer	mother to make	Mother — Maker
Marcatambo[100]	#9	marka = pueblo tanpu = albergue	town lodge	Town Lodge
Marcatampu[101]	Ch. 7:3	marka = pueblo tanpu = albergue	town lodge	Town Lodge

Huaca Name	Number[2]	Quechua/Spanish	English	English Name
Margauiche	#6	marq'arichiy = hacer llevar en los brazos	to have someone carry something in one's arms	Carry (Stone) in Arms
Mascaguaylla	Co. 5:7	maska = borla roja[102] waylla = prado	red fringe headdress meadow	Royal Headdress Meadow
Mascata urco	Cu. 8:6	maska = borla roja urqu = cerro	red fringe headdress hill	Royal Headdress Hill
Matarapacha	Cu. 11:1	matara = enea[103] phaqcha = cascada	cattails, rushes waterfall	Waterfall — Rushes
Matoro[104]	Co. 7:5	matoro = ?	?	?
Maychaguanacauri	An. 4:7	maych'a = herbolario[105] wanap = del escarmiento yawrin = cetro real	herbalist of expiation royal scepter	Herbalist — Royal Scepter of Expiation
Mayu	Co. 1:9	mayu = río	river	River
Membilla puquiu	Co. 5:2	winpilla = la horca[106] puquiu = manantial	the gallows spring	(Place of the) Gallows Spring
Micaya puquiu	Co. 1:5	mik'aya[107] =ciénaga puquiu = manantial	bog spring	Bog — Spring
Micaypuquiu	Co. 6:8	mik'aya =ciénaga puquiu = manantial	bog spring	Bog — Spring
Micayurco	Cu. 9:2	mika uya[108] = cara redonda urqu = cerro, montaña	round-faced hill, mountain	Round Face Hill
Michosamaro[109]	Ch. 1:1	michuq[110] = juez amaru = serpiente	judge serpent	Judge — Serpent
Mollaguanca	Ch. 3:6	mullu[111] = concha marina wanka = piedra mármol	marine shell marble stone	Sacred Marine Shell Stone
Muchayllapuquiu	Ch. 7:8	much'ay = venerar illa = tesoro puquiu = manantial	to worship treasure spring	Venerable Treasure Spring
Mudca	Co. 8:3	mut'ka = mortero	mortar	Mortar
Mudcapuquiu	Co. 1:2	mut'ka = mortero puquiu = manantial	mortar spring	Mortar — Spring
Nina	Ch. 3:1 and #32	nina = llama de fuego[112]	flame	Flame
Ñan	Ch. 6:3	ñan = senda, camino	path, road	Road
Oma chilligues[113]	#15	uma = agua[114] chiri = frío	water cold	Cold Water (Plain)
Omanamaro[115]	Ch. 7:1	uma = agua[116] amaru = serpiente	water serpent	Water Serpent
Omatalispacha	Co. 2:4	uma = agua[117] qhalli = sano phaqcha = cascada	water healthy waterfall	Healthy Water Cascade
Omotourco[118]	Co. 5:10	umutu = enano urqu = cerro	dwarf hill	Dwarf Hill

Huaca Name	Number[2]	Quechua/Spanish	English	English Name
Orcopacla	Cu. 6:3	urqu = cerro pallqa = partido	hill cleft	Cleft Hill
Orocotopuquiu	Ch. 8:6	uru/khuru = gusano qutu = montón puquiu = manantial	worm pile spring	Worm — Pile — Spring
Oscollo	Co. 2:5	usqullu = gato cerval	mountian lion	Mountain Lion
Otcuropuquiu[119]	Cu. 14:2	otcuro = uqururu[120] puquiu = manantial	watercress spring	Watercress Spring
Oyaraypuquiu	An. 5:5	uyariy = escuchar puquiu = manantial	to listen spring	Listening — Spring
Oznuro[121]	Cu. 14:1	usnu- = altar, asiento real	altar, royal seat	Altar
Pacaypuquiu	An. 7:3	pakay = esconder puquiu = manantial	to hide spring	Hidden Spring
Pactaguañui	Co. 9:3	paqtataq = cuidado wañuy = muerte	be careful death	Careful, Death!
Pacha	An. 1:5	phaqcha = cascada	waterfall	Waterfall
Pachachiri	Cu. 8:12	phaqcha = cascada chiri = frío	waterfall cold	Cold Waterfall
Pachapuquiu	Cu. 6:4	phaqcha = cascada puquiu = manantial	waterfall spring	Waterfall — Spring
Pachatosa[122]	An. 2:2	pacha = tierra tusa = sostén de la	earth support	Supporter of the Earth
Pachayaconora[123]	An. 5:4	phaqcha = cascada yaku = agua uray = abajo	waterfall water below	Waterfall — Downhill
Palpancay puquiu	Co. 2:7	pallqa = partido qaylla = cerca puquiu = manantial	cleft near spring	Near Cleft Spring
Pampasona	Co. 3:2	panpa = llano hina = como un	plain like a	Like a Plain
Pantanaya	Cu. 14:4	pantanayay = estar a punto de equivocarse de camino	about to lose one's way	Fork in the Road
Patallacta	Ch. 1:2	pata = andén llaqta = pueblo	terrace town	Terrace Town
Paylla llanto	Cu. 2:3	palla = mujer principal llanthu = sombra	principal woman shade	Shade — Principal Woman
Picas	An. 8:10	picas = ?	?	?
Piccho [?]	Ch. 9:2	piqchu = montaña, picacho	peaked mountain	Peaked Mountain
Pilcopuquiu	An. 8:7	pillku = de varios colores puquiu = manantial	multicolor spring	Many-Colored Spring
Pilcopuquiu	Cu. 10:1	pillku = de varios colores puquiu = manantial	multicolor spring	Many-Colored Spring

Huaca Name	Number[2]	Quechua/Spanish	English	English Name
Pilcopuquiu	Ch. 1:3 and #36	pillku = de varios colores puquiu = manantial	multicolor spring	Many-Colored Spring
Pilcourco	An. 8:11	pillku = de varios colores[124] urqu = cerro	multicolor hill	Many-Colored Hill
Pillolliri	Ch. 9:11	pillu = corona[125] churi = tamaño de niño	crown child-sized	Child-Sized Diadem (Stone)
Pillo lluri[126]	Cu. 2:2	pillu = corona churi = tamaño de niño	crown child-sized	Child-Sized Diadem (Stone)
Pirpoyopacha[127]	Co. 3:3	llirpu- = espejo phaqcha = cascada	mirror waterfall	Mirror Waterfall
Pirquipuquiu	An. 8:2	pirqui = ? puquiu = manantial	? spring	? — Spring
Pitopuquiu[128]	Cu. 8:13	pitu = junto, pareja puquiu = manantial	beside, pair spring	Pair of Springs
Piuni guaca	#31	piuni = ? wanka = piedra mármol	? marble stone	? — Marble Stone
Pomacorco	Ch. 3:5	puma = puma kurku = agachado	puma crouched	Crouched Puma (Hill)
Pomacucho	Ch. 9:4	puma = puma k'uchu = rincón	puma corner	Puma Corner
Poma chupa[129]	Cu. 1:3	puma = puma chupa = cola	puma tail	Puma Tail
Pomaguaci	Cu. 13:4	puma = puma wasi = casa	puma house	Puma House
Pomamarca	An. 6:6	puma = puma marka = pueblo	puma town	Puma Town
Pomapacha	Co. 4:1	puma = puma phaqcha = cascada	puma waterfall	Puma Waterfall
Poma urco	An. 5:10	puma = puma urqu = cerro del	puma hill of the	Puma Hill
Poroypuquiu	Ch. 8:12	puru- = sapillo[130] puquiu = manantial	small frog spring	Small-Frog Spring
Pucamarca	Ch. 5:2	puka = rojo marka = pueblo	red town	Red Town
Pucamarca	Ch. 6:2	puka = rojo marka = pueblo	red town	Red Town
Pucamarca quisuarcancha	#21	puka = rojo marka = pueblo kishwar = árbol andino[131] kancha = cercado	red town Andean tree enclosure	Red Town — Kishwar Tree Enclosure
Puncu	Co. 9:13	punku = portal	portal	Portal (Hill)
Puntuguanca	Cu. 1:14	pintuna = mortaja[132] wanka = piedra mármol	shroud marble stone	Shrouded Marble Stone
Puñui	Ch. 4:2	puñuy = sueño	sleep	(Giver of) Sleep

Huaca Name	Number[2]	Quechua/Spanish	English	English Name
Puquin[133]	Co. 8:7	puquiu = manantial	spring	Spring
Puquincancha[134]	Cu. 10:2	puqu- = madurar kancha = cercado	to ripen enclosure	(Festival of Crop) Ripening — Enclosure
Puquinpuquiu[135]	Cu. 11:3	puqu- = madurar puquiu = manantial	to ripen spring	(Festival of Crop) Ripening — Spring
Puquiu	An. 2:8	puquiu = manantial	spring	Spring
Pururauca	Co. 1:1	purun = balas de piedra awqa = enemigo	stone projectiles enemy	Enemy — Stone Projectiles
Pururauca	Cu. 4:1	purun = balas de piedra awqa = enemigo	projectile stones enemy	Enemy — Stone Projectiles
Queachili[136]	Ch. 9:8	khuska = en medio chiri = frío	in between cold	Cold (Plain) in between (Hills)
Quiacas amaro	Cu. 8:8	killaka = en forma de media luna amaru = serpiente	halfmoon shaped serpent	Half-Moon Serpent
Quiangalla[137]	Ch. 6:9	qiyan = herrumbre qaylla = cerca	rust-colored near	Near the Rust-Colored (Sunset)
Quicapuquiu	Co. 9:4	kisa = ortiga[138] puquiu = manantial	nettles spring	Nettles Spring
Quicasunto	#20	kinsa[139] = tres runtu = huevo	three egg	Three Egg (-Shaped Stones)
Quiguan	Cu. 1:15	kinsa = tres wanka = piedra mármol	three marble stone	Three Marble Stones
Quilca	Cu. 12:2	Quilca = nombre de un señor	name of a lord	(Sepulchre of) Lord Quilca
Quillcai cancha	#2	inkill = jardín qaylla = cerca kancha = cercado	garden near enclosure	Near Garden (of Gold) Enclosure
Quillo[140]	Co. 9:10	k'iru = diente	tooth	Tooth (-Shaped Stone)
Quingil	Cu. 1:2	quri = oro inkill = jardín[141]	gold garden	Golden (Maize Plants) Garden
Quinoacalla	Ch. 9:3	kinua = quinoa[142] qaylla = cerca	quinoa near	Near Quinoa
Quinoapuquiu	An. 1:10	kinua = quinoa, puquiu = manantial	quinoa spring	Quinoa Spring
Quinoapuquiu	Ch. 3:10	kinua = quinoa, puquiu = manantial	quinoa spring	Quinoa Spring
Quintiamaro	Co. 5:3	q'inti = picaflor amaru = serpiente	hummingbird serpent	Hummingbird — Serpent
Quiquijana	Co. 6:9	quiquijana = ?	?	?
Quiquijana	Ch. Extra:4	quiquijana = ?	?	?
Quirarcoma	Co. 6:4	k'irukuna = dientes	teeth	Tooth (-Shaped Stones)
Quiropiray	Co. 9:12	k'iru = diente piray = ?	tooth ?	Tooth (-Shaped Stone)

Huaca Name	Number[2]	Quechua/Spanish	English	English Name
Quisco	Ch. 6:8	khiska = espino[143]	spiny plant	Spiny Plant
Quiscourco	An. 1:11	khiska = espino urqu = cerro	spiny plant hill	Spiny Plant Hill
Quishuarpuquiu	Ch. 9:9	kishwar = árbol andino[144] puquiu = manantial	native Andean tree spring	Kishwar Tree Spring
Quispiquilla	Co. 4:3	qispi = transparente, cristal killa = luna	transparent, crystal moon	Transparent Moon
Quizquipuquiu	Co. 6:10	khuska = en medio puquiu = manantial	in the middle spring	Spring in the Middle
Racramirpay	Ch. 2:2	rakra = hendido[145] wirp'a = labio inferior	cleft lower lip	Cleft Lip (Stone)
Raquiancalla	Co. 2:2	raki = división[146] tiyana = asiento qaylla = cerca	division seat near	Near Seat (of Idols from the Four) Divisions
Rauaraya	Cu. 2:4	rawrarayay = arder continuamente[147]	to burn continually	Burning Continually
Rauaypampa	Cu. 14:3	rawray = arder panpa = llano	to burn plain	Burning Plain
Raurao quiran	Co. 4:7	rawra- = arder k'iru = diente	to burn tooth	Tooth (-Shaped) Flame (Hill)
Rocrocmuca	Cu. 7:2	rakra- = engullir[148] muqu = coyuntura del cuerpo	to swallow whole articulation of the body	Swallowing Whole, Necklike (Stone)
Rondao	Co. 5:9	runtu = piedra[149] khuya- = adorar	stone to adore	Adored Stones
Rondoya	An. 5:9	runtu = piedra khuya- = adorar	stone to adore	Adored Stones
Sabacurinca	Ch. 5:6	sapa = único quri = oro inka = inca	unique gold Inca	Unique Golden Inca
Sabaraura[150]	An. 5:3	sapay = único rawra = llama de fuego	unique flame	Unique Flame
Sabaraura	An. 8:5	sapay = único rawra = llama de fuego	unique flame	Unique Flame
Sabaraura	Cu. 1:1	sapay = único rawra = llama de fuego	unique flame	Unique Flame
Sacasaylla puquiu	An. 8:1	saqsa = jaspeado waylla = prado puquiu = manantial	speckled meadow spring	Speckled Meadow Spring
Sanca[151]	#5	sanq'ay = cárcel	prison	Prison
Sancacancha	Co. 8:1	sanq'ay = cárcel kancha = cercado	prison enclosure	Prison Enclosure
Sanca cancha[152]	Ch. 7:2	sanq'ay= cárcel kancha = cercado	prison enclosure	Prison Enclosure

Huaca Name	Number[2]	Quechua/Spanish	English	English Name
Sanopuquiu	Co. 3:8	sañu = loza cocida[153] puquiu = manantial	tiles spring	Clay Spring
Sanotuiron[154]	An. 6:4	sañu = loza cocida[155] tuyru = señal	tiles marker	Clay Marker
Santocollo	Co. 7:1	suntu = redondo, amontonado qullu = morro	round, piled up hill	Round Hill
Sausero	Co. 2:3	sausero = ?	?	?
Sico cayan[156]	#37	sico = ? qayllan = cerca	? near	Near — ?
Sinayba	Co. 4:9	saywa = señal	marker	Marker
Sinopampa	Co. 3:7	sañu = loza cocida[157] panpa = llano	tiles plain	Clay Plain
Sonconancay	Ch. 1:5	sunqu = corazón nanay = dolor	heart pain	Heart Pain
Sucanca	Ch. 8:7	sukana = cresta	crest	Crest
Suchique	#16	suchi- = dar plata[158]	to exchange silver for employment	Exchange Silver for Employment
Sumeurco	Co. 4:10	sumaq = lindo urqu = cerro	beautiful hill	Beautiful Hill
Sunchupuquiu	An. 2:5	sunch'u[159] = planta herbácea puquiu = manantial	herbaceous plant spring	Herbaceous Plant Spring
Suramapuquiu	An. 9:2	surama = ? puquiu = manantial	? spring	? — Spring
Suriguaylla	Co. 3:6	suri = avestruz[160] waylla = prado	ostrich meadow	Ostrich Meadow
Susumarca	An. 5:8	suqus = caña brava[161] marka = pueblo	reeds town	Reed Town
Sutirmarca	Cu. 7:4	sut'i = verdadero, visible marka = pueblo	clear, visible town	Clearly Visible Town
Tambomachay	An. 1:9	tanpu = albergue mach'ay = cueva	lodge cave	Lodge Cave
Tampucancha	Co. 3:1	tanpu = albergue kancha = cercado	lodge enclosure	Lodge Enclosure
Tampucancha	Co. 6:1	tanpu = albergue kancha = cercado	lodge enclosure	Lodge Enclosure
Tampucancha	Co. 9:1	tanpu = albergue kancha = cercado	lodge enclosure	Lodge Enclosure
Tampuvilca	Co. 9:5	tanpu = albergue willka = sagrado	lodge sacred	Sacred Lodge
Tampu vrco	Cu. 11:4	tanpu = albergue urqu = cerro	lodge hill	Lodge Hill
Tanancuricota	Cu. 8:1	chanaq = valiente[162] quri = oro kuka = coca	valiant gold coca	Valiant, Gold Coca (Warrior Woman)

Huaca Name	Number[2]	Quechua/Spanish	English	English Name
Tancarvilca	Co. 9:2	t'ankar = zarzamora[163] willka = sagrado	blackberry bush sacred	Sacred Blackberry Bush
Taucaray	Co. 4:2	tawqarayay = amontonarse	to pile	(Funerary Bundle) Continually Piling Up
Taxanamaro[164]	Ch. 7:4	taksan = mediano amaru = serpiente	medium size serpent	Medium-Sized Serpent
Ticicocha	Ch. 3:3	tiqsi = cimiento del mundo qucha = lago	foundation of the world lake	Foundation of the World Lake
Tipcpuquiu[165]	An. 1:8	t'inpuq = que hierve puquiu = manantial	which boils spring	Boiling Spring
Tiucalla	Cu. 5:2	t'iyu = arena qaylla = cerca	sands near	Near the Sands
Tocacaray	Co. 5:6	tawqarayay = amontonarse	to pile	(Funerary Bundle) Continually Piling Up
Tocoripuquiu	Ch. Extra:2	tukuy rikuq = gobernador de provincias puquiu = manantial	provincial governor spring	Provincial-Governor Spring
Totorgoaylla[166]	Ch. 9:12	t'otora = carrizo lacustre[167] waylla = prado	reed meadow	Reed Meadow
Tucanamaro[168]	#10	taksan = mediano amaru = serpiente	medium size serpent	Medium-Sized Serpent
Tuino urco	Co. 2:6	tuyru = señal urqu = cerro	marker hill	Hill Marker
Turuca	An. 1:2	taruka = venado andino[169]	Andean deer	Deer (Stone)
Uman amaro[170]	#4	uma = agua[171] amaru = serpiente	water serpent	Water Serpent
Unugualpa	An. 7:6	unu = agua[172] wallpa = juez	water judge	(Irrigation) Water Judge
Urcomilpo	An 3:10	urqu = cerro millp'uy = tragar	hill to swallow	Swallow — Hill
Urcopuquiu	An 8:6	urqu = cerro puquiu = manantial	hill spring	Hill Spring
Urcoscalla[173]	Ch. 8:9	urqu = cerro qaylla = cerca	hill near	Near Hill
Urcos calla uiracocha[174]	#14	urqu = cerro qaylla = cerca Wiraqucha	hill near name of an Inca king and the Creator God	Near Wiraqucha Hill
Urcoslla amaro	Ch. 7:5	urqu = cerro qaylla = cerca amaru = serpiente	hill near serpent	Near Serpent Hill
Uscucalla[175]	#25	khuskan = junto qaylla = cerca	in the middle near	Near the Middle (of River)

Huaca Name	Number[2]	Quechua/Spanish	English	English Name
Usno	#26	usnu- = altar, asiento real	altar, royal seat	Altar
Usno	An. 5:1	usno = altar, asiento real	altar, royal seat	Altar
Uspa	Co. 7:7	uchpa = ceniza	ash	Ash
Uxi	Cu. 1:4	usiyay = terminar, límite[176]	to finish, terminus	Terminus (in Cusco of road from Tambo)
Vicaribi	Ch. 9:5	willka = sagrado lliwi = boleadora	sacred animal snare	Lord Sacred Snare
Vilcacona	An. 2:1	willkakuna = seres sagrados	sacred beings	Sacred Beings
Vilcaraypuquiu	Co. 7:6	willka = sagrado arpay = sacrificio[177] puquiu = manantial	sacred sacrifice spring	Sacred-Sacrifice Spring
Viracocha	An. 4:4	Wiraqucha	name of Inca king and the creator god	Wiraqucha
Viracochacancha	Co. 6:5	Wiraqucha kancha = cercado	name of Inca king and the creator god enclosure	Wiraqucha Enclosure
Viracochapuquiu	An. 6:5	Wiraqucha puquiu = manantial	name of Inca king and the creator god spring	Wiraqucha Spring
Viracochaurco	Cu. 10:4	Wiraqucha urqu = cerro	name of Inca king and the creator god hill	Wiraqucha Hill
Vircaypay	Co. 7:4	willka = sagrado arpay = sacrificio[178]	sacred sacrifice	Sacred Sacrifice
Viroypacha[179]	Ch. 2:4	wiruy = gentil hombre phaqcha = cascada	handsome man waterfall	Handsome Waterfall
Yamarpuquiu	Cu. 1:11	yawar = sangre puquiu = manantial	blood spring	Blood-Colored Spring
Yancaycalla[180]	An. 3:9	yunqay = zona tropical qaylla = cerca	tropical zone near	Near Tropical Zone
Yauirac[181]	#12	apu = gran señor yawira = ?	great lord ?	Lord Yawira
Yllanguaiqui[182]	#3	illapa = relámpago warqi = ondulado	lightning wavy	Wavy Lightning
Yuncaypampa	An. 3:8	yunqay = zona tropical panpa = llano	tropical zone plain	Tropical Zone Plain
Yuyotuyro	Ch. 9:10	yuyu = nabo[183] tuyro = señal	wild turnip greens marker	Wild-Turnip-Greens Marker

Shrines with No Names

An. 3:2
Co. 8:8

Notes

1. Introduction

1. ". . . Ciudad del Cuzco era casa y morada de dioses, e ansí no avía en toda ella fuente ny paso ny pared que no dixesen que tenya mysterio . . ." (Polo de Ondegardo 1916c:55 [1571]).

2. For extensive discussions of the term *huaca,* see Albornoz (1984 [ca. 1582]), Van de Guchte (1990:237–271, 312–320), and MacCormack (1991).

3. ". . . a todos los lugares sagrados diputados para oración y sacrificios llamaban los indios peruanos *guacas,* así como a los dioses e ídolos que en ellos adoraban" (Cobo 1956:167 [1653: Bk. 13, Ch. 12]).

4. "Del templo del sol salian como de centro ciertas lineas, que los indios llaman, ceques: y hacianse quatro partes conforme a los quatro caminos Reales que salian del cuzco; y en cada uno de aquellos ceques estauan por su orden las Guacas, y adoratorios que hauia en el cuzco, y su comarca, como estaciones de lugares pios, cuya veneracion era general a todas" (Cobo 1980:14 [1653:Bk. 13, Ch. 13]).

5. "Començando pues por el camino de chinchaysuyu, que sale por el barrio de carmenga, hauia en el nueue ceques, en que se comprendian ochenta y cinco Guacas . . ." (Cobo 1980:14 [1653:Bk. 13, Ch. 13]).

6. This assumption, as discussed in Chapter 9, is supported by Albornoz's clockwise description of the Chinchaysuyu huacas.

7. ". . . toda la jente que con la *Capaccocha* que por otro nombre se llama *Cachaguaes,* . . . apartada los unos de los otros, sin ir por camino real derecho, sino sin torcer a ninguna parte, atravesando las quebradas y cerros que por delante hallavan hasta llegar cada uno a la parte y lugar que . . . estavan esperando para revevir los dichos sacrificios . . ." (Molina 1989:126–127 [ca. 1575]).

2. The Original Ceque System Manuscript

1. "La sesta Guaca se llamaua, sabacurinca, era un asiento bien labrado, donde se sentauan los incas; el qual fue mui venerado, y se le hacian solennes sacrificios; y por respeto desto asiento se adoraua toda la fortaleça; que deuiera de estar dentro, o junto a ella" [Cobo 1980:22 (1653:Bk. 13, Ch. 13)].

2. As Rowe (1980:6) notes, "Apparently, in 16th-century Cuzco, properties were commonly identified by the name of an early owner who was prominent during the wars of the Spanish conquest."

3. "La quinta era un llano dicho, Oscollo, que fue de Garcilaso; ofrecianle lo ordinario" (Cobo 1980:42 [1653:Bk. 13, Ch. 15]).

4. "La quarta era una plaça grande llamada, colcapampa, donde se hiço la parroquia de los Martires; al cabo de la qual estaua una piedra, que era idolo principal, a quien se ofrecian niños con lo demas" (Cobo 1980:36 [1653:Bk. 13, Ch. 14]).

5. Leaders of this movement preached that the traditional Andean huacas would soon rise and defeat the Spanish invaders and their god (Molina 1989 [ca. 1575]; Millones 1973, 1990; Ossio 1973; Wachtel 1977; Stern 1982).

6. "Hallé más de otras dos mil guacas visitando esta provincia, que las que pude aver, mandé quemar y deshazer, y dejé memoria en los libros de fábricas que hize en las dotrinas" (Albornoz 1984:207 [ca. 1582]).

7. See Chapter 9 for a comparison of the Cusco shrine information provided by Albornoz and by Cobo.

8. Parts of this lost manuscript are preserved in Cabello de Balboa's (1951:26 [1586]) *Miscelánea antártica.*

9. "Heran tantos los lugares que dedicados tenían para sacrificar en el Cuzco, que si se ubiesen de poner aquí sería mucha prolijada, y porque en la Relación de las guacas que a Vuestra Señoría Reverendísima di, están puestos todos de la manera que se sacrificauan, no lo pongo aquí" (Molina 1989: 126 [ca. 1575]).

10. Polo de Ondegardo (1872:59 [1571], cited by Rowe 1980:7), mentions that the Creator had women.

11. Rowe (1980:5), citing the works of Zimmerman (1938:103, 173) and Esquivel y Navía (1980), states that Polo de Ondegardo was corregidor of Cusco from 2 December 1558 to 19 December 1560 and from August 1571 to October 1572.

12. "Y como el Cuzco y su comarca tenía gran suma de Idolos, huacas, villcas, adoratorios ó mochaderos constituydos en diferentes partes, assí también tenían en cada prouincia particulares huacas y adoratorios, y cada vna otra cosa más particular que adoraua, y cada familia, cuerpos de difuntos que venerar. Finalmente cada tierra y prouincia tenía mucha di-

uersidad de mochaderos, y si agora se an desecho los Idolos, piedras, é instrumentos de sacrifiçios y otras cosas muchas que tenían para sus ritos, con todo están en pié los cerros, collados, fuentes, manantiales, ríos, lagunas, mar, angosturas, peñas, Apachetas, y otras cosas assí: cuya veneración aún dura todavía y es necesario que allá mucha vigilancia para desterrar de sus coraçones esta impía veneración. Las Huacas y adoratorios del Cuzco y algunas leguas alrededor del, son, 340, de diuersos nombres, y deuía de auer otras más. De todo lo qual muçha parte se á oluidado: más con todo no dexará de auer algún rastro y en especial donde ay viejos y viejas, y más donde ay principales y Curacas inclinados á estos ritos" (Polo de Ondegardo 1916b:43 [1585]).

13. An encomienda consisted of exclusive rights granted by the Spanish Crown to the labor or produce from specific communities.

14. Perhaps this is the report that Molina gave to Sebastián de Lartaun, the bishop of Cusco.

15. ". . . paresçerá por la carta que yo hize de los zeques y adoratorios de la çiudad del Cuzco, que se hallara en poder de muchos Religiosos de aquel pueblo, avía en aquella çiudad, y legua y media a la Redonda quatroçientos y tantos lugares donde se hazían sacrifiçios, y se gastava mucha suma de hazienda en ellos para diferentes effectos que los indios tienen ymaginado, . . ." (Polo de Ondegardo 1940:183–184 [1561]).

16. The Spanish word *carta* is problematic because it can be translated as map (or chart), document, or letter. Rowe (1980:7) suggests that Polo de Ondegardo would have used the word *relación* had he indeed written a narrative account of the system, and thus concludes that Polo de Ondegardo made a map of the ceque system rather than a written report.

17. These divisions of Cusco, and the empire, are generally written as Collasuyu, Chinchaysuyu, Antisuyu, and Cuntisuyu.

18. ". . . alliende de otra diuisión más general que llamaron estos, *taguantinsuyo,* que quiere decir quatro partes en que todo el rreyno estaua dividido, que llamaron *colca* suyo, *zincha* suyo, *ande* suyo, *inde* suyo, la qual división empieça dende el Cuzco, del qual salen quatro camynos cada vno para vna parte destas, como paresçe en la carta de las Guacas; . . ." (Polo de Ondegardo 1916c:133–134 [1571]).

19. ". . . Ciudad del Cuzco era casa y morada de dioses, e ansí no avía en toda ella fuente ny paso ny pared que no dixesen que tenya mysterio como paresçe en cada manyfestaçión de los adoratorios de aquella Ciudad y carta que dellos manifestaron que pasauan de quatrocientos y tantos: todo esto duró hasta que vinyeron los españoles y hasta oy se haçe veneración a cada vno quando no los ven y toda la tierra guarda y venera las guacas que los yngas les dieron y yo por sus mysmos rregistros para ensayar la manifestaçión saqué muchas que las provinçias del Omasuyo y Collasuyo . . ." (Polo de Ondegardo 1916c:55 [1571]).

20. Pocona is located in the Department of Cochabamba in Bolivia. For additional historical and archaeological information on this village, see Ramírez Valerde (1970 [1557]), Toledo (1975:28 [1583]), and Céspedes Paz (1982).

21. ". . . En cada pueblo puso la mysma horden y dividió por çeques y rrayas la comarca, e hiço adoratorios de diversos asdvocaçiones, todas las cosas que paresçían notables de fuentes y manantiales y puquios y piedras ondas y valles y cumbres quellos llaman apachetas, e puso á cada cosa su gente e les mostró la orden que avían de tener en sacrificar cada vna de ellas, y para qué efeto e puso quien se lo enseñase y en qué tiempo e con qué género de cosas: finalmente, avnque en nynguna parte fueron tantos los adoratorios como en el Cuzco, pero es la orden vna mysma e vista la carta de las guacas del Cuzco en cada pueblo por pequeño que sea la pintaron de aquella misma manera y mostraron los çeques y guacas y adoratorios fijos, que para sauerlo es negocio ymportantisimo para su conbersión, que yo la tengo ensayada en más de cien pueblos, y el Señor Obispo de las Charcas dudando el si aquello fuese tan vnyversal, quando vinymos juntos al negoçio de la perpetuydad por mandado de Su Magestad se lo mostró en Pocona e los mysmos yndios le pintaron allí la mysma carta, y en esto no hay duda porque se hallaron, como digo, sin falta y por ser negoçio general se a de tener en más averse descuvierto . . ." (Polo de Ondegardo 1916c:56–57 [1571]).

22. In this case, it seems more appropriate to translate *carta* as "letter" rather than "map" because the sentence mentions an account.

23. Here Polo de Ondegardo is discussing a map.

24. ". . . pongo ésto para que se entienda que ansí son sus ymaginaçiones en cada cosa, e quán fáçiles y desventurados son. Otros munchos barones y hembras tienen cargo de las guacas fixas de que esta hecha particular rrelaçión en la carta general del Cuzco, ques común en todo el rreyno e contiene todos los lugares que se diferençian de los otros en algo alrededor del pueblo hasta las cumbres, si es tierra áspera que llaman estos, *apachetas,* como algunas piedras grandes e todos los puquios y nascymientos de agua, o algunos llanos que haçen en alguna questa o algunos árboles señalados, ó las partes a donde siembran el mayz para los sacrifiçios: porque todas estas cosas estan dividas por sus çeques e rrayas en el torno de cada pueblo y están a cargo de personas que hagan en ellos sacrifiçios diferentes e para diversos efetos; en vnas para que se empreñen las mugeres, en otras que dizen que de allí sale el yelo o el granizo, y en otras que llueva; ansí desta manera les enseña el Ynga esta diuisión de lugares en todo lo que conquistó, hechándole grandísimo cargo del venefiçio que rresçivían en darles notiçia a cada vno en su tierra de lo que tenyan e se podian aprovechar para sus nesçesidades; lo qual el dia de oy haçen por su mysma horden y tienen señalada gente que entiende en ello; e ansi es neçesario en todos los

pueblos haçerles que pinten la carta, y viendo la del Cuzco luego lo haçen, . . ." (Polo de Ondegardo 1916c:114 [1571]).

25. I have been unable to find such a manuscript in the Biblioteca Nacional. It is possible that the work that Means was told about was destroyed in the fire that swept through the library on 10 May 1943.

26. "Iten, mirar con mucha advertencia si en los pueblos donde . . . hay alguna huaca ó adoratorio; y para más información, os informaréis de los caciques y más antiguos del dicho repartimento y de los muchachos de la dotrina ó alguaciles; y no os dando claridad os aprovecharéis de una traza y orden en que este reino los ingas tenían de las huacas y adoratorios que en cada provincia había y del modo que tenían en los sacrificios y demás ceremonias que en su gentilidad hacían y no obstante que os digan que están destruidas y que no hay memoria ni rastro de ellas, veréis personalmente por la traza los lugares donde estaban y si están destruidas y quién las destruyó; preguntando por los ritos y ceremonias que cada una de estas hacían y quién es el hechicero ó hechiceros que á cada una tenía y qué oficio hacían en la dicha huaca y lo que daban á los dichos hechiceros sacerdotes; y si tenían en particular chácaras, oro, ó otras cosas é que se ha hecho de ello. De todo lo cual haréis entera relación poniendo por escripto los nombres de las huacas, hechiceros para que se tenga cuenta que no reincidan y haya enmienda y se pongan en ellas cruces, siendo lugar decente para ello" (Córdoba Mexía 1900: 395–396 [ca. 1572]).

27. Part of a report by Pedro Córdoba Mexía (1925:269–288 [1582]) was used by Cobo as an unreferenced source.

28. ". . . primero quitarles las *huacas* y adoratorios que tienen, e idolos que reverencian, cosa que hasta agora no se ha hecho, aunque el Licenciado Polo de Ondegardo, vecino y encomendero de esta ciudad, hombre de muy buen entendimiento, y que ha servido muy bien en este Reino a Su Magestad, siendo Corregidor en el Cuzco averiguó todas las *huacas* e idolos que tienen los indios, a que adoraban, por los quipos de los Ingas y supersticiones que usaban, lo cual tiene escrito de mano . . ." (Matienzo 1967:119 [1567:Ch. 36]).

29. ". . . están tan en vigor entre los indios, que no se pueden contar los géneros de sacrilegios y guacas: montes, cuestas, rocas prominentes, aguas manantiales útiles, ríos que corren precipitados, cumbres altas de las peñas, montones grandes de arena, abertura de un hoyo tenebroso, un árbol gigantesco y añoso, una vena de metal, la forma rara y elegante de cualquier piedrecita; finalmente, por decirlo de una vez, cuanto observan que se aventaja mucho sobre sus cosas congéneres, luego al punto lo toman por divino y sin tardanza lo adoran. De esta peste perniciosa de la idolatría están llenos los montes, llenos los valles, los pueblos, las casas, los caminos y no hay porción de tierra en el Perú que esté libre de esta superstición. Pues las víctimas, las libaciones, el orden de las ceremonias con que

seguían todos estos cultos los principales de los Ingas, sería infinito contarlo; lea quien quiera la historia que cuidadosamente escribió de esto el licenciado Polo [de Ondegardo], varón grave y prudente; verá que sólo dentro de los términos de la ciudad del Cuzco había más de trescientas sesenta guacas contadas, a todas las cuales se daban honores divinos, a unas ofrecían frutos de la tierra a otras, vellones preciosos y oro y plata, y en honor de otras se derramaba en sacrificio mucha sangre de niños inocentes" (Acosta 1954a:560–561 [1580:Bk. 5, Ch. 9]).

30. ". . . las Guacas e Idolos de esta dicha ciudad y algunas leguas alrededor de ella eran más de cuatrocientas y cincuenta de diversos nombres, y debía de haber otras muchas más, que cada uno, tomando devoción, usaba [para] hacer sacrificios e ceremonias, así cuando estaban enfermos, como cuando se querían morir. . . ." (Murúa 1946:78 [1590:Pt. 1, Ch. 14]).

31. "La rrelacion que vuestra magestad manda de las guacas y lo por mi hordenado y proueido se ynbia con este despacho" (Toledo 1924:394 [1572]).

32. Cobo also notes in this chapter that he had access to the works of Acosta and Garcilaso de la Vega, and he mentions elsewhere that he had a copy of a report by Pedro Pizarro.

3. Huacas

1. "La primera Guaca se decia, Guaracince, la qual estaua en la plaça del templo del sol llamada chuquipampa (suena llano de oro) era un pedaçuelo de llano que alli estaua; en el qual decian que se formaua el temblor de tierra. Hacian en ella sacrificios para que no temblase, y eran mui solennes [*sic*]; porque quando temblaua la tierra se matauan niños; y ordinariamente se quemauan carneros, y ropas, y se enterraua oro, y plata" (Cobo 1980:16 [1653:Bk. 13, Ch. 13]).

2. "La tercera Guaca era una fuente llamada, Aucaypata [paccha], que estaua junto a donde aora es la casa de cabildo, en la qual decian los sacerdotes de chucuilla que se bañaua el Trueno, y fingian otros mil disparates" (Cobo 1980:26 [1653: Bk. 13, Ch. 13]).

3. "La nouena se llamaua, Cascasayba; eran ciertas piedras que estauan en el cerro de Quisco: era Guaca principal, y tenia cierto origen largo que los indios quentan; ofrecianle de todas las cosas, y tambien niños" (Cobo 1980:32 [1653:Bk. 13, Ch. 14]).

4. Shrines related to Manco Capac and the mythical first Incas are Ch. 1:1, Ch. 9:6, An. 7:4, Co. 1:6, Co. 2:3, Co. 6:1, Co. 6:7, Co. 7:5, Co. 7:6, Cu. 5:1, Cu. 7:1, and perhaps Co. 3:4.

5. Shrines that are specifically listed as Pururaucas are Ch. 4:1, Ch. 5:3, Ch. 6:1, Ch. 7:1, Co. 1:1, Co. 7:2, Co. 9:2, Co. 9:12, Cu. 1:1, Cu. 4:1, Cu. 5:2, Cu. 6:1, Cu. 6:3, and Cu. 8:1. To these can be added Ch. 2:2. There are no Pururaucas listed in Antisuyu. Rowe (1980:9) noted that the majority of the stone-warrior shrines are located in or near the Temple of the Sun (the exceptions are Co. 7:2, Co. 9:12, Cu. 5:2, Cu 6:3, and Cu. 8:1).

6. Susumarca (An. 5:8), a spring at which Pachacuti Inca Yupanqui had a vision on the eve of the war, can be added to the list of shrines related to the Chanca War.

7. Huaca descriptions that mention Pachacuti Inca Yupanqui are Ch. 1:2, Ch. 1:3, Ch. 2:2, Ch. 2:3, Ch. 2:4, Ch. 2:6, Ch. 3:4, Ch. 3:6, Ch. 3:9, Ch. 3:10, Ch. 4:4, Ch. 5:1, Ch. 5:5, Ch. 7:3, Ch. 7:4, Ch. 8:1, Ch. 8:11, An. 1:9, and An. 5:9. All but two of the shrines are in Chinchaysuyu. There are no shrine descriptions that mention this Inca in Hurin Cusco.

8. Huayna Capac is listed in relation to Ch. 3.5, Ch. 6:5, Ch. 8:4, Ch. 9:2, and Co 6:7. The tomb of a brother of Huayna Capac is described in Ch. 5:8. Paullu is mentioned in the descriptions of Ch. 4:4, Co. 2:3, and Co 6:7.

9. Huacas associated with the Capac Raymi festival include Cu. 10:2, Cu. 10:3, and Cu. 12:1. Those connected with the Warachikoy ritual are Ch. 3:8, Ch. 5:7, Ch. 9:3, Ch. 9:6, An. 5:1, An. 6:4, Co. 6:8, Co. 7:5, Cu. 1:7, and Cu. 2:4.

10. "La nouena Guaca se llamaua, cugiguaman, era una piedra a manera de halcon, que dijo inca yupanqui hauersele aparecido en una cantera, y mando que se pusiese en este ceque, y se le hiciesen sacrificios" (Cobo 1980:18 [1653:Bk. 13, Ch.]).

11. "La segunda se decia, Mancochuqui, era una chacara de Huanacauri, y lo que della se cogia le sacrificauan" (Cobo 1980:26 [1653:Bk. 13, Ch. 13]).

12. For more information on Inca offerings, see Molina (1989 [ca. 1575]), Polo de Ondegardo (1916b [1585], 1916c [1571]), Guaman Poma de Ayala (1980 [1615]), Arriaga (1968 [1621]), Cobo 1990 [1653]), as well as Reinhard (1985b) and McEwan and Van de Guchte (1992).

13. "... vuelto el rostro para ellos o para sus templos y guacas, inclinaban la cabeza y cuerpo con una humillación profunda, y extendiendo los brazos para adelante, igualmente distante el uno del otro desde el principio hasta el cabo, con las manos abiertas y levantadas en alto un poco más que la cabeza, y las palmas hacia fuera, hacían con los labios cierto sonido como quien besa, y llegando tras esto las manos a la boca, las besaban por la parte de dentro, hacia las extremidades de los dedos" (Cobo 1956:204 [1653:Bk. 13, Ch. 23]).

14. "A ti, señor, que criaste todas las cosas y entre ellas tuviste por bien de criarme a mí y a esta agua desta fuente para mi sustento, te suplico hagas que no se seque, sino que salga como lo ha hecho otros años, para que cojamos el fruto que tenemos sembrado.... Oh nacimiento de agua que tantos años ha que me riegas mi heredad y mediante este beneficio que me haces yo cojo mi comida haz lo mismo este año, y antes acrecienta más agua, para que la cosecha sea más copiosa!" (Cobo 1956:200 [1653:Bk. 13, Ch. 21]).

15. "... no le ofrecian otra cosa que la coca que echauan de la boca los que pasauan" (Cobo 1980:57 [1653:Bk. 13, Ch. 16]).

16. See Cu. 4:5, Co. 8:8, Co. 9:4, as well as Ch. 6:10.

17. "Ofrecíanle conchas de todos colores conforme a los tiempos" (Cobo 1980:34 [1653:Bk. 13, Ch. 14]).

18. "... ponia en el dicho cerro muchos hacian ciertos sacrificios; y para ellos ponian en el dicho cerro muchos haces de leña labrada vestidos como hombres, y mugeres; y gran cantidad de maçorcas de maiz hechas de palo, y despues de grandes borracheras quemauan muchos carneros con la leña dicha, y matauan algunos niños" (Cobo 1980:32 [1653:Bk. 13, Ch. 14]).

19. "... matauan niños; y ordinariamente se quemauan carneros, y ropa, y se enterraua oro, y plata" (Cobo 1980:16 [1653:Bk. 13, Ch. 13]).

20. "... sacrificauan ó ofrecían conchas de la mar que llaman Mollo. Y ofrecíanlas á las fuentes y manantiales, diziendo que las conchas eran hijas de la mar, madre de todas las aguas. Tienen diferentes nombres según la color, y assí siruen á diferentes efectos, vsauan destas conchas casi en todas las maneras de sacrificios, ..." (Polo de Ondegardo 1916b:39 [1585]).

21. Exceptions to this statement are the 1990 and 1991 Instituto Nacional de Cultura excavations at Puquincancha (Cu. 10:2), which yielded a variety of Inca offerings (Justo Torres, pers. com. 1992).

22. Formerly the Archivo Histórico del Cusco.

4. The Social Organization of Cusco and Its Ceque System

1. Principal sources for this chapter include Zuidema (1964), Rowe (1985), and my own readings of the *Relación de las huacas*.

2. See Zuidema (1964, 1977c) for additional discussions on the terms *collana, payan,* and *cayao,* and how this tripartition may be related to the quadripartitioning of the Cusco Valley into suyus.

3. "Carurunamacij: es lejano pariente ú deudo en el quarto grado.

"Collana: es el que no es tan lejano deudo, ó pariente.

"Payan: es el mas cercano pariente.

"Cayaurunamacij: es el ultimo de los deudos ó parientes, mucho mas cercanos, que los otros dos primeros.

"Hucayllulla, (...) hacpanacalla: son todos los que son de una familia y casta." (Pérez Bocanegra 1631:613)

4. "Gobernábanse conforme á lo quel inga tenia puesto, que era, por sus *ayllos* é parcialidades nombraba de cada *ayllo* un cacique, y eran tres *ayllos,* llamados *Collona, Pasana, Cayao;* cada *ayllo* destos tenia trescientos indios y un principal á quien obedecian, y estos tres principales obedecian al cacique principal, que era sobre todos. Tenia el cacique principal mando y poder sobre todos los demás principales, los cuales le eran obedientísimos en todo lo que mandaba, asi en las cosas de la guerra como en las cosas de justicia y castigo de delitos. Era

este cacique puesto por el inga y subcedian sus hijos y á falta dellos sus hermanos, aunque eran preferidos en la herencia el hermano legítimo del cacique á su hijo, aunque fuese legítimo" (Ulloa Mogollón 1885:45 [1585]).

5. For information on Amaru Topa Inca, see Sarmiento de Gamboa (1906:77, 84–86 [1572:Ch. 37, Ch. 42, 43]), Cabello de Balboa (1951:334 [1586:Pt. 3, Ch. 18]), and Pachacuti Yamqui Salcamayhua (1950:245–246 [1613]).

6. The Yacanora lived near the modern community of San Sebastián in Antisuyu, while the Ayarmaca were located in both Chinchaysuyu and Antisuyu.

7. "Y cada ceque estaua a cargo de las parcialidades, y familias de la dicha ciudad del cuzco; de las quales salian los ministros, y siruientes, que cuidauan de las Guacas de su ceque, y atendian a ofrecer a sus tiempos los sacrificios estatuidos" (Cobo 1980:14 [1653:Bk. 13, Ch. 13]).

8. "El primer ceque se decia, cayao, estaua a cargo de la parcialidad, y Ayllo de Goacaytaqui, y tenia los cinco Guacas siguientes" (Cobo 1980:14 [1653:Bk. 13, Ch. 13]).

9. In this work I use the word *ayllu* as a gloss for "descent group" and the word *panaca* for a group of individuals who claimed descent from a specific Inca ruler. This reflects the modern scholarly uses of these Quechua terms and not their original indigenous meanings (Zuidema 1964:7 n. 5).

10. Zuidema (1983a) has proposed that each king of Hanan Cusco matched with a king of Hurin Cusco. See Gose (1996) for a critical review of this theory.

11. Cobo (1990:123 [1653:Bk. 12, Ch.8]) states that Manco Capac was the "head and trunk of both tribal groups of Hanan Cuzco and Hurin Cuzco . . . ," suggesting that the first king should not be included in either of these divisions.

12. Also see lists provided in Gutiérrez de Santa Clara (1963:214 [ca. 1600]) and Pachacuti Yamqui Salcamayhua (1950 [1613]). It should be noted that Betanzos (1987 [1557]) indicates that an additional Inca called Yamque Yupanqui may have ruled after Topa Inca Yupanqui, but Betanzos provides no information on the existence of a panaca for Yamque Yupanqui.

13. Juan de Betanzos, one of the translators present at this inquest, wrote an important chronicle on the Incas several years later.

14. "Heran estos yndios que llevavan estas boces hacia *Collasuyo*, los que salían del Cuzco de la generaçion de Uscaymataayllo, Yapo may ho ayllo, Yahuaymin ayllu y *Sutic* y *Marasaylla, Cuycussa ayllo*.

"Los que salían hacia el poniente que es a *Chinchaysuyo*, salían dando las mesmas boces y éstos heran de la generaçion *Capacayllu* y *Atunaillu* y *Uicaquicao* y *Chaueticuzco ayllu* y *Arayraca Ayllu* y otros de *Uro* . . .

"Los que llevavan las boces a la parte del *Antisuyo* heran de las generaciones siguientes: *Cuscupanaca ayllo, Aucaylli ayllo, Tarpuntai aillu, Sano aillu* . . .

"Los que yban a la parte de *Contisuyo* heran de las generaciones siguientes: *Raurapanaca aillu* y *Chinapanaca aillu* y *Mascapanaca aillu* y *Quesco ayllu*, . . . " (Molina 1989:74–75 [ca. 1575])

15. "El ego o punto de referencia del sistema representado ha debido ser Wayna Qhapaq, el onceno monarca, quien fue hijo de Thupa 'Inka. Para Wayna Qhapaq, los miembros de la parcialidad de su padre serían efectivamente kayaw, los miembros de la parcialidad de su abuelo Pachakuti payan, y los miembros de la parcialidad de su bisabuelo Wiraqocha 'Inka qollana" (Rowe 1985:43).

16. The works of Cieza de León (1976 [1553]) and Betanzos (1987 [1557]) also contain information on some of the nonroyal ayllus of Cusco.

17. "A lo cual por el interés se movieron diez parcialidades ó *ayllos*, que quiere decir entre estos bárbaros linaje ó bando; los nombres de los cuales son estos que se siguen:

"Chauin Cuzco Ayllo: del linaje de Ayar Cache; hay hoy deste bando en el Cuzco algunos, las cabezas de los cuales se llaman Martín Chucumbi y Don Diego Guaman Paucar,

"Arayraca Ayllo
Cuzco-callan: hay agora desde ayllo Juan Piçarro Yupangui, Don Francisco Quipi, Alonso Tarma Yupangui del linaje de Ayar Uchu,

"Tarpuntay Ayllo: hay agora deste ayllo en el Cuzco,

"Guacaytaqui Ayllo: de los cuales agora viven [en] el Cuzco algunos,

"Sañoc Ayllo: destos hay en el Cuzco.

"Estos cinco bandos, son Hanancuzcos, que quiere decir el bando de lo alto del Cuzco.

"Sutic-toco Ayllo: que es la generación, que salió de la una de las ventanas, llamada Sutic-toco, como arriba es dicho; hay destos en el Cuzco agora algunos, y las cabezas, que los conservan, son Don Francisco Avca Micho Avri Sutic y Don Alonso Gualpa,

"Maras Ayllo: estos son los que dicen [que] salieron de la ventana Maras-toco; hay destos algunos en el Cuzco, mas los principales son Don Alonso Llama Oca y Don Gonçalo Ampura Llama Oca,

"Cuycusa Ayllo: hay destos algunos en el Cuzco y la cabeza es Cristóual Acllari,

"Masca Ayllo: hay deste linaje en el Cuzco Juan Quispi -

"Oro Ayllo: hay deste linaje hoy Don Pedro Yucay.

"Digo, que de todos estos linajes se han conservado de tal manera que no se ha perdido la memoria dellos, y puesto que hay más de los dichos, pongo solas cabezas, que son protectores y principales del linaje, que son en quien se van conservando. Y cada uno destos tienen cargo y oligación de amparar á los demás y saber las cosas y hechos de sus pasados." (Sarmiento de Gamboa 1906:34 [1572:Bk. 11])

18. After interrogating members of Sauasiray Ayllu, Antasayac Ayllu, and Aray Ucho Ayllu, Gabriel de Loarte questioned members of the Hualla. Although the Hualla are among the most famous "pre-Inca" groups of the Cusco Valley, and are mentioned in the *Relación de las huacas* (An. 1:4 and An. 2:2), their relation to the nonroyal ayllus of Cusco and their role in maintaining shrines in the Cusco ceque system are not known.

19. Quesco Ayllu was absorbed into the new Spanish community called Belén. In 1825 it contained twenty-six members (AHD/Judiciales Civiles: Leg. 15).

20. A group called Uro is mentioned by Toledo (1975:196 [1583]) as having been resettled into San Jerónimo during his *reducción* movement. There are also many documents in the AHD that describe Uro lands near the eastern end of the Cusco Valley, in the region of San Jerónimo.

21. Several other nonroyal ayllus are also mentioned in the *Relación de las huacas* in relation to specific huacas of the ceque system, including Alcaviza (Co. 9:1), Anatasaya (Ch. 4:4), and Maras (Ch. 9:5).

22. "Los que yban a la parte de *Contisuyo* heran de las generaciones siguientes: *Raurapanaca aillu* y *Chinapanaca aillu* y *Mascapanaca aillu* y *Quesco ayllu,*. . ." (Molina 1989:75 [ca. 1575]).

23. It has been suggested that Guacaytaqui Ayllu was also called Uro Ayllu (Zuidema 1964:8).

24. It should also be noted that Cobo writes that Antasaya Ayllu worshipped a stone on Ch. 4, and that Loarte (1882:229 [1572]) indicates that the names of Antasaya and Quesco were synonymous.

5. The Huacas and Ceques of Chinchaysuyu

1. Also see Sarmiento de Gamboa (1906:83 [1572:Ch. 41]).

2. For a detailed description of the Patallacta area, see Van de Guchte (1990:98–103).

3. Van de Guchte (1990:100) suggests that the spring of Pilcopuquio was in the Chunchul Ravine.

4. Llanllakuyoc is also presented as a possible location for Amaromarcaguaci (An. 1:7).

5. It should be noted that storms in the Cusco area generally originate in the northwest.

6. Another possible candidate for Ch. 1:4 is a small cave on the western side of the Chuspiyuc ravine, between Salonpuncu

and Puca Pucara, which was identified by one informant as a place where modern offerings are made to the rain, hail, and thunder. This cave, however, is in Antisuyu.

7. "Tenía también el trueno templo aparte en el barrio de *Totocacha,* en el cual estaba una estatua suya de oro en unas andas de lo mismo, que hizo el Inca *Pachacútic* en honor del trueno, y llamó *Intiillapa;* a la cual tomó por hermano, y mientras vivió la trajo consigo en la guerra. Fué tenido este ídolo en gran veneración y servido con grande majestad y aparato" (Cobo 1956:160–161 [1653:Bk. 14, Ch. 7]).

8. This coincides with information presented in Acosta (1954:201 [1590:Ch. 21]) said to have been copied from Polo de Ondegardo.

9. These two drawings by Guaman Poma de Ayala show a number of other huacas besides Viroypacha (Ch. 2:4). The first drawing, "Canciones i Mucica" (Songs and Music), illustrates two young men playing flutes on a hill labeled with three names: Cinca Urco (Ch. 5:9), Guean Calla (Quiangalla Ch. 6:9), and Pingolona Pata zerro (cerro). At the base of the hill, Guaman Poma de Ayala (1980:289 [1615:316 (318)]) depicts two women swimming in the Uatanay River (Huatanay, Co. 1:9), which flows from the Uaca Punco (Huaca Punco). In the background are the names of three other major water sources for Cusco: Uiroy Paccha (Viroypacha, Ch. 2:4), Collquemachacuay (Cu. 9:1), and Cantoc Uno. (Also see Guaman Poma de Ayala [1980:119 (1615:141)]).

Uiruy Paccha (Viroypacha, Ch. 2:4) is also marked in the upper right-hand corner of Guaman Poma de Ayala's (1980:970 [1615:1051 (1059)]) map of Cusco. This map also includes the shrines of Cinco Urco (Cinca, Ch. 5:9), Aucaypata (Ch. 5:4), Poma Chupan (Poma Chupa, Cu. 1:3), Cuci Chanca (Cusicancha, Ch. 5:1), and Cori Cancha.

10. The river has a number of different names including Choquechaca and Tullumayo.

11. See Van de Guchte (1990:91–93) for a detailed description of Sapantiana.

An alternative location for Ch. 2:4 is a spring downstream from Sapantiana marked as an ancient fountain on Wiener's (1880) map of Cusco. This spring still flows inside a house along Choquechaca Street.

12. Chuquibamba is mentioned several times in "Real Cédula de Don Carlos Quito y Doña Juana su Madre sobre concesión de merced y amparo de posesión a favor de Felipe Topa Yupanqui. . ." [1552]. For excerpts from this document, see Rostworowski (1962) and Sherbondy (1982:171, 192 n. 83).

13. "Hacíanle asímismo todas las mañanas un fuego de leña muy labrada, y en saliendo en el cielo, le pegaban fuego y le traían allí su comida guisada como al Inca, y parte echaban en el fuego, diciendo: 'Como desto, *Apu-Inti,* en reconocimiento que somos tus hijos. . .'" (Cobo 1956:202 [1653 Book 13, Ch. 21]).

14. "El fuego para los sacrificios que se hacían en el Cuzco se

encendía en un brasero de piedra que estaba junto al templo del sol, y no se podía tomar de otra parte; el cual no se encendía y cebaba con cualquiera leña, sino de cierto género della, olorosa y muy labrada y muy pintada" (Cobo 1956:204 [1653 Bk. 13, Ch. 22]).

15. "Aquí (Templo del Sol) había fuego que llamaban eterno, al modo de los romanos, porque había de estar encendido de noche y de día perpetuamente . . ." (*Antigüedades* 1992:59 [1590]).

16. "El principal oficio destas [Aclla] era guardar y conservar el fuego de los sacrificios, que ellos llamaban nina villka, fuego sagrado" (*Antigüedades* 1992:90 [1590]).

17. This shrine should not be confused with the Tecse Cocha Street to the northwest of the Plaza de Armas.

18. Sarmiento de Gamboa (1906:102 [1572:Ch. 54]) states that the ashes of Atahuallpa's general, Calcuchimac, were found in a large jar at Calispuquiu.

19. "E ordenó que estos treinta días cumplidos se juntasen allí en la plaza los parientes destos noveles e trujesen los noveles allí consigo e que hincada el alabarda y estando ellos en pie tomasen con las manos el alabarda e ansi tendidos los brazos los parientes les disen con unas hondas en ellos para que tuviesen memoria e se acordasen desta fiesta y que esto hecho fuesen de allí a una fuente que dicen Calizpuquio que dice el manantial del caliz y siendo ya allí que se laven todos a la cual fuente han de ir ya que quiera anochecer e siendo ansi lavados . . ." (Betanzos 1987:69 [1557:Pt. 1, Ch. 14]).

20. "Ya los veinte y un días del dicho mes, todos los que se avían armado cavalleros se yban a bañar a una fuente llamada Calixpuquio, que está detrás de la fortaleza del Cuzco, casi un quarto de legua, adonde se quitauan aquellas uestiduras con que se avían armado cavalleros, y se vestían otras que se llamavan *uauaclla,* de color negro y amarillo y en medio una cruz colorada; y de allí se bolvían a la plaza . . ." (Molina 1989:109 [ca. 1575]).

21. "Cómo tenía grandes fortalesas llamado Sacsa Guaman y Puca Marca, Suchona, Callis Pucyo, Chingana el agugero de deuajo de la tierra le llega hasta Santo Domingo, Curi Cancha del Cuzco. Éstos fue la gran fortalesa y *pucara* del Ynga, hecho de todo el rreyno" (Guaman Poma de Ayala 1980:310 [1615:337 (339)]).

22. A small lake near the center of the flat area is called Mollacocha.

23. Manuel Chávez Ballón (pers. com. 1991) states that the ex-owner of the hacienda beside the Sacsahuaman Plain specifically told him that these springs are called Calispuquio. Van de Guchte (1990:130, 140, 283) has also reached a similar conclusion regarding the location of Calispuquio (Ch. 3:8). Italo Oberti Rodríguez (1982), on the other hand, suggests that Calispuquio was located on the other side of Sacsahuaman, near the Hacienda Llaullipata.

24. A declaration from the grandchildren (*nietos*) of Topa Inca, written in 1569, confirms the ownership by this Inca of land near Callispuquio (AGN/Títulos de Propiedad: Leg. 2, c. 50, f. 28, 1597).

25. See Ch. 3:2 and Ch. 3:3.

26. "La tercera Guaca se llamaua, curiocllo, era una casa de curiollo [*sic;* debe decir curiocllo] muger que fue de Amaro topa inca, la qual estaua en colcapata; y adorauan tambien una fuente que estaua junto a ella" (Cobo 1980:20 [1653:Bk. 13, Ch. 13]).

27. Valencia Zegarra (1984) excavated in Colcapata and recovered both Inca and pre-Inca (Qotacalle) remains.

28. Loarte (1882:229 [1572]) indicates that Andasaya Ayllu was believed to have controlled this area of Cusco before the arrival of Manco Capac.

29. Colcapata (or Collcapata) is also said to be the palace of Manco Capac. Garcilaso de la Vega (1945 [1609:Vol. 1, Bk. 2, Ch. 22; Vol. 1, Bk. 5, Ch. 2; Vol. 1, Bk. 6, Ch. 4; Vol. 1, Bk. 7, Chs. 7 and 8]) describes the location of Colcapata, several of its buildings, and celebrations that took place there.

30. Van de Guchte (1990:93) suggests that the carved rock of Sapatiana, on the slope of Sacsahuaman, may represent Guamancancha (Ch. 4:5).

Two references indicate that a second place called Guamancancha was located in the Carmenca area. The first, a shrine called Guamancancha, described as a pile of stones above Carmenca, is included in Albornoz (1984:204 [ca. 1582]), and the second is mentioned by Molina (1989:106–107 [ca. 1575]), who describes an important area called Guamancancha at the base of Yauira (i.e., Apuyauira, Ch. 9:6) on the slope of Picchu, which was near Carmenca. Since the name Guamancancha is a common Quechua toponym, it is possible that there were two such areas near Cusco.

31. "El cuarto y último de los maestros se llamó Calla Cúnchuy; en tiempo déste truxeron la piedra cansada, a la cual puso el maestro mayor su nombre por que en ella se conservasse su memoria, cuya grandeza también, como de las demás sus iguales, es increíble. Holgara poner aquí la medida cierta del gruesso y alto della; no he merescido haverla precisa; remítome a los que la han visto. Está en el llano antes de la fortaleza; dizen los indios que del mucho trabajo que passó por el camino, hasta llegar allí, se cansó y lloró sangre, y que no pudo llegar al edificio" (Garcilaso de la Vega 1945:152 [1609:Vol. 1, Bk. 7, Ch. 29]).

32. Garcilaso de la Vega (1966:185 [1609:Vol. 1, Bk. 3, Ch. 23]) describes the importance of a street that leads from the Coricancha to the central plaza; however, he does not mention any stones along its course.

33. This may be related to the shrine that Albornoz (1984:204 [ca. 1582]) calls Uscucalla (#25).

34. For another reference to the Cabildo, see Ch. 8:3.

35. Van de Guchte (1990:10, 72, 123) also suggests that this carving is Ch. 5:6.

36. "Empezábanse a hacer mucho antes grandes prevenciones de vestidos, galas y lo demás necesario para tan solemne fiesta. Ante todas cosas cogían un buen número de doncellas nobles desde doce hasta trece o catorce años, que, vestidas ricamente, sirviesen en ella; las cuales, algunos días antes, se estaban en el cerro de Chacaguanacauri hilando el hilo para los rapacejos de las *guaras* que se habían de poner los muchachos que se armaban orejones o caballeros; y ellos también iban al dicho cerro por cierta paja que habían de llevar en los bordones; y la que sobraba de la que traían, repartían sus parientes entre sí; y todo el tiempo que las dichas doncellas gastaban en esta ocupación en aquel cerro, estaba puesta en él la *guaca* o ídolo de Guanacauri. Lo demás que para esta solemnidad era menester prevenían los padres y parientes de los mancebos, . . ." (Cobo 1956:208 [1653:Bk. 14, Ch. 25])

37. Sherbondy (1982:175, 199 n. 124) has found references to another Guamanguachanca somewhere near the pass of Llancaycalla (Yancaycalla, An. 3:9).

38. "Había demás desta casa á la redonda del pueblo algunas guacas que eran la de Guanacauri y otra llamada Anaguarqui, y otra llamada Yauira y otra dicha Cinga y otra Picol y otra que se llamaba Pachatopan . . ." (Sarmiento de Gamboa 1906:69 [1572:Ch. 31]).

These mountains, all of which surround the city of Cusco, are presented in a clockwise order.

39. Albornoz (1984:205 [ca. 1582]) also states that there was a shrine called Catungui in Chinchaysuyu.

40. Alternatively, Rowe (1980:23) proposes that the name of Ch. 6:2 should be Quishuarcancha because it is listed as the temple of Pachayachachic. Rowe's suggestion is based on information from Molina (1989:59 [ca. 1575]), who states that the temple of the Creator was called Quishuar Cancha. Cobo (1956:79, 156; 1981:135; 1990:23 [1653:Bk. 12, Ch. 12 and Bk. 13, Ch. 4]) also writes that the temple of the Creator was called Quishuarcancha. However, this information was extracted from Molina. Quishuarcancha is traditionally thought to have been beneath the Cusco Cathedral or adjacent to the Triunfo Church (Hyslop 1990; Rowe 1991:86–87). This location for Quishuarcancha is supported by Molina (1989:59 [ca. 1575]), who states that Quishuarcancha was where Hortiz de Guzmán built his house, and by Urbano and Duviols (1989:59 n. 17), who indicate that Guzmán owned land beside the cathedral and the Triunfo Church.

41. Perhaps this should be read as Tecsecocha, a name that also appears on a street between the Plaza de Armas and the Saphy Ravine. Archival research provided a number of documents that mention the area of Tecsecocha, the earliest of which dates to 1614 (AHD/Colegio Ciencias: Leg. 10, c. 11).

42. Sarmiento de Gamboa (1906:104 [1572:Ch. 58]), Cobo (1956:89, 93; 1979:154, 161 [1653:Bk. 11, Chs. 16 and 17]), Cabello

de Balboa (1951:361 [1586:Ch. 21]) and Pizarro (1921 [1571]). Also see Hyslop (1990:41–42) and Rowe (1990).

43. "En mi tiempo abrieron los españoles una calle, que dividió las escuelas de las casas reales; de la que llamavan Cassana alcancé mucha parte de las paredes, que eran de cantería ricamente labrada, que mostravan haver sido aposentos reales, y un hermosíssimo galpón, que en tiempo de los Incas, en días lloviosos, servía de plaça para sus fiestas y bailes. Era tan grande que muy holgadamente pudieran sesenta de a cavallo jugar cañas dentro en él. Al convento de San Francisco vi en aquel galpón, que, porque estava lexos de lo poblado de los españoles, se passó a él desde el barrio Tococachi. . . . También vi derribar el galpón y hazer en el barrio Cassana las tiendas con sus portales, como hoy están, para morada de mercaderes y oficiales" (Garcilaso de la Vega 1945:110 [1609:Vol. 1, Bk. 7, Ch. 10]).

44. Garcilaso de la Vega (1966:321 [1609:Vol. 1, Bk. 6, Ch. 4]) writes that the Cassana was large enough to hold three thousand people. However, he mistakenly associates it with Pachacuti rather than Huayna Capac.

45. Squier's (1877:428) map of Cusco shows a location high on the eastern slope of Saphi, near the terraces of Sacsahuaman, labeled as "Bath of the Inca."

46. A light scatter of Killke and Inca pottery can be found at the base and on the slope of this hill.

47. There may be a brief record of its looting: "En 26 de Agosto de 1613, registro una guaca Francisco de Loyola y entierro en el asiento de zape y otra en la parroquia de San Cristobal y otra en una pampa arriba del matadero junto a San Antonio . . ." (AGN/Superior Gobierno, Causas Ordinarias: Leg. 2, c. 32, f.26).

48. Archival research found two references to Quiancalla. Because this shrine is of considerable importance to the study of Inca astronomy, these references are presented in full. The first dates to 1541, only ten years after the initial arrival of the Spanish in Peru:

"La estancia y tierras de quiancalla ullucobamba que comienzan desde zape hasta ipocava que todas ellas con cerros y quebradas, por una parte lindan con tierras de los indios cañares ucusichas y adelante con tierras de don Gomez de Tordoya y al principio con las tierras de Alco Baca y a las espaldas con las tierras de los yanaconas que fueron del marqués don Francisco Pizarro, las cuales dichas tierras le cupo al dicho mi padre en la repartición que se hizo por el marqués don Francisco Pizarro cuando se dieron a los conquistadores por cerca de sesenta años que las poseemos el dicho mi padre y yo de las cuales dichas tierras tengo mandamiento de amparo de las justicias de esta ciudad del Licenciado de la Gama Teniente de Gobernador que fué en este reyno su fecha a 6 de Junio de 1541 años y otro amparo que me dio el Capitán Juan Ramón corregidor de esta ciudad su fecha a 4 de Febrero de setenta años. " (AHD/Justiciales Civiles: Leg. 73, f. 1v)

The second reference to the lands of Quiancalla dates to 1595 and mentions Guamanguachanca (Ch. 5:8) and Cinca (Ch. 5:9):

"Otro si el dicho Luis Ramírez medidor dijo y declaro haber medido unas tierras del dicho Juan de Cellorigo llamadas cape quiangalla, sondor guazi guaman guachanca angabamba ullucobamba ucuchacara ruquerilinga chuquechaca y otros nombres que por una parte linden hacia las cabezadas con las faldas del cerro singa y por la frontera hacia la guasavara con tierras de Hernando Machicado y el camino real de Jaquijaguana y por otro lado con tierras de Don Gómez de Tordoya y por el otro tierras de Don Pedro Ucusicha comienzan desde un cerro llamado ipocava hasta una quebrada que baja de la una y viene al arroyo de sapi que se llama guaman guachanca y sondorguazi y pasa por las dichas tierras del camino alto de Yucay quedaron amojonadas por todas partes y declaro el dicho Luis Ramírez haber debajo de los mojones suso dichos setenta fanegadas de tierra de la medida ordinaria que se usa en la ciudad de los reyes asi mismo dijo." (ADC/Justiciales Civiles: Leg. 73, f. 4v)

49. This shrine is missing from the Cobo (1964) edition.

50. A survey of this hill found no evidence of prehistoric remains.

51. Co. 8:1 is also called Sanca Cancha.

52. The areas of Ticatica and Callanca appear on Arechaga y Calvo's 1771 map of Hacienda Picchu (AHD/ Colegio Ciencias: Leg 10a, c. 83, f. 20v; Macera 1968). The spring of Ticatica is mentioned by Betanzos (1987:260 [1557:Pt. 2, Ch. 19]).

53. Possible locations for several of these shrines have been proposed by Aveni (1981a) and Zuidema (1982a).

54. It should be noted that there was a secular and an ecclesiastical Cabildo in Cusco, and both of these institutions had several locations over time. Assuming that the ceques ran in straight lines, Zuidema (1982a) speculates that one of the Cabildos was located south of the Plaza de Armas, where the Palacio de Justicia now stands. For additional information on the Cabildos of Cusco, see Rowe (1990).

55. A 1569 reference to a field called Chacuaytapara can be found in Rowe (1986:203).

56. The Hacienda Picchu became the property of the Jesuits in 1576 as the result of a land donation by Doña Teresa de Bargas (Gutiérrez et al. 1981:64).

57. A place called Yaguira is marked on Arechaga y Calvo's 1771 map of Hacienda Picchu (Macera 1968).

58. Molina writes:

"Y aquella noche se quedavan a dormir al pie del cerro en un lugar llamado *Guamancancha;* y a la mañana, al amanecer se levantavan y suvían al cerro llamado *Yauira,* como dicho es, que está media legua del Cuzco, ado venía el Ynca señor, el qual yba allí este día, a hacer mercedes a los que se avían armado cavalleros, dándoles unas orejas de oro y mantas coloradas con unas borlas açules y otras cosas por vía de grandezco.

"Esta guaca *Yauira* heran dos alcones de piedra puestos en un altar en lo alto del cerro, la qual guaca ynstituyó Pachacuti Ynca Yupanqui para que allí fuesen a recevir los saraguelles o bragas, que ellos llaman *guara.* Hera esta guaca, primero de los yndios de Maras, y Guascar Ynca hizo poner los dichos alcones por ermosear la dicha guaca. El sacrificio que se le hacía hera quemar cinco corderos y derramar chicha, pediendo al Hacedor, Sol, Trueno y Luna que aquéllos que se armavan cavalleros fuesen valientes guerreros y venturosos, y que todas las cosas en que pusiesen mano se les hiziesen bien, que nunca fuesen vencidos; el qual sacrificio hacía el sacerdote de la dicha guaca *Yauira,* y también rogando a la guaca por los dichos mancevos, los hiziese venturosos. Y acavado de quemar el dicho sacrificio, el *guacamayo* que hera el sacerdote, dava a cada uno de los dichos mancevos unos panetes que llaman *guarayanos.* . . ." (Molina 1989:106–107 [ca. 1575])

It should be noted that the transcriptions of Molina's description of the shrine of Yauira offered by Urbano and Duviols (1989:106) and by Romero et al. (1943:43–44) are significantly different.

59. "E otro día salgan de la ciudad do yo ansimesmo mañana señalaré otra guaca en la cual llamara Yavirá la cual será el ídolo de las mercedes e siendo ya en ella hagan hacer un gran fuego e ofrezcan a esta guaca e al sol estas ovejas e corderos degollándolos primero con la sangre de los cuales les sea hecha una raya con mucha reverencia por los rostros que les tome de oreja e ofezcan ansimismo en este fuego mucha maíz e coca todo lo cual sea hecho con gran reverencia e acatamiento ofreciéndolo al sol . . ." (Betanzos 1987:67 [1557:Pt. 1, Ch. 14]).

60. For discussions of Manco Capac, Tambo Toco, and the Pacariqtambo origin myth of the Inca, see Urbano (1981), Urton (1989, 1990), and Bauer (1991, 1996).

61. At the time of our research, several houses were being built on this flat area.

62. Cieza de León (1976:225–226 [1554:Ch. 95]) implies that the battle between the Chanca and the Inca *began* near Carmenca, but in the same context he also mentions the Vilcaconga area.

63. Rowe (1980:9) errs in relating the name of Ayavira with that of Apuyauira.

64. The pass of Vilcaconga is also mentioned by many of the earlier writers, including Callapiña et al. (1974:56 [1542/1608]), Cieza de León (1979:135, 225 [1553:Pt. 1, Ch. 41, 1554:Pt. 2, Ch. 95]), Segovia (1943 [1553]), and Santillan (1950 [1564]). Albornoz (1984:205–206 [ca. 1582]) lists it as one of the shrines of the Anta area (Bauer and Barrionuevo Orosco 1997).

65. This huaca may be related to Albornoz's (1984:205 [ca. 1582]) shrines of Hananchaca and Hurinchaca: two springs that help to irrigate Hanan Cusco.

66. "Al octavo mes llamaban *chahuahuarquiz.* En él se quemaban cien carneros pardos como los del mes precedente, sin los cuales llevaban el primer día a quemar otros dos a la

guaca de Tocori, el uno donde empezaba, y el otro donde acababa de regarse el valle, por la conservación de aquella agua. Instituyó este sacrificio *Inca-Roca,* de quien cuentan los indios esta fábula: que saliendo antes muy poca agua por aquel manantial, después de haber este Inca hecho ciertos sacrificios, metió el brazo por él y fué causa que manase tanta como ahora mana; lo cual tenían por tan averiguado, que los de su parcialidad y linaje pretendieron por esta razón regar solos ellos con aquel agua; y en tiempo de los Incas salieron con ello; . . ." (Cobo 1956:216 [1653:Bk. 13, Ch. 28]).

67. Cobo miscounted the number of ceques in the system. There are either forty-one or forty-two lines, depending on whether one counts the eighth ceque of Cuntisuyu as one or two ceques.

6. The Huacas and Ceques of Antisuyu

1. For a historical reference to this shrine, see Sherbondy (1982:171, 194 n. 89).

2. Also see An. 2:2.

3. Sherbondy (1982:100) also suggests that An. 1:4 and An. 1:5 were in the Chunchul Ravine.

4. This shrine may also be recorded as "Topa Amaro" in Albornoz's (1984:216 [ca. 1582]) description of the six most important shrines of the Cusco area.

5. Zuidema (1977b:20) initially believed that Amaro-marcaguaci (An. 1:7) was situated in or near the Inca ruins of Puca Pucara. This location appears, however, to be too distant from Cusco to be An. 1:7 and may represent An. 1:9.

6. The dual-channel fountain of Puca Pucara is also a possible candidate for An. 2:8.

7. We were told by only one person that this stone serves as a landmark. He was, however, the president of the community of Tambomachay and was quite certain of its role.

8. "A este adoratorio lleuauan en cierto tiempo del año todas las Guacas, e idolos de la ciudad del Cuzco, y alli juntas les sacrificauan, y luego las voluian a sus lugares; era Guaca mui solenne; ofrecianle cestos mui pequeños de coca" (Cobo 1980:30 [1653:Bk. 13, Ch. 14]).

9. ". . . son de la decendencia y orígen de los indios Guallas del pueblo de Payatusan, que es á las espaldas de San Blas, en esta ciudad, hácia donde sale el sol, por la acera de los andenes que salen de San Blas hácia las Salinas" (Loarte 1882:240 [1572]).

10. Sherbondy (1982:195 n.92) found a reference to a different location called Ampato Suchiuna or Ampato Suchuna, which appears to be closer to Cusco. (Also see Villanueva and Sherbondy 1979:127).

11. Also see An. 1:10.

12. There is an area called Macaycalla approximately sixteen kilometers from Cusco along the Cusco–Huchuy Cusco trail. This pass appears, however, to be located too far from Cusco to be An. 2:10. In addition, the physical setting of the pass, best described as a high open plain, does not match that of An. 2:10, which is depicted as a steep mountain pass.

13. Queser Qasa is on the IGM map Calca (1970:27s) 1:100,000.

14. Named for Francisco Peces.

15. This shrine is recorded as Manducalla in Albornoz (1984:216 [ca. 1582]).

16. Some of this information appears to be extracted from Molina (1989:69 [ca. 1575]), who provides a similar, although not identical, description of Inca activities at Mantocalla.

17. "El séptimo mes respondía a junio y llamábanse *aucaycuzqui.* En él se hacía la fiesta principal del sol, que se decía *Inti-Raymi.* El primer día se ofrecían cien carneros pardos del ganado del sol en la forma que arriba se ha hecho relación. Hacían esta fiesta y sacrificio en el cerro de Manturcalla, al cual iba el Inca y asistía hasta que se acababa, bebiendo y holgándose. Hacíanla sólo los Incas de sangre real, y no entraban en ellas ni sus propias mujeres, sino que se quedaban fuera en un patio. Dábanles de beber las *mamaconas* mujeres del sol, y todos los vasos en que comían y bebían eran de oro. Ofrecíanse a las estatuas sobredichas de parte de los Incas treinta carneros: diez a la del *Viracocha,* otros diez a la del sol y otros diez a la del trueno; y treinta piezas de ropa de *cumbi* muy pintada. Otrosí hacían en aquel mismo cerro gran cantidad de estatuas de leña de *quishuar,* labrada, y vestidas de ropas ricas; éstas estaban allí desde el principio de la fiesta, al fin de la cual les ponían fuego y las quemaban. Llevábanse al dicho cerro seis *aporucos,* que se quemaban con lo demás. Después de toda la cantidad de sacrificios, para empezar el baile llamado *cayo,* que se hacía en esta fiesta cuatro veces al día, se dividían todos los indios, y la mitad quedaban allí bailando y bebiendo; y de la otra mitad parte iban a Chuquicancha, y parte a Paucarcancha; en los cuales cerros repartían otros seis *aporucos,* y eran sacrificados con la misma solemnidad.

"En esta fiesta enviaba el sol por sus estatuas con los que tenían cuidado dellas dos corderos pequeños, el uno de plata y el otro de oro, a Paucarcancha, y otros dos hechos de conchas a Pilcocancha, y otros dos al cerro de Manturcalla, y todos se enterraban en estos cerros después de haberlos ofrecido. En acabando de hacer el dicho baile del *cayo,* enviaban las estatuas del sol dos carneros grandes hechos de cierta confección, y dos corderos, a este cerro de Manturcalla; llevábanlos con grande acompañamiento puestos en unas andas y en hombros de señores principales ricamente vestidos; iban delante las insignias reales del *sunturpáucar,* y un carnero blanco vestido de una camiseta colorada, y con zarcillos de oro. Llegados al dicho cerro, los ofrecían al *Viracocha* y quemaban con muchas ceremonias." (Cobo 1956:215–216 [1653:Bk. 13, Ch. 28])

18. Yuncaypata is on the IGM map Calca (1970:27s) 1:100,000.

19. The pass of Yuncaycalla is also known as San Martín Pass and is so labeled on the IGM map Calca (1970:27s) 1:100,000.

20. There are a number of impressive springs on the plain of Chita.

21. The earliest archival reference found to Cariurco dates to 1623 (BN/Virreynato, Real Audiencia, Asuntos Judiciales, B701).

22. Of these four shrines, only Callachaca is mentioned in other chronicles. Santa Cruz Pachacuti Yamqui Salcamayhua (1950:237, 247 [1613]) associates Callachaca with two different Incas. He writes that Pachacuti Inca Yupanqui had a vision near Callachaca at the height of the Chanca War, and that Amaro Topa Inca owned Callachaca.

A 1594 document suggests that Pachacuti Inca Yupanqui owned land in Choquequirau and Callachaca (BN/Virreynato, Real Audiencia, Asuntos Judiciales, B701, f. 3).

23. For a detailed description of these ruins see Niles (1987).

It should be noted that there is a large quarrying area approximately one kilometer uphill from the Chuquiquirao complex.

24. In 1991 Manuel Chávez Ballón gave me photocopies of two documents concerning Hacienda Pumamarca, which will be referred to as Document 1 and Document 2 of the Chávez Ballón Archive. The first of these documents is five pages long and dates to 1972. It records the sale and ownership of land near Hacienda Pumamarca in 1897, 1908, 1938, 1940, 1941, 1943, and 1972. The second document, signed in 1971, is eighty-two pages long and records land sales around Hacienda Pumamarca in 1677, 1678, and 1842.

25. The mountain Huanacauri near Chita Pampa is marked as such on the IGM map Calca (1970:27s) 1:100,000, while the mountain of Maycha is labeled as Chanquicruz.

26. The Inca concept of "usnu," related to a centrally located rock, platform, or pillar monument in Inca communities, is discussed in Zuidema (1980) and Hyslop (1990).

27. It should be noted that while the usnu in Limacpampa was on An. 5, the area of Limacpampa is listed as being on Co. 2.

28. Niles notes her equally frustrated attempts to find Pachayacanora (An. 5:4), Oyaraypuquiu (An. 5:5), and Arosayapuquiu (An. 5:6): "There are no especially good candidates for the water shrines in this series, but there is no shortage of possible ones. This part of Callachaca has reliable springs that run all year, several canals, and two reservoirs providing additional water from above. This is the part of the hill that, even in drought years, appears to be bushy and lush when viewed from below" (1987:196).

29. "Y estando un día en Susurpuquio en gran aflicción, pensando el modo que tendría para contra sus enemigos, le apareció en el aire una persona como Sol, consolándole y animándole á la batalla. Y le mostró un espejo, en que le señaló las provincias, que había de subjetar; y quél había de ser el mayor de todos sus pasados; y que no dudase, tornase al pueblo, porque vencería á los Chancas, que venían sobre el Cuzco" (Sarmiento de Gamboa 1906:62 [1571:Ch. 27]).

30. Garcilaso de la Vega (1966:231 [1609:Vol. 1, Bk. 4, Ch. 21]) also presents a similar myth; however, he indicates that it involved Viracocha Inca and took place on Chita Pampa.

31. This section of Molina can also be found in Cobo (1979:133–134 [1653:Bk. 11, Ch. 12]).

32. "Dizen que antes que fuese señor, yendo a visitar a su padre Viracocha Ynca que estava en Sacsahuana, cinco leguas del Cuzco, al tiempo que llegó a una fuente llamada Susurpuquio, vido caer una tabla de cristal en la misma fuente, dentro en la qual vido una figura de yndio . . ." (Molina 1989:60 [ca. 1575]).

33. In an early work, Zuidema (1977b) suggested that Susurmarca (An. 5:8) was located in the Cachimayo ravine near an elaborately carved rock called Inca Carcel or Inquilltambo. He has since suggested that this is not the case (Zuidema 1982b:228 n. 20; 1990b:635 n. 5).

34. The earliest reference to Susumarca dates to 1579 and states that it was a large area of land that was formerly owned by the Incas (Guevara Gil 1993:375).

35. Co. 5:9 (Rondao) and An. 5:9 (Rondoya) share similar names.

36. Zuidema (1977b:212–213), basing his work on earlier investigations by Müller (1972), suggests that Auriauca was some sort of window, doorway, or street that was directed at the June solstice sunrise.

37. Cobo (1956:223; 1990:156 [1653:Bk. 13, Ch. 32]) notes in another section of his chronicle, which appears to be based on information provided by Molina, that offerings were made at Chuquicancha during the coronation of an Inca.

38. ". . . y así enterravan los cuerpos juntamente con todos los demás sacrifiçios, en un lugar llamado *Chuquicancha*, que es un cerro pequeño que está encima de San Sebastián, que será media legua del Cuzco, como ya está dicho, y luego los sacerdotes del Sol, por la mesma horden, recevían los que para el Sol estavan dedicados, y en el mismo lugar dicho hacían el sacrificio al Sol, . . .

"Y asimismo al Trueno que llaman *Chuqueylla*, los sacerdotes que a cargo tenían su figura, que era de la forma ya dicha, recevían las criaturas y demás sacrificios que para ello tenían dedicado, y lo enteravan por la misma horden en el lugar ya dicho, llamado *Chuquicancha,* y por la misma horden, en el mismo lugar se enteravan los sacrificios para la Luna, rogándole que al Ynga siempre le diese salud u prosperidad, y que siempre venciese a sus enimigos." (Molina 1989:123–125 [ca. 1575]).

39. Like Co. 2, Co. 3, and Co. 7, which contain the huacas of Sausero (Co. 2:3), Guanipata (Huanaypata, Co. 3:4), and Matoro (Matahua, Co. 7:5), An. 7 contains several shrines related to Manco Capac's mythical conquest of the Cusco Valley.

40. A 1569 reference to a place called Yallipampa (Ayllipampa [An. 7:1]?) can be found in Rowe (1985b:229). Ayllipampa is also described in detail in documents dating to 1708 and 1795 (AHD/Cajas de Censos, Leg 5, f. 2, 1707–1708; AHD/Cajas de Censos, Leg. 16, f. 69, f. 7, 1791–1795).

41. The spring of Huamantiana is mentioned by Cabello de Balboa (1951:269 [1586:Bk. 3, Ch. 10]), Santa Cruz Pachacuti Yamqui Salcamayhua (1950:216 [1613]), and Murúa (1987:55 [ca. 1615]).

42. Sherbondy (1982:53) reports a similar location for the spring of Huamantiana and suggests that Pacaypuquiu is close to San Sebastián.

43. Colcapampa (An. 7:4) should not be confused with Colcapata (Ch. 4:4) between Cusco and Sacsahuaman.

44. "Y despues se bajó hacia Collcapampa, y con sus hermanos juntos, desde el pueblo de Sañuc, les bió desde lejo vn bulto de persona, y corrio uno de sus hermanos, entendiendo que era algun yndio, y llegado, dizen que le bió sentado como á un yndio mas fiero y cruel, los ojos colorados. Luego como llegó vno de los hermanos, que fue el menor, el dicho que parecia persona, le llamó junto assí, y luego como lo llegó, los tento de la cabeça, diciendo: 'muy bien abeis benido en mi busca, al fin me hallasteis, que yo tambien os andaba en busca vuestro, al fin estais ya en mi mano.' Y el dicho *Mancocapac,* como su hermano tardó tanto, enbió á su hermano para que lo llamase; y lo mismo se quedó el vno y el otro, ojeado dequel uaca de Sañuc. Y por el dicho *Mancocapac* viendo quel vno y el otro se tardaban tanto, bino con gran enojo en donde halló á los dos ermanos ya medio muertos, les preguntó como se tardaba tanto, y entonces dizen que el vno y el otro le respondio con çeñas quejandose de una piedra questaba allí enmedio de los dos; y oydo aquello, llegó junto á ellos á preguntarle de qué se quejaua; y como les dijo que aquel ydolo y guaca lo auian hecho aquel mal, entonces el dicho *Apomancocapac* dió coçes á la dicha piedra y uaca con grande enojo, dandole con la bara de *topayauri* en la cabeza al dicho ydolo; y luego, dentro de aquella piedra començó á hablar como si fuera persona, y cabizbajo, y començó á decir al dicho Mancocapac: 'que si no obieras traido aquella bara que os dejó aquel viejo boçenglero, no os perdonara, que tambien os heziera á mi gusto. Andad,

que abeis alcanzado gran fortuna, que á este tu ermano y ermana lo quiera gozar, porque sí pecaron gravemente pecado carnal, y asi conbiene que esté en el lugar donde estubiere yo;' el qual se llamaria *pituçiray, sauasiray . . .*" (Santa Cruz Pachacuti Yamqui Salcamayhua 1951:214–215 [1613]).

45. Aucaylli Ayllu owned a large amount of land at Collcabamba in 1649 (AHD/Corregimiento, Pedimentos: Leg. 82, 1600–1669c).

46. There is a clear transcription error in Cobo's work concerning the name of Sacas[gu]aylla Puquiu (An. 8:1).

47. The name of this riverbed comes from only one informant. A small burnt offering, containing pieces of cloth, was found in this riverbed just above Pirquipuquiu.

48. The lands of Auacos (An. 8:4) and Pirqui (An. 8:2) appear under the names of Aquacoec, Ahuaccoas, Aguacoc, and Ppirque, Pirque, Pirqui in descriptions of Hacienda Pumamarca dating from 1677 to 1842 (PA/Chávez Ballón: Document 2).

49. The town of Larapa is mentioned several times in a document dating to 1559 that was signed by Polo de Ondegardo (Guevara Gil 1993:337).

50. This area is marked on the IGM map Cuzco (1973:28s) as Rau Rau.

51. It appears that Zuidema (1982b, 1982c, 1990a) believes a street in the town of San Jerónimo currently called Andamachay represents this shrine, because his drawing of An. 8 runs through the center of this community.

52. For a description of Racay-Racayniyoc, see Niles (1987).

53. Picas is also mentioned in Document 2 of the Chávez Ballón Archive.

54. The top of Huayna Picol contains a 2 × 7 × 1.5 m looters' trench cut into bedrock.

55. Llampa Huayco is on the IGM map Cuzco (1973:28s) 1:100,000.

56. Surama Ravine is labeled as Quebrada Jocopuquio on the IGM map Cuzco (1973:28s) 1:100,000. The ravine is, however, widely known as Surama Huayco. The area of Surama is discussed in two documents (AHD/Corregimiento, Causas Ordinarias: Leg. 18, 1671–1673 and AMAC/ Community File for Collana Chahuancusco) as being owned by the descendants of Amaro Topa Inca in 1595.

57. This ridge runs between the ravine of Surama and the Hacienda Angostura. Its summit is labeled as Inti Churucana on the IGM map Cuzco (1973:28s) 1:100,000.

58. The location of Pachatusan is marked on the IGM map Cuzco (1973:28s) 1:100,000.

59. If Pachatusan does represent the final shrine of An 9, then An. 9:3 (Corcorpuquiu) and An. 9:4 (Churucana) may be listed in an incorrect order. The ceque may have run from Lampapuquiu (An. 9:1) to Suramapuquio (An. 9:2), and then climbed the northern slope of Angostura to An. 9:4 (Churu-

cana). It may have then continued to 9:3 (Corcorpuquiu) on the northwest slope of Pachatusan and then terminated at its summit.

60. The area northwest of Pachatusan is marked on the IGM map Calca (1970:27s [1:100,000]) as Atas Cerro.

61. Zuidema is not consistent in his depictions of An. 7, An. 8, and An. 9. In his general diagram of the ceque system, Zuidema (1982b, 1982c, 1990a) suggests that these three ceques formed a continuous line. In his article on the Inca calendar, Zuidema (1977a) depicts An. 8 as projecting out of Cusco in the direction of the Pachatusan.

7. The Huacas and Ceques of Collasuyu

1. Sections of this chapter have appeared in "Ritual pathways of the Inca: An analysis of the Collasuyu ceques in Cuzco," *Latin American Antiquity* 3(3):183–205. They are reprinted here by permission of the Society of American Archaeology (copyright 1992).

2. Mudcapuquiu was also the name for a group, or *beaterio,* of devout women of Cusco (Zárate 1921:46–47). Wiener (1880) has marked a specific spot on his Cusco map, near the midsection of Ahuacpinta Street, as "Recolimiento del Mudcapuccio," which most likely marks the house of the beaterio.

3. Paz Soldán (1865) and Zárate (1921) place Mudcapuquiu one street to the west of Tullumayu, near the end of Ahuacpinta, south of the Temple of the Sun.

4. The name Churucana (or Churuncana) is a common name for a shrine. Each of the four suyus contains one huaca with this name.

5. In 1990 parts of Churucana were destroyed by a bulldozer. While I saw no artifacts on the hill, I did see several *in situ* Inca stone blocks along its base near the hacienda. Dwyer (1971:37) reports finding Killke pottery on the south side of this hill.

6. There is an area called Caribamba between Cusco and San Sebastián. The earliest record we have for this area dates to ca. 1640 (AHD/Cabildo: Leg. 4, 1640–1645).

7. Cayra is currently owned by the Universidad San Antonio Abad del Cusco. It is shown on the IGM map of Cusco (1973:28s) 1:100,000 as Granja Rayra.

8. The earliest reference we found to this spring dates to 1595 (AHD/Corregimiento, Causas Ordinarias: Leg. 26, c. 8, f. 55v, 1691–1692).

9. The name Acpitan is also found in a document dating to 1690 (AHD/Justiciales Civiles: Leg. 10)

10. There are several small Inca ruins within and above the Angostura.

11. "... salían a vever y bailar a *Aucaypacta,* adonde llaman agora los españoles *Limapampa,* que es avajo de Sancto Domingo; y allí los sacerdotes del Hacedor quemavan por la mañana un carnero blanco y maíz y coca y plumas de pájaros de colores de [*sic:* y] *mullo,* que es concha de la mar, como dicho está, rogando al Hacedor diese buen año, . . ." (Molina 1989:72 [ca. 1575]).

12. "Yendo todavía con el cerco al mediodía, se sique otro gran barrio, que llaman Rimacpampa: quiere dezir la plaça que habla, porque en ella se apregonavan algunas ordenanças, de las que para el govierno de la república tenían hechas. Apregonávanlas a sus tiempos para que los vezinos las supiessen y acudiessen a cumplir lo que por ellas se les mandava, y porque la plaça estava en aquel barrio, le pusieron el nombre della; por esta plaça sale el camino real que va a Collasuyu" (Garcilaso de la Vega 1945:104 [1609:Vol. 1, Bk. 7, Ch. 8]).

13. Also see An. 5:1.

14. "Que este mes entran a trauajar; aran y rronpen tierras cimple para senbrar mays. En este mes sacrificauan en los y dolos, *uacas,* pobres deste rreyno con lo que podían, con *cuuies* [conejo de Indias] y *mullo* [conchas] y *zanco* y chicha y carneros. . . .

"En este mes haze *haylle* [cantos de triunfo] y mucha fiesta de la labransa el *Ynga* y en todo el rreyno y beuen en la *minga* [prestación colectiva de tradajo a una autoridad] y comen y cantan *haylli* y *aymaran* [canto al romper la tierra], cada uno su natural *haylli.* Y se conbidan; comen y beuen en lugar de paga.

"Y comiensan a senbrar el mays hasta el mes de enero, conforme el rrelojo y rruedo del sol y del temple de la tierra; ci es *yunga* [zona andina cálida], tarde, ci es cierra, tenprano, como conbiene en este mes." (Guaman Poma de Ayala 1980:225 [1615: 251[253]])

15. Cobo states here and in the *Relación de las huacas* that Sausero was a field of the Sun, while Molina indicates that it belonged to Mama Huaco. This discrepancy has led Rowe (1980:8) to suggest that Molina was not the original author of the ceque system manuscript.

16. "En el noveno mes, llamado *yapaguiz,* se quemaban cien carneros castaños sin mancha alguna, con las ceremonias más arriba dichas; y hacían una fiesta llamada *guayara,* pidiendo en ella bueno y abundante año. Repartían quince carneros para todas las *guacas* del contorno del Cuzco, los cuales eran del ganado del Inca y del sol; y con este sacrificio se sembraba la *chácara* de *Sausero,* la cual sementera hacían con mucha solemnidad; porque esta *chácara* era del sol, y lo que se cogía della era para los sacrificios ordinarios que se le hacían allende de los arriba dichos; y en tanto que se sembraba, estaba en medio della un carnero blanco con sus orejeras de oro, y con él cantidad de indios y *mamaconas* del sol, derramando mucha chicha en nombre del dicho carnero. Ya que se iba acabando la sementera, traían de todas las provincias por cuenta mil *cuíes,* como cabía a cada una, conforme el repartimiento que estaba hecho, y con gran solemnidad los degollaban y guemaban todos en esta *chácara,* excepto cierto número dellos, que

en nombre del sol se repartían por las *guacas* y adoratorios de la ciudad. Dirigían este sacrificio al hielo, al aire, al agua y al sol y a todo aquello que les parecía a ellos que tenía poder de criar y ofender los sembrados. Los sacerdotes *tarpuntaes* ayunaban no comiendo más que *maíz* cocido y yerba sin sal, y no bebían sino *chicha* turbia, que llaman *concho,* hasta que el *maíz* salía de la tierra un dedo en alto" (Cobo 1956:216–217 [1653:Bk. 13, Ch. 28]).

17. "Los que se habían armado caballeros salían a cierta *chácara* llamada *Sausero,* que está camino de San Sebastián, a traer el *maíz* que en ella se había cogido. Acarreábanlo en unos costales pequeños con un cantar llamado *Araví.* El primer día lo traían solos los dichos caballeros noveles galanamente vestidos, y los demás días acudía a lo mismo toda la gente del Cuzco. Poco después iban a la misma *chácara* con sus arados todos los señores y principales y gran suma de gente con ellos, y la araban; lo cual acabado, volvían a la plaza mayor con gran regocijo, vestidos de las camisetas que habían ganado en la guerra" (Cobo 1956:215 [1653:Bk. 13, Ch. 27]).

18. "Al mes de abril llamavan Ayriguay. Coxían las chácaras en él y tanbién las encerravan y recogían, a lo qual llamavan Aymoray. Y los que se avían armado cavalleros salían a la chácara de Sausiro a traer el maíz que en ella se avía cojido, ques por bajo del arco ado dizen Mamaguaco, hermana de Mango Capac, el primer Ynga, sembró el primer maíz, la cual chácara veneficiavan cada año para el cuerpo de la dicha Mamaguaca, haciendo dél la chicha que hera necessaria para el vicio [servicio] del dicho cuerpo . . ." (Molina 1989:118 [ca. 1575]).

19. The earliest land document we found that mentioned the "lands and corn fields" of Sausero dates to 1575 (BN/Virreynato Cacicazgo:B561, 1685, f. 29r and f. 34).

20. Oscollopampa may be found on the IGM map Cuzco (1973:28s) 1:100,000.

21. There are several references to Tuino Pampa near Cayra dating to 1595 (AHD/Corregimiento, Causas Ordinarias: Leg. 19, c. 15, 1672–1675; AMAC/Community File for Collana Chahuancusco, 1656, f. 99v).

22. There are many documents in Cusco that refer to the Palpancay area. The earliest one we found dates to 1595 (AHD/Corregimiento, Causas Ordinarias: Leg. 10, c. 15, 1637–1642).

23. A document dating to 1595 places Collollacta in the territory of Sucso Panaca (AHD/Corregimiento, Causas Ordinarias: Leg. 26, c. 8, f. 54v, 1691–1692).

24. There are frequent references to the area of Lirpuypacha in the Cusco archives. The earliest document we recovered naming this place dated to 1595 (AHD/Colegio Ciencias: Leg. 10, c. 6, 1595).

25. "Despues desto estuvieron en Matagua dos años, intentando pasar el valle arriba á buscar buena y fértil tierra. Mama Guaco, que fortísima y diestra era, tomó dos varas de oro y

tirólas hacia el norte. La una llegó como dos tiros de arcabuz á un barbecho llamado Colcabamba y no hincó bien, porque era tierra suelta y no bancal; y por esto conoscieron que la tierra no era fértil. Y la otra llegó más adelante cerca del Cuzco y hincó bien en el territorio que llaman Guanaypata, de donde conoscieron ser tierra fértil. Otros dicen, questa prueba hizo Mango Capac con la estaca de oro que traía consigo, y que así conoscieron la fertilidad de la tierra, cuando hincándola una vez en un territorio llamado Guanaypata, dos tiros de arcabuz del Cuzco, . . ." (Sarmiento de Gamboa 1906:38 [1572:Bk. 13]).

26. Sherbondy (1982) has reached a similar conclusion regarding the possible location of Huanaypata (Co. 3:4).

27. Numerous documents record land sales at Añaypampa, including one dating to 1659 (AHD/Cabildo: Leg. 15, f. 2, 1708–1715) that records the sale of forty *topos* of land.

28. "Las aves, para que se criassen mejor, las tenían fuera de la ciudad, y de aquí se llamó Surihualla, que es prado de abestruzes, un heredamiento que está cerca de una legua del Cuzco, al mediodía, que fué de mi ayo Juan de Alcobaça, y lo heredó su hijo Diego de Alcobaça, presbítero, mi condiscípulo" (Garcilaso de la Vega 1945:243–144 [1609:Vol. 1, Bk. 5, Ch. 10]).

29. The location of Hacienda Suriguaylla is shown on the IGM map Cuzco (1973:28s) 1:100,000.

30. The town of Sañu is mentioned in a number of different chronicles, including Betanzos (1987:21 [1557:Pt. 1, Ch. 5]), Cieza de León (1976:193 [1554:Pt. 2, Ch. 31]), Cabello de Balboa (1951:263 [1586:Ch. 9]), and Cobo (1983:109 [1653:Bk. 11, Ch. 4]). Numerous archival documents and field interviews indicate that Sañu Ayllu once controlled much of the area now found within the limits of San Sebastián.

31. A hill called Tocacary (Taucaray) is listed as a shrine on Co. 5. Taucaray is marked on the IGM map Cuzco (1973:28s) 1:100,000.

32. There are many references to the area of Quispiquilla in the Cusco archives. The earliest we found dates to 1584 (AHD/Protocolos Notariales, Pedro Cerbantes: Prot. 3, 1580–1582, f. 1589].

33. Hacienda Quispiquilla is on the IGM map Cuzco (1973:28s) 1:100,000.

34. We were unable to identify definitively any of the shrines named Cuipan (Co. 4:4, Co. 6:6, and An. 8:8) in the *Relación de las huacas.* However, one possibility remains to be explored through further archival and ethnographic research. Interviews suggest that the communities now called Quircas Bajo and Quircas Alto, on the north slope of Huanacauri, may have formerly been called Ccopana (also see the IGM map Cuzco [1973:28s] 1:100,000). It is possible that the term "Cuipan," recorded in Cobo's document for a number of different shrines, is in some way related to the group that once occupied the Ccopana (Quircas) region.

35. "Y en otra india hermosa llamada Curi Chulpa, de nación

Ayavilla del valle del Cuzco, hubo dos hijos varones, el uno llamado Inga Urcon y el otro Inga Çocço . . ." (Sarmiento de Gamboa 1906:57 [1572:Bk. 24]).

36. The area of Ayavillay is mentioned in a document dating to 1658 (AHD/Corregimiento, Causas Ordinarias: Leg. 16, c. 8, 1657–1663).

37. An alternative location for Co. 4:9 and a highly speculative possibility for Co. 4:10 are worth noting. Adjacent to the town of Lucre are two mountains called Sayhua (also Caballitoyoc) and Cuzco Jahaurina. The mountain of Cuzco Jahaurina is especially impressive because it consists of twin peaks, on which small stone platforms stand with scattered remains of Inca pottery. It is possible that the mountain of Sayhua is the shrine called Sinayba, and that Cuzco Jahaurina, with its twin peaks, represents the final huaca of this ceque.

38. The spring is upslope from Wimpillay's museum. Although the spring is now seasonal, surveyors were told that it flowed year-round before the 1950 earthquake.

39. A small ravine called Ancas Cocha between the communities of Quesallay and Huilcarpay may be related to this shrine.

40. Quesallay is on the IGM map Cuzco (1973:28s) 1:100,000. The hill of Taucaray faces this community, as well as the site of Qotakalli.

41. This area is mentioned by Santa Cruz Pachacuti Yamqui Salacamayhua (1950:82 [1613]) as he notes that the wife of Lloque Yupanqui, Mama Tancarayacchi, was the daughter of a huaca in the village of Tancar.

42. The slopes of Taucaray contain the remains of Inca structures and terraces, and its summit is marked by a number of small looters' pits and a light scatter of Inca pottery.

43. The Masca were a large ethnic group who lived south of Cusco in the province of Paruro (Bauer 1992; Poole 1984). The town of Mascaguaylla is misspelled on the IGM map Cuzco (1973:28s) 1:100,000 as Aschahuaylla. The earliest reference to Mascaguaylla found during our archival research dates to 1595 (AHD/Corregimiento, Causas Ordinarias: Leg. 26, c. 8, f. 54, 1691–1692).

44. The area of Inti Pata is marked on the IGM map Cuzco (1973:28s) 1:100,000.

45. The location of Rondobamba is marked on the IGM map Cuzco (1973:28s) 1:100,000.

46. There is also a small Inca ruin, consisting of a set of terraces and corrals on the mountain of Pinta, above the village of Cayra. These archaeological remains are called Motocancha and may also be related to Co. 5:10.

47. Also see Co. 9:1.

48. "La setima se llamaua, Huanacauri; la qual era de los mas principales adoratorios de todo el reyno; el mas antiguo que tenian los incas despues de la ventana [cueva] de Pacaritampu, y donde mas sacrificios se hicieron. esta es un cerro que dista

del Cuzco como dos leguas y media por este camino en que vamos de collasuyu; en el qual dicen que uno de los hermanos del primer inca se voluio piedra por raçones que ellos dan: y tenian guardada la dicha piedra, la qual era mediana, sin figura, y algo ahusada. estubo encima del dicho cerro hasta la venida de los españoles, y hacianle muchas fiestas. Mas luego que llegaron los españoles, aunque sacaron deste adoratorio mucha suma de oro, y plata, no repararon en el idolo por ser, como he dicho, una piedra tosca; con que tubieron lugar los indios de esconderla, hasta que vuelto de chile Paullu inca le hiço casa junto a la suya. y desde entonces se hiço alli la fiesta del Raymi, hasta que los cristianos la descubrieron, y sacaron de su poder. hallose con ella cantidad de ofrendas, ropa /f. 239/ pequeña de idolillos, y gran copia de oregeras para los mancebos que se armauan caualleros. lleuauan este idolo a la guerra mui de ordinario, particularmente quando yua el Rey en persona; y Guayna capa lo lleuo a Quito, de donde lo tornaron a traer con su cuerpo. Porque tenian entendido los incas que hauia sido gran parte en sus vitorias. Ponianlo para la fiesta del Raymi ricamente vestido, y adornado de muchas plumas encima del dicho cerro de Huanacauri" (Cobo 1980:46 [1653: Bk. 13, Ch. 15]).

49. On the IGM map Cuzco (1973:28s) 1:100,000, this area is labeled as Ccescce.

50. For a plan of Qotakalli, see Niles (1987:37–40). A place called "cotacay[a]" is mentioned in a 1669 document (BN/Virreynato, Bienes, B405, f. 8v).

51. The ravine of Chachaquiray separates the communities of Quijallay and Huilcarpay. On the IGM map Cuzco (1973:28s) 1:100,000, the ravine is spelled Chajchacaray. The area of Chachaquiray is mentioned numerous times in a document dating to 1595 (AHD/Corregimiento, Causas Ordinarias: Leg. 19, c. 15, 1672–1675).

52. Other documents (AHD/Corregimiento, Causas Ordinarias: Leg. 19, c. 15, f. 51, 1672–1675; Leg. 51, c. 6, f. 6, 1769–1770; AGN/Compañia de Jesús, Título de Propiedad, Leg. 69) confirm that Chachapoyas were living near Huilcarpay.

53. Matahua is mentioned by Cabello de Balboa (1951: 263, 264, 268 [1586:Ch. 9]) in his description of Manco Capac's arrival in the Cuzco Valley; however, this information has been extracted from Sarmiento de Gamboa (1906:38 [1572:Bk. 13]) or a shared source. It is also mentioned by Betanzos (1987:19 [1557:Pt. 1, Ch. 4]).

54. ". . . bajaron al pie del cerro, adonde comenzaron á entrar en el valle del Cuzco, y llegaron á un sitio llamado Matagua, adonde asentaron y hicieron chozas para estar algún tiempo" (Sarmiento de Gamboa 1906:37–38 [1572: Bk. 13]).

55. "Antes de entrar el Inca en el Cuzco, le había nacido un hijo de su mujer *Mama-Huaco*, en un pueblo llamado Matagua, que distaba una legua del Cuzco, a quien puso *Cinchi-Roca* y crió con mucho cuidado, como al que le había

de suceder en el reino que fundaba; y para que los suyos lo reconociesen por su heredero y respetasen, ordenó que en cierto día se juntasen en el mismo pueblo de Matagua los principales y que allí se celebrase el *Rutuchico,* ceremonia nueva nunca usada antes, la cual inventó en esta ocasión el Inca, para cortar el primer cabello a su hijo, y desde entonces quedó introducida.

"Hízose esta fiesta con mucho concurso y aparato, llegando cada uno de los nobles por su orden y grados de nobleza a cortar parte del cabello del príncipe, ofreciéndole juntamente ricos dones de ropas finas y joyas de oro y plata, y reverenciándolo como a nieto del mismo sol, a quien ellos adoraban por Dios. Inventáronse para más solemnizar esta fiesta nuevas músicas, cantares y danzas, en lo cual y en comer y beber de banquete gastaron diez días.

"No fué de menor majestad y aparato la solemnidad con que se celebró el día en que el Inca mozo *Cinchi-Roca* se armó de caballero y recibió las insignias de noblezas. Para cuya fiesta se juntó en el sobredicho pueblo de Matagua mucho mayor número de gente que en la fiesta pasada; aderezóse el camino que va del Cuzco a él con curiosos arcos de flores, y sacáronse para este día diversas invenciones de bailes y regocijos; iban en este acompañamiento el Inca mozo ricamente vestido, y los reyes, sus padres, y el sacerdote que le había de armar caballero junto a ellos, todos cuatro en andas y los demás a pie. Llegados al lugar señalado, el sacerdote, haciendo primero al príncipe un breve razonamiento que llevaba estudiado, le vistió las ropas reales y dió las demás insignias que desde entonces comenzaron a usar los que habían de suceder en el reino. " (Cobo 1956:65 [1653:Bk. 12, Ch. 4])

56. "Cada uno de los que así se avían de armar cavalleros tenía ya aparejado un carnero para hacer sacrificio, e yban ellos y los de su linage al cerro llamado *Guanacauri.* Y este día dormían al pie del cerro en un lugar que se llama Matagua; y otro día siguiente, al salir del Sol, que es el décimo día, todos en ayunas, porque ayunavan este día, suvían al cerro arriva hasta llegar a la guaca *Guanacauri.* Dexavan los carneros, que para el sacrificio llevavan, al pie del dicho cerro en Matagua; . . ." (Molina 1989:100–101 [ca. 1575]).

57. Sanca Cancha is mentioned by a number of other chroniclers, including Loarte (1882:234 [1572]), Albornoz (1984:204 [ca. 1582]), Cabello de Balboa (1951:353 [1586]), and Guaman Poma de Ayala (1980:970 [1615:1051(1059)]).

58. Pucamarca was south of the Plaza de Armas; see Ch. 5:2.

59. There is a 1690 reference to a place called Cuicosi near Huanacauri (AHD/Justiciales Civiles: Leg 10, 1825).

60. The Alcaviza are said to have been the original occupants of the Cuzco Valley.

61. Also see Co. 3:1 and Co. 6:1.

62. Two informants from San Sebastián stated that Muyu Urco was formerly called Vilcacolca.

63. Test excavations and surface collections on the hill of Muyu Urco by students and staff of the Universidad San Antonio Abad del Cuzco have found evidence of a continuous occupation dating back to Chanapata times (±700–400 B.C.).

64. The location of Chacapahua is marked on the IGM Cuzco (1973:28s) 1:100,000 map.

65. Rowe (1944:43) suggests that there were once three bridges in this area.

66. The area between the spring and the bridges contains Killke and Inca pottery fragments, several small terraces, and the remains of a structure.

67. A 1638 document refers to an area called Chanquiri Pampa that may be related to Cupaychangiri Puquiu (AMAC/Community File for Collana Chahuancusco, 1656, f. 106).

68. This shrine may be related to the place that Cieza de León calles Tampu Quiru (1976:33 [1554:Pt. 2, Chs. 6–7]).

8. The Huacas and Ceques of Cuntisuyu

1. It is said that Pachacuti Inca Yupanqui took a woman named Mama Anaguarque, a native of Chocco, as his wife (Callapiña et al. 1974:39 [1542/1608]; Sarmiento de Gamboa 1906:72 [1572:Ch. 34]; Cabello de Balboa 1951:303 [1586:Pt. 3, Ch. 15]; Garcilaso de la Vega 1989:392 [1609:Pt. 1, Bk. 6, Ch. 34]; Santa Cruz Pachacuti Yamqui Salcamayhua 1950:247 [1613]; Guaman Poma de Ayala 1980:89, 114, 115 [1615:109, 136, 137]; Murúa 1946:137 [1590:Pt. 2, Ch. 13]; Montesinos 1882 [1630:Ch. 5]; and Cobo 1979:133 [1653:Bk. 12, Ch.12]). Also see La Lone (1985:55–65) and Rostworowski (1962, 1966).

Anaguarque Mountain is marked on the IGM map Cuzco (1973:28s) 1:100,000.

2. There are two other shrines in the ceque system called Sabaraura, An 5:3 and An 8:5.

3. Molina (1989:100 [ca. 1575]) reports that the huaca of the moon, Passamama, had her quarters where the belvedere (*mirador*) of Santo Domingo was built.

4. "Passado el barrio de Rimacpampa, está otro, al mediodía de la ciudad, que se dize Pumapchupan: quiere dezir cola de león, porque aquel barrio fenesce en punta, por dos arroyos que al fin dél se juntan, haziendo punta de escuadra" (Garcilaso de la Vega 1945:104–105 [1609:Pt. 1, Bk. 7, Ch. 8]).

5. "Y el día siguiente que hera a los diez y nueve del dicho mes, salían a la plaça del Cuzco llamada *Haucaypata,* como dicho es, el Ynca y toda la demás jente, y asimismo sacavan todas las demás guacas y los cuerpos de los muertos embalsamados, do echa la reverencia acostumbrada, empeçavan a hacer el sacrificio llamado *Moyucati* por la horden siguiente:

"En el Cuzco por medio dél, pasa un río pequeño llamado *Capimayo* y *Guacapancomayo,* el qual baxa de unas quebradas que están en lo alto del Cuzco hacían en él unas represas a trechos del agua para tener la represada, no obstante que hera ynvierno, para que con más fuerça llevase los sacrificios que en él se avían de hechar. Y así para este día tenían aparejado todos los géneros y maneras de comidas que ellos usavan, todas las maneras de ajíes, gran cantidad de cestos de coca, todas las maneras de ropas de colores que ellos uestían, y calçados de que usavan, *llautos* y plumas que se ponían en la caveça; ganados, flores, oro, plata y de todas las cosas que ellos usauan, todas las ceniças y carvones que guardados tenían de los sacrificios que en todo el año avían hecho; todo lo qual hechavan en el dicho río y soltando la primera presa bajava con tanta fuerça que ella misma yba quebrando las demás y llevando los sacrificios. Quémase este día en sacrificio un cordero, hechando las ceniças dél y carbón, con lo demás, en el dicho río. Estavan de la una parte y de la otra, mucha jente, al remate de la ciudad del Cuzco, en un lugar que llaman *Pomapichupa*, adonde hechavan los dichos sacrificios. Héchanlos una ora poco menos antes que se pusiese el Sol y los yndios que estavan de la una parte del río y de la otra, en echando los sacrificios en el río, el Ynca señor, que presente estava, les mandava fuesen con el dicho sacrificio hasta Ollantaytambo, . . . " (Molina 1989:114–115 [ca. 1575])

6. "Seis días después de la luna llena, habiendo hecho en el arroyo que pasa por la plaza unas represas a trechos, sacaban las cenizas y carbones que tenían guardados de lo que había sobrado de los huesos de los sacrificios de todo el año, molíanlos con dos cestos de *coca*, muchas flores de diversos colores, *ají*, sal y *mani* quemado, y así junto y hecho polvos, sacada cierta cantidad, que ponían en el depósito, llevaban lo demás a la junta que abajo del barrio de *Pumachupa* hace el dicho arroyo con otro. Acompañaban este sacrificio las estatuas del sol y demás dioses que solían poner en la plaza las fiestas grandes, el mismo Inca con toda la corte hasta el lugar dicho, y particularmente doscientos hombres con bordones en las manos. En llegando a la dicha junta de los arroyos, los indios que llevaban bordones, dejándolos, tomaba cada uno dos vasos de *chicha* y ofrecía el uno al agua de aquel riachuelo y el otro se bebían ellos; y habiendo bailado un rato con gran regocijo alrededor de las estatuas, poco antes de anochecer, echaban en el arroyo toda aquella ceniza, lavando mucho las vasijas en que iba, para que no quedase nada della; y tomados sus bordones en las manos y puestos en ambas orillas del río, les mandaba el Inca que fuesen con aquel sacrificio el río abajo hasta el pueblo de Tambo . . ." (Cobo 1956:213–214 [1653:Bk. 13, Ch. 26]).

7. ". . . y de allí vayan a una guaca que yo mañana señalaré la cual se llamará Anaguarque y llegados allí hagan su sacrificio ofreciéndole cierta chicha y haciendo delante della un fuego en el cual fuego le ofrezcan algún maiz e coca e sebo e cuando ansi allí fueren lleven los parientes deste novel que casi querían imitar a padrinos unas alabardas grandes y altas de oro e plata y siendo ya el sacrificio hecho aten en lo alto de los hierros de estas alabardas aquella paja que en las manos ansi lleven col-gando de los tales hierros aquella lana que ansí cuelga de la paja y estando ya ansi atada esta paja den a cada uno de sus noveles una alabarda destas en las manos y esto ya hecho júntenlos todos a estos noveles que allí se hallaren y mándenles que partan de allí corriendo todos juntos con sus alabardas en las manos bien ansi como si fuesen siguiendo alcance de enemigos y este correr sea desde la guaca hasta un cerro do se parece esta ciudad . . ." (Betanzos 1987:67 [1557:Ch. 14]).

8. ". . . y así yban caminando hasta llegar al cerro llamado *Anaguarque,* que será dos leguas del Cuzco, a dar a la guaca que en lo alto del cerro estava, llamada del dicho nombre. Hera guaca de los yndios del pueblo de *Chocco* y *Cachona*. La raçón porque yban desta guaca a hacer deste sacrificio, hera porque este día se avían de provar a correr quien más corriese, porque hacían esta ceremonia; y dicen que esta guaca desde el tiempo del diluvio quedó tan ligera, que corría tanto como un alcón bolava; ado llegados los mancevos, ofrecían a la dicha guaca un poco de lana que en las manos llevavan y los sacerdotes del Sol, no el principal, y los de las demás guacas ya dichas llamados *tarpuntaes,* sacrificavan cinco corderos, quemándolos al Acedor, Sol y Trueno y Luna y por el Ynca, a cada uno suyo con las raçones otras veces ya dichas; y los parientes tornavan [a] açotar con las dichas *guaracas* a los moços ya cavalleros, refiriéndoles tuviesen gran cuenta con el balor y balentía de sus personas. Acavado lo qual se asentava la jente y hacían el *taqui* llamado *guarita* con las *guayllaquepas* y caracoles ya dichos; y mientras se hacían, estavan en pie los cavalleros, teniendo en las manos el dicho bordón llamado *yauri* que eran las armas que se les dava y sus a (. . .) que estavan en los bordones; algunas heran de oro y otras de cobre, cada uno como podía" (Molina 1989:104–105 [ca. 1575]).

9. These two communities are also mentioned by Cobo in his descriptions of the fifth, sixth, seventh, and eighth ceques of Cuntisuyu.

10. We found the remains of an Inca road on the northern slope of Anaguarque and several burnt offerings along its summit.

11. The upper end of the Chachaquiray Ravine is also locally known as Jug'i or Chilla Hauyco.

12. A burnt-corn offering was found near this spring during our survey work.

13. See Rowe (1986:204) for a 1569 reference to a place called Chuquimatoro.

14. "Lexos deste barrio, al poniente dél, havía un pueblo de más de trezientos vezinos llamado Cayaucachi. Estava aquel pueblo más de mil passos de las últimas casas de la ciudad; esto era el año de mil y quinientos y sesenta; ahora, que es el año de mil y seiscientos y dos, que escrivo esto, está ya (según me han dicho) dentro, en el Cozco, cuya poblazón se ha estendido tanto que lo ha abraçado en sí por todas partes" (Garcilaso de la Vega 1945:105 [1609:Pt. 1, Bk. 7, Ch. 8]).

15. The parroquia de Cayaocache de Nuestra Señora de Belén was founded on 26 February 1560 (González Punana 1982:106).

16. The area of Chocoracay is mentioned in two documents (AHD/Protocolos Notariales, Solano, Hernando: Prot. 303, 1674–1676; AGN/Derecho Indígena, c. 180, f. 8, 1698).

17. The location of Hacienda Churucalla is marked on the IGM map Cuzco (1973:28s) 1:100,000.

18. This hill is also called Pucara.

19. Perhaps Cu. 6:3 should read Urcopacha.

20. Pacha Puquiu is a common Quechua place-name. A 1720 document mentions a Pacha Puquiu as being in the area of Matara (AHD/Corregimiento, Causas Ordinarias: Leg. 32, c. 2, 1735–1739), which seems too close to central Cusco for this shrine.

21. On this ridge there are numerous stone wall alignments, several well-cut Inca stone blocks, and a field called Intihuasi.

22. A place called Inticancha is mentioned by Sarmiento de Gamboa (1906:41 [1572:Ch. 14]).

23. Ritual battles are widely reported to have taken place between closely related villages or groups throughout the Andes. For example, Molina (1989 [ca. 1575]) and Betanzos (1987 [1557:Ch. 14]) write that such a battle occurred between the youths of Hanan and Hurin Cusco. Tinkus are known to have taken place during the Colonial period (Hopkins 1982) and still occur in the province of Canas, department of Cusco (Gorbak and Muñoz 1962).

24. Zuidema (1977c:100) presents alternative courses for Cu. 8(cayao) and Cu. 8(collana).

25. Legends of Chañan Cori Coca's battle with the Chanca continued after the Spanish invasion. Images of this heroine standing victoriously above Chanca warriors can be found in a Colonial period painting in the Museo de Arqueología del Cusco (Urton 1990:54–61) and on a number of wooden *keros* (drinking vessels) held in private collections (Chávez Ballón, pers. com. 1991).

26. "Y los que entraron por un barrio del Cuzco llamado Chocoscachona, fueron valerosamente rebatidos por los de aquel barrio; adonde cuentan que una mujer llamada Chañan Curycoca peleó varonilmente y tanto hizo por las manos contra los Chancas, que por allí habían acometido, que los hizo retirar" (Sarmiento de Gamboa 1906:63 [1572:Ch. 27]).

27. There is a second Chinchay Puquiu (Co. 9:7) in the ceque system and two other Cor Cor Puquius (Ch. 5:10 and An. 9:3).

28. This spring is called Cor Cor because of the sound the bubbles make as they rise from the depths of the spring.

29. The name Mascata may be related to the Masca ethnic group who occupied the northern reaches of the province of Paruro at the time of the Spanish invasion (Poole 1984; Bauer 1992a).

30. Another trail from Huamancharpa to Cachicalla crosses through a pass called Puca Qasa, approximately one kilometer east of Llaulli Qasa. This second pass is a less likely possibility for Cu. 8:7 because Cusco is not visible from it.

31. The community of Cachicalla is situated one to two kilometers west of the location marked for it on the IGM map Cuzco (1973:28s) 1:100,000.

32. The earliest reference found for Huacaracalla dates to 1591 (PA/Chávez Ballón, Document 3; also see AMAC/Fundo File for Carhis).

33. The summit of the hill contains a looters' pit and fragments of Inca pottery.

34. The mountain of Cimon is marked as Señal Cerro Quepan on IGM map Tambobamba (1977:28r) 1:100,000.

35. See Co. 13:1.

36. "... Cerca de aquel camino están dos caños de muy linda agua, que va encañada por debaxo de tierra; no saben dezir los indios de dónde la llevaron, porque es obra muy antigua, y también porque van faltando las tradiciones de cosas tan particulares. Llaman *collquemachác-huay* a aquellos caños: quiere dezir culebras de plata, porque el agua se asemeja en lo blanco a la plata y los caños a las culebras, en las bueltas que van dando por la tierra" (Garcilaso de la Vega 1945:105 [1609:Pt. 1, Bk. 7, Ch. 8]).

37. The pit, dug into the bedrock of the ridge, measures 2 × 3 × 2 m.

38. A group called the Alcaviquiza are mentioned by Cieza de León (1976:197–198 [1554:Pt. 2, Ch. 33]) and Villena Aguirre (1987:52). A confusing reference to the road to Alca is also contained in Albornoz's (1984:205 [ca. 1582]) description of a shrine called Catunqui.

39. A document records the sale of land at Haquira in the mid-1600s (AHD/Corregimiento, Causas Ordinarias: Leg. 14, c. 6, 1654–1656), and it is also mentioned in Arechaga y Calvo's 1771 description of Hacienda Picchu (AHD/Colegio Ciencias: Leg 10a, c. 83, f. 20; Macera 1968:48). The area of Haquira is marked as Jaquira on the IGM map Tambobamba (1977:28r) 1:100,000.

40. Agurto Calvo (1980:126) places Puquincancha to the east of Killke near Picchu in his plans of ancient Cusco. Zuidema (1977a:256; 1982c:65) suggests that the Inca observed the sunrise on the December solstice from Puquincancha. However, he provides no information on its location. See Bauer and Dearborn (1995:91–92) for an examination of the Puquincancha–December solstice hypotheses.

41. "El postrero día del mes iban a la plaza del cerro de Puquin, llevando dos carneros grandes, uno de plata y otro de oro, seis corderos y otros tantos *aporucos* vestidos, con seis corderos de oro y plata, conchas de la mar, treinta carneros blancos y otras tantas piezas de ropa, y lo quemaban todo en el dicho cerro, excepto las figuras de oro y plata. Y con esto se daba fin a la fiesta de *Cápac-Raymi*, que era la más grave y solemne de todo el año" (Cobo 1956:212 [1653:Bk. 13, Ch. 25]).

42. Molina also mentions Puquincancha at the beginning of

his report, stating that painted boards showing various scenes of Inca mythic history were housed there: "Y para entender donde tuvieron origen sus ydolatrías, porque es así que éstos no usaron de escritura, y tenían en una casa de el Sol llamada Poquen Cancha, que es junto al Cuzco, la vida de cada uno de los yngas y de las tierras que conquistó, pintado por sus figuras en unas tablas y qué origen tuvieron y entre las dichas pinturas tenían asimismo pintada la fábula siguiente . . ." (Molina 1989: 49–50 [ca. 1575]). This passage was later paraphrased by Cobo (1979:99 [1653:Bk. 12, Ch. 2]) and included in his chronicle.

43. "A los veinte y tres días del dicho mes, llevavan la estatua del Sol llamada *Huayna Punchao* a las casas del Sol llamadas *Puquin*, que abrá tres tiros de arcabuz, poco más, del Cuzco. Está en un cerrillo alto y allí sacrificavan y hacían sacrificio al Hacedor, Sol y Trueno y Luna por todas las naciones, para que multiplicase las jentes y todas las cosas fuesen prósperas. Y entendían en estos días en bever y holgarse, acavados los quales bolvían la estatua del Sol, lleyando delante el *suntur paucar* y dos carneros de oro el uno y el otro de plata, llamados *cullquenapa, curinapa*, porque heran las insinias que llevava la estatua del Sol doquiera que yba, y así se acavava esta pascua y mes llamado *Capa raymi*" (Molina 1989:110 [ca. 1575]).

44. An area called Viracochaurco is marked on Arechaga y Calvo's 1771 map of Hacienda Picchu and is mentioned in his description of the hacienda (AHD/Colegio Ciencias: Leg. 10a, c. 83, f. 20v; Macera 1968:48). The location of Viracochaurco, spelled as Hueracocha, is marked on the IGM map Tambobamba (1977:28r) 1:100,000.

45. The earliest archival reference to Cuchir[i]guaylla dates to 1622 (AHD/Protocolos Notariales, Domingo de Oro: Prot. 249, f. 245v, 1622).

46. Several informants suggest that a spring once located just above the area is thought to be Puquincancha (Cu. 10:2).

47. Rowe (1944:52) also notes an archaeological site at this location.

48. For a more extensive description of Chinchincalla and its possible role as a sunset marker, see Bauer and Dearborn (1995:76–80).

49. Aveni (1981a:308–309) discusses locations of various shrines on Cu. 14 and the general projection of this ceque.

50. A 1569 reference to a place called vxruro, which may be related to Cu. 14:1, is found in Rowe (1986).

51. "La otra [fuente], hacia la parte de septentrión, se decía Ocorura Puquiu, fuente de berros, que es Conte Suio . . ." (Murúa 1987:332 [ca. 1615:Bk. 1, Ch. 91]).

52. This second reference to the area of Chinchincalla may help to clarify the location of the December solstice markers. The ceque system document indicates that the currently unidentified shrine of Rauaypampa (Cu. 14:3) was located in the area between Hacienda Picchu and the known shrine of Pantanaya (Cu. 14:4), on the slope of the hill of Chinchincalla. Killke Hill, one possible location for Chinchincalla and the De-

cember solstice markers, is situated across a very large ravine from Hacienda Picchu and Pantanaya. On the other hand, the area above Llamacancha, the second possible location for Chinchincalla, where the sun sets on the December solstice as seen from the Plaza, is adjacent to Pantanaya and above Hacienda Picchu.

53. The area of Pantanavi is marked on Arechaga y Calvo's 1771 map of Hacienda Picchu and mentioned in the text (AHD/Colegio Ciencias: Leg. 10a, c. 83, 1770, f. 20; Macera 1968:47). It can also be found in various land documents concerning the bounderies of Picchu (AGN/Títulos de Propiedad: Leg. 34, c. 660, 1620).

9. Albornoz and the Cusco Ceque System

1. This study builds on Rowe's (1980) discussion of Albornoz's work.

2. "Ase de advertir que, en todas las más guacas questán en los cerros y en llanos, tienen alrededor de sí unas señales que llaman Ceques o cachauis, que son señales de los ofrescimientos que a las tales guacas hazían y tienen sus nombres en renombre cada señal del que allí ofresció hijo o carnero de oro o plata o de mollo. Hallarán los ofrescimientos en los tales ceques o cachauis. Es necesario destruirlos juntamente con las guacas y con todo el cuidado" (Albornoz 1984:218 [ca. 1582]).

3. Albornoz states that lines of huacas were called *ceques* or *cachauis*. Duviols (1984:222 n. 2) suggests that the word *cachauis* is related to that of *chachaguaco*, a term that Molina (1989:128 [ca. 1575]) uses in his description of the Capac Cocha ritual of the Inca.

4. Albornoz's life is discussed in Guibovich Pérez (1990).

5. Duviols provides three different transcriptions of Albornoz's *Instrucción para descubrir* . . . . The first was printed in 1968. However, two shrines in the Chinchaysuyu region of Cusco, Margauiche (#6) and Tucanamaro (#10), were not included, and Albornoz's description of Agmoasca (#7) is confused with that of Sanca (#5). Duviols's (1984) second transcription of Albornoz's work corrects these errors. His third version, presented in Urbano and Duviols (1989), is missing an entire page of text with the names and physical descriptions of twenty-one shrines in the Cusco area. In this study, I use Duviols's second transcription of Albornoz.

6. Rowe (1980:74) notes that the original document might have read "bolo" (ninepin) rather than "bola" (ball).

7. It seems unlikely, however, that both Albornoz and the author of the original ceque system document should made similar mistakes: Albornoz calls this shrine "Pucamarca Quisuarcancha," and states that it was the house of the Creator and the Thunders, while the *Relación de las huacas* lists two shrines as Pucamarca, but relates their functions to the Creator and the Thunder.

8. "Y asimismo conquistó á Caytomarca cuatro leguas del

Cuzco, y descubrió y encañó las aguas de Hurinchacan y las de Hananchacan, ques como decir las "aguas de arriba" y las "aguas de abajo" del Cuzco, con que hasta el día de hoy se riegan las sementeras del Cuzco; y así las tienen y poseen sus hijos y descendientes agora" (Sarmiento de Gamboa 1906:49 [1572: Ch. 19]).

9. ". . . y vasallos acordo buscar orden como meter Acequias de agua en aquel valle para que se pudiessen aprovechar las tierras que por falta de riego estavan ociosas, y baldias, y ansi saco las que oy llaman Hananchaca y Urinchaca que a sido y será obra de mucha importancia para toda aquella republica" (Cabello de Balboa 1951:294 [1586:Pt. 3, Ch. 13]).

10. "Y quentan estos yndios que al tienpo que le fueron rasgadas las orejas a este Ynga para poner en ellas aquel redondo que oy día tra[e]n los orejones, que le dolió mucho la una dellas, tanto que salió de la çibdad con esta fatiga y fue a un çerro questá çerca della muy alto, a quien llaman Chaca, adonde mandó a sus mugeres y a la Coya, su hermana Nicay Coca, la qual en vida de su pardre avía reçibido por muger, que con él se estuviesen. Y quentan en este paso que çusedió un misterio fabuloso, el qual fue que como en aquel tienpo no corriese por la çibdad ni pasase ningún arroyo ni río . . . y estando en este çerro el Ynga desviado algo de su jente, començó a hazer su oración al gran Tiçiviracocha y a Guanacaure y al Sol y a los Yngas, sus padres y abuelos, para que quisiesen declaralle cómo y por dónde podrían, a fuerças de manos de hombres, llevar algún río o açequia a la çibdad; y que estando en su oración, se oyó un trueno grande, tanto que espantó a todos los que allí estavan; y quel mismo Ynga, con el miedo que reçibió, abaxó la cabeça hasta poner la oreja ysquierda en el suelo, de la qual le corría mucha sangre; y que súpitamente oyó un gran ruydo de agua que por debaxo de aquel lugar yva; y que, visto el misterio, con mucha alegría mandó que viniesen muchos yndios de la çibdad, los quales con prieça grande cavaron por aquella sierra hasta que toparon con el golpe de agua, que aviendo abierto camino por las entrañas de la tierra, yva caminando sin dar provecho" (Cieza de León 1984:105–106 [1554:Pt. 2; Ch. 35]).

11. For additional information on the usnu in the central plaza of Cuzco, see Zuidema (1980), Aveni (1981a), and Hyslop (1990).

10. Systems of Huacas and Ceques: Past and Present

1. For other overviews of radial systems in the Andes, see Reinhard (1985a, 1988), Sherbondy (1986), and Urton (1990).

2. For a comprehensive analysis of Capac Cocha rituals, see Duviols (1968) as well as McEwan and Van de Guchte (1992).

3. "Concluído con los sacrificos de todas las *guacas* del Cuzco, mandaba el Inca a los sacerdotes extranjeros llevasen a ofrecer a las de sus tierras lo que se les había señalado en la repartición hecha, y ellos salían al punto a ponello por obra, caminando por este orden: el ganado solo iba por el camino real, y el golpe de la gente que llevaba los otros sacrificios, por fuera de camino en cuadrillas algo apartadas y puestas en ala con los sacrificios por delante; iban derechos hacia el lugar que caminaban sin torcer a ninguna parte, atravesando montes y quebradas, hasta llegar cada una a su tierra. Los niños que podían andar, iban por su pie, y a los muy pequeños llevaban a cuestas con el oro y demás cosas. De cuando en cuando alzaban gran vocería, empezando uno que para este efecto estaba señalado . . ." (Cobo 1964:223 [1653:Bk. 13, Ch. 32]).

4. "Y por esta horden yban caminando por toda la tierra que el Ynga conquistada tenía, por las quatro partidas, y haciendo los dichos sacrificios hasta llegar cada uno por el camino do yba a los postreros límites y mojones que el Ynga puesto tenía.

"Tenían tanta cuenta y raçón en esto, y salía tan bien repartido del Cuzco . . . , que aunque hera en cantidad el dicho sacrificio y los lugares do cavía de hazer sin número, jamás avía yerro ni trocavan de un lugar para el otro. Tenía en el Cuzco el Ynga para este efecto, yndios de los quatro *Suyos* o partidas, que cada uno dellos tenía quenta y raçón de todas las guacas por pequeñas que fuesen, que en aquella partida de que él hera *quipocamayo* o contador, que llaman *uilcacamayo;* y avía yndio que tenía a cargo casi quinientas leguas de tierra. Tenían éstos la raçón y cuenta de las cosas que a cada guaca se avía de sacrificar, . . ." (Molina 1989:127–128 [ca. 1575])

5. "La undecima, y ultima Guaca deste ceque se llamaua, Pilcourco, era otra piedra a quien hacian gran veneracion, la qual estaua en un cerro grande cerca de larapa, quando hauia inca nueuo le sacrificauan demas de lo ordinario una muchacha de doce años abajo" (Cobo 1980:38 [1653:Bk. 13, Ch. 14]).

6. In this same article, Zuidema discusses a long-distance ceque that ran from Cusco to Tiahuanaco. The existence of this ceque is more speculative.

7. Hyslop (1985, 1990) also suggests that the site of Inkawasi held a number of astronomical alignments similar to those that Zuidema suggests for the Cusco ceque system. Furthermore, Martha Anders (1986a, 1986b) proposes that the architectural layout of the Huari site of Azángaro reflects a number of attributes that Zuidema proposes for the Inca calendar. These hypotheses were alluring at their time of formation, but they need to be critically reexamined in light of recent research on the Inca calendar (Bauer and Dearborn 1995).

8. For overviews of Nazca research, see Reinhard (1985a, 1988), Aveni (1990a), and Silverman (1993).

11. An Overview of the Cusco Ceque System

1. A similar mistake can be found in Cobo (1954, 1964): Ch. 6:11 is missing from these editions.

Appendix 2

1. This translation first appeared in Rowe (1980). It is reproduced here with permission from *Ñawpa Pacha* and John H. Rowe.

Appendix 3

1. Santa Cruz Pachacuti Yamqui Salcamayhua (1993:98 [1613]) writes: "... eran tres ventanas que significavan la cassa de sus padres de donde descendieron, los quales se llamaron: el primero Tampo Ttoca, el 2 Maras Ttoco, el 3 Sutic Ttoco, que fueron de sus tios aguelos maternos y paternos que son como este: Incap Tampo Tocon o pacarinan, yurinan cacpa unanchan, en lengua general se llaman Pacaric Tampo Toco."

2. Huacas with suyu classifications (Ch., An., Co., Cu.) are from Cobo, while those with # are from Albornoz.

3. González Holguín (1901:103 [1608]): Hachha runa = Montañés, salvaje, sin cultura, sin rey ni ley. Bertonio (1984:107 [1612]): Haccha = Fuertemente, recio.

4. The three adjectives, *hacha, añay,* and *warqi,* pertain to the hawk numen that the warrior initiates emulated during competitive races in the Warachikuy festival. Molina (1989:105 [ca. 1575]): "... esta quaca desde el tiempo del diluvio quedó tan ligera, que corría tanto como un alcón bolava ..." [this shrine, at the time of the flood, became so swift that it ran as fast as a hawk could fly].

5. This name, possibly of Quechua origin, has entered the Andean Spanish lexicon (Arguedas 1973:11).

6. This is the same shrine as Yauirac (#12). There are many spellings of this name, including Yauira (Cieza de León 1976:35 [1554:Pt. 2, Ch. 6]; Sarmiento de Gamboa 1906:69 [1572:Ch. 31]; Molina 1989:106 [ca. 1575]); Yaguira (Macera 1968 [1771]); Yavira (Betanzos 1987:67 [1557:Pt. 1, Ch. 14]).

7. González Holguín (1989:39 [1608]): Ayar = La quinoa silvestre. Bot. *Chenopodium hircinum* (Zimmerer 1996).

8. Aran (Aymara) or araq (Quechua).

9. In colonial documents, *d* can represent *i, y,* or *w*. In this case, it could be aspakay = fiesta con inmolación [celebration with sacrifice] (Lara 1978:52) or aspacacuni = hazer sacrificio con conbite [sacrifice with celebration] (González Holguín 1989:35 [1608]). See also Santa Cruz Pachacuti Yamqui Salcamayhua (1993:201 [1613]): "aspacay cortándole la cabeza y echando la sangre en el fuego para que el humo lo llegasse al Hacedor del cielo y tierra" [aspacay beheading and throwing the blood in the fire so that the smoke reaches the Maker of the sky and the earth].

10. There are a number of spellings for this shrine: Alpitan (Cobo 1964:179); Apitay (Murúa 1946:51 [1590:Pt. 1, Ch. 2]); Atpian (AHD/Corregimiento, Causas Ordinarias: Leg. 26, c. 8, f. 53v, [1691–1692]); Acpitan (ADC/Judiciales Civiles: Leg. 10

[1690]); Acpita (modern community name); and perhaps Aepiran (Molina 1989:68 [ca. 1575]).

11. Ancapapirqi (Cobo 1964:176). This name could also be glossed as ankapa apiriqin = el arriero del águila [herder of eagles]. Lara (1978:49): apiri = arriero, and Bertonio (1984:24 [1612]): apiratha (Aymara) = Coger como el que limpia el trigo [pick out as in cleaning wheat].

12. This is the same shrine as Haucaypata (#8).

13. Antuiturco (Cobo 1964:175).

14. Bot. *Capiscum annum.* González Holguín (1989:393 [1608]): Agi. Hayac uchu = el que quema.

While we rely on Jaroslav Soukup (1980) for the primary Latin names of the plants in the list, we do not attempt to also supply the botanical species names for each one.

15. González Holguín (1901:42 [1608]): Aypachini = dar en el blanco, hacer alcanzar lo que se distribuye.

16. When the shrine involves water, we translate Cobo's word *pacha* as phaqcha (waterfall) rather than pacha (earth).

17. Kacha (kachay = to send), along with chaski, was used for "messenger." It is probable that the "cachauis" (see Churucani guanacauri #17), stones placed around a central stone deity, represented the subordinates (servants, messengers, or warriors) of that personage. Betanzos (1996:83 [1557:Ch. 18]): caccha = idol, god of battles. Also, Albornoz (1989:180 [ca. 1582]): sacred objects from the four quarters sent to the huaca Vilca conga in the Xaquixaguana Valley, "le hazía todo el Pirú cacchaui y le ofrecían y servían" [all of Peru brought cacchaui and made offerings to it and served it].

18. Cobo describes this huaca as three stones placed on a small hill. These stones, cacha- (kacha or kachakuna; Guaman Poma de Ayala 1980:179 [1615:203(205)]), may have represented "cachauis" (see Cacchacuchui [#11]).

19. This was probably an enclosure where potatoes were processed into ch'uñu by freeze-drying and stored for the consumption of the royal household.

20. Calizpuquiu (Betanzos 1996:63 [1557:Pt. 1, Ch. 14]), Calixpuquio (Molina 1989:109 [ca. 1575]), Callis Pucyo (Guaman Poma de Ayala 1980:310 [1615:337 (339)]).

21. Calla[nca]chaca may have been the complete phrase such as in the following huaca, Callancapuquiu, where large quarried stones (kallanka) were employed in the construction of residential and ceremonial enclosures and in public works. González Holguín (1952:44 [1608]): Callancarumi = Piedras grandes labradas, de sillería para cimientos y umbrales; Callanca huaci = Cosa fundada sobre ellas.

22. This is the same shrine as Capi (Ch. 6:7).

23. This is the same shrine as Capa (#27).

24. Capipachan (Cobo 1964:172).

25. Sapay rawra, as also in nina rawra (ardor del fuego [heat of fire]), was a venerated eternal flame. Also see Nina #32. González Holguín (1989:50, 151 [1608]): Caqquey = Mi

hazienda mis bienes; Caqueycak capuqueycak = Lo que tengo, lo que es mio; Haqquini = Dexar algo por erencia el difunto en sustento. Dexar, o no lleuar.

26. Carvinca cancha (Cobo 1964:184).

27. Karu may be a lineage term. See Domingo de Santo Tomás (1995:173 [1560]). Also, Zuidema (1989d:71) writes, "Advertimos que para formar un grupo con la extensión caru, tanto la posición de ego como la de altar es extendida a lo largo de cuarto generaciones, cada una en la línea de su propio sexo."

28. Cascajillo, Spanish loan word to Quechua. González Holguín (1989:631 [1608]): Piedrecillas, o chinas = Silla silla rumi cascajillo.

29. Illa, in this case, refers to a resplendent and sacred object such as a bright star or planet.

30. See Catungui (#22).

31. Since this huaca in Albornoz refers to stones representing warriors (awki) located on a road, qhatu (in modern Quechua "market post" or "stall") would refer to a cluster of stone warriors.

32. The original name may have been Qhawana Qaylla [near the lookout].

33. Cavas (Cobo 1964:184). This huaca was the burial place of a person named Qhawa, possibly of Mama Cava, the wife of Capac Yupanqui, whom Murúa (1946:91 [1590:Bk. 1, Ch. 20]) describes as an intelligent and serious woman ("mujer cuerda y grave"). Others state that she was wife of Lloque Yupanqui (Sarmiento de Gamboa 1906:45 [1572:Ch. 17]; Garcilaso de la Vega 1966:113 [1609:Bk. 2, Ch. 20]; Cobo 1979:116 [1654:Bk. 13, Ch. 6]).

34. González Holguín (1989:631 [1608]): Piedra larga = Cayturumi. Also González Holguín (1989:185 [1608]): Huasca chacra, o huascca huaci = Chacra, o cosa larga y angosta.

35. Cobo describes this huaca as a resting place ("descansadero"). González Holguín (1989:194 [1608]): Huaynaricuna = Los entretenimientos y recreaciones.

36. The initial c in Cicui might have been written as a cedilla (ç) in prior documents; likewise in Cinca (Cu. 8:10), Cirocaya (Ch. 1:4), and Cupaychangiri (Co. 9:9). Sicuy (ADH/Protocolos notariales, Varios escribanos, 1683–1720 [Antonio Moreno Notario #313, f. 889]).

37. Also, Sikuwa, Siquya, Bot. Stipa ichu (R.&P.) Kunth.

38. This is the same shrine as Sico cayan (#37).

39. There is a 1595 reference to a spring called Cuapacha (AMAC/Community File for Collana Chahuancusco, 1656, f. 101).

40. Colcabamba (Sarmiento de Gamboa 1906:30 [1572:Ch. 13]); Cullca Bomba (Cabello de Balboa 1951:269 [1586:Pt. 3, Ch. 10]); Collcapampa (Santa Cruz Pachacuti Yamqui Salcamayhua 1950:214–215 [1613]).

41. Garcilaso de la Vega (1966:470 [1609:Vol. 1, Bk. 7, Ch. 29]) writes that the name of the mason of the Weary Stone was Calla Cunchuy [kallanka kuchuy = sillería, cortar].

42. Corcorchaca could also be rendered as Qonqorchaki [qunqurchaki = kneeling] (AMLQ 1995:464). Although the three Corcors and the E con con in Cobo are springs, these huaca names appear to refer to a stone located near or at the edge of them. See Albornoz (1984:181 [ca. 1582]) for a description of a huaca named Corcor in the province of Quichuas that "era una piedra questava junto a una fuente cercana del pueblo Toto" [it was a stone that was beside a spring near the town of Toto].

43. Catacalla (Cobo 1964:181).

44. González Holguín (1989:70 [1608]): ccotto ccotto [qutu qutu] = Montones.

45. Cuchirguaylla (AHD/Protocolos Notariales, Domingo de Oro: Prot. 249, f. 245v, 1622), modern place called Cuchiriguaylla.

46. González Holguín (1989:51 [1608]): Ccolqueyta rantiypac catichicuni, o suchicuni = Dar plata en encomienda para emplear, o a compañía para emplear.

47. Cuycusa (Sarmiento de Gamboa 1906:34 [1572:Ch. 11]), name of an ayllu in Hurin Cusco. Cobo describes this huaca as composed of three (cuico [quinsa or kinsa]) round stones.

48. There are five cuipans. While not all of them may have denoted qullpa (see Co. 6:6), this is a likely candidate because saltpeter (sulfato ferroso, salitre) is a common ingredient used in curing illnesses, ritual offerings, and textile dyeing. González Holguín (1989:665 [1608]): Salitre = Collpa, o çuca.

49. This huaca consisted of "tres piedras en el llano de quicalla" [kinsa qaylla = near the three]. The name Cuipan could have been combined with kinsa and a word for stone such as wanka (see Cu. 1:15, quiguan = kinsa wanka, and Co. 8:5, cuicosa). Wanka is a large, light-colored, slablike stone embedded naturally in the ground. See Sarmiento de Gamboa (1906:39 [1572:Ch. 13]): "mojón de piedra mármol" [marker of marble stone].

50. Kunpi has entered the Andean Spanish lexicon as Cumbe or Cumbi.

51. González Holguín (1901:57 [1608]): cumpa galgas = piedras que se echan cuesta abajo; González Holguín (1989:531 [1608]): Galga piedra desgalgada = Cumpa o cumpamusccarumi.

52. Bot. Opuntia exaltata.

53. Mama Curi Ocllo, wife of Amaro Topa Inca.

54. Curipaxapuquiu (Cobo 1964:183).

55. González Holguín (1989:70 [1608]): ccororumpa rumi o cullu = bola de piedra o palo; González Holguín (1989:320 [1608]): Curu rumpa = Palo, piedra maciza redonda.

56. This is the same shrine as Cusicancha pachamama (#19).

57. This is the same shrine as Cusicancha (Ch. 5:1).

58. This may be the same shrine as Uscucalla (#25).

59. This is the same shrine as Chacan guanacauri (#29).

60. This is the same shrine as Chaca guanacauri (Ch. 5:7).

61. The area of this shrine, currently called Chacapahua (chakapa - wa-?), is a later elaboration on the original name.

62. Chaquaytapara (Cobo 1964:173; Rowe 1986:203); Chacuaytapara and Chanaytapra (AHD/Protocolos Notariales, Domingo de Oro: Prot. 255, f. 477, 1627; Beltrán Lucero Alonso: Prot. 3, f. 347, 1634).

63. Bot. *Escallonia resinosa*.

64. Bot. *Escallonia corymbosa* (R.65P.) Pers.

65. Haquira (AHD/Corregimiento, Causas Ordinarias: Leg. 14, c. 6, 1654–1656); Jaquira (modern community name).

66. See Achatarque (Cu. 1:9).

67. Chaquillchaca (Garcilaso de la Vega 1966:420–421 [1609:Vol. 1, Bk. 7, Ch. 10]), a sector of Cusco.

68. Zoo. *Felis Pardalis aequarorialis*.

69. Cobo describes this huaca as an enclosure next to the Temple of the Sun. It was probably the place where the llamas of all types were kept and separated from the herd for sacrifice.

70. See the illustration and description for chuku in *Antigüedades* (1992:66–69 [1590]).

71. Chuqui (or chuque, choqui) can also be translated as "lance"; however, following Cobo (1990:54 [1653:Bk. 13, Ch. 13]), we translate it as "gold."

72. González Holguín (1952:361): Piedra chata no redonda = Ppalta rumi.

73. Although the morphology of the term may be intact, this huaca name is not glossed because the two possible definitions do not correspond to features in the terrain existent today: (1) churakuna, a substantive from the verb churakuy = establecer, colocar [to put, place]. González Holguín (1989:122 [1608]): Churana o churaccuna = La caxa alazena o donde se guarda algo. Guaman Poma de Ayala (1980:302 [1615:329 (331)]): Churakuna wasi = storage houses. Today, churana is used for "box," "niche," or "shelf." (2) Churukuna, the plural substantive churukuna, meaning "a place or the ground between rivers, as in a delta, where two or three rivers converge."

74. Churcana (Guevara Gil 1993:361 [1544]).

75. This is the same shrine as Churuncana (Ch. 7:7).

76. This is the same shrine as Churucani guanacauri (#17).

77. Chusaccachi (Cobo 1964:175).

78. Econcopuquio (Cobo 1964:184).

79. The letter *E* has been retained from a prior transcription of the name embedded in a Spanish phrase.

80. This is the same shrine as Guayra (Ch. 6:4).

81. Huamantiana (Cabello de Balboa 1951:269 [1586:Bk. 3, Ch. 10]; Murúa 1987:55 [ca. 1615]); Guaman tianca (Santa Cruz Pachacuti Yamqui Salcamayhua 1950:216 [1613]).

82. This is the same shrine as Guaracinci (#33). It was probably associated with the Warachikuy.

83. This is the same shrine as Guaracince (Ch. 2:1).

84. González Holguín (1989:631 [1608]): Piedras medianas manuales = Huaru huaru rumi.

85. This is the same shrine as Guairaguaca (#28).

86. This is the same shrine as Aucaypata [paccha] (Ch. 8:3).

87. Also see Sanca cancha.

88. Ch. 6:11, missing in Cobo (1954, 1964). Apart from illa re-ferring to a resplendent object in the heavens, and to divine personages, such as Illa Tiqsi Wiraqucha, other meanings are: González Holguín (1989:336–337 [1608]): Ylla = a precious stone; Yllayoc runa = a person who possesses precious goods (tesoro); Ylla huaci = a house containing abundant riches; Ylla = antique treasured goods. Also Cieza de León (1985:92 [1554: Pt.2, Ch. 30]): Ylla = a deceased personage of great virtue; and *Antigüedades* (1992:91 [1590]): illay tanta = sacred ceremonial bread.

89. This is the same shrine as Yllanguaiqui (#3).

90. González Holguín (1989:367 [1608]): Yllappa = Rayo, arcabuz, artilleria.

91. Inca Roca, also the name of the second king of Cusco. Garcilaso de la Vega (1966:103 [1609:Vol. 1, Bk. 2, Ch. 16]) writes, ". . . Padre Valera says that roca means 'a prudent and astute prince' . . ."

92. This is the same shrine as Michosamaro (Ch. 1:1).

93. Sarmiento de Gamboa (1906:61, 63, 64 [1572:Ch. 26 and 27]): quillis-cachi = Urco Guaranca, a messenger for Viracocha Inca; also see Betanzos (1996:22 [1557:Ch. 6]): Quilescache = Urcoguaranca; Guaman Poma de Ayala (1980:281): Quiles Cachi cimi apac = jués de comisiones. Santa Cruz Pachacuti Yamqui Salcamayhua (1993:251, 261 [1613]) refers to the Quilliscachi as an ethnic group. González Holguín (1901:297 [1608]): Quilli quilli = El cernícalo, ave de rapiña.

The name also could be rendered as Llipi qhilli q'achu (all dirty grass). In this case, the name, Lord Fleet Kestrel Messenger, had taken on a ludic and pejorative meaning similar to those recorded for the messengers of Inca Atahuallpa: Ciquinchara [Wet Backsides] (Betanzos 1996:247–250 [1557:Pt. 2, Ch. 20]) and Waylla Wiksa [Meadow - Belly] in the dramas of the death of Atahuallpa (Beyersdorff 1997).

94. González Holguín (1989:348 [1608]): Tturu = Lodo, barro.

95. This is the same shrine as Mararoray (#13).

96. Manturcalla (Cobo 1990:142–143 [1653:Bk. 13, Ch. 28]); Manducalla (Albornoz 1984:216 [ca. 1582]); Mantucalla (AHD/Cajas de Censos: Leg. 2, 1656–1675).

97. González Holguín (1989:229 [1608]): Mantur huan passicuni hauicuni = Afeytarse la muger; González Holguín (1989:431 [1608]): Bermellon. Fruto de arbol con que se afeytan = Mantur.

98. Mantocallaspa (An. 3:5) is described as a spring on the hill of Mantocalla near Chuquimarca. The name may have been Mantocallaspa[qcha].

99. This is the same shrine as Mamararoy (Ch. 8:8).

100. This is the same shrine as Marcatampu (Ch. 7:3).

101. This is the same shrine as Marcatambo (#9).

102. Maska: name of an ethnic group.

103. Bot. *Loricaria* Wedd. González Holguín (1989:515 [1608]): Matara = Enea o espadaña, yerba.

104. Matahua or Matagua (Betanzos 1987:19 [1557:Pt. 1, Ch. 4]; Sarmiento de Gamboa 1906:38 [1572:Bk. 13]; Molina

1989:100–101 [ca. 1575]; Cabello de Balboa 1951:263, 264, 268 [1586:Ch. 9]). It may also be related to the modern community of Matao and to the legendary Matagua where Manco Capac stopped on his descent from Huanacauri to the Cusco Valley.

105. Bot. *Senecio vulgaris.*

106. González Holguín (1989:353 [1608]): Vinpilla = La horca en que dauan trato de cuerda por vn dia.

107. AMLQ (1995:320): Mik'aya = Manantial de agua. González Holguín (1989:241 [1608]): Miqqui = Humedad, cosa humeda lienta &c; Miqquicun = Humedecerse algo, o miqquiyan.

108. González Holguín (1989:237 [1608]): Micca uya = Cari ancho, cari redondo.

109. This is the same shrine as Luchus Amaro (#34).

110. Guaman Poma (1980:249 [1615]).

111. Bot. *Spondylus.*

112. Nina villka (*Antigüedades* 1992:90 [1590]).

113. This is the same shrine as Queachili (Ch. 9:8). In the copy of Albornoz that has survived, the -gues, a contraction of "que es" (which is), in the name Oma Chilli-gues has been appended to the original Quechua toponym. See Rowe 1980:73.

114. Uma (Aymara).

115. This is the same shrine as Uman Amaro (#4).

116. See note 114.

117. See note 114.

118. Omoto Yanacauri (Molina 1989:68 [ca. 1575]).

119. Ocorura Puquiu (Murúa 1987:332 [ca. 1615:Ch. 91]).

120. Bot. *Mimulus L.* González Holguín (1989:431 [1608]): Berros = Occo ruru.

121. vxruro (Rowe 1986).

122. Payatusan (Loarte 1882:240 [1572]); Pachatusan in modern usage.

123. The Yaconora were a kin group residing near San Sebastián.

124. Pillku = pájaro andino (Andean bird). González Holguín (1989:285 [1608]): Apillco ppichu = Un pájaro de los Andes colorado preciado por las plumas.

125. Cobo records this huaca as a stone that according to legend had jumped ("saltado") from one hill to another as if "crowning it."

126. Pillo Churi (Cobo 1964:183).

127. Lirpuypacha (AHD/Colegio Ciencias: Leg. 10, c. 6, 1595).

128. This spring and Pachachiri (Cu. 8:12) formed a pair.

129. Poma Chupan (Guaman Poma de Ayala 1980:970 [1615:1051 (1059)]; Betanzos 1987:60, 77 [1557:Pt.1, Ch. 13, 16]); Pumapchupan (Garcilaso de la Vega 1966:420 [1609:Vol. 1, Bk. 7, Ch. 8]); Pumachupa (Molina 1989:114–115 [ca. 1575]).

130. González Holguín (1989:298 [1608]): Puru challua = Sapillos que se hacen de renacuajos.

131. Bot. *Buddleia incana R.&P.*

132. González Holguín (1989:39, 286 [1608]): Aya pintuna = Mortaja. Pinttuni = Embolūer niño, o cobijarle con la ropa, o amortajar.

133. Puquiu (Cobo 1964:182).

134. This name is probably a contraction of *puqu-* and another word, possibly *killa* or *inti.* Both Puquincancha (Cu. 10:2) and Puquinpuquiu (Cu. 11:3) were probably associated with the Capac Raymi festival during the month of December, pucoi quilla raime quis [puquy killa raymi khuska]. This celebration, marking the beginning of the year, was dedicated to the sowing and ripening of crops (Betanzos 1996:65 [1557:Pt. 1, Ch. 15]). Molina (1989:49–50, 110 [ca. 1575]): Poquen and Puquin.

135. See note 134.

136. Quzachili (Cobo 1964:174). This is the same shrine as Oma Chilligues #15.

137. Quean calla (Guaman Poma de Ayala 1980:289 [1615:316 (318)]). González Holguín (1989:300,301 [1608]): Qqillay = El hierro; Qquillaypa acan = La escoria o herrumbre o orin; Quillay tacak = Herrero.

138. Bot. *Urtica andicola* Wedd.

139. Although Albornoz writes that this huaca was "a stone like a ball, which they had in a public place to revere it," we render *qui-* as *kinsa* (three) here, as in Quiquan (Cu. 1:15). Prior to the time Albornoz described it, this huaca probably had been composed of three stones.

140. Cieza de León (1985:15 [1554:Pt. 2, Ch. 6]) mentions a "Tanbo Quiro, que en nuestra lengua querrá dezir 'dientes de aposento' o 'de palacio'" [Tanbo Quiro, that in our language means "teeth of a dwelling" (architectural adornment of points) or of a palace]. According to Cieza de León, the Ayar brothers, after leaving Ayar Ucho in the cave, descended from Guanacauri to Tanbo Quiro and settled there for awhile.

141. See Pedro Pizarro (1986:92 [1571:Ch. 15]) for a description of the garden of golden maize plants near the Coricancha. Also Cobo (1964:169 [1653:Bk. 13, Ch. 12]) writes, "Delante desta capilla [Coricancha] tenían hecha una huerta, en la cual, los días que se hacía fiesta del sol, hincaban cañas de maíz con sus hojas y mazorcas hechas de oro finísimo . . ." [Before this chapel (Coricancha) they had made a garden, in which, on the days when they celebrated the sun, they thrust corn stalks with their leaves and cobs made with fine gold . . .].

142. Bot. *Chenopodium quinoa.*

143. Bot. *Berberis lobbiana* Schneid. González Holguín (1989:307 [1608]): Quichca quichca = Espinal. Origin lodge, lineage of Lord Quisco Cinchi [spiny plant - strong], Polo de Ondegardo (1920:134 [1572]).

144. Bot. *Buddleia incana R.&P.*

145. González Holguín (1989:311 [1608]): Rakra = Hendidura resquebrajadura.

146. González Holguín (1989:313 [1608]): Raquini, o raquitani = Repartir, dar porciones o apartar vno de otro. This huaca was near a field where idols from the four suyus were kept during the annual Situa festival in Cusco. *Antigüedades* (1992:59 [1590]): "Había en el Cuzco un templo, que era como el Panthéon de Roma, donde colocaban todos los ídolos de

todas las naciones y pueblos subjetos al inga . . ." [There was a temple in Cusco, that was like the Pantheon of Rome, where they placed all of the idols of all the nations and towns subject to the Inca . . .].

147. Raurawa (Molina 1989:104 [ca. 1575]).

148. González Holguín (1989:311 [1608]): Rakrani rakraycuni = Engullir medio mascado, o entero. González Holguín (1989:631 [1608]): Tragadero = Ttoncor nuez cunca mucu.

149. González Holguín (1989:321 [1608]): Runtu = Huevo, o granizo gordo, piedra. Murúa (1946:68, 96 [1590:Bk. 1, Chs. 10 and 22]): Mama yunto cayan (Runtu Khuyan). This personage, also named Mama Anahuarque, was the wife of Pachacuti Inca Yupanqui.

150. Sauaraura (Cobo 1964:177).

151. Also see Sanca Cancha (Ch. 7:2) and Hurin Sanca (Ch. 7:2).

152. Sancay Uaci (Guaman Poma de Ayala 1980:970 [1615:1051 (1059)]); Sanzahuaci (Loarte 1882:234 [1572]); Cangaguase (Betanzos 1987:95 [1557:Pt. 1, Ch. 19]); Sanca (Cabello de Balboa 1951:353 [1586:Ch. 20]; Albornoz 1984:204 [ca. 1582]). Also see Hurin cancha.

153. González Holguín (1989:324 [1608]): sañutturu = La loca cozida.

154. Sanoctuyro (Guevara Gil 1993:389 [1570]).

155. See note 153.

156. This is the same shrine as Cirocaya (Ch. 1:4).

157. See note 153.

158. González Holguín (1989:51 [1608]): Ccolqueyta rantiypac catichicuni, o suchicuni = Dar plata en encomienda para emplear, o a compañia para emplear. For an explanation of -gues, see note 113 above.

159. Bot. *Viguinera lanceolata* Britt.

160. Zoo. *Rhea darwini*.

161. Bot. *Phragmites adans*.

162. González Holguín (1901:69 [1608]): Chanaq chanaq = Con brío, con insolencia.

163. Bot. *Berberis conmutata* Eichl.

164. This is the same shrine as Tucanamaro (#10).

165. Timpucpuquiu (Cobo 1964:175).

166. Totorgo aylla (Cobo 1964:175).

167. Bot. *Scirpus totora* Koyama.

168. This is the same shrine as Taxanamaro (Ch. 7:4).

169. Zoo. *Hippocamelus antisensis* d'Orbigny.

170. This is the same shrine as Omanamaro (Ch. 7:1).

171. See note 114.

172. González Holguín (1989:174 [1608]): Unucta hualpapaya = Dar el riego por igual y repartir bien el agua a todos. Also Itier (1993:167): Runa wallpa, "el que dota a los hombres de lo necesario para un fin determinado" [divine giver of all necessities to humanity for a determined end].

173. This is the same shrine as Urcos calla uiracocha (#14).

174. This is the same shrine as Urcoscalla (Ch. 8:9). Following traditional usage, we retain Wiraqucha as a proper name here. See Beyersdorff (1992) for an etymological analysis of the term.

175. This may be the same shrine as Cuzcocalla (Ch. 5:3).

176. Domingo de Santo Tomás (1951:372 [1560]): Usianigui = Fenecer o acabar obra.

177. González Holguín (1989:34 [1608]): Arpay = Sacrificio, obra de sacrificar.

178. See note 177.

179. Uiroypaccha (Guaman Poma de Ayala 1980:289, 970 [1615:316 (318), 1051 (1059)]). González Holguín (1989:353, 532 [1608]): Viruy mana = gentil hombre, hombre bien tallado.

180. Yuncaycalla (Cobo 1964:176).

181. This is the same shrine as Apuyauira (Ch. 9:6).

182. Although this is the same huaca as Illanguarque (Ch. 8:1), Albornoz may have recorded an alternate name, *wayqi* (brother or male companion) instead of *warqi*, rendering the term Brother Lightning.

183. Bot. *Brassica compestris* Linneo.

Glossary

The glossary includes Aymara [A], English [E], Spanish [S], and Quechua [Q] terms used in this work. For more extensive definitions of the Quechua terms, see the early colonial dictionary of Domingo de Santo Tomás (1951 [1560]), the anonymous vocabulary titled *Arte y vocabulario en la lengua general del Perú llamada Quichua y en la lengua española* (1951 [1586]), and the extensive work of González Holguín (1989 [1608]). Important modern dictionaries include those written by Middendorf (1890), Lira (1944), and Cusihuamán (1976). For expanded definitions of the Aymara terms, see Bertonio (1984 [1612]).

Abuela [S] = Grandmother.

Aguini Ayllu [Q] = A little-known kin group of the Cusco Valley.

Alcaviza [Q] = Believed to be one of the original kin groups of the Cusco Valley. They may also have been known as Arayraca Ayllu.

Altiplano [S] = High mountain plain of Bolivia and Peru.

Alto [S] = Upper.

Amaru Topa Inca [Q] = The older brother of Topa Inca and the eldest son of Pachacuti Inca Yupanqui. It is said that Pachacuti Inca Yupanqui selected Topa Inca as his successor rather than Amaru Topa Inca.

Anaguarque (Anahuarque) [Q] = The wife of Pachacuti Inca Yupanqui, and the name of an important mountain near Cusco.

Angostura [S] = The Narrows, an area at the eastern end of the Cusco Valley.

Anta [Q] = Copper.

Antasaya (Andasaya) Ayllu [Q] = Believed to be one of the original kin groups of the Cusco Valley. Antasaya Ayllu was also called Quisco Ayllu, and it was associated with Cuntisuyu.

Antisuyu [Q] = The northeast quadrant of Cusco and, by extension, of the Inca Empire.

Antizenith [E] = Zuidema (1981b, 1988b) refers to the date when the sun sets 180 degrees from the position where it rises on the zenith passage day as the "antizenith passage date."

Apacheta [Q] = Sacred cairn.

Apu (Apo) [Q] = Mountain lord; a sacred mountain.

Apu Mayta Panaca [Q] = Descendants of Capac Yupanqui, the fifth Inca.

Aravi (Yaraví) [Q] = A song about an important past event.

Arayraca Ayllu [Q] = Kin group of Cusco that held ritual responsibilities associated with Chinchaysuyu. They may also have been known as Alcaviza Ayllu.

Atahualpa (Atawallpa) [Q] = Inca ruler killed by the Spaniards at Cajamarca in 1532.

Aucaylli (Aucailli, Aqqaylli) Panaca [Q] = Descendants of Yahuar Huacac, the seventh Inca.

Aucaypata [Q] = *See* Haucaypata.

Ayllu (Ayllo) [Q] = Kin group, clan, lineage, community.

Aymara [A] = Indigenous language of much of Bolivia.

Aymaran [Q] = Song to break the earth.

Bajo [S] = Lower.

Bamba [Q] = *See* Pampa.

Beatería [S] = Group of devout women.

Braza [S] = Fathom, the length of two outstretched arms.

Cachi (Cache) [Q] = Salt.

Cacique [A] = Leader.

Cacra [Q] = A misspelling by Cobo of "Carya."

Camayocs [Q] = Attendants, specialists.

Cancha [Q] = An enclosure that may contain several rooms.

Capac [Q] = Royal.

Capac Panaca [Q] = Descendants of Topa Inca Yupanqui, the tenth Inca.

Capac Raymi [Q] = A festival month associated by most colonial authors with the December solstice and the beginning of a new year. During this month the Warachikoy ritual took place.

Carmenca (Carmenga, Karminka) [Q] = An area of ancient Cusco now called Santa Ana.

Cayao (Kayaw) [Q] = Unknown term.

Cayaocache [Q] = A community outside ancient Cusco where Belén is now.

Cayra (Kayra) [Q] = A community at the east end of the Cusco Valley.

Ceque [Q] = Line, border. In Cusco it was also used to designate a group of shrines.

Cerro [S] = Mountain.

Cestos [S] = Bundles.

Chaca [Q] = Bridge, leg.

Chacara (Chacra) [Q] = Agricultural field.

Chanca [Q] = An ethnic group that lived in the area of Andahuaylas.

Chanca War [Q] = A legendary war fought between the Inca and the Chanca.

Chañan Cori Coca [Q] = A heroine of the Chanca War.

Chavin Cusco [Q] = Kin group of Cusco that held ritual responsibilities associated with Chinchaysuyu.

Chicha [S (Carib)] = The Carib name for a fermented drink generally made of corn. This name was introduced into the Andean region by the Spaniards. The Quechua term for corn beer is *aka*.

Chico [S] = Small.

Chima Panaca [Q] = Descendants of Manco Capac, the first Inca.

Chinchaysuyu [Q] = The northwest quadrant of Cusco and, by extension, of the Inca Empire.

Chincheros Canal [E] = A major canal that brought water to colonial Cusco.

Chinchincalla [Q] = A hill with twin pillars that represented the third shrine of the thirteenth ceque of Cuntisuyu (Cu. 13:3). The approximate positions of these pillars include the locations where the sun is seen to set on the December solstice as viewed from the Coricancha and from the central plaza of Cusco.

Chirao [Q] = Clear, burning.

Chulpa [Q] = Burial tower.

Cinca (Senca, Cinga, Singa) [Q] = Nose.

Citua Raymi [Q] = The Inca celebration of expelling evils from Cusco, held in the ninth month of the year corresponding most closely with September. (Also called Coya Raymi).

Cocha (Qocha) [Q] = Lake.

Collana (Qollana) [Q] = An excellent, first, or principal thing.

Collas [Q] = An ethnic group that inhabited the Lake Titicaca region.

Collasuyu [Q] = The southeast quadrant of Cusco and, by extension, of the Inca Empire.

Collcampata [Q] = A terraced area of Cusco on the slope of Sacsahuaman.

Collque [Q] = Silver.

Cori (Curi) [Q] = Gold.

Coricancha [Q] = An enclosure in Cusco containing the principal Sun temple. This enclosure was called the Templo del Sol (Temple of the Sun) by the Spaniards.

Corregidor [S] = Chief Magistrate.

Coya [Q] = Queen, sister/wife of an Inca.

Coya Raymi [Q] = *See* Citua Raymi.

Cuis (Kuis, Cuuies) [Q] = Guinea pigs.

Cuntisuyu [Q] = The southwest quadrant of Cusco and, by extension, of the Inca Empire.

Curaca (Kuraka) [Q] = Head, leader, chief.

Cusco (Cuzco, Qosco) [Q] = Exact meaning unknown. Capital city of the Inca.

Cusi (Kusi) [Q] = Happy.

Cuycusa [Q] = Kin group of Cusco that held ritual responsibilities associated with Collasuyu.

December solstice [E] = The date on which the apparent solar motion reaches its farthest southerly extension, and the sun begins moving northward. As the north/south motion is very slow at this time, the sun appears to rise and set in the same position for a few days. On this date the sun passes directly above the Tropic of Capricorn.

Encomienda [S] = Exclusive rights, granted by the Spanish Crown, to the labor or produce from specific communities.

Equinox [E] = Dates near 21 March and 22 September when the sun crosses the equator and the days and the nights are of equal length. The dates of the equinoxes are shifted from the dates midway between the solstices by a few days.

Estado [S] = The height of an average man, about 1.5 meters.

Fathom [E] = The length of outstretched arms, usually taken to be six feet, or a little short of two meters.

Grande [S] = Large.

Guaca [Q] = *See* Huaca.

Guacaytaqui (Goacataqui) [Q] = A kin group mentioned by Cobo and Sarmiento.

Hahuanina Panaca [Q] = Descendants of Lloque Yupanqui, the third Inca.

Hanan (Anan) [Q] = Upper.

Hanan Cusco [Q] = Upper Cusco.

Hanansaya [Q] = Upper part.

Hatun [Q] = Great.

Hatun Panaca [Q] = Descendants of Pachacuti Inca Yupanqui, the ninth Inca. Also called Iñaca.

Haucaypata (Aucaypata) [Q] = Central plaza of Cusco.

Haylle (Haylli) [Q] = Song of triumph.

Huaca (Guaca) [Q] = Sacred location or object, shrine.

Huaci (Guaci, Wasi) [Q] = House.

Huamanga [Q] = An area of the central highlands of Peru now called Ayacucho.

Huanacauri [Q] = A large mountain, and one of the most important shrines in the Cusco Valley.

Huascar [Q] = Son of Huayna Capac and half brother of Atahualpa.

Huayco (Huaycco) [Q] = Ravine.

Huaylla (Guaylla) [Q] = Meadow.

Huayna [Q] = Young.

Huayna Capac [Q] = The last undisputed Inca ruler. He is believed to have died of a plague that swept the Inca Empire, leading to a civil war between the half brothers Atahualpa and Huascar.

Huchuy [Q] = Small.

Hurin (Urin) [Q] = Lower.

Hurin Cusco [Q] = Lower Cusco.

Hurinsaya [Q] = Lower part.

IGM [S] = Acronym for Instituto Geográfico Militar.

INC [S] = Acronym for Instituto Nacional de Cultura.

Inca Roca [Q] = The sixth Inca king.

Inca Yupanqui [Q] = *See* Pachacuti Inca Yupanqui.

Inti [Q] = Sun.

Inti Illapa [Q] = Thunder/Lightning.

Inti Raymi [Q] = A festival associated with the June solstice.

Iñaca (Incaca) Panaca [Q] = Descent group for Pachacuti Inca Yupanqui. Also called Hatun Panaca.

June solstice [E] = The date on which the apparent solar motion reaches its farthest northern extent, and the sun begins to move south. As the north/south motion is very slow at this time, the sun appears to rise and set in the same position for a few days. On this date the sun passes directly above the Tropic of Cancer.

Kenko [Q] = Curved, zigzagged.

Killke pottery [E] = Pottery produced in the Cusco Valley from around A.D. 1000 to A.D. 1400. Also known as Early Inca pottery.

Kinsa [Q] = Three.

Lacco [Q] = A set of ruins northeast of Cusco that are also known as Salon Punco.

League [E] = The average distance traveled by a person on a horse in an hour, a distance equal to about 5.50 kilometers.

Licenciado [S] = Lawyer.

Limacpampa (Rimacpampa) [Q] = A large flat area on the eastern edge of ancient Cusco at which a number of important festivals were held.

Llacta (Llaqta) [Q] = Community.

Llautu (Llauatu) [Q] = Headbands.

Machacauy [Q] = Snake.

Machay [Q] = Cave.

Mama [Q] = Mother.

Mamacona [Q] = Holy women.

Manco Capac [Q] = The first mythical Inca.

Maras [Q] = Kin group of Cusco that held ritual responsibilities associated with Collasuyu.

Mayu (Mayo) [Q] = River.

Membilla (Wimpillay) [Q] = A community near Cusco.

Minga [Q] = Communal work for an authority.

Mitima [Q] = Colonist.

Mitta (Mita) [Q] = Turn, rotation; used for public labor.

Moco (Moqo) [Q] = Mountain, hill.

Moiety [E] = One of two equal parts. Andean communities were commonly divided into two sectors called the "upper part" and the "lower part."

Mojón [S] = Boundary marker.

Mollo (Mullu) [Q] = *Spondylus* shells.

Mujeres (Mugeres) [S] = Women.

Muyu [Q] = Round.

Napa [Q] = Sacred, frequently white, llamas.

Niña [Q] = Flame.

Northern Sea [E] = Atlantic Ocean.

Ñan [Q] = Road, trail.

Ñusta [Q] = Princess.

Orejones [S] = Spanish term for Incas of high rank.

Pacari (Paccari, Paqari) [Q] = Morning.

Pacarina (Paqarina) [Q] = Origin place, location from which mythical ancestors emerged from the earth.

Pacariqtambo [Q] = Origin place of the Inca. It lies due south of Cusco in Cuntisuyu.

Paccha (Phaqcha)[Q] = Waterfall, swiftly moving water.

Pacha [Q] = Time, earth.

Pachacuti Inca Yupanqui [Q] = The ninth king of Cusco, traditionally believed to be responsible for the initial expansion of the empire.

Pampa [Q] = Flat area.

Panaca [Q] = Royal kin group; the descendants of an Inca.

Pata [Q] = Terrace, flat area, plain.

Paullu Inca [Q] = An Inca who ruled the empire under Spanish direction.

Payan [Q] = Unknown term.

Picchu [Q] = Mountain; a hill northwest of Cusco.

Pisac [Q] = A town northeast of Cusco.

Plaza de Armas [S] = Central square of a town.

Puma (Poma) [Q] = Puma, mountain lion.

Puna [Q] = High grassland.

Punchao (Punchau) [Q] = Dawn, the day, sunlight; a gold idol held in the Coricancha.

Puncu (Punco) [Q] = Entrance.

Puquín [Q] = A hill south of Cusco.

Puquín Cancha [Q] = A temple of the Sun on the hill of Puquín where part of the Capac Raymi celebration took place.

Puquiu (Puquio, Pucyo) [Q] = Spring, fountain.

Pururaucas [Q] = Stones that were magically transformed into soldiers to help the Inca battle the Chanca.

Quechua [Q] = Language of the Inca. It is still spoken in parts of Peru, Ecuador, Bolivia, Chile, and Argentina.

Quiancalla (Quiangalla) [Q] = A hill with two pillars that were the ninth shrine of the sixth ceque of Chinchaysuyu (Ch. 6:9). Cobo states that they marked the beginning of summer, though substantial arguments can be made that they marked the June solstice.

Quilla [Q] = Moon, month.

Quipu (Khipu) [Q] = A knotted cord for encoding information.

Quipucamayocs [Q] = People who kept and read quipus.

Quisco Ayllu [Q] = Believed to be one of the original kin groups of the Cusco Valley. Quisco Ayllu was also called Andasaya (Antasaya) Ayllu and was associated with Cuntisuyu.

Raqay (Racay) [Q] = Ruins.

Raurau Panaca [Q] = Descendants of Sinchi Roca, the second Inca.

Raymi (Raimi) [Q] = Festival.

Redondo/a [S] = Round.

Reducción [S] = Resettlement village organized by the Spaniards.

Relación [S] = Report.

Rimay [Q] = To speak.

Rumi [Q] = Stone.

Sacsahuaman (Sacsayhuaman) [Q] = A large fort/temple above Cusco.

Sañoc [Q] = Kin group of Cusco that held ritual responsibilities associated with Antisuyu.

Sauasiray [Q] = Believed to be one of the original kin groups of the Cusco Valley. May have also been called Sutic Ayllu.

Sayhua (Sayba) [Q] = Marker.

Serpi [Q] = Frog.

Solstice [E] = The most northerly and southerly points along the path that the sun appears to follow in the sky. The arrival of the sun at these locations defines the beginning of summer and winter.

Sucanca [Q] = Cobo and Polo de Ondegardo used this name for solar pillars on the Cusco horizon.

Suchuna [Q] = Sliding place. A large, smooth rock adjacent to Sacsahuaman.

Suscu (Cubcu, Çusçu, Zukzu) Panaca [Q] = Descendants of Viracocha Inca, the eighth king of Cusco.

Sutic [Q] = Kin group of Cusco that held ritual responsibilities associated with Collasuyu.

Suyu [Q] = Division, region of the empire. The Cusco region, and the empire as a whole, was divided into four suyus called Chinchaysuyu, Antisuyu, Collasuyu, and Cuntisuyu.

Tahuantinsuyu (Tawantinsuyu) [Q] = Name of the Inca Empire (the four parts together).

Tambo (Tampu) [Q] = Lodging place.

Tambo Tocco [Q] = The origin cave of the Inca.

Taqui [Q] = Dance.

Tarpuntaes [Q] = Kin group of Cusco that held ritual responsibilities associated with Antisuyu.

Tinku [Q] = A ritual battle between related villages or groups.

Tocco [Q] = Cave, window.

Tocco Cachi (Toto Cache) [Q] = Cave of salt. The area of Cusco now called San Blas.

Topa Amaru [Q] = Last legitimate heir to the Inca crown. He was captured and executed in Cusco under the orders of Viceroy Toledo in 1572.

Topa Inca [Q] = The tenth king of Cusco and the younger son of Pachacuti Inca Yupanqui.

Tullumayo [Q] = Bone river.

Tumi Bamba Panaca [Q] = Descendants of Huayna Capac, the eleventh king of Cusco.

Urco [Q] = Hill.

Uro [Q] = Kin group of Cusco that held ritual responsibilities associated with Chinchaysuyu.

Usca Mayta Panaca [Q] = Descendants of Mayta Capac, the fourth Inca.

Usno (Osno, Usnu, Ushnu) [Q] = A centrally located dais of ritual importance in Inca settlements.

Vara [S] = A Castilian yard, equal to about 85 centimeters.

Vicaquirao [Q] = Descendants of Inca Roca, the sixth Inca.

Vilca [Q] = Sacred.

Viracocha [Q] = *See* Wiraqucha.

Yauri [Q] = A long narrow staff; a large needle.

Yunga [Q] = Lowland, lowlander; applied to both the coast and tropical forest areas of Peru and Bolivia.

Warachikoy (Huarachikcoy) [Q] = A ritual in which the elite young men were recognized as adults. It took place in December.

Wiraqucha (Viracocha) [Q] = Name of the last undisputed Inca king and of the creator god.

Zenith [E] = The point in the sky directly overhead. In tropical regions (between the Tropics of Capricorn and Cancer), the sun will pass through the zenith on two days of the year.

Bibliography

Archival Sources

Archivo General de la Nación, Lima (AGN)

Archivo Agrario, Miscelánea: Hacienda Larapa,
   Venta de 27/1/1616. Otorga: Gerónimo Pastos. A favor: Juan
   Florencio.
Compañía de Jesús, Título de Propiedad, Leg 69.
   Autos hechos a pedimento del Colegio de la Compañía de
   Jesús de ciudad del Cuzco, sobre la donación de Domingo
   Gonzales y posesión de las tierras de Calquiña en el valle de
   Amaybamba [1572].
Derecho Indígena, c. 180, 1698.
   Testimonio hecho en la ciudad del Cuzco, por el Justicia
   Mayor, por comisión particular de los señores de la Real Au-
   diencia de Lima, en el pleito que tiene el Colegio de la San-
   tísima Trinidad de niñas huérfanas, hijas de indios de la ciu-
   dad del Cuzco con los indios que dicen ser del aillo
   Uscamayta y Sutec de la parroquia de Belén de dicha ciudad.
   Sobre las tierras y aguas pertenecientes al dicho colegio y a
   su rectora y maestra sus fundadoras.
Real Audiencia, Causas Civiles: Leg. 6, 1561.
   Venta de censos sobre unas casa, huerta, viña, solares y
   chacaras en el Cuzco. Otorga: Pedro Portocarrero y su mujer
   María de Escobar. A favor de los herederos de Pedro Muñiz
   de Godoy.
Real Hacienda, Tribunal de Cuentas, Composición de tierras de
   indígenas: Leg. 5, 1643–1717.
   Visita y composición de tierras en Zurite, Abancay.
Superior Gobierno: Leg. 2, c. 32, 1613.
   Libro donde se asientan las denuncias de huacas y entierros
   de tesoros y otras cosas mencionándose entre otras cosas las
   siete parroquias del Cuzco.
Superior Gobierno, Causas Ordinarias: Leg. 2, c. 32, f.26, 1613.
   Libro donde se registran las denuncias de guacas y entierros
   de tesoros y otras cosas.
Títulos de Propiedad: Leg. 1, c. 3, 1557.
   Títulos de la hacienda y tierras de Amantuy junto al pueblo
   de Maras Obispado del Cuzco, las mismas que pertenecieron
   a doña Mariana de la Cuba Centano. Por una presentación
   hecha el año de 1555 ante el cabildo del Cuzco por don
   Alonço Loayza, vecino y encomenderos de aquella ciudad,
   consta que aquellas tierras pertenecieron primitivamente a
   Topa Inga Yupanque, y se encontraban abandonadas y
   baldías cuando el dicho Loayza tomó posesión de ellas y
   comenzó a formar la referida hacienda de Amantuy.

Títulos de Propiedad: Leg. 2, c. 50, 1597.
   Títulos de las tierras de Callispuquio, sitas junto a la fortaleza
   de la ciudad del Cuzco, que obtuvo en remate Diego Espinosa
   de Villasante, vecino y regidor de aquella ciudad, quién después remató a Diego Felipe de Medina.
Títulos de Propiedad: Leg. 3, c. 58, 1599.
   Títulos de las tierras de Pilco Puquio, Amaro y otras que
   están en las alturas de la parroquia de San Blas de la ciudad
   del Cuzco y que habiendo pertenecido a Da. Juana Mara-
   chimbo Coya y al Cap. Juan Balsa, vinieron después a ser
   propiedad de los padres de la Compañía de Jesús.
Títulos de Propiedad: Leg. 7, c. 47, 1648.
   Testimonio de la escritura de compra-venta que Don Pedro
   Alonso Carrasco otorgó a favor del Presbítero Don Juan
   Lizaraso, de una tierras con 300 topos más o menos que
   poseía junto a la fortaleza antigua del Cuzco y frente a las
   tierras llamadas Chuquibamba.
Títulos de Propiedad: Leg. 19, c. 387, 1627.
   Títulos de la estancia de Callispuquio jurisdicción de la ciudad del Cuzco.
Títulos de Propiedad: Leg. 34, c. 660, 1620.
   Títulos de las tierras y punas denominadas Picchu, en términos y jurisdicción del Cuzco, que Da. Teresa de Vargas,
   Vda. del Cap. Tomás Vázquez, vecino que fue de aquella ciudad, donó por escritura ínter vivos otorgada el 14 de agosto
   de 1579 al Colegio de la Compañía de Jesús, que a la razón se
   fundaba, en cuya donación comprendieron todas las tierras,
   chacaras, arboledas y punas que integraban aquella propiedad.

Archivo Histórico Departamental (AHD).
(Formerly Archivo Histórico del Cusco [AHC])

Cabildo: Leg. 1, 1569–1605.
   Provisión para que los bienes y haciendas del mayorazgo de
   Don Juan Francisco Maldonado, se arrienden con los pre-
   gones de derecho . . .
Cabildo: Leg. 4, 1640–1645.
   Información sobre posesión de tierras por Juan Fernández,
   como testigo.
Cabildo: Leg. 15, 1708–1715.
   Colegio de la Compañía de Jesús, sobre se de mandamiento
   de ejecución sobre las tierras de Anaypampa, por unos im-
   puestos sobre ellas en favor de dicho colegio.
Cajas de Censos: Leg. 2, 1656–1675.
   Sin carátula, comienza: Yo Don Francisco de Rosas y de Valle
   tesorero del papel sellado desta ciudad . . .

Cajas de Censos: Leg. 4, 1687–1697.
  Sobre las haciendas nombradas Quiachille y Ychubamba que posee el maestro de campo Don Felipe Gutiérrez de Toledo.
Cajas de Censos: Leg. 5, 1707–1708.
  Imposición de censo sobre tierras en Ayllipampa . . .
Cajas de Censos: Leg. 16, 1791–1795.
  Autos ejecutivos seguidos contra las tierras de Ayllipampa.
Cajas de Censos: Leg. 20, 1802–1809.
  Sobre las haciendas, tierras, casas y alfalfar que tengo y poseo que están en los altos de la fortaleza de esta ciudad nombradas Llaullipata, Mascabamba y Sacsahuaman . . .
Colegio Ciencias: Leg. 9, c. 3, 1595.
  Títulos de las tierras de Oscollopampa, a los cofrades de la cofradía de Jesús.
Colegio Ciencias: Leg. 10, c. 6, 1595.
  Documento sobre un trueque de dos topos de tierra entre Sancho de Orozco y Angela de Córdoba en Lirpuypaccha.
Colegio Ciencias: Leg. 10, c. 9, 1601–1624.
  Sin carátula, al margen: Venta de unos terrenos papales de la fortaleza hecha por Melchor Carlos Inga.
Colegio Ciencias: Leg. 10, c. 11, 1601–1624.
  Testamento de Doña Inés Chimbo.
Colegio Ciencias: Leg. 10, c. 18, 1642.
  Testimonio de las escrituras de venta de las casas de Muscapucyo y Pumacchupan y Limacpampa.
Colegio Ciencias: Leg. 10a, c. 83, 1770.
  Sin carátula, comienza: Pedimento (al margen) Señores de la Real Junta de Temporalidades, Don Bernardo Peralta, Teniente de Caballería . . .
Corregimiento, Causas Ordinarias: Leg. 10, c. 15, 1637–1642.
  Autos seguidos por Doña Leonor Costilla Gallinato y Don Jerónimo Costilla su hermano contra los herederos de Pedro Costilla Nocedo.
Corregimiento, Causas Ordinarias: Leg. 14, c. 3, 1654–1656.
  Remate de se hizo a Don Luis Enríquez de Monroy de las haciendas de Colquemachaguay, Puquín y Rocco y casas de la Calle San Agustín y Santa Catalina con sus tiendas, año de 1655.
Corregimiento, Causas Ordinarias: Leg. 14, c. 6, 1654–1656.
  Sin carátula, al margen: Pedimento de los hijos de Mellado para vender las casas y chacras de sus padres.
Corregimiento, Causas Ordinarias: Leg. 16, c. 8, 1657–1663.
  Autos seguidos por Cristóbal Ramos hacendado en el Valle de Oropesa, contra Doña María Arias viuda de Juan de Santiago de la Vaca, por unas punas que están encima del cerro Hurpo, que será como una fanega de tierras en el asiento de Ayavillay.
Corregimiento, Causas Ordinarias: Leg. 16, 1658–1664.
  Sin carátula, al margen: Doña Ana Cusi Mantor contra Antonio Basurto sobre unas casas.
Corregimiento, Causas Ordinarias: Leg. 18, 1671–1673.
  Expediente sobre las tierras de la quebrada de Sorama en la parroquia de San Gerónimo del Cuzco. [Currently missing from the archive.]

Corregimiento, Causas Ordinarias: Leg. 19, c. 15, 1672–1675.
  Autos seguidos por el Protector de Naturales, por lo que toca a Juan Cusi Guaman, cacique principal, y en nombre de los indios de los Ayllus Vicaquirao y Apomayta, reducidos en la parroquia de San Sebastián, sobre la propiedad de 6 topos de tierras nombradas Muchuicuibi, Chimbomarca, Pacaiguaico, Caramasca, Sunchobamba y otros nombres que están en términos de dicha parroquia. [Contiene: repartición y acomodamiento que hizo el Capitán Don Francisco de Loayza, visitador, en los indios del Ayllu Vicaquirao de la encomienda del Capitán Martín de Olmos, reducidos en la parroquia de San Sebastián. Cusco, 5 de marzo de 1640 (1595).]
Corregimiento, Causas Ordinarias: Leg. 23, c. 17, 1684–1686.
  Autos seguidos por Don Diego Sapiro y Don Martín Chayata, caciques principales de los indios Cañares de la parroquia de Santa Ana, contra Don Alonso Ugusicha y Cristóbal Ugusicha su hijo, sobre la posesión de las tierras nombradas Conchapata, Collana, Pocoban, Chullumbuy, Ticatica, Purumpampa y Quescaurco y otros nombres de la parroquia de Santa Ana.
Corregimiento, Causas Ordinarias: Leg. 24, c. 10, 1686–1689.
  Petición que presenta Andrés Quispe, marido y conjunta persona de Juana Sisa, sobre la posesión de las tierras de Añaypampa en la parroquia de San Sebastián, 1687.
Corregimiento, Causas Ordinarias: Leg. 26, c. 8, 1691–1692.
  Autos ordinarios seguidos por los indios de la parroquia de San Jerónimo con Don Guillermo Balladares sobre la propiedad de 18 topos de unas tierras nombradas Oscollopampa y otras en dicha parroquia. [Contiene la posesión de unas tierras que piden los caciques y común de los Ayllus Sucso y Aucaylli reducidos en la parroquia de San Jerónimo y de los Ayllus Señor de Atarpuntay de la parroquia de Señor San Sebastián. También el testimonio de la comisión que tuvo del Señor Licenciado Alonso Maldonado de Torres del Consejo de su Majestad y su Oidor que fue en la Real Audiencia de la ciudad de los Reyes, 1595.]
Corregimiento, Causas Ordinarias: Leg. 27, c. 12, 1693–1699.
  Expediente sobre tierras en la parroquia del Hospital. Autos seguidos por Don Martín Tisoy Sayre Topa ynga, cacique principal y gobernador de la parroquia del Hospital, Don Juan Paucar Tito, cacique de dicha parroquia, Don Ignacio Quispi Curo y Don Diego Chuque Consa Ynquiltopay y por los demás indios de ellos, sobre la propiedad de unos solares y tierras nombradas Gualpancaguase, Champacocha, Puquin huque.
Corregimiento, Causas Ordinarias: Leg. 28, c. 20, 1700–1711.
  Autos seguidos por Don Jerónimo Cusirimache Luna, cacique principal de la parroquia de San Jerónimo y en nombre del común de indios de los Ayllus Sucso Aucaylli, contra Don Lucas Orcoguaranca cacique que fue del dicho Ayllu Aucaylli, por la posesión de las tierras nombradas Puma Urco.
Corregimiento, Causas Ordinarias: Leg. 32, c. 2, 1735–1739.
  Autos seguidos por Don Felipe Cusiguaman, principal de la

parroquia del Hospital de los Naturales, contra Don Matías Villegas, por cobro de pesos por la venta de unas casas que están en el barrio de Matará.

Corregimiento, Causas Ordinarias: Leg. 51, c. 6, 1769–1770.
Autos seguidos por Doña Juana Uglucama viuda, cacique y gobernadora de los ayllus Chachapoyas y Yanaconas, reducidos en la parroquia de Santa Ana, sobre restitución de una capilla en que se celebraba la fiesta del patrón de dichos ayllus San Francisco Javier y se enseña a los párvulos la Doctrina Cristiana, que fue arruinada por omisión de su antecesor Don Pablo Soria Condorpusa para que la reedifique a sus costas.

Corregimiento, Causas Ordinarias: Leg. 53, c. 3, 1771–1772.
Autos seguidos por Don Gregorio Alvaro, y Don Pedro Samata, caciques ambos del Ayllu Tupa Yupanqui, parroquia del Hospital, y en nombre del común de indios, contra Bartolomé de Araujo, dueño de la hacienda nombrada Sarzuela, los indios del Ayllu Cachona de la parroquia de Santiago, entre otros; sobre el derecho a la acequia y aguas de Pacpachiri.

Corregimiento, Causas Ordinarias: Leg. 55, c. 17, 1773–1774.
Autos sobre la presentación de los títulos pertenecientes a las tierras nombradas Tamburque, Moyo Urco, sitas en la parroquia de Belén y de otros 3 topos de tierras en la parroquia de San Sebastián propias de Don José Aucapuri Quispe Ynga y de sus autores según califican los instrumentos.

Corregimiento, Pedimentos: Leg. 82, 1600–1669.
Sin carátula, comienza: Don Francisco Chillitupa, principal de la parroquia de San Sebastián, como legítimo de María Paucar Ocllo . . .

Corregimiento, Pedimentos: Leg. 82, 1600–1669a.
Sin carátula, comienza: Catalina Tocto, viuda de Antón Gaquiva y Juana Tocto . . .

Corregimiento, Pedimentos: Leg. 82, 1600–1669b.
Ordinaria el común de los indios de la parroquia de Santa Anade los Cañares, contra Don Diego Sapiru y otros, sobre las tierras de Tica Tica y otros nombres (al margen).

Corregimiento, Pedimentos: Leg. 82, 1600–1669c.
Sin carátula, comienza: Juan Cuollo de Herrera, en nombre de Juan de Bejar Marido de (. . .) Leonarda de Sanabria . . .

Corregimiento, Pedimentos: Leg. 85, 1753–1765.
Sin carátula, comienza: Don Tomás Chara, hijo legítimo de Diego Chara y de Da. Lorenza Suta aza [sic] . . .

Intendencia, Real Hacienda: Leg. 177, 1786–1787.
Expediente formado por el cacique Don Rafael Amau para que se declaren a sus ayllus de Nobles Pumamarca y Ayarmaca reducidos a la parroquia de San Sebastián . . .

Justiciales Civiles: Leg. 10, 1825.
Repartición de tierras de San Sebastián.

Justiciales Civiles: Leg. 15, 1830.
Demanda sobre despojo e injurias de Don Juan Guallpa, al subdelegado Don Agustín Rosel.

Justiciales Civiles: Leg. 73, 1851.
Instrumento del Señor Campero.

Libro de Cabildos del Cuzco, 1559–1560: f. 63v, cited by Rowe 1981a: 213.

Protocolos Notariales, Cerbantes, Pedro: Prot. 3, 1580–1582.
Concierto: al margen dice: entre los indios de San Sebastián y San Jerónimo. En la parroquia de Sr. de San Jerónimo a 16 días del mes de febrero de 1584, Don García Atao Yupanqui cacique principal de la dicha parroquia. Don Jerónimo Tito Topa, Don Cristóbal Cusiguaman, Don Francisco Guaman Rimachi, Don Diego Quispi, Don Juan Tito Topa, Don Felipe Cusi Rimache cacique de Yanaconas . . .

Protocolos Notariales, Domingo de Oro: Prot. 249, f. 245v, 1622.
Venta, Otorga: Miguel Matupi indio natural de la parroquia del Hospital Yanacona de la Compañía de Jesús. A favor de: Pantaleón Guamán Cusi del Pueblo de Oropesa.

Protocolos Notariales, Domingo de Oro: Prot. 253, f. 1489, 1625.
Venta, Otorga: Pedro Hernández indio de la Cofradía de Ntra. Sra. de la Consolación fundada en esta compañía. A favor de: Domingo Camara indio natural de la parroquia de San Blas.

Protocolos Notariales, Domingo de Oro: Prot. 255, f. 477, 1627.
Venta, Otorga: Pedro Carrillo de Tomani. A favor de: Luisa Pasña india natural de esta ciudad viuda de Domingo Poma indio sastre.

Protocolos Notariales, Domingo de Oro: Prot. 257, f. 680, 1629.
Venta. Otorga: María Sisa india viuda de Don Diego Inga Yupanqui. A favor de: Pedro Jiménez.

Protocolos Notariales, Beltrán Lucero Alonso: Prot. 3, f. 347, 1634.
Venta. Otorga: Pedro Atau Poma natural del pueblo de San Agustín de Cotabambas y Paula Suyo su mujer panaderos residentes en esta ciudad. A favor de: Bernabé Quispe y Catalina Pacha su mujer.

Protocolos Notariales, Solano, Hernando: Prot. 303, 1674–1676.
Fundación del recogimiento de las muchachas huérfanas de la Santísima Trinidad del Cuzco y de la Capellanía de Patronazgo.

Protocolos Notariales, Varios escribanos, 1683–1720 [Moreno, Antonio, Notario #313, f. 889].
Don Lorenzo Pomacatunque Sairetopa natural de la parroquia de San Cristóbal desta ciudad del ayllo libre (sic) vende al capitán Juan Ximeñez Pilares vecino desta dicha ciudad . . . un topo de tierra de sembrar máis y otra legumbres que tiene y posee en el asiento de Cachona nombrado sicuy, que el pertenece desta manera.

Archivos del Ministerio de Agricultura del Cusco (AMAC)

Community Files

File for Collana Chahuancusco.
File for San Jerónimo.

Fundo Files

File for Carhis.
File for Larapa.
File for Lirca y Andamachay.

File for San Jerónimo.

Biblioteca Nacional, Lima (BN)

Virreynato, Bienes, B405, 1669.
Testimonio del expediente sobre la composición de tierras y estancias efectuadas entre el oidir Lic. Alonso de Torres Maldonado en nombre de su majestad y Miguel Merino de Lezana adjuntase algunas composición de tierras situadas en Andahuaylas. Incompleto.

Virreynato, Cacicazgo, B561, 1685.
Expediente sobre la petición presentada por Melchor Pacheco, Procurador de Naturales en nombre de Gabriel Túpac Yupanqui, cacique Principal y Gobernador de la parroquia de San Blas a fin de que se le restituyan unas tierras de las que ha sido despojado.

Virreynato, Real Audiencia, Asuntos Judiciales, B701, 1666.
Expediente sobre la petición presentada por Francisco Roldán para que se le ampare en la posesión de unas tierras de su propiedad.

Private Archives (PA)

Bauer, Brian S.
Chocco Document [1555–1591].

Chávez Ballón, Manuel
Document 1 [1972]: Various records of land sales near Hacienda Pumamarca in 1897, 1908, 1938, 1940, 1941, 1943 and 1972.

Document 2 [1971]: Various records of land sales near Hacienda Pumamarca in 1677, 1678, and 1842.

Document 3 [1613]: La causa seguida entre el convento de nuestra señora de las Mercedes, el cacique, gobernador e indios de las parroquias de nuestra señora de Belén i Santiago sobre las tierras de Cachona i otros nombres.

Printed Sources

Academia Mayor de la Lengua Quechua (cited as AMLQ)
1995   *Diccionario Quechua-Español-Quechua/Qheswa-Español-Qheswa Simi Taqe.* Municipalidad del Qosqo, Qosqo.

Acosta, José de
1954a   *De procurinda indorum salute, o Predicación del evangelio en las Indias* [1580]. In *Obras del P. José de Acosta de la Compañía de Jesús,* ed. P. Francisco Mateos. Biblioteca de Autores Españoles (continuación), vol. 73, 390–608. Madrid: Ediciones Atlas.

1954b   *Historia natural y moral de las Indias* [1590]. In *Obras del P. José de Acosta de la Compañía de Jesús,* ed. P. Francisco Mateos. Biblioteca de Autores Españoles (continuación), vol. 73, 3–247. Madrid: Ediciones Atlas.

Aguilar, Romualdo
1913   Huanacauri o Huaynacauri? *Revista Universitaria* 6:39–45. Cusco: Universidad San Antonio Abad del Cusco.

Agurto Calvo, Santiago
1980   *Cusco: Al traza urbana de la ciudad Inca.* Cusco: UNESCO, Instituto Nacional de Cultura del Perú.

1987   *Estudios acerca de la construcción, arquitectura y planeamiento Incas.* Lima: Cámara Peruana de la Construcción.

Albó, Javier
1972   Dinámica en la estructura inter-comunitaria de Jesús de Machaca. *América Indígena* 32(2):773–816.

Albornoz, Cristóbal de
1968   Instrucción para descubrir todas las guacas del Pirú y sus camayos y haziendas [ca. 1582], ed. Pierre Duviols. *Journal de la Société des Américanistes* 56:17–39.

1984   Instrucción para descubrir todas las guacas del Pirú y sus camayos y haziendas [ca. 1582]. In "Albornoz y el espacio ritual andino prehispánico," ed. Pierre Duviols. *Revista Andina* 2(1):169–222.

1989   Instrucción para descubrir todas las guacas del Pirú y sus camayos y haziendas [ca. 1582]. In *Fábulas y mitos de los Incas,* ed. Henrique Urbano and Pierre Duviols, 162–198. Crónicas de América series. Madrid: Historia 16.

Anders, Martha B.
1986a   *Dual organization and calendars inferred from the planned site of Azángaro.* Ann Arbor, Mich.: University Microfilms.

1986b   Wari experiments in statecraft: A view from Azángaro. In *Andean archaeology: Papers in memory of Clifford Evans,* ed. Ramiro Matos Mendieta, Solveig A. Turpin, and Herbert H. Eling, Jr. Monograph 27, 201–224. Los Angeles: Institute of Archaeology, University of California at Los Angeles.

Anonymous Chronicler
1906   Discurso de la sucesión y gobierno de los yngas [ca. 1570]. In *Juicio de límites entre el Perú y Bolivia; Prueba peruana presentada al gobierno de la República Argentina,* ed. Víctor M. Maúrtua, vol. 8, 149–165. Madrid: Tipografía de los Hijos de M. G. Hernández.

***Antigüedades del Perú* [1590].**
1992   In *Relación de las costumbres antiguas de los naturales del Piru,* ed. Henrique Urbano and Ana Sánchez. Crónicas de América series. Madrid: Historia 16.

Ardiles Nieves, Percy E.
1986   Sistema de drenaje subterráneo prehispánico. *Allpanchis* 18(27):75–97.

Arguedas, José María
1973   *Todas las sangres.* Buenos Aires: Losada.

Arriaga, Pablo José de
1968a   *La extirpación de la idolatría del Pirú* [1621]. In *Crónicas peruanas de interés indígena,* ed. Francisco Esteve Barba. Biblioteca de Autores Españoles (continuación), vol. 209, 191–277. Madrid: Ediciones Atlas.

1968b   *The extirpation of idolatry in Peru* [1621]. Translated and edited by L. Clark Keating. Lexington: University of Kentucky Press.

Arte y vocabulario en la lengua general del Perú llamada Quichua y en la lengua española [1586].
1951   Lima: Antonio Ricardo. Facsimile edition, Publicaciones del Cuarto Centenario. Lima: Facultad de Letras, Instituto de Historia, Universidad Nacional Mayor de San Marcos.

Aveni, Anthony F.

1980 *Skywatchers of ancient Mexico.* Austin: University of Texas Press.

1981a Horizon astronomy in Incaic Cuzco. In *Archaeoastronomy in the Americas,* ed. R. A. Williamson, 305–318. Los Altos, Calif.: Ballena Press.

1981b Comment. *Latin American Research Review* 16(3):163–166.

1987 On seeing the light (a reply to "Here comes the sun" by D. Dearborn and K. Schreiber). *Archaeoastronomy* 10:22–24.

Aveni, Anthony F., ed.

1990a *The Lines of Nazca.* Philadelphia: The American Philosophical Society.

1990b An assessment of previous studies of the Nazca Lines. In *The Lines of Nazca,* 1–40. Philadelphia: The American Philosophical Society.

1990c Order of the Nazca Lines. In *The Lines of Nazca,* 41–113. Philadelphia: The American Philosophical Society.

Aveni, Anthony F., and Helaine Silverman

1991 Between the lines: Reading the Nazca markings as rituals writ large. *The Sciences* (The New York Academy of Science, New York City) 31(4):36–42.

Azevedo, Paulo O. D. de

1982 *Cusco ciudad histórica: Continuidad y cambio.* Lima: Ediciones PEISA.

Bandelier, Adolph F. A.

1910 *The islands of Titicaca and Koati.* New York: The Hispanic Society of America.

Barthel, Thomas S.

1959 Ein Frühlingsfest der Atacameños. In *Zeitschrift für Ethnologie* 84:25–45.

Bauer, Brian S.

1991 Pacariqtambo and the mythical origins of the Inca. *Latin American Antiquity* 2(1):7–26.

1992a Ritual pathways of the Inca: An analysis of the Collasuyu ceques in Cuzco. *Latin American Antiquity* 3(3):183–205.

1992b *The development of the Inca state.* Austin: The University of Texas Press.

1992c Caminos rituales de los Incas: Un análisis de los ceques del Collasuyu (Cuzco). In *Avances en arqueología andina,* ed. Brian S. Bauer, 15–40. Cusco: Centro de Estudios Rurales Andinos "Bartolomé de las Casas."

1996 The legitimization of the Inca state in myth and ritual. *American Anthropologist* 98(2):327–337.

Bauer, Brian S., and Wilton Barrionuevo Orosco

1998 Reconstructing Andean shrine systems: A test case from the Xaquixaguana (Anta) region of Cusco, Peru. *Andean Past* Vol. 5.

Bauer, Brian S., and David S. P. Dearborn

1995 *Astronomy and empire in the ancient Andes.* Austin: The University of Texas Press.

Beorchia Nigris, Antonio

1973 La arqueología de Alta Montaña en la prov. de San Juan, y su relación con los yacimientos de altura de la cordillera de los Andes. *Revista del Centro de Investigaciones Arqueológicos de Alta Montaña* (San Juan, Argentina) 1:5–48.

1978 Análisis comparativo, descripción de los santuarios de altura y conclusiones provisorias en base a los antecedentes conocidos hasta junio de 1978. *Revista del Centro de Investigaciones Arqueológicos de Alta Montaña* (San Juan, Argentina) 3:11–16.

1987 El enigma de los santuarios indígenas de Alta Montaña. Centro de Investigaciones Arqueológicas de Alta Montaña. *Revista del Centro de Investigaciones Arqueológicos de Alta Montaña* (San Juan, Argentina) vol. 5 [1985].

Betanzos, Juan de

1987 *Suma y narración de los Incas* [1557], ed. María del Carmen Martín Rubio. Madrid: Ediciones Atlas.

1996 *Narrative of the Incas* [1557], trans. and ed. Roland Hamilton and Dana Buchanan. Austin: University of Texas Press.

Beyersdorff, Margot

1992 Ritual gesture to poetic text in the Christianization of the Andes. *Journal of Latin American Lore* 18(2):125–161.

1997 *Historia y drama ritual en los Andes bolivianos, siglos XVI–XX.* La Paz: Plural.

Bingham, Hiram

1922 *Inca land: Explorations in the highlands of Peru.* Cambridge, Mass.: Riverside Press.

Cabello de Balboa, Miguel

1951 *Miscelánea antártica, una historia del Perú antiguo* [1586], ed. L. E. Valcárcel. Lima: Universidad Nacional Mayor de San Marcos, Instituto de Etnología.

Calancha, Antonio de la

1981 *Corónica moralizada del Orden de San Agustín en el Perú* [1638], ed. Ignacio Prado Pastor. Lima: Universidad Nacional Mayor de San Marcos, Editorial de la Universidad.

Callapiña, Supno, and other Quipucamayos (cited as Callapiña et al.)

1974 *Relación de la descendencia, gobierno y conquista de los Incas* [1542/1608], ed. Juan José Vega. Lima: Ediciones de la Biblioteca Universitaria.

Céspedes Paz, Ricardo

1982 La arqueología del área Pocona. Cuadernos de Investigación, Serie Arqueología, no. 1, 89–99. Cochabamba, Bolivia: Instituto de Investigaciones Antropológicas, Museo Arqueológico, Universidad Mayor de San Simón.

Chávez Ballón, Manuel

1970 Ciudades incas: Cuzco, capital del imperio. *Wayka* 3:1–15.

Cieza de León, Pedro de

1976 *The Incas of Pedro Cieza de León* [Part 1, 1553, and Part 2, 1554]. Translated by Harriet de Onís and edited by Victor W. von Hagen. Norman: University of Oklahoma Press.

1984 *Crónica del Perú: Primera parte* [1553]. Introduction by Franklin Pease G. Y. and notes by Miguel Maticorena E. Lima: Academia Nacional de la Historia and Pontificia Universidad Católica del Perú.

1985 *Crónica del Perú: Segunda parte* [1554]. Introduction by Franklin Pease G. Y. and notes by Miguel Maticorena E. Lima: Academia Nacional de la Historia and Pontificia Universidad Católica del Perú.

Clarkson, Persis B.

1990 The archaeology of the Nazca Pampa: Environmental and cultural parameters. In *The Lines of Nazca,* ed. Anthony F. Aveni, 117–172. Philadelphia: The American Philosophical Society.

Cobo, Bernabé

1956 *Historia del Nuevo Mundo* [1653]. In *Obras del P. Bernabé Cobo de la Compañía de Jesús,* ed. P. Francisco Mateos. Biblioteca de Autores Españoles (continuación), vols. 91 and 92. Madrid: Ediciones Atlas.

1964 *Historia del Nuevo Mundo* [1653]. In *Obras del P. Bernabé Cobo de la Compañía de Jesús,* ed. P. Francisco Mateos. Biblioteca de Autores Españoles (continuación), vols. 91 and 92. Madrid: Ediciones Atlas.

1979 *History of the Inca Empire: An account of the Indians' customs and their origin together with a treatise on Inca legends, history, and social institutions* [1653]. Translated and edited by Roland Hamilton. Austin: University of Texas Press.

1980 Relación de las guacas del Cuzco [1653]. In "An account of the shrines of ancient Cuzco." Translated and edited by John H. Rowe. *Ñawpa Pacha* 17(1979):2–80.

1981 Relación de las guacas del Cuzco [1653]. In "Una relación de los adoratorios del antiguo Cuzco." Introduction by John H. Rowe. *Histórica* 5(2):209–261.

1990 *Inca religion and customs* [1653]. Translated and edited by Roland Hamilton. Austin: University of Texas Press.

Córdoba Mexía, Pedro de

1900 Instrucción de lo que ha de hacer el Licenciado Pedro Mexía, clérigo presbítero de la Compañía de Jesús en la visita general que el muy Excmo. Señor Don Francisco de Toledo, Virrey de estos reynos, . . . [ca. 1572]. *Revista de Archivos y Bibliotecas Nacionales* 3(4):387–404.

1925 Información hecha en el Cuzco, por orden del Rey y encargo del Virrey Martín Enríquez acerca de las costumbres que tenían los Incas del Perú, antes de la conquista española, en la manera de administrar justicia civil y criminal . . . [1582]. In *Gobernantes del Perú: Cartas y papeles, siglo XVI, Documentos del Archivo de Indias,* ed. D. Roberto Levillier, vol. 9, 268–288. Colección de Publicaciones Históricas de la Biblioteca del Congreso Argentino. Madrid: Imprenta de Juan Pueyo.

Cornejo Bouroncle, Jorge de

1957 Tierras de la fortaleza. *Revista del Archivo Histórico del Cuzco* 8:199–202.

Cusihuamán Gutiérrez, Antonio

1976 *Diccionario Quechua: Cuzco-Collao.* Lima: Ministerio de Educación, Instituto de Estudios Peruanos.

Dearborn, David S. P.

1987 Blinded by the light (a reply to "On seeing the light" by A. Aveni). *Archaeoastronomy* 10:24–27.

Dearborn, David S. P., and Katharina J. Schreiber

1986 Here comes the sun: The Cuzco-Machu Picchu connection. *Archaeoastronomy* 9:15–37.

1989 Houses of the rising sun. In *Time and calendars in the Inca Empire,* ed. M. S. Ziólkowski and R. M. Sadowski, 49–75. BAR International Series 454. Oxford: British Archaeological Reports.

Dearborn, David S. P., and Raymond E. White

1983 The "torreón" at Machu Picchu as an observatory. *Archaeoastronomy* (A supplement to the *Journal for the History of Astronomy*) 5:S37–S49.

Dearborn, David S. P., Katharina J. Schreiber, and Raymond E. White

1987 Intimachay, a December solstice observatory. *American Antiquity* 52:346–352.

Domingo de Santo Tomás

1951 *Lexicón, o vocabulario de la lengua general del Perú* [1560]. Facsimile edition. Lima: Instituto de Historia, Universidad Nacional Mayor de San Marcos.

1995 *Gramática o arte de la lengua general de los indios de los reynos del Peru.* Cusco: Centro de Estudios Rurales Andinos "Bartolomé de las Casas."

Dorn, Ronald I., Persis B. Clarkson, Margaret F. Nobbs, Lawrence L. Loendorf, and D. S. Whitley

1992 New approach to the radiocarbon dating of rock varnish, with examples from drylands. *Annals of the Association of American Geographers* 82(1):136–151.

Duviols, Pierre

1968 Un inédit de Cristóbal de Albornoz: Instrucción para descubrir todas las guacas del Pirú y sus camayos y haziendas [c. 1582]. *Journal de la Société des Américanistes* 56(1):7–39.

1984 Instrucción para descubrir todas las guacas del Pirú y sus camayos y haziendas [c. 1582]. In "Albornoz y el espacio ritual andino prehispánico." *Revista Andina* 2(1):169–222.

1986 *Cultura andina y represión: Procesos y visitas de idolatrías y hechicerías Cajatambo, siglo XVII.* Archivos de Historia Andina Rural 5. Cusco: Centro de Estudios Rurales Andinos "Bartolomé de las Casas."

Dwyer, Edward Bridgman

1971 The early Inca occupation of the Valley of Cuzco, Peru. Ph.D. diss., Department of Anthropology, University of California, Berkeley.

Espinoza Galarza, Max

1973 *Topónimos Quechuas del Perú.* Lima: Comercial Santa Elena.

Esquivel y Navía, Diego de

1980 *Noticias cronológicas de la gran ciudad del Cuzco* [1749]. Edición, prólogo y notas de Félix Denegri Luna con la colaboración de Horacio Villanueva Urteaga y Cesar Gutiérrez Muñoz, vols. 1 and 2. Lima: Fundación Augusto N. Wiese, Banco Wiese Ltdo.

Farrington, Ian S.

1992 Ritual geography, settlement patterns and the characterization of the provinces of the Inka heartland. *World Archaeology* 23(3):368–385.

Fernández, Diego ("El Palentino")

1876 *Primera y segunda parte de la historia del Perú* [1571]. Documentos Literarios del Perú, vols. 8 and 9. Lima: Imprenta del Estado.

1963 *Primera y segunda parte de la historia del Perú* [1571]. In *Crónicas del Perú*, ed. Juan Pérez de Tudela Bueso. Biblioteca de Autores Españoles (continuación), vols. 164 and 165. Madrid: Ediciones Atlas.

Garcilaso de la Vega, Inca

1945 *Comentarios reales de los Incas* [1609]. 2d ed. Notes by Ricardo Rojas. Buenos Aires: Emecé Editores.

1966 *Royal commentaries of the Incas and general history of Peru, Parts 1 and 2* [1609]. Translated by H. V. Livermore. Austin: University of Texas Press.

Gasparini, Graziano, and Luise Margolies

1980 *Inca architecture.* Translated by P. J. Lyon. Bloomington: Indiana University Press.

González Holguín, Diego

1901 *Arte y diccionario qquechua-español, cor. y aumentado por los RR. PP. Redentoristas al que en 1608 publicó el Rvdo. P. Diego González de Holguín S. J. en esta Ciudad de los Reyes.* Lima: Imprenta del Estado.

1989 *Vocabulario de la lengua general de todo el Perú llamada lengua Qquichua o del Inca* [1608]. Presentación de Ramiro Matos Mendieta. Prólogo de Raúl Porras Barrenechea. Lima: Universidad Nacional Mayor de San Marcos, Editorial de la Universidad.

Gorbak, Celina, Martha Lischetti, and Carmen Muñoz

1962 Batallas rituales de Chiaraje y del Tocto de la Provincia de Kanas (Cuzco–Perú). *Revista del Museo Nacional* (Lima) 31:245–304.

Gose, Peter

1996 The past is a lower moiety: Diarchy, history and divine kingship in the Inka Empire. *History and Anthropology* 9(4):383–414.

Guaman Poma de Ayala, Felipe

1980 *El primer nueva corónica y buen gobierno* [1615], ed. J. V. Murra, R. Adorno, and Jorge I. Urioste. 3 vols. Mexico City: Siglo Veintiuno.

Guevara Gil, Jorge A.

1993 *Propiedad agraria y derecho colonial: Los documentos de la Hacienda Santotis Cuzco (1543–1822).* Lima: Pontificia Universidad Católica del Perú, Fondo Editorial.

Guibovich Pérez, Pedro M.

1990 Nota preliminar al personaje histórico y los documentos. In *El retorno de las huacas: Estudios y documentos sobre el Taki Onqoy siglo XVI,* comp. Luis Millones, 23–40. Lima: Instituto de Estudios Peruanos.

Gutiérrez, Ramón, Paulo de Azevedo, Graciela M. Viñuelas, Esterzilda de Azevedo, and Rodolfo Vallin

1981 *La casa cusqueña.* Resistencia, Argentina: Departamento de Historia de la Arquitectura, Universidad Nacional del Noreste.

Gutiérrez de Santa Clara, Pedro

1963 *Historia de las guerras civiles del Perú y de otros sucesos de las Indias* [ca. 1600]. Biblioteca de Autores Españoles, (continuación), vols. 165–167. Madrid: Ediciones Atlas.

Hadingham, Evan

1987 *Lines to the Mountain Gods: Nazca and the mysteries of Peru.* Norman: University of Oklahoma Press.

Hemming, John

1970 *The conquest of the Incas.* New York: Harcourt Brace Jovanovich Press.

Hernández Príncipe, Rodrigo

1986 Visitas de Rodrigo Hernández Príncipe [1621]. In *Cultura andina y represión: Procesos y visitas de idolatrías y hechicerías Cajatambo, siglo XVII,* ed. and transcribed by Pierre Duviols, 461–482. Cusco: Centro de Estudios Rurales Andinos "Bartolomé de las Casas."

Heyerdahl, Thor, Daniel H. Sandweiss, and Alfredo Narváez

1995 *Pyramids of Tucumé: The quest for Peru's forgotten city.* New York: Thames and Hudson.

Hopkins, Diane

1982 Juego de enemigos. *Allpanchis* (Cusco) 17(20):167–187.

Hyslop, John

1985 *Inkawasi: The new Cusco.* BAR International Series 234. Oxford: British Archaeological Reports.

1990 *Inka settlement planning.* Austin: University of Texas Press.

Kirchhoff, Paul

1949 The social and political organization of the Andean peoples. In *Handbook of South American Indians,* vol. 5, *The comparative ethnology of South American Indians,* ed. Julian Steward. Bureau of American Ethnology Bulletin 143, 293–311. Washington, D.C.: U.S. Government Printing Office.

Kosok, Paul

1965 *Life, land and water in ancient Peru.* Brooklyn, N.Y.: Long Island University Press.

La Barre, Weston

1947 The Uru-Chipaya. In *Handbook of South American Indians,* vol. 2, *The Andean civilizations,* ed. Julian Steward. Bureau of American Ethnology Bulletin 143, 575–585. Washington, D.C.: U.S. Government Printing Office.

La Lone, Mary Burkheimer

1985 Indian land tenure in southern Cuzco, Peru: From Inca to colonial patterns. Ann Arbor, Mich.: University Microfilms.

Lara, Jesús

1978 *Diccionario Quechua.* Cochabama, Bolivia: Los Amigos del Libro.

Lehmann-Nitsche, Robert

1928 Coricancha: El Templo del Sol en el Cuzco y las imágenes de su altar mayor. *Revista del Museo de La Plata* 31:1–256.

Lira, Jorge A.

1944 *Diccionario Kkechuwa-Español.* Tucumán, Argentina: Universidad Nacional de Tucumán.

1982 *Diccionario Kkechuwa-Español.* 2d ed. Cuadernos Culturales Andinos No. 5. Bogotá, Colombia: Secretaría Ejecutiva del Convenio "Andrés Bello," Instituto Internacional de Integración, and Instituto Andino de Artes Populares.

Lizárraga, Reginaldo de

1909 *Descripción breve de toda la tierra del Perú, Tucumán, Río de Plata y Chile* [1605], ed. M. Serrano y Sanz. Historiadores de Indias, vol. 2. Nueva Biblioteca de Autores Españoles, vol. 15, 485–660. Madrid: Bailly Bailliére e hijos.

Loarte, Gabriel de

1882 Información hecha en el Cuzco a 4 de enero de 1572. In *Informaciones acerca del señorío y gobierno de los Incas hechas por mandado de Don Francisco de Toledo, Virrey del Perú (1570–1572).* Colección de Libros Españoles Raros ó Curiosos, ed. Marcos Jiménez de la Espada, vol. 16, 223–243. Madrid: Imprenta de Miguel Ginesta.

López de Velasco, Juan

1894 *Geografía y descripción universal de las Indias, desde el año 1571 al de 1574,* ed. Justo Zaragoza. Madrid: Real Academia de la Historia.

MacCormack, Sabine

1991 *Religion in the Andes: Vision and imagination in early colonial Peru.* Princeton: Princeton University Press.

Macera, Pablo

1968 *Mapas coloniales de haciendas cuzqueñas.* Lima: Universidad Nacional Mayor de San Marcos, Seminario de Historia Rural Andina.

Matienzo, Juan de

1967 *Gobierno del Perú* [1567], ed. Guillermo Lohmann Villena. Lima: L'Institut français d'études andines.

McEwan, Colin, and Maarten Van de Guchte

1992 Ancestral time and sacred space in Inca state ritual. In *The ancient Americas: Art from sacred landscapes,* ed. Richard F. Townsend, 359–371. Chicago: The Art Institute of Chicago.

Means, Philip Ainsworth

1925 *A study of ancient Andean social institutions.* Transactions of the Connecticut Academy of Arts and Sciences 27, 407–469. New Haven: Connecticut Academy of Arts and Sciences.

1928 *Biblioteca Andina: The chroniclers, or, the writers of the sixteenth and seventeenth centuries who treated of the pre-Hispanic history and culture of the Andean countries.* Transactions of the Connecticut Academy of Arts and Sciences 29, 271–525. New Haven: Connecticut Academy of Arts and Sciences.

Mejía Xesspe, Toribio

1940 Acueductos y caminos antiguos de la Hoya del Río Grande de Nazca [1927]. In *Actas y Trabajos Científicos,* vol. 1, 559–569. Lima: 27th Congreso Internacional de Americanistas.

Métraux, Alfred

1935 Les Indiens Uro-Cipaya de Carangas. *Journal de la Société des Américanistes* (Paris) 27:325–415.

Mexía, Pedro. *See* Córdoba Mexía, Pedro de.

Millones, Luis

1973 Un movimiento nativista del siglo XVI: El Taki Onqoy. In *Ideología mesiánica del mundo andino,* ed. Juan A. Ossio M., 83–94. Lima: Edición de Ignacio Prado Pastor.

Millones, Luis, comp.

1990 *El retorno de las huacas: Estudios y documentos sobre el Taki Onqoy siglo XVI.* Lima: Instituto de Estudios Peruanos.

Molina (el Cusqueño), Cristóbal de

1943 Relación de las fábulas y ritos de los Incas [1575]. In *Las crónicas de los Molinas,* ed. Carlos A. Romero, Raúl Porras Barrenechea, and Francisco A. Loayza. Los Pequeños Grandes Libros de Historia Americana, 1st ser., vol. 4. Lima: Imprenta D. Miranda.

1989 Relación de las fábulas i ritos de los Ingas . . . [ca. 1575]. In *Fábulas y mitos de los Incas,* ed. Henrique Urbano and Pierre Duviols, 47–134. Crónicas de América series. Madrid: Historia 16.

Montesinos, Fernando de

1882 *Memorias antiguas historiales y políticas del Perú* [1630]. Colección de Libros Españoles Raros ó Curiosos, ed. Marcos Jiménez de la Espada, vol. 16. Madrid: Imprenta de Miguel Ginesta.

1920 *Memorias antiguas historiales del Perú* [1630], trans. and ed. Philip Ainsworth Means. Introduction by Clements R. Markham. Hakluyt Society Publications, 2d ser., vol. 48. London: The Hakluyt Society.

Morris, Craig

1990 Arquitectura y estructura del espacio en Huánuco Pampa. *Cuadernos* 12:27–45. Buenos Aires: Instituto Nacional de Antropología.

Morris, Craig, and Donald E. Thompson

1985 *Huánuco Pampa: An Inca city and its hinterland.* London: Thames and Hudson.

Morrison, Tony

1978 Pathways of the gods: The mystery of the Andes lines. New York: Harper and Row.

Morúa, Martín de. *See* Murúa, Martín de.

Moscoso, J. Maximiliano

1950 Los ayllus reales de San Sebastián. *Revista Universitaria* 99:151–170.

Müller, Rolf

1972 *Sonne, Mond und Sterne über dem Reich der Inka.* Verständliche Wissenschaft Bd. 110, Naturwissenschaftliche Abteilung. Berlin: Springer Verlag.

Murúa, Martín de

1946   *Historia del origen y genealogía real de los reyes Inças del Perú* [1590]. Introduction and notes by Constantino Bayle. Biblioteca "Missionalia Hispánica," vol. 2. Madrid: Instituto Santo Toribio de Mogrovejo. (Loyola Manuscript).

1987   *Historia general del Perú* [ca. 1615], ed. Manuel Ballesteros-Garbrois. Crónicas de América series. Madrid: Historia 16. (Wellington Manuscript).

Niles, Susan A.

1987   *Callachaca: Style and status in an Inca community.* Iowa City: University of Iowa Press.

Oberti Rodríguez, Italo

1982   Exploración arqueológica en Llaullipata Cuzco. In *Arqueología de Cuzco,* comp. Italo Oberti Rodríguez, 41–64. Cusco: Instituto Nacional de Cultura.

Ossio M., Juan A., ed.

1973   *Ideología mesiánica del mundo andino.* Lima: Edición de Ignacio Prado Pastor.

Pachacuti Yamqui Salcamayhua, Juan de Santa Cruz

1950   Relación de antigüedades deste reyno del Perú [ca. 1613]. In *Tres relaciones de antigüedades peruanas,* ed. Marcos Jiménez de la Espada, 207–281. Asunción del Paraguay: Editora Guaranía.

1993   *Relación de antigüedades deste reyno del Piru,* ed. Pierre Duviols and César Itier. Cusco: Centro de Estudios Rurales Andinos "Bartolomé de las Casas."

Pardo, Luis A.

1941   Un hallazgo en la zona arqueológica del Ausangati (Cuzco). *Revista del Museo Nacional* 10(1):110–112.

Paz Soldán, Carlos Enrique

1951   Cuzco, la ciudad herida, un reportaje gráfico. Lima: Imprenta Torres Aguirre.

Paz Soldán, Mariano Felipe

1865   *Atlas Geografía del Perú.* Paris: Librería de Agusto Durand.

Pérez Bocanegra, Juan de

1631   *Ritual formulario e institución de curas para administrar a los naturales de este reyno los santos sacramentos.* Lima: Geronymo de Contreras.

Pizarro, Pedro

1921   *Relation of the discovery and conquest of the kingdoms of Peru* [1571], trans. and ed. Philip Ainsworth Means. New York: The Cortes Society.

1986   *Relación del descubrimiento y conquista de los reinos del Perú* [1571]. Lima: Pontificia Universidad Católica del Perú.

Polo de Ondegardo, Juan

1872   *Relación de los fundamentos acerca del notable daño que resulta de no guardar a los Indios sus fueros* [1571], ed. Horacio H. Urteaga. Colección de Documentos Inéditos . . . de América y Oceanía, vol. 16, 5–177. Madrid: Imprenta del Hospicio.

1916a   *Informaciones acerca de la religión y gobierno de los Incas.* Colección de Libros y Documentos Referentes a la Historia del Perú, ser. 1, vol. 3. Lima: Sanmartí.

1916b   *De los errores y supersticiones de los indios, sacados del tratado y averiguación que hizo el Licenciado Polo* [first published in 1585, researched ca. 1559], ed. Horacio H. Urteaga. In Vol. 3, *Informaciones acerca de la religión y gobierno de los Incas.* Colección de Libros y Documentos Referentes a la Historia del Perú, ser. 1, 3–43. Lima: Sanmartí.

1916c   *Relación de los fundamentos acerca del notable daño que resulta de no guardar a los indios sus fueros* [1571], ed. Horacio H. Urteaga. In Vol. 3, *Informaciones acerca de la religión y gobierno de los Incas.* Colección de Libros y Documentos Referentes a la Historia del Perú, ser. 1, 45–189. Lima: Sanmartí.

1916d   *Instrucción contra las ceremonias y ritos que usan los indios conforme al tiempo de su infidelidad* [1567], ed. Horacio H. Urteaga. In Vol. 3, *Informaciones acerca de la religión y gobierno de los Incas.* Colección de Libros y Documentos Referentes a la Historia del Perú, ser. 1, (Appendix A), 189–204. Lima: Sanmartí.

1916e   *Supersticiones de los indios, sacadas del Segundo Concilio Provincial de Lima* [first published in 1567, researched ca. 1559], ed. Horacio H. Urteaga. In Vol. 3, *Informaciones acerca de la religión y gobierno de los Incas.* Colección de Libros y Documentos Referentes a la Historia del Perú, ser. 1 (Appendix B), 205–208. Lima: Sanmartí.

1917   *Del linaje de los Ingas y como conquistaron,* ed. Horacio H. Urteaga. Colección de Libros y Documentos Referentes a la Historia del Perú, ser. 1, vol. 4, 45–94. Lima: Sanmartí.

1920   Información hecha en el Cusco a 4 de enero de 1572. In *Información sobre el antiguo Perú.* Colección de Libros y Documentos Referentes a la Historia del Perú, ser. 2, vol. 3. Lima: Sanmartí.

1940   Informe del Licenciado Juan Polo de Ondegardo al Licenciado Briviesca de Muñatones sobre la perpetuidad de las encomiendas en el Perú [1561]. *Revista Histórica* 13:125–196.

1965a   On the errors and superstitions of the Indians, taken from the treatise and investigation done by Licentiate Polo. Translated by A. Brunel, John Murra and Sidney Muirden. New Haven, Conn.: Human Relations Area Files.

1965b   On the errors and superstitions of the Indians, taken from the treatise and investigation done by Licentiate Polo [first published in 1585, researched ca. 1559], trans. A. Brunel, John Murra, and Sidney Muirden, 1–53. New Haven, Conn.: Human Relations Area Files.

1965c   A report on the basic principles explaining the serious harm which follows when the traditional rights of the Indians are not respected [1571], trans. A. Brunel, John Murra, and Sidney Muirden, 53–196. New Haven, Conn.: Human Relations Area Files.

1965d   Instruction against the ceremonies and rites that the Indians practice in conformance with the stage of their infidelity [1567], trans. A. Brunel, John Murra, and Sidney Muirden (Appendix A), 196–208. New Haven, Conn.: Human Relations Area Files.

1965e Superstitions of the Indians, taken from the Second Provincial Council of Lima [first published in 1567, researched ca. 1559], trans. A. Brunel, John Murra, and Sidney Muirden (Appendix B), 209–211. New Haven, Conn.: Human Relations Area Files.

Poole, Deborah

1984 *Ritual economic calendars in Paruro: The structure of representation in Andean ethnography.* Ann Arbor, Mich.: University Microfilms.

Porras Barrenechea, Raúl, ed.

1962 *Los cronistas del Perú (1528–1650).* Edición auspiciada por Grace y Cía. Lima: Sanmartí.

Ramírez Valerde, María

1970 Visita a Pocona [1557]. *Historia y Cultura* (Museo Nacional de Historia, Lima) 4:269–308.

Reinhard, Johan

1983 High altitude archaeology and Andean mountain gods. *American Alpine Journal* 25:54–67.

1985a *The Nazca Lines: A new perspective on their origin and meaning.* Lima: Los Pinos.

1985b Sacred mountains: An ethno-archaeological study of high Andean ruins. *Mountain Research and Development* 5(4): 299–317.

1988 The Nazca lines, water and mountains: An ethnoarchaeological study. In *Recent studies in pre-Columbian archaeology,* ed. Nicholas J. Saunders and O. de Montmoll, 363–414. BAR International Series 421. Oxford: British Archaeological Reports.

1992a An archaeological investigation of Inca ceremonial platforms on the volcano Copiapo, central Chile. In *Ancient America: Contributions to New World archaeology,* ed. Nicholas J. Saunders, 145–172. Oxford: Oxbow Books.

1992b Underwater archaeological research in Lake Titicaca, Bolivia. In *Ancient America: Contributions to New World archaeology,* ed. Nicholas J. Saunders, 117–143. Oxford: Oxbow Books.

Ricardo, Antonio

1586 See *Arte y vocabulario en la lengua general del Perú llamada Quichua y en la lengua española* [1586].

Romero, Carlos A., Raúl Porras Barrenechea, and Francisco A. Loayza, eds.

1943 Relación de las fábulas y ritos de los Incas [ca. 1575]. By Cristóbal de Molina (el Cusqueño). In *Las crónicas de los Molinas.* Los Pequeños Grandes Libros de Historia Americana, ser. 1, vol. 4. Lima: Imprenta D. Miranda.

Rostworowski de Diez Canseco, María

1960 Succession, cooption to kingship, and royal incest among the Incas. *Southwestern Journal of Anthropology* 16(4): 417–427.

1962 Nuevos datos sobre tenencia de tierras reales en el Incario. *Revista del Museo Nacional* 31:130–164.

1964 Nuevos aportes para el estudio de la medición de tierras en el Virreynato e Incario. *Revista del Archivo Nacional de Perú* 28:1–31.

1966 Las tierras reales y su mano de obra en el Tahuantinsuyu. XXXVI Congreso Internacional de Americanistas (Sevilla, 1964), *Actas y Memorias* 2:31–34.

1970 Los Ayarmaca. *Revista del Museo Nacional* 36:58–101.

1988 Conflicts over coca fields in XVIth-century Peru. *Memoirs of the Museum of Anthropology.* Studies in Latin American Ethnohistory and Archaeology, Joyce Marcus, General Editor, vol. 4, no. 21. Ann Arbor: University of Michigan.

Rowe, John H.

1944 An introduction to the archaeology of Cuzco. In *Papers of the Peabody Museum of American Archaeology and Ethnology,* vol. 27, no. 2. Cambridge, Mass.: Harvard University.

1946 Inca culture at the time of the Spanish Conquest. In *Handbook of South American Indians,* vol. 2, *The Andean civilizations,* ed. Julian Steward. Bureau of American Ethnology Bulletin 143, 183–330. Washington, D.C.: U.S. Government Printing Office.

1967 What kind of settlement was Inca Cuzco? *Ñawpa Pacha* 5:59–75.

1978 La fecha de la muerte de Wayna Qhapaq. *Histórica* 2(1):83–88.

1979 Archaeoastronomy in Mesoamerica and Peru. *Latin American Research Review* 14(2):227–233.

1980 Relación de las guacas del Cuzco [1653]. In "Account of the shrines of ancient Cuzco," trans. and ed. John H. Rowe. *Ñawpa Pacha* 17(1979):2–80.

1981a Una relación de los adoratorios del antiguo Cuzco. *Histórica* 5(2):209–261.

1981b Reply. *Latin American Research Review* 16(3):171–172.

1985 La constitución Inca del Cuzco. *Histórica* 9(1):35–73.

1986 Probanza de los Incas nietos de conquistadores. *Histórica* 9(2):193–245.

1990 Los monumentos perdidos de la plaza mayor del Cuzco incaico. *Saqsaywaman* 3:81–109.

Salazar, Antonio

1867 Relación sobre el período de gobierno de los virreyes Don Francisco de Toledo y Don García Hurtado de Mendoza [1596]. In *Colección de documentos inéditos relativos al descubrimiento, conquista y organización de las antiguas posesiones españolas de América y Oceanía* 8:212–421. Madrid: Imprenta de Frías y Compañía.

Sallnow, Michael J.

1987 *Pilgrims of the Andes: Regional cults in Cusco.* Washington, D.C.: Smithsonian Institution Press.

1991 Pilgrimage and cultural fracture in the Andes. In *Contesting the sacred: The anthropology of Christian pilgrimage,* ed. John Eade and Michael J. Sallnow, 137–153. London: Routledge.

Santa Cruz Pachacuti Yamqui Salcamayhua, Juan de. *See* Pachacuti Yamqui Salcamayhua, Juan de Santa Cruz.

Santillán, Hernando de

1950 Relación del origen, descendencia política y gobierno de los Incas. . . [ca. 1564]. In *Tres relaciones de antigüedades peruanas,* ed. Marcos Jiménez de la Espada. Asunción del Paraguay: Editorial Guaranía.

Santo Tomás, Domingo de. *See* Domingo de Santo Tomás.

Sarmiento de Gamboa, Pedro

1906 Segunda parte de la historia general llamada Indica . . . [1572]. In *Geschichte des Inkareiches von Pedro Sarmiento de Gamboa,* ed. Richard Pietschmann. Abhandlungen der Königlichen Gesellschaft der Wissenschaften zu Göttingen, Philologisch-Historische Klasse, Neue Folge, vol. 6, no. 4. Berlin: Weidmannsche Buchhandlung.

Schobinger, Juan

1991 Sacrifices of the high Andes. *Natural History* 100(4):62–68.

Segovia, Bartolomé de

1943 Relación de las muchas cosas acaecidas en el Perú . . . [1553]. In *Las crónicas de los Molinas.* Los Pequeños Grandes Libros de Historia Americana, ser. 1, vol. 4, first document, 1–88. Lima: Librería e Imprenta D. Miranda. [Incorrectly attributed to Cristóbal de Molina (el Almargrista)].

Sherbondy, Jeanette

1982 The canal systems of Hanan Cuzco. Ann Arbor, Mich.: University Microfilms.

1986 Los ceques: Código de canales en el Cusco incaico. *Allpanchis* 27:39–73.

1987 Organización hidráulica y poder en el Cuzco de los incas. *Revista Española de Antropología Americana* 17:117–153.

Soukup, Jaroslav

1980 *Vocabulario de los nombres vulgares de la flora peruana y catálogo de géneros.* Lima: Ed. Salesiana.

Squier, E. George

1877 *Peru: Incidents of travel and exploration in the land of Incas.* New York: Harper and Brothers Publishers.

Stern, Steve J.

1982 El Taki Onqoy y la sociedad andina (Huamanga, siglo XVI). *Allpanchis* 16(19):49–77.

Tito Cussi Yupangui, Diego de Castro

1988 Instrucción del Ynga D. Diego de Castro Tito Cussi Yupangui para el muy ilustre señor el Licenciado Lope García de Castro, gobernador que fue destos reinos del Pirú, tocante a los negocios que con su majestad en su nombre por su poder ha de tratar, la cual es estaque se sigue [1570]. In *En el encuentro de dos mundos: Los Incas de Vilcabamba,* ed. María del Carmen Martín Rubio. Madrid: Atlas.

Toledo, Francisco de

1882 *Informaciones acerca del señorío y gobierno de los Ingas hechas por mandado de Don Francisco de Toledo, Virrey del Perú, 1570–1572.* Colección de Libros Españoles Raros ó Curiosos, ed. Marcos Jiménez de la Espada, vol. 16, 223–243. Madrid: Imprenta de Miguel Ginesta. (Also see Loarte, Gabriel de.)

1920 *Informaciones sobre el antiguo Perú* [1572–1575]. Colección de Libros y Documentos Referentes a la Historia del Perú, ser. 2, vol. 3. Lima: Sanmartí.

1924 Carta del Virrey D. Francisco de Toledo a S. M. sobre materias de gobierno, hacienda, guerra y eclesiásticos, en respuesta a cartas del Rey del año anterior [1572]. *Gobernantes del Perú: Cartas y papeles, siglo XVI, Documentos del Archivo de Indias,* ed. D. Roberto Levillier, vol. 4, 380–403. Colección de Publicaciones Históricas de la Biblioteca del Congreso Argentino. Madrid: Imprenta de Juan Pueyo.

1940 Informaciones que mandó levantar el Virrey Toledo sobre los Incas . . . [1570–1572]. In *Don Francisco de Toledo, supremo organizador del Perú: Su vida, su obra (1515–1582),* ed. D. Roberto Levillier. Buenos Aires: Espasa-Calpe. (Also see Loarte, Gabriel de.)

1975 *Tasa de la visita general de Francisco de Toledo.* Introducción y versión paleográfica de Noble David Cook, y los estudios de Alejandro Málaga Medina, Thérèse Bouysse Cassagne. Lima: Dirección Universitaria de Biblioteca y Publicaciones, Universidad Nacional Mayor de San Marcos, Seminario de Historia Rural Andina.

Ulloa Mogollón, Juan de

1885 Relación de la provincia de los Collaguas para la descripción de las Yndias que su Magestad manda hacer [1586]. In *Relaciones geográficas de Indias Perú,* ed. Marcos Jiménez de la Espada, vol. 2, 38–50. Madrid: Ministerio de Fomento.

Urbano, Henrique

1981 *Wiracocha y Ayar: Héroes y funciones en las sociedades andinas.* Cusco: Centro de Estudios Rurales Andinos "Bartolomé del las Casas."

Urbano, Henrique, and Pierre Duviols, eds.

1989 *Fábulas y mitos de los incas.* Crónicas de América series. Madrid: Historia 16.

Urteaga, Horacio H., ed.

1916 *Informaciones acerca de la religión y gobierno de los Incas.* Colección de Libros y Documentos Referentes a la Historia del Perú, ser. 1, vol. 3. Lima: Sanmartí.

Urton, Gary D.

1984 Chuta: El espacio de la práctica social en Pacariqtambo, Perú. *Revista Andina* 2(1):7–56.

1989 La historia de un mito: Pacariqtambo y el origen de los Incas. *Revista Andina* 7(1):129–216.

1990 *The history of a myth: Pacariqtambo and the origin of the Inkas.* Austin: University of Texas Press.

Urton, Gary D., and Anthony F. Aveni

1983 Archaeoastronomical fieldwork on the coast of Peru. In *Calendars in Mesoamerica and Peru: Native American computations of time,* ed. A. F. Aveni and G. Brotherston, 221–234. BAR International Series 174. Oxford: British Archaeological Reports.

Vaca de Castro, Cristóbal

1920 *Discurso sobre la descendencia y gobierno de los Incas . . .* [1542]. Colección de Libros y Documentos Referentes a la Historia del Perú, ser. 2a, vol. 3. Lima: Sanmartí.

Valcárcel Vizquerra, Luis Eduardo

1934a *Cuzco: Capital arqueológica de Sud América (1534–1934).* Lima: Torres Aguirre.

1934b Los trabajos arqueológicos del Cusco. Sajsawaman redescubierto II. *Revista del Museo Nacional* 3:3–36, 211–233.

1935 Los trabajos arqueológicos en el Departamento del Cusco. Sajsawaman redescubierto III–IV. *Revista del Museo Nacional* 4:1–24, 161–203.

1946 The Andean calendar. In *Handbook of South American Indians,* vol. 2, *The Andean civilizations,* ed. Julian Steward. Bureau of American Ethnology Bulletin 143, 471–476. Washington, D.C.: U.S. Government Printing Office.

Valencia Zegarra, Alfredo

1984 Arqueología de Qolqampata. *Revista del Museo e Instituto de Arqueología* 23:47–62.

Valencia Zegarra, Alfredo, and Arminda Gibaja Oviedo

1990 *Excavaciones y puesta en valor de Tambomachay.* Cusco: Instituto Nacional de Cultura.

Van de Guchte, Maarten J.

1984 El ciclo mítico andino de la Piedra Cansada. *Revista Andina* 2(2):539–556.

1990 Carving the world: Inca monumental sculpture and landscape. Ann Arbor, Mich.: University Microfilms.

Vázquez de Espinosa, Antonio

1948 *Compendio y descripción de las Indias Occidentales* [1628]. Transcribed from the original by Charles Upson Clark. Smithsonian Miscellaneous Collections, vol. 108. Washington, D.C.: Smithsonian Institution.

Villanueva, Horacio, and Jeanette Sherbondy

1979 *Cuzco: Aguas y poder.* Cusco: Centro de Estudios Rurales Andinos "Bartolomé de las Casas."

Villena Aguirre, Arturo

1987 *Qorilazo y región de refugio en el contexto andino.* Cusco: Papelería Peñarol.

Wachtel, Nathan

1973 Estructuralismo e historia: A propósito de la organización social del Cuzco. In *Sociedad e ideología: Ensayos de historia y antropología,* 23–58. Lima: Instituto de Estudios Peruanos.

1977 *The vision of the vanquished: The Spanish conquest of Peru through Indian eyes, 1530–1570.* New York: Barnes and Noble Press.

1990 *Le Retour des ancêtres: Les indiens urus de Bolivie.* Paris: Editions Gallimard.

Wiener, Charles

1880 *Pérou et Bolivie. Récit de voyage suivi d'études archéologiques et ethnographiques et de notes sur l'écriture et les langues des populations indiennes.* Paris: Hachette et Cie.

Wittfogel, K. A.

1957 *Oriental despotism: A comparative study of total power.* New Haven: Yale University Press.

Zárate, R.

1921 *El Cuzco y sus monumentos: Guía del viajero.* Lima: Sanmartí.

Zimmerer, Karl S.

1995 *Changing fortunes: Biodiversity and peasant livelihood in the Peruvian Andes.* Berkeley: University of California Press.

Zimmerman, Arthur Franklin

1938 *Francisco de Toledo, fifth viceroy of Peru, 1569–1581.* Caldwell, Idaho: The Caxton Printers, Ltd.

Zuidema, R. Tom

1964 *The ceque system of Cuzco: The social organization of the capital of the Inca,* trans. Eva M. Hooykaas. International Archives of Ethnography, supplement to vol. 50. Leiden: E. J. Brill.

1969 Hierarchy in symmetric alliance systems. *Bijdragen tot de Taal-, Land- en Volkenkunde* 125:134–139.

1973 Kinship and ancestor cult in three Peruvian communities: Hernández Príncipe's account in 1622. *Bulletin de l'institut français d'études andines* 2(1):16–23.

1977a The Inca calendar. In *Native American astronomy,* ed. Anthony F. Aveni, 219–259. Austin: University of Texas Press.

1977b La imagen del sol y la huaca de Susurpuquio en el sistema astronómico de los Incas en el Cuzco. *Journal de la Société des Américanistes,* n.s., 63:199–230.

1977c The Inca kinship system: A new theoretical view. In *Andean kinship and marriage,* ed. R. Bolton and E. Mayer, Special Publication No. 7, 240–281. Washington, D.C.: American Anthropological Association.

1980 El Ushnu. *Revista de la Universidad Complutense, Madrid* 28(117):317–362.

1981a Anthropology and archaeoastronomy. In *Archaeoastronomy in the Americas,* ed. Ray A. Williamson, 29–31. Los Altos, Calif.: Ballena Press.

1981b Inca observations of the solar and lunar passages through zenith and anti-zenith at Cuzco. In *Archaeoastronomy in the New World,* ed. Ray A. Williamson, 319–342. Los Altos, Calif.: Ballena Press.

1981c Comment. *Latin American Research Review* 16(3):167–170.

1982a Bureaucracy and systematic knowledge in Andean civilization. *The Inca and Aztec states, 1400–1800: Anthropology and history,* ed. G. A. Collier, R. I. Rosaldo, and J. D. Wirth, 419–458. New York: Academic Press.

1982b Catachillay: The role of the Pleiades and of the Southern Cross and α and β Centauri in the calendar of the Incas. In *Ethnoastronomy and archaeoastronomy in the American Tropics,* ed. A. F. Aveni and G. Urton, 203–229. New York: Annals of the New York Academy of Sciences, vol. 385.

1982c The sidereal lunar calendar of the Incas. In *Archaeoastronomy in the New World,* ed. Anthony F. Aveni, 59–107. Cambridge: Cambridge University Press.

1982d Myth and history in ancient Peru. In *The logic of culture: Advances in structural theory and methods,* ed. I. Rossi, 150–175. South Hadley, Mass.: Bergin and Garvey Publishers.

1983a Hierarchy and space in Incaic social organization. *Ethnohistory* 30(2):49–75.

1983b Towards a general Andean star calendar in ancient Peru. In *Calendars in Mesoamerica and Peru: Native American computations of time,* ed. Anthony F. Aveni and G. Brotherston, 235–262. BAR International Series 174. Oxford: British Archaeological Reports.

1985 The lion in the city. *Animal myths and metaphors in South America: An anthology,* ed. G. Urton, 183–250. Salt Lake City: University of Utah Press.

1986a *La Civilisation Inca au Cuzco.* Paris: Presses Universitaires de Frances, Collège de France.

1986b Inka dynasty and irrigation: Another look at Andean concepts of history. In *Anthropological history of Andean polities,* ed. J. V. Murra, N. Wachtel, and J. Revel, 177–200. Cambridge: Cambridge University Press.

1988a A quipu calendar from Ica, Peru, with a comparison to the ceque calendar from Cuzco. In *World archaeoastronomy: Acts of the second Oxford conference on archaeoastronomy,* ed. Anthony F. Aveni, 341–351. Cambridge: Cambridge University Press.

1988b The pillars of Cuzco: Which two dates of sunset did they define? In *New directions in American archaeoastronomy,* ed. Anthony F. Aveni, 143–169. BAR International Series 454. Oxford: British Archaeological Reports.

1989a The moieties of Cuzco. In *The attraction of opposites: Thought and society in the dualistic mode,* ed. Maybury Lewis, D. Almagor, and U. Almagor. Ann Arbor: University of Michigan Press.

1989b At the king's table: Inca concepts of sacred kingship in Cuzco. In *Anthropology and history,* ed. J. C. Galey, vol. 4, 249–274. Great Britain: Harwood Academic Publishers.

1989c Cuzco, quipu, and quadrant. In *World art: Themes of unity in diversity. Acts of the XXVIth International Congress of the History of Art,* ed. Irving Lavin, vol. 1, 193–198. University Park: The Pennsylvania State University Press.

1989d *Reyes y guerreros: Ensayos de cultura andina.* Lima: Fomciencias.

1990a *Inca civilization in Cuzco,* trans. Jean-Jacques Decoster. Austin: The University of Texas Press.

1990b Ceques and chapas: An Andean pattern of land partition in the modern valley of Cuzco. *Circumpacifica: Festschrift für Thomas S. Barthel,* ed. Bruno Illius and Matthias Laubscher. Sonderdruck: Peter Land.

Zuidema, R. Tom, and Deborah Poole

1982 Los límites de los cuatro suyus incaicos en el Cuzco. *Bulletin de l'institut français d'études andines* 2(1–2):83–89.

Zuidema, R. Tom, and Gary Urton

1976 La constelación de la Llama en los Andes peruanos. *Allpanchis* 9:59–119.

General Index

Acamana, 14
Acosta, José de, 15, 16, 19–20, 21, 50, 140, 155, 156
Aguini, 45, 47, 48, 96
Agurto Valvo, Santiago, 10
Albornoz, Cristóbal de, 15, 21, 24, 25, 38, 73, 143, 155, 156, 157; camayocs, 8; description of ceques, 5, 135; huacas of Chinchaysuyu, 49, 50, 51, 53, 54, 55, 58, 61, 63, 64, 65, 66, 67, 69, 70, 135–142; shrines in Anta, 146–147
Alcaviza, 44, 114
Alonso Carrasco, Perdo, 30, 70
Altamirano, Antonio, 124
Amaru Cancha, 96
Amaru Topa Inca, 25, 37, 56, 68, 75, 76
Anaguarque, Mama, 25, 37, 38, 48
Andamachay, 93, 95
Andasaya, 56
Angostura, 30, 94, 98, 102, 103, 116
Anta, 138, 143, 146–147, 156
Antasayac, 44
Antigüedades (anonymous writer), 54–55, 139
Antisuyu, 6; ceque clusters in, 35, 38; ceques and huacas in, 7, 75–95; nonroyal ayllus of, 44–45; panacas of, 41–42; research in, 10, 11
Apachetas, 16, 17, 18, 19
Apu Mayta (Capac Yupanqui: 5th Inca), 40–43, 45, 103
Apurimac River, 146
Arayraca, 40, 43–45
Aray Ucho, 44
Ardiles Calvo, Percy, 101
Arriaga, Pablo José, 5, 26
Arte y vocabulario en la lengua general del Perú, 36; definition of ceque, 5

Aucaylli (Yahuar Huacac: 7th Inca), 41–43, 45, 83
Aveni, Anthony, 10, 11, 50, 63, 64, 65, 69, 70, 81, 82, 131, 150, 159
Ayarmaca, 37, 38, 47, 62, 92
Ayaviri, 71
Ayllu, 9, 37
Aymara, 15
Aytocari, 125

Bachicao, Hernando, 80
Bandelier, Adolph, 30
Barrionuevo Orosco, Wilton, 146–147
Betanzos, Juan, 50, 54, 55, 61, 66, 70, 137, 139; Anaguarque, 120; Cayaocache, 124; Poma chupa, 118; Rauaraya, 124
Bingham, Hiram, 69, 70, 145

Cabello de Balboa, Miguel, 66, 71, 91, 137, 138, 139
Cachimayo, 84, 86, 90, 94
Cachona, 120, 125, 126, 127, 128, 129, 134
Cachua, Mama, 127
Calendar, 14, 159–160
Callapiña et al., 40
Cañete, 150
Capac (Topa Inca: 10th Inca), 37, 38, 40–43, 45
Capac Cocha, 143–145, 154, 156, 161; child sacrifices, 27; Cobo's description of, 143–144; Molina's description of, 10, 87, 143–144
Capac Raymi, 25, 55, 61, 67, 70, 108, 124, 129, 131, 137, 200n.9
Capac Yupanqui, 39, 41–42, 103, 106, 127
Cari, 47, 48, 93
Carmenga, 7, 66, 68, 70, 137, 138
Catunque, 51

Cayao, 7; classification of ceques into, 38 definition of, 35–37
Cayaocache, 124, 125, 126, 128, 129, 130, 131
Cayo, Diego, 79
Cayra, 14, 96, 97, 101, 102, 108, 109
Ccorca, 131
Ceque(s): definition of, 5; directions, 38; Inca calendrics, 159–160; lengths of, 158; maintenance of, 9, 38, 39–48, 157, 160; numbering and naming of, 11–12, 163; number of, 7; offerings along, 27; order of, 7; pervious studies, 9–10; relation with nonroyal ayllus, 43–47, 157, 160; relation with panacas, 40–43, 47, 157; resource tenure, 160; straight lines, 10; straightness of, 10–11, 94–95, 157
Ceque clusters, definition of, 7, 35; distribution of, 42, 156, 157; hierarchy of, 38; Tambocancha, 117
Chachapoya, 110
Chanan, 32, 61, 62
Chañan Cori Coca, 127
Chanca, 15, 24, 63, 71, 87, 89, 96, 127, 138, 147
Cháven Ballón, Manuel, 9, 10
Chavin Cusco, 40, 43–45
Chillón Valley, 144, 145
Chima (Manco Capac: 1st Inca), 41–43, 45, 125
Chincana, 55
Chincha, 136
Chinchaysuyu, 6; Albornoz's shrines in, 15, 49, 135–142; ceque clusters in, 35, 38; extra huacas in, 71, 72, 73; nonroyal ayllus of, 44–45; order of ceques, 7; panacas of, 41–42; research in, 10, 49–73

Index of Huaca Names

Index of Ceques